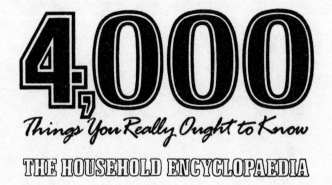

4,000

Things You Really Ought to Know

THE HOUSEHOLD ENCYCLOPAEDIA

Books by Ginette Chevallier

1,000 Things You Ought to Know about Stains and Fabrics
1,000 Things You Ought to Know

Ginette Chevallier

4,000

Things You Really Ought to Know

THE HOUSEHOLD ENCYCLOPAEDIA

GUILD PUBLISHING

LONDON · NEW YORK · SYDNEY · TORONTO

This edition published 1988 by
Guild Publishing London
by arrangement with
Bantam Press
a division of Transworld Publishers Ltd

Reprinted 1989
Third reprint 1989
Fourth reprint 1990
Fifth reprint 1991

Printed in Great Britain by
St Edmundsbury Press Ltd
Bury St Edmunds, Suffolk

CN 9016

CONTENTS

HOUSEHOLD HINTS

ACID
Wrap bottles containing acid and other dangerous liquids from top to bottom with transparent surgical tape or sellotape. If the bottle is dropped, the tape will hold the pieces of glass together and the liquid will not escape.

When acid has taken the colour out of a fabric, apply ammonia to the stain or the rinsing water to restore the colour. Alternatively make a strong solution of bicarbonate of soda and water and apply to the stain; then rinse.

ACRYLIC (PLEXIGLASS, PERSPEX)
To clean acrylic surfaces (e.g. tray, bath etc.), use warm soapy water to which a few tablespoons of vinegar have been added.

Scratches; light scratches on acrylic can be removed by rubbing them with metal polish. If the scratches are deep, use some very fine wet sandpaper and rub until the scratches have disappeared. Next, gently rub with metal polish. This method is also good for removing stubborn stains.

ADHESIVE
Where applying clear adhesive, if one surface is absorbent and the other is not (e.g. fabric on plastic), apply the adhesive to the plastic only. Epoxy resin is a very strong adhesive which takes five to seven hours to dry. If the material to be glued is heat-resistant, the drying time can be reduced by placing the glued object near a radiator or in a warm oven.

To prevent a tube of quick-drying adhesive drying out while you are using it, stick the opening of the tube on a long nail which has been half buried point up in a ball of plasticine. Stick the ball somewhere on your work table.

If your fingers get stuck together while using one of those colourless, runny, 'handy around the house' glues, roll a pencil between them and they will slowly and painlessly free themselves. Anywhere else on your skin, soften the glue with a wet piece of cottonwool.

To remove adhesive labels: rub with a piece of cottonwool dipped in nail-varnish remover (acetone). Alternatively, soak the label in water, or cover with a wet cloth until the paper is soaked, then remove with methylated spirit.

When the adhesive in a bottle starts to get low, store the bottle upside down in a jar so that you do not have to wait for it to come out when you want to use it.

Use warm vinegar to loosen glued wooden joints. Brush the vinegar over the joints as many times as required.

ADHESIVE PAPER

To undo the end of a roll of clear adhesive (Sellotape), hold it for a few seconds over the steam of a kettle.

AEROSOL SPRAY

Before throwing away an empty aerosol spray, detach the nozzle (if possible – some do not come off). Keep these spares in a box: they will come in very handy when one of your half-empty aerosols gets a clogged nozzle. Just slip the nozzle off and replace it with one of your collection. Nozzles from paint aerosol sprays can be kept in a jar filled with paint-thinner (remember to put the lid on because otherwise the thinner will evaporate). To unclog the nozzle, throw it into boiling water for a few seconds.

ALABASTER

To clean alabaster, rub softly with a cloth dipped in turpentine. This will clean and polish simultaneously. For a better polish, once the alabaster is clean and dry, rub it with chamois leather dipped in talcum powder, or wax it with a natural-colour wax and shine with a soft cloth.

ALARM CLOCK

If you fail to hear the alarm clock most mornings, stand the clock in a pan with some small coins in it.

ALUMINIUM

Aluminium pans are not suitable for boiling the water for tea as the metal gives the tea a disagreeable colour. Some foods (for example, white soups or white sauces) are slightly discoloured if cooked in aluminium owing to a small, harmless chemical reaction.

Do not wash aluminium pans in water mixed with washing soda. It would damage the protective film put on the aluminium to prevent corrosion.

To clean aluminium, use a piece of crumpled kitchen foil. When rubbed over the aluminium it restores a bright new look.

To clean aluminium utensils rub them with a mixture of salad oil and methylated spirit. Use equal quantities of both and it will clean the aluminium perfectly.

Wood ash made into a thin paste with a little lemon juice or vinegar is also very good for cleaning and polishing aluminium. Use a wire pad dipped in wood ash to get rid of any brown stains.

To clean a burnt aluminium saucepan, fill with water, add an onion and boil. The burn will soon loosen and come to the surface, leaving the pan clean and bright.

Another way is to invert the burnt saucepan on top of a pan full of boiling water, keeping the water boiling until the burn can be removed easily.

Or boil a pint of water to which four tablespoons of bleach have been added in the saucepan. Do this in a well-ventilated room. Wash thoroughly.

Stained aluminium cooking utensils not responding to the usual cleansing treatment can be restored to a bright new look by cooking apples or apple peel in them. This does not affect the taste or do any harm to the apples. Rhubarb or lemon can be used with the same result. Another method is to mix one tablespoon of cream of tartar with one pint/half a litre of water, bring to the boil and continue boiling for five minutes. A third alternative is to add two teaspoonsful of vinegar to the water in which eggs have been boiled.

To give a black patina to an aluminium object, one has first to rub the object with a fine sandpaper and then cover it with olive oil. Next warm the metal lightly over a flame (gas, oil-lamp etc.). Repeat the process. The black tint appears very rapidly. Leave to cool off by dipping the object in olive oil.

ALUMINIUM WINDOW FRAMES (DOUBLE GLAZING)
To clean the aluminium, use a cloth dipped in paraffin oil, then wipe off the excess. This will also prevent it from rusting.

AMBER
To tell real amber from false, rub the amber on the palm of your hand. Real amber will give off an aromatic smell, the false one will not.

Another test is to rub against wool. The real amber will attract any small light particles, the false will not. Real amber will not be scratched by the false one, but the false will be scratched by the real one. When run over a flame the amber swells and the false crumbles easily.

Clean amber with soap and water, rinse and dry with a soft cloth.

To clean dirty amber, rub it gently with a piece of cottonwool dipped in methylated spirit and then polish it with a chamois leather.

To maintain clean amber, rub a little almond oil over it and polish with a chamois leather. Jeweller's rouge is also good.

AMETHYST
Clean in warm soapy water using a soft toothbrush. Rinse well, then dip in surgical spirit and dry with a soft cloth.

ANIMAL HAIR
To remove animal hair from clothes, upholstery etc., wrap some Sellotape round the fingers of one hand, sticky side outward and rub it over the hairs. Or instead of the Sellotape use a foam rubber sponge or slide a brush inside a nylon stocking and brush over the material.

You can vacuum-clean your dog, using the soft brush on the vacuum-cleaner; he will love it.

ANTIMONY

A soft chamois leather is all you need to clean objects made of antimony. Stains will disappear if rubbed with crushed chalk.

ANTS

In the house, put a container where a handful of lavender is soaking in white vinegar near their hills – or a saucer upside down with a spoon of honey on top will drown the ants; a bunch of fresh chervil or a saucer full of cloves and paraffin will make them run. Some essence of peppermint on a piece of cotton wool is also a good ant-deterrent.

To deter ants in the home, sprinkle bicarbonate of soda or powdered borax of cloves on shelves and in drawers.

To destroy ants, pour boiling water into the anthills.

AQUARIUMS

Fish need oxygen to live, and they take this from the water in which they live. The water in turn gets oxygen from its contact with the air, so the larger the area of water in contact with the air the more oxygen there is in the water and the healthier the fish. If you have a round goldfish bowl, only fill it half-full with water. Then the surface area of the water will be greater than if filled to the top, but as a general rule, do not keep a fish in a round bowl for long; a rectangular container is better.

When filling a fish tank with water, in order not to disturb the gravel on the bottom leaving a bare patch, stand a teacup on the bottom of the tank and gently pour the water into the cup. The water will slide down the sides of the cup onto the gravel.

If stones from the garden or beach are used to decorate the bottom of the tank, sterilize them first by pouring boiling water over them to avoid poisoning the water.

To remove the rubbish from an aquarium without emptying it, use a syphon method. Take a piece of rubber tube, put one end in the aquarium down to the bottom and suck the air out through the other end until you feel the water coming. Immediately put the end into a container placed near the tank, but slightly below it. Vacuum clean the bottom of the aquarium by holding the end of the tube (the one in the water) and running it over the stones and gravel. When the rubbish has been sucked away remove the tube and do not forget to replace the water that has been siphoned off. The water to be added should be approximately the same temperature as that already in the tank.

To help keep your aquarium clean, put a few water snails in it (they feed on carrion).

ARTICIFIAL FLOWERS

Brush them often with a soft brush. When dirty, and if washable, dip them a few times in warm soapy water. Non-washable artificial flowers made of silk or linen can be restiffened by holding them over steam from a kettle and then pressing carefully, petal by petal. Other non-washable flowers can be cleaned by putting them in a plastic bag with 3 or 4 tablespoons of salt. Shake well, then remove the flowers from the bag and with a soft brush dust away any remaining salt.

Pink or red plastic flowers can be given a fresh look with a coat or two of nail varnish.

ASH

Cigarette or cigar ash can easily start a fire, so do not empty ashtrays into wastepaper baskets. Use a large tin (coffee tins are good for this), empty the ashtrays into it and put the lid on tightly. The ash can then be used to remove heat marks on polished tables (see p. 231).

Ashes from coal, when sifted, are perfect for scouring stone surfaces. Ashes from burnt wood, when sifted, are very good for scouring pans. Keep some handy in a tin or plastic box (let them cool first) near the sink.

Ash stains on china ashtrays can be removed by rubbing the stains with a cork dipped in slightly dampened salt.

Some alcohol stains on wood can be removed with ash (see p. 231).

ASHTRAY

To stop cigarette ends burning in an ashtray at home and in the car and to minimize the smell of stale tobacco, place a thin coat of baking soda or baking powder in the ashtray.

BAKELITE

To clean bakelite and celluloid, use silver or brass metal polish (the woolly impregnated pad is especially good). Polish with a soft cloth after rubbing.

BAKING TINS

Boil stained and greasy tins in a strong solution of water and washing soda crystals for five minutes. Rinse and dry well to prevent rusting. (This treatment is no good for non-stick or aluminium baking tins). Do not rub tinware with scouring powder or wire wool because it will remove the tin plating on top of the iron.

Remove rust on tinware by rubbing it with a cut raw potato dipped in scouring powder (this is the only time you need scouring powder), then rinse and dry. Place the tins in the oven to get them really dry. Another way to clean tins is to put some wood ash (three to four handfuls, or more if the tin is very dirty) in a container, add a gallon (4 litres) of water and bring to the boil. When it boils dip the baking tins in and rub them with a nylon brush. When the tin has brightened, rinse and dry.

To prevent (or at least delay) a new tin from rusting, rub it, both inside and out, with lard and place it in a moderate oven for forty-five minutes. Do not use before it is cool and has been wiped thoroughly with a paper towel.

BALLOON

Before blowing up a ballon stretch it and rub it between your hands and it will inflate more easily.

A balloon is good for retaining the shape of a woollen hat or beret after washing. Dry the hat or beret stretched over the inflated balloon.

BALLPOINT PEN

When a ballpoint is clogged up with too much ink, stick the point into a cigarette filter and twist it round a few times.

If a ballpoint pen refuses to work, warm the point (without burning the plastic casing) with a match or dip it in very hot water for a few minutes.

The plastic casing of a useless ballpoint is a very good small pill-carrier. Just remove the empty ink catridge, wash the barrel, let it dry or dry it with a hair-dryer, and fill it up with the small pills.

BAMBOO

To clean bamboo, wash it with a sponge or cloth soaked in warm soapy and salty water; use a soft brush if needed. Rinse and dry. Shine with a wax polish.

BARBECUE

Line the base and sides of your barbecue with aluminium foil, shiny side up, to intensify the heat.

Wrap your briquettes for the barbecue in brown paper bags. When ready to barbecue place a bag or two in the barbecue and light.

Soak your barbecue grill in some left-over brewed coffee for a good clean.

BARRELS

To clean a barrel, wash thoroughly with a mixture of washing soda and boiling water (two tablespoons of soda to one gallon/four litres of water), then rinse well.

BASKETWARE – See also **Cane**; and **Wicker**

To clean dusty basketware, brush with a soft brush, then wash vigorously using a brush dipped in a solution of warm water and a little washing soda. Rinse with cold water and wipe with a soft cloth.

Creaking basketware chairs can be cured by putting a few drops of liquid paraffin on the joints.

To stop baskets becoming brittle, give them a good wetting with the garden hose or the bathroom shower from time to time. Then shake them to get the excess water off and leave to dry naturally.

BATHING CAP

To prevent water penetrating your bathing cap, wear a narrow band of chamois leather under it.

BATHROOM MIRROR
Rub the bathroom mirror with a few drops of shampoo to stop it steaming up.

BATHROOM SCALES
Give new life to your shabby bathroom scales by covering them with a toilet-lid cover and cutting the material around the dial.

BATH
Scratch marks on an acrylic bath (or basin) will disappear if rubbed with a cloth with some metal polish on it. This should not be done too often, because metal polish is abrasive.

Neglected porcelain bathtubs will look as good as new if rubbed all over with a cloth dampened in paraffin. Or, using a hard brush, scrub the bath with a paste made of cream of tartar and peroxide, then rinse thoroughly. For persistent stains add a few drops of ammonia to the paste, apply to the stains and leave for a few hours before scrubbing.

If your bath (or basin) has stains caused by a dripping tap, rub the stains with a paste made of salt and lemon juice and then rinse. If the stains are old and resistant, make a paste of cream of tartar and peroxide. Rub the stain with a brush (an old toothbrush will do) and then rinse.

Another good recipe for cleaning the bathtub is to wash it with a mixture of one teacupful of ammonia, half a teacupful of vinegar, a quarter of a teacupful of bicarbonate of soda and four pints/two litres of hot water. Rinse well. Wear rubber gloves and ventilate the room.

Rust stains on baths can be removed with lighter fluid.

Use an old toothbrush to clean the scale around the bathroom taps.

To avoid too much steam when running a bath, run the cold water first.

BATH MATS – See Rubber mats

BATH SALTS
A small container (saucer, open jar, open box) of perfumed bathsalts left in a wardrobe or linen cupboard acts as a delicious air-freshener.

BATTERIES
If the batteries inside your radio, tape recorder etc., are too loose because of a defective spring, take a little piece of foil and push it in at one end of the battery to secure it and restore the contact.

The life of batteries can be prolonged by placing them in a warm place when they become weak. Put them on a radiator, or hot-water bottle, in a slightly warm oven for half an hour or in the sun, but do not put them in contact with a naked flame or allow them to get too hot.

To prevent batteries getting rusty from humidity before putting them into your radio, torch etc., wrap them individually in paper, leaving the ends open for circuit contact. Or coat the terminals lightly with vaseline (petroleum jelly).

BEADS

To restring a bead necklace with a worn-out string, easily and quickly, stick the new thread to the old one with nail varnish or glue and pull the old thread out carefully.

When knots are to be tied between each bead, secure the knot with a little nail varnish.

To keep decreasing sizes of beads in order when re-stringing a necklace, stick them on a strip of sellotape fixed sticky-side up on a table. Or use a piece of corrugated paper.

A very fine fishing line is ideal for restringing some beads.

Children love threading beads, but often the limpness of the thread discourages them. Dip the end of the thread in nail varnish and leave it to dry, or rub it with soap. The thread will be stiff enough to pass through the beads easily. Better still use a long shoe-lace. Dental floss is good for stringing beads.

Dip different-shaped macaroni in a variety of food colourings to make beads for children.

BED-MAKING

When making a bed, fold the corners of each sheet and blanket separately, neat and tidy; do the 'hospital corners'.

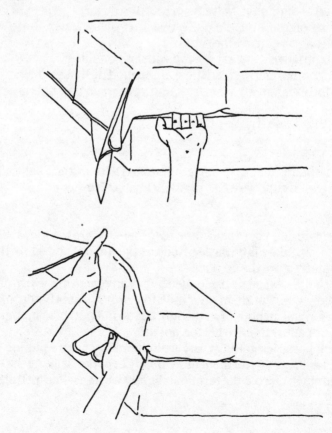

When making a bed for a child, make a large box-pleat in the centre of the top sheet and blanket. This will allow the child to move about during the night without the bed coming untucked.

If there is any dampness in a bed the following test will tell: place a hot-water bottle in the bed between the sheets for five minutes. Next hold a mirror inside the bed. If any mist appears on the mirror, the bed is damp.

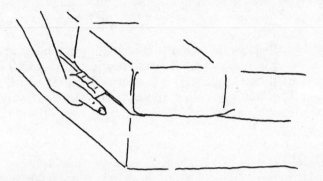

BEES (and WASPS)
One way of getting rid of a bee in the house is to present the bee with a long-stemmed flower, wait until it settles on it, then shake the flower out of the window until the bee flies away.

Another way is to use a hair spray which will harden the bees' wings and stop it flying away.

If you are bothered by bees or wasps when sitting outside, fill up one or two bottles or saucers with sugared water, or better still honeyed water; their greediness will prove fatal! Or keep them away with a few saucers here and there filled with ammonia.

BICYCLE
A plastic dish or jar cover or a shower cap will protect the seat of a bicycle on a rainy day.

BLANKET
If after washing and drying an old blanket looks a little tired and flat, fluff it up by brushing it with a wire brush.

BLEACH – See also **Care of fabrics** pp. 270–80 and **Cleaning Agents** p. 265
To get rid of the smell of bleach on your hands, rub them with vinegar and then rinse.

BLENDER
To clean a blender thoroughly, fill it with warm water, add a drop or two of washing-up liquid, cover and switch on for a few seconds. Rinse and dry.

BLINDS

To clean canvas or linen roller blinds, sponge them with warm soapy water to which ammonia has been added (one teaspoon to one pint/half a litre of water). Do not get the blind too wet, rinse with a damp cloth and hang to dry. Wait until it is completely dry before rolling the blind again.

Non-washable blinds can be cleaned with some dough made with flour (four tablespoons), white spirit (two tablespoons) and water. Rub a piece of the dough over the blind until it gets dirty and then replace it with a clean piece.

To clean Venetian blinds, use a plastic spatula wrapped in a soft cloth. Wipe the slats with the spatula damped in one of the following: an equal solution of linseed oil and paraffin oil, neat methylated spirit, a solution of cold water and ammonia (one tablespoon to one pint/half a litre of water).

To mend a broken Venetian blind slat, tape along the under-side with transparent surgical tape.

BLOCKED PIPE

Expanding curtain wire can be of immense help when it comes to cleaning a blocked pipe.

BLOWING SOAP BUBBLES

Children's soap bubbles will be more colourful if a few drops of glycerine are added to the soap solution.

BOARD

A crooked wooden board can be straightened by putting it on a flat surface and leaving it covered with a wet cloth for at least twenty-four hours.

BOAT KEYS

Boat keys should always be attached to a floating key-holder in case they drop in the water. A fishing cork or bottle cork will do; choose one according to the weight of the key. Insert a closed-eye screw into the cork and attach the key with the key chain to the screw. Try it in a bucket of water first.

BOAT

Stop mice, rats etc., walking along the rope and getting onto the boat when it is moored, by sliding a large funnel halfway up the rope, head facing the mooring.

BOLT

An obstinate bolt, hard to undo, can be made loose by pouring some coca-cola over it.

BONE – See also **Ivory**

Bone can be cleaned in soapy water, rinsed and dried, but handle with care. Bone is soft and breaks quite easily when wet. Give it a sheen by rubbing it very gently with jeweller's rouge and a soft cloth.

BOOKS

To dust the top of books, use a wide, clean paintbrush.

Books should be kept upright on the shelf, not leaning at an angle, which is bad for their bindings. Leave a gap between the wall and the books for the air to circulate.

A few sprigs of thyme here and there behind the books on a shelf will help to keep insects (e.g. silver fish) away.

Pages can be repaired, if not too badly torn, with the white of an egg. Place the torn pieces in position and smear lightly with the egg white. Leave the book open to dry.

A hole in a page of a book can be mended by chewing a piece of paper until it is soft enough to press into the hole, and then pressing the page with a warm iron.

To remove greasy spots from a page, put a piece of blotting paper on either side of the page and press with a warm iron.

A soft pencil-eraser will work if the pages are not too dirty.

Surface dirt on book pages can be removed with fresh bread kneaded into a ball and rubbed gently over the paper.

To get rid of dampness on book pages, sprinkle each page with talcum powder or cornflour, close the book and place a weight on top of it. When all the damp has been absorbed by the talc/cornflour, shake and brush the book.

To repair the spine of a book, use carpet tape.

To clean the edges of a book, place a heavy weight on top of the closed book and rub the edges with a soft cloth dampened with methylated spirit and a few drops of ammonia. Wipe with a clean dry cloth and leave to dry, before removing the weight.

If the leather binding is in good condition, polish twice a year with one of the following: colourless wax, petroleum jelly, saddle soap or leather wax. Leave to dry several hours before replacing the book upon the shelf.

Dirty leather bindings can be cleaned with a milky solution of flour-paste and water. Rub the binding gently with the solution, then dry lightly before applying some natural colour leather wax.

A dirty leather binding will regain its patina if cleaned with a mixture of one stiffly beaten egg white and a few drops of vinegar.

To stop leather-bound books getting dry, wipe them with a cloth dampened in a solution of warm soapy water and glycerine (one teaspoon of glycerine to one pint/half a litre of water), then while still damp, wax with natural colour leather wax and leave the binding to dry before polishing.

Another way to stop the leather getting dry is to rub it a few times a year with a mixture of lanolin (see Cleaning Agents, p. 267) and neatsfoot oil (from a sadler's shop) in equal quantities. Mix the lanolin and the neatsfoot to a smooth paste in a container which has been placed in a warm water bath. On old dry leather after rubbing the paste in, wait a few days before buffing.

BOTTLES

When packing bottles of liquid, always stick a piece of adhesive plaster over the cork or stopper to prevent accidents, and always pack bottles between soft items.

When emptying bottles, shake with a circular motion; they will empty much quicker.

Glass bottles containing oily liquid are sometimes slippery and difficult to hold. Get a good, safe grip by putting a few rubber bands around it.

If you find it impossible to unscrew a screw-top bottle or jar, give a firm tap to the bottom of the container. The top will then unscrew easily.

To clean a dirty bottle, pour just enough flour into the bottle to line the bottom. Then fill it up slowly and carefully with hot water. Leave to stand for a few hours; longer if the bottle is very dirty.

Toilet-bowl cleaner is good to clean small glass bottles or vases with a narrow opening. Fill up two-thirds with water, one third with toilet-bowl cleaner, and leave it to stand for an hour. Rinse well.

Strong smells in a bottle (e.g. scent, spirit etc.) can be removed by filling up the bottle with cold water to which four teaspoons of dry mustard have been added. Leave to stand for at least half a day. Rinse well.

BRAN

Hot bran absorbs dirt and grease and freshens up fur or felt. Do not treat light-coloured felt with bran. Lace and other delicate fabrics can be washed in bran water, which is a very gentle cleanser. To make bran water, fill a muslin bag with a teacupful of bran, tie the bag and put in six pints/three litres of water, bring to the boil and boil for ten minutes. Squeeze the bag before removing it. The water will look cloudy; leave to cool before soaking and washing any fabric in it.

BRASS

To find out if an object is made of brass or brass-plated steel, use a magnet. The magnet will not cling to real brass but will stick to brass-plated steel (because of the steel).

To clean brass:

1. Soak it in a solution of bicarbonate of soda (one teacupful) and boiling water (four pints/two litres). Let it stand in the solution until it is cool.
2. Wash it in liquid detergent, then rub with a mixture of $1\frac{1}{2}$ tablespoons of soap, $2\frac{1}{2}$ tablespoons of vinegar and one pint/half a litre of water.
3. Brush the brass with a mixture of fine salt and vinegar made into a paste, then wash in soapy water, rinse, dry and shine.
4. Half an onion or half a lemon dipped in fine salt and rubbed on the brass is also a good cleaner. Wash afterwards in soapy water, rinse, dry and shine.

5. Use the water in which haricot beans have been cooked. Wash and rub the brass; dry and shine with a soft cloth.

6. Worcester sauce does a good job cleaning brass.

7. Old delicate brass pieces can be cleaned with a paste made of jeweller's rouge and paraffin which makes a gentle cleaner.

8. Lacquered or varnished brass still needs to be cleaned sometimes. Apply a thick paste of lemon juice and cream of tartar over the brass. Leave on for ten minutes, wash with warm water, dry and buff.

To remove old polish from engraved brass, use an old toothbrush dipped in ammonia.

Old varnish on brass can be removed with the finest steel wool dipped in acetone or a paint-remover, or methylated spirits, then wash the brass in water and household ammonia (one tablespoon of ammonia to two pints/ one litre of water) or in mild soapy hot water; rinse and dry. If any corrosion shows up after the removal of the varnish, rub it with brass polish.

To remove lacquer from brass soak in boiling water or rub the brass with surgical spirit.

Brass will need less cleaning if, after polishing, it is rubbed with a thin layer of beeswax polish, linseed oil, paraffin or vaseline, to preserve the shine.

To clean brass curtain-hooks and rings, soak them in very hot water and ammonia for a while (two pints/one litre of water to two tablespoons of ammonia).

To clean brass on furniture without damaging the wood, just rub with water to which a little salt or vinegar has been added, then dry immediately.

Brass finger-plates and door handles can be cleaned without damaging the area surrounding them if a piece of cardboard is cut to fit exactly round the plate or handle and is then put in place while polishing.

Fingerprints on brass will rub off with some bicarbonate of soda on a dry cloth.

Corroded brass will respond to the following treatment: brush with vinegar in which some salt has been added (one teacupful of vinegar to three tablespoons of salt), then wash in soapy water, rinse, dry and polish.

For badly neglected and corroded brass: soak the brass overnight in a mixture of washing soda and hot water (three teacupsful to one gallon/four litres), rinse thoroughly, dry and polish. When in a hurry to clean brass, use the same mixture but add one teacupful of salt. Immerse the brass and bring to the boil, simmer for an hour or two, then rinse, dry and polish.

To clean a sooty brass pot, immerse it in a solution of hot water, detergent and ammonia (one gallon/four litres of hot water, half a teacup of detergent, to four tablespoons of ammonia), rinse, dry and polish with brass polish.

To keep brass clean longer, apply a little salad oil or some furniture polish over the brass after polishing them. Finish off with a soft cloth.

Another way to keep brass bright a long time after cleaning is to rub with a little flour on a clean soft cloth.

To give a patina to new brass, dip the piece in water in which mushrooms have been cooked, or dab the brass with wine vinegar.

When an engraving on a brass article is fading away, avoid damaging it further by rubbing it with vegetable oil instead of brass cleaner.

Make your own brass cleaner by mixing three tablespoons of flour, six tablespoons of salt, the white of an egg and some vinegar to a soft paste. After cleaning the brass with this mixture, wash the article in hot soapy water, rinse, dry and shine with a soft cloth. This mixture can be stored in an airtight jar or tin for the next time.

BRICKS

To cut a brick neatly and easily, lay it on a bed of sand, fill the hollow space in the top of the brick with sand and, using a hammer, lightly tap the brick until it cuts.

To clean slightly dirty bricks around a fireplace, use a piece of broken brick or pumice stone and rub the discoloured area. If the bricks need to be thoroughly cleaned, scrub them with a brush and some malt vinegar, then rinse.

When cleaning brick flooring, do not soak the floor with too much water, and make sure it is as dry as possible after rinsing. Excess water dissolves the soluble salts in the bricks and brings them to the surface, giving the floor an unattractive, whitish look. (If this warning comes too late, wash your floor immediately, as above, taking care to dry it well).

BRONZE

To clean bronze:

1. Use soap and water applied with a soft brush. After rinsing, warm the bronze article on a radiator and apply natural wax (liquid) with a paintbrush. Leave it to dry and then rub off any excess wax. When the bronze is cold, shine it with a soft cloth. Brown shoe polish in place of natural wax can also be used to polish bronze and improve the sheen.

2. Make a paste of equal quantities of salt, flour and vinegar.Apply the paste with a soft cloth, rub well, wash in warm soapy water, rinse, dry and shine.

3. Cooking water from haricot beans is also very good for cleaning bronze. Leave to dry on a radiator or dry it with a hair-dryer and wax as above.

4. Dirty bronze is best washed first with hot vinegar, then rinsed and waxed.

5. Rub very dirty bronze with turpentine, then rinse and shine with a chamois leather or with a solution of equal quantities of malt vinegar, ammonia and water, rinse, dry and shine.

To give a nice patina to bronze, rub it with an infusion of chicory (two tablespoons of chicory for one teacup of boiling water). Leave it to dry before shining the bronze with soft, clean, dry cloth.

BROOM

When the threaded handle of a broom won't fit tight any more, wrap some adhesive tape around it and screw the handle into its socket. It should then fit perfectly.

Make the bristles of your new broom last longer by soaking them in strongly salted water for twelve hours. Leave to dry before using for the first time. This treatment is also good for a new straw broom.

The soft bristles of a broom can be hardened by soaking them overnight in water to which a little ammonia has been added.

Brushes that are too soft will become hard again if the bristles are soaked for a while in an equal solution of water and white vinegar.

BRUSHES – See **Clothes brush** and **Hair brush**

BULB

When a light bulb breaks at the socket, it is very difficult to remove the base of the bulb from the socket. Here is a successful method: first unplug the lamp, then take a large raw carrot or potato, force it into the broken base and twist it out.

A flickery light bulb, if not caused by a loose wire, could be faulty at the socket base (a worn-out base which doesn't connect completely with the bulb). A drop of solder on each contact point of the socket base will solve the problem.

BURGLARY PREVENTION

A lock can be opened sometimes by slipping a thin plastic card in it. To prevent this, push two or three drawing-pins into the wooden frame of the door in front of the lock; push them in deep enough so that it does not stop the door from closing.

Trick the burglar by placing a wooden stick on the back of your sliding door. Cut it to fit the track exactly. That way, even if the burglar manages to open the lock, he won't be able to slide the door open.

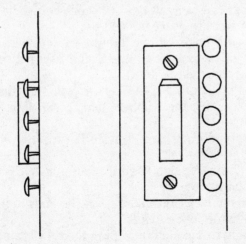

BUTTON

Metal buttons on jackets and blazers will be clean and shine again if rubbed with a piece of cottonwool dampened with vinegar.

CAMEO

A cameo can be cleaned by brushing gently with an old, clean toothbrush dipped in warm soapy water. Rinse and dry well.

A cotton bud dipped in methylated spirit is also very good.

CAMPING

To clean a greasy pan or pot while camping, use green foliage, or sand if you are near a beach – it will clean perfectly.

To stop ants and other small insects climbing up the legs of the camp bed or table when camping, place each leg in an empty tin of fruit juice, beer, food etc. and fill it up halfway with water. The insects will drown in the water.

CAN

When emptying a flat gallon can, make another hole in the top to allow the liquid to flow smoothly and avoid dribbling.

CANDLE

To make candles last twice as long, hold them by the wick and coat them with a clear varnish. Leave to dry and harden. The varnish forms a hard coat which prevents the grease from running. Alternatively, put them in the freezer for a few hours before using.

To prevent candles dripping, soak them overnight in salted water, or sprinkle a little household salt around the top of the candle before lighting it. Another solution is to rub them with slightly damp soap.

If candles are difficult to light, dip the wicks into some methylated spirit for a short while before they are needed.

Avoid burning your fingers when lighting candles with a match, by lighting a long piece of uncooked spaghetti and using it to light the candle (especially useful on birthday cakes!).

A rubber band fitted around the candle will stop the candle burning: as soon as it reaches the rubber band, the flame will extinguish itself.

A candle will spread more light if placed in front of a mirror or a large piece of silver foil.

A bent candle can be straightened if soaked in hot water until soft and rolled back on a flat surface.

To make candles fit into candlesticks, dip the ends in hot water until soft enough to mould to the required size.

Soiled candles can be cleaned by wiping them (when not lit) with a piece of cloth or cottonwool dampened with methylated spirit.

Small pieces of left-over candle can be melted together with furniture wax to give an extra shine to the furniture. Left-over candle wax can also be melted down and used as firelighters. Melt the candle in a container and dip some tightly rolled newspaper (two pages at a time) into the wax. Put them aside to dry, and store them until you need them.

To remove the wax from glass candle holders, wash them in soapy water to which a few drops of ammonia have been added.

Silver candlesticks, when coated with wax, will clean easily if put in the freezer for two to three hours before the wax is peeled off. Alternatively, hold the candlestick in hot water until the wax melts.

To twist and give your candles unusual shapes, warm them gently in the oven beforehand.

CANE – See **Basketware** and **Wicker**

To treat sagging cane seats of chairs, clean thoroughly on both sides with soap and hot water and dry in the open air. This will cause the cane to shrink and will often make it as firm as when new. When it is dry rub the cane with linseed oil to prevent any cracking.

If you cannot bring the chairs out in the open air, cover the sagging seat with a damp cloth for at least two hours. Centrally heated houses make wicker and cane very dry and brittle, so even if the seat does not sag, a damp cloth applied from time to time will help prevent it.

Baskets made of cane should be washed regularly in warm water. Cane is stronger and more supple when kept moist.

CANVAS

Clean your canvas from time to time with a solution of water and ammonia (two tablespoons of water to one tablespoon of ammonia) to keep the colours vivid.

CAR

When driving into your garage, avoid bumping the front or back of your car (depending on how you go in) on the back wall by hanging an old tyre against the back wall. When your bumper touches the tyre, you know that your car is well positioned. Alternatively, hang a tennis ball on a string from the garage roof in such a way that it will knock the back window when the car is well parked.

To clean a very dirty car, use a mixture of water and methylated spirit (one gallon/four litres of water to one pint/half a litre of methylated spirit. Do not rinse. Give the car a good rub with a chamois leather or soft cloth, and in no time your car will be gleaming.

You can also use a mixture of paraffin oil ($\frac{3}{4}$ pint/400 ml) and methylated spirit ($\frac{1}{4}$ pint/130 ml). Then wash, dry and polish with a chamois leather or a soft cloth. Both these methods will give the car a wax finish which will protect it from rain smears.

To remove insects which have stuck to the car windscreen, take a plastic mesh bag (used in supermarkets for fruit and vegetables) and roll it into a ball. Then rub it over the windscreen and it will collect the dead insects. Another way is to scrub the windscreen with a damp cloth dipped in washing soda.

To clean the chrome on the car, dip a damp sponge or cloth in bicarbonate of soda and rub over the surface. Rinse, dry and shine.

A few drops of liquid detergent in the windscreen washer container will clean muddy or dusty windscreens.

To clean the rubber floor mats, apply liquid furniture wax to them. Then brush and shine.

Vinyl car upholstery will clean well with a solution of dishwashing liquid detergent (one teacup) and warm water (four pints/two litres). Make lots of suds with an egg-beater, and apply them with a sponge. Scrub with a soft brush, rinse and dry.

Small, freshly rusted areas can be removed by rubbing them with a cork dipped in cooking oil. Older rusted spots should be dabbed with olive oil – repeat this for a few days, rub with emery paper and then with fine steel wool. Finish with a chamois leather.

To prevent rust on the chrome parts of your car, coat it with linseed oil, wax polish, vaseline or petroleum jelly.

To cover up small scratches on the bodywork, rub them with a matching wax colour crayon – it will also protect it from rusting.

Tears or holes in a convertible top can be mended with press-on clothes patches. Put the patch on top of the cut material, hold a book or a piece of wood covered with a cloth on the wrong side of the patch and apply a hot iron over the patch.

To repair split piping around the edge of a seat, slide a matchstick coated with adhesive half-way into one of the hollow ends of the piping. Slide the other, hollow end of the split piping over the protruding matchstick so that the two split ends meet. Leave to set.

Keep the battery of your car free from corrosion by scrubbing both cap and terminal with a wire brush dipped in a strong solution of bicarbonate of soda and water. Then smear them with vaseline or petroleum jelly.

A broken fan-belt can be replaced in an emergency by a stocking tied very tightly around the pulley wheels. When you have done this, drive slowly and carefully to the nearest garage.

A temporary replacement for a stolen or broken aerial can be made from a straightened wire coat-hanger.

To stop cigarette ends burning in the ashtray and to prevent the smell of stale tobacco in the car, coat the bottom of the ashtray with bicarbonate of soda.

To prevent ice forming on the windscreen in freezing weather, cover the glass with newspaper or the rubber mats from the inside of the car. Hold them firmly against the windscreen with the wipers or some waterproof tape.

To prevent the locks freezing, put a few drops of liquid paraffin in them, or cover them with adhesive tape. If you didn't take these precautions and your locks are frozen, warm the car key with a match or a cigarette lighter and gently easy it into the lock.

To prevent frozen doors and boot, coat the rubber seals with vegetable oil or talcum powder.

Keep a small muslin bag full of salt in your car; it will be very useful for cleaning a frozen windscreen. Just rub it over the glass.

A frozen carburettor can be started by blowing hot air on it with a hair-dryer.

In winter keep old blankets or a small bag or two of fine sand in the boot. If the car gets stuck in snow or ice, put the car mats covered with the old blankets in front of the rear wheels or spray the sand in front of the rear wheels.

As an additional safety precaution, stick some reflector tape onto different parts of your car, so that, if you have to pull up on a dark road, other motorists can see you. The most obvious places are inside the door so that it can be seen when the door is opened and on the front and back of the car.

CARBON PAPER
Worn-out carbon paper will last a little longer if left for a few minutes on top of a warm place (heater, hot-water bottle, radiator).

CARDS
To clean playing cards, rub them with talcum powder, jeweller's sawdust or fine breadcrumbs. Wipe each card after cleaning. Finger marks can be removed by rubbing them with a piece of bread or a piece of cottonwool dipped in cold milk.

CARPET
To restore a carpet pile which has been pressed flat by furniture legs etc., place a piece of wet cloth folded three or four times over onto the flattened carpet. Then take a hot iron and hold it lightly on top of the cloth; the steam will lift the pile. Finally, brush the carpet with a nail brush.

Crushed pile marks on the carpet can be restored by leaving an ice cube to melt on the mark, then brushing up the pile.

To clean small pieces of carpet or small rugs, rub them with half a cabbage. Vacuum or brush away any particles of cabbage dropped during the rubbing.

To get rid of moths in carpet immerse a cloth in hot water (half a pint/a quarter of a litre) to which one tablespoon of ammonia has been added. Wring out the cloth, fold into four and place over the carpet on the patch affected by moths. Then with a hot iron (not too hot) go over and over the cloth until dry. It will kill moths and eggs at the same time.

To cut foam rubber backed carpet easily, use an electric carving knife, but be careful: it's very quick.

Sparks from an open fire may make slight burns on the carpet. A good rubbing with the cut surface of a raw onion will very often make them disappear.

For a method of preventing the edges of carpets curling up, see **MATS** on p. 59.

CASSETTE TAPES
Join the ends of a broken cassette tape with a small dot of nail varnish.

CASTING
To cut a piece of casting, first heat a handsaw until red-hot: the casting will cut like wood.

CAST-IRON POTS
The outside can be cleaned by spraying with oven-cleaner, but make sure it is only on the outside, and let it set for at least two hours before wiping.

New cast-iron pans should be treated before being used for the first time. Heat some oil (preferably vegetable oil) in it to deep-frying heat, then leave to cool. Empty the pan and rub it with salt. Next wipe with a paper towel or a soft clean cloth.

CELLULOID
To clean collars and cuffs made of celluloid, rub them with a soft, fine cloth dipped in acetone. Work in rapidly and dry. Rub and shine with a soft cloth.

CEMENT
Dirty cement floors will respond well to a good rubbing with hot white vinegar.

CERAMIC COOKER TOPS
To remove stains from a ceramic cooker top, dab them with some hot white vinegar. Leave the vinegar for at least five minutes (more if it is very badly stained) before wiping it off.

CERAMIC FLOOR
To get rid of shoe marks on a ceramic floor, rub the marks with white spirit or turpentine.

CERAMIC TILES
Give them a good clean with a solution of one teacupful of ammonia to half a teacupful of vinegar, half a teacupful of washing soda and four pints/two litres of warm water. Make sure you wear rubber gloves when applying the mixture and ventilate the room. Rinse the tiles and dry them.

CHALK
Children can go through an amazing quantity of chalk in no time by breaking them up into small pieces. Put a stop to this by wrapping the chalks from the

bottom to near the top with surgical transparent tape. The tape can be peeled off as the chalks are used.

CHAMOIS

To clean chamois when it is hard and dirty, soak in warm suds to which half a cup of cooking oil has been added. Soften well with your hands, and, unless the chamois is used for cleaning windows or mirrors, do not rinse or wring but press in a towel to dry (do not hang it outside). If the chamois *is* needed for cleaning windows and mirrors, rinse it before drying.

One can also clean chamois leather in warm soapy water and ammonia (one litre/two pints of warm soapy water to two tablespoons of ammonia). Do not rub, give it a good rinse, press it in a towel to dry, and stretch it from time to time while it is drying.

CHEST OF DRAWERS

To clean underneath a heavy chest of drawers which has very short legs, take the bottom drawer out, revealing the hollow base through which you can vacuum-clean the carpet with the long nozzle attachment.

CHILDREN'S PARTIES

A bunch of lollipops stuck in a potato and placed inside a bowl will make an attractive centrepiece for a child's party.

Mark each child's place around the table at a birthday party by attaching a balloon to the back of each chair with the name of the child written on it with a felt pen.

Make-up on children's faces can be taken off easily after a party with baby oil.

CHIMNEY FIRE

If a chimney fire occurs, first shut all doors and windows. Seal the bottom of the chimney with a piece of wet blanket so that the draught is stopped; the burning soot will be extinguished for lack of air. If every fireplace were provided with a damper or shutter made of iron or tin plate, large enough to seal it thoroughly, chimney fires would not be such a problem.

Quickly put some wet newspaper on the fire, and the steam will extinguish a chimney fire.

Throw about 1 lb/500 g of washing soda, well dampened, on the fire and the fumes will extinguish the flames.

A cure for smoking chimneys is to fill a large ox-bladder with air and tie it by the neck to the middle of a stick placed across the inside of the chimney, about three feet/one metre from the top. The rising air keeps the bladder continually moving in a circular motion, which prevents a rush of air down the chimney.

CHINA

To mend a small piece of broken china, colourless nail varnish is very good.

To clean a crack in china where dust and grease have collected, bleach it with a cottonwool pad dipped in hydrogen peroxide and then rinse. Sometimes the pad has to be left on for a few days. Cover it with a plastic bag or a piece of transparent clingfilm to keep the moisture on longer. Wet the pad as soon as it starts getting dry.

A crack in a china plate will disappear if the plate is immersed in a container full of milk, brought to the boil and kept boiling slowly for forty minutes or a little longer if necessary. Then carefully bring the plate out, let it cool off a little and rinse under warm water.

Badly stained coarse china can be cleaned by soaking in neat domestic bleach for a few days. Rinse well.

A paper napkin or a paper plate placed between china plates when storing them will help prevent cracking and chipping.

To make decorative plates look their best, wash them in warm soapy water, rinse, dry well, then rub with a soft cloth dampened with methylated spirit; leave to dry and buff with a soft rag.

CHRISTMAS CARDS

Display your Christmas cards, but keep them out of the way, by sliding the back of the card between books on the bookshelves, leaving the front of the card showing.

CHRISTMAS DECORATIONS

Make a hanging ball of holly by sticking the holly in a large potato and using it as a base.

To make a Christmas wreath, use a wire hanger shaped into a circle; push the wire through the centre of some raw potatoes (the circle when closed should be covered with raw potatoes) and stick stems of holly in the potatoes. The potatoes will keep the holly fresh over the holidays.

CHRISTMAS TREE

Keep your Christmas tree looking fresh and happy throughout the festivities by standing it in a container filled with two parts water to one part glycerine.

Use pipe-cleaners as a quick and easy way of attaching decorations and presents to the tree.

CHROME

To clean chrome, rub a soft cloth dampened in vinegar over it and polish dry with a clean soft cloth.

Or rub the chrome with a damp cloth dipped in bicarbonate of soda or cigarette ash. Rinse and polish.

Very dirty chrome will shine again if rubbed with paraffin on a damp cloth. Neat ammonia will also clean dirty chrome.

To shine your chrome bathtaps after cleaning and drying them, rub them over with an old pair of nylon tights rolled into a ball.

To stop outside chromium door knobs becoming blackish and dull during bad weather, rub them from time to time with a little paraffin.

CHROMIUM
To take the tannin out of your chromium tea or coffee-pot, rub it with a cloth dampened with vinegar and dipped in salt. Rinse well, as salt left on chromium would be damaging to it after a while.

Small rusty spots on chromium will disappear if rubbed with a piece of crumpled wet aluminium foil.

Revive dull-looking chromium with a good rubbing of paraffin oil or bicarbonate of soda on a wet cloth.

CIGARETTE BURNS
Burns on bakelite (plastic) can be removed by rubbing metal polish or paste on the marks.

To mend a cigarette burn on a lightweight fabric garment, one needs a small piece of material to match the fabric of the garment. First, trim away all the burnt edges. Next place the damaged fabric face down on a piece of brown paper. Cut a patch of material larger than the burnt hole and a piece of transparent polythene bag (the same size as the patch). Neatly place the polythene patch over the hole; then the fabric patch. Press lightly with a hot iron, causing the polythene to melt and binding together the patch and the fabric to a clean invisible mending.

On wood, rub with metal polish if the mark is light, or rub with some turpentine if the wood has a wax finish.

CIGARETTE/CIGAR SMOKE
A few candles burning in a room where people are smoking will absorb the smoke.

CIGARS AND TOBACCO
Place a quarter of a fresh apple in the tobacco or cigar box to keep them moist. Renew the apple when it starts getting dry.

A good Havana cigar should not crackle to the touch when you rub it between your fingers. If it does crackle it is not in good condition, not humid enough. A good Havana cigar is slightly elastic to the touch. Cigars should be kept in a humidor, but if you do not have one, put them in a wooden box with a cup of water next to it – they should not become dry.

Dutch cigars do crackle to the touch – this is quite normal.

Cut, slit, but do not pierce a cigar as this will make the smoke too hot and the taste bitter. You can also bite the end neatly.

CLAY
Before working with modelling clay, wash your hands with soap. The clay will be easier to handle.

CLOCK

A screw-on bottle top filled with paraffin and placed inside a clock (grandfather clock, carriage clock, any wooden-case clock) will keep the parts from getting rusty. Refill the container when the paraffin has evaporated.

To clean the face of a clock, brush it with a soft paint-brush dipped in a thick mixture of water and cream of tartar. Next wipe with a sponge dampened in cold water. Dry with a soft cloth.

CLOTHES BRUSH

To clean, dip the brush in some lightly dampened bran. Rub the bran well in between the bristles with your fingers. Rinse under water and leave to dry.

COAL

Keep your coal in a dark place, as sunlight causes it to crumble to dust.

To make your coal go further, sprinkle it with a solution of water (four pints/two litres) and washing soda ($\frac{1}{2}$lb/225 grams) when it is stored in the cellar.

Fill cardboard eggboxes with coal dust, then wet them and let them dry. Place on the fire and it will keep in for hours.

COFFEE TABLE

A handsome trunk of metal or wood will make a very attractive coffee table and can also be used for storage.

COLLARS AND CUFFS

To remove the dirty rings around shirt collars and cuffs, either cover them with a paste made of bicarbonate of soda and white vinegar or rub in a little hair shampoo, before washing by hand or in the washing machine.

Sometimes only the collar of a coat or a dress needs to be cleaned. This can be done by rubbing it with powder of magnesia; if you have no magnesia, use a piece of stale bread or rub with ammonia.

COMB

Clean your combs in warm soapy water with a discarded toothbrush or a nailbrush. Add a few drops of ammonia or washing soda to the soapy water.

CONTACT LENSES

To find a contact lens lost in the carpet, tie a piece of nylon tight over the nozzle of the vacuum cleaner. Switch on the vacuum cleaner and pass the nozzle over the area where the lens was lost. It will stick to the nylon.

CONTACT PAPER

Old contact paper can easily be unstuck from shelves, panels, drawers etc. if a warm iron is applied to it before pulling off. This also works for removing sellotape. Use methylated spirits to wipe off the gummy residue.

Before using the paper place it in the refrigerator for two to three hours.

As the paper is likely to shrink when it is put in position, this will ensure that the shrinkage occurs in the refrigerator first.

Before sticking contact paper down, get the correct fit by cutting newspaper or brown paper to the correct measurement. Transfer the newspaper or brown paper to the contact paper, secure with pieces of sellotape and cut.

To stop air pockets forming when you are applying contact paper, rub the surface to be covered with a cloth dampened in cooking oil. If this precaution has not been taken and air pockets appear, puncture them with a needle or make a small cut with a razor blade and rub with a clean cloth to flatten the surface.

COOKING SMELLS

Get rid of cooking smells by boiling one teaspoon of ground cinnamon or ground cloves in half a pint/a quarter of a litre of water for fifteen minutes.

Kitchen or cigarette smells in the house will disappear immediately if the room is sprayed with a mixture of half water/half ammonia. (A spray plastic bottle normally used for spraying household plants or for dampening the linen when ironing is the perfect container.)

COPPER

To clean any copper utensils dulled or blackened by fire, rub them with half a lemon dipped in salt. Wash them afterwards in water to prevent the acid corroding the copper.

To clean very dirty old copper, bring some bleach to the boil and dip the object in it. Remove it immediately as the bleach will strip metal left in it too long.

Tarnished copper equipment can be cleaned with a mixture made of one part flour, one part silver sand and one part fine salt, adding enough vinegar to make a paste. When the copper is cleaned, rinse thoroughly and dry.

Another way is to use a spraying bottle filled with white vinegar ($\frac{1}{2}$ pint/ 250 ml) to which four tablespoons of salt have been added and spray the copper utensils. Leave it to set for a short while, then rub and wash before drying.

To clean copper utensils, soak them in the water in which potatoes have been cooked. Then wash and rub the copper, dry and shine with a soft cloth.

Ketchup also does a good job cleaning copper.

The inside of copper cooking utensils should be rubbed with one tablespoon each of salt and vinegar or salt mixed with the juice of half a lemon. Rinse and dry no more than two hours before cooking in them.

To give an old look to new copper, brush it with wine vinegar.

To remove the greenish stains left by a cleaning product on an outside wall around a brass or copper doorbell or a plaque, rub them with hydrogen peroxide (obtainable from a chemist).

CORAL

Clean in warm soapy water, rinse and dry. If it is not possible to wash it take the soft crumbs from a thick slice of bread, roll them into a ball and rub the coral with it. It will gradually absorb the dirt. Brush away any little pieces of bread left after cleaning with a soft toothbrush. Rub with a chamois leather.

Coral needs to be fed with a mixture of one tablespoon of turpentine or white spirit to three tablespoons of almond oil. Rub gently, then wipe with tissue paper and leave for one day before polishing with a chamois leather.

To clean a coral necklace, soak it in water (one teacup) to which a tablespoon of bicarbonate of soda has been added. Then leave to dry on blotting paper or an absorbent cloth.

CORKS

Cork swells, and sometimes a cork will not fit back into a bottle. Just drop it into boiling water for a minute or two; it will become soft and easy to fit back into the bottle.

One can also use a nail file to rasp the cork.

When a cork has been pushed inside an empty bottle:

1. Take a button that will slide through the neck of the bottle. Run a strong thin string through the two holes of the button. Holding the two ends of the string, push the button inside the bottle, tilt the bottle until the cork falls into the right position at the neck. Holding the two ends, pull the string until the button is lying flat against the bottom of the cork, gently pull the string and lift out the cork.

2. Using a string with a knot tied in the middle, rest the knot underneath the cork and pull.

3. Pour a little ammonia into the *empty* bottle, just enough for the cork to float in. Close the bottle with another cork and wait until the cork inside disintegrates into small pieces (this will take a few days). Pour out the contents and rinse well.

To cut a cork easily, drop it in warm water for a few minutes first.

Objects made of cork can be cleaned by rubbing them with a fine sandpaper.

CORK MATS

To clean cork mats, do not wash them but rub them hard with coarse sandpaper. They will look like new.

To clean a very dirty cork mat, do not use soap and warm water; instead place it in cold water and rub it with a pumice stone (obtainable from a chemist). Rinse under cold running water. Wipe it and leave to dry in a cool place.

CORKSCREW

An improvised corkscrew can be made by attaching a piece of strong string to an ordinary screw or by running some very hot water over the neck of the bottle – sometimes it will force the cork to pop out.

CORK TILES

To repair holes or chips in cork tiles (wall or flooring), mince some pieces of cork finely with a knife or scissors and mix them with glue to a thick paste. Press the paste hard into the damaged area. Leave to dry and harden completely before smoothing with sandpaper.

COSTUME JEWELLERY

A drop of natural-colour nail varnish will set a loose stone on costume jewellery back in place.

Costume jewellery blackens the skin sometimes. Brush the part touching the skin with a transparent nail varnish, leave to dry and it won't mark your skin or clothes any more.

If you keep a piece of chalk in your costume jewellery box, your jewellery won't tarnish.

Use warm soapy water to clean costume jewellery but do not leave it to soak as it might soften the glue or cement.

COTTON REEL

Cotton reels will be kept tidy in the sewing box if they are slipped onto a knitting needle or a skewer with a cork at the sharp end. A string or a rubber band run through the reels, with the two ends knotted together, will also do.

COTTON WOOL

Double the quantity of your roll of cotton wool: unroll the cotton wool and place it in a slightly warm oven with the door half closed for half an hour. Then cut it into layers before storing it.

CRÊPE SOLES

Crêpe soles can become dangerously slippery sometimes; rub them on the coarse kitchen grater.

If your crêpe-soled shoes are slippery in wet weather, it may be that the tread of the soles has worn out. Renew the tread by using a razor blade to cut shallow V-shaped grooves across the soles.

CROCODILE SKIN

To clean crocodile skin (handbags, shoes, belts etc.), rub the skin gently with a little almond oil on a pad of cotton wool. Then polish with a soft cloth.

CRYSTAL

Vases, glasses etc. will sparkle if a few drops of ammonia are added to the washing water and some vinegar is added to the rinsing water.

CUPBOARD

To prevent dampness in a linen cupboard:

1. Fill a saucer with cloves and place it inside the cupboard.
2. Fill a box with lime and place it on a shelf. This will absorb any dampness and also keep the air in the cupboard sweet.
3. A jar full of salt is also very efficient against dampness.
4. A tin full of charcoal briquettes will prevent dampness (a coffee tin will do well).

Musty odours in a cupboard can be got rid of by placing a bowl of perfumed bathsalts in the bottom of the cupboard. Replace when the perfume fades away.

Stop the cupboard door opening by itself, if it is loose, by sticking a drawing-pin into one of the edges.

CURTAINS

When putting new rods into curtains, wax the rods with a bar of soap before fixing them. They will slide much more easily.

When threading a rod through the top hem of a curtain, a thimble placed on the end of the rod will allow it to run through smoothly without continually catching on the fabric. A cut-off rubber glove finger or the cut-off corner of a plastic bag will also do.

CUSHION STUFFING

To stop the foam stuffing settling in one end of your cushion, put in two or three large pieces of foam when you stuff the cushion. They will help distribute the small pieces more evenly.

DAMPNESS – See also Bed-making

To find out if dampness on a wall is caused by condensation or comes from outside, place a sheet of silver foil over the damp area inside the room. If condensed water appears on the front surface of the foil, it is caused by the air in the room being more humid and warmer than the walls. If on the contrary the foil is wet on the side touching the wall, the damp comes from outside. The remedy for this is to call professional help. For the condensation inside the room, a better ventilation (e.g. an extractor fan on the windows) would be the solution.

When dampness is felt in a room, put a piece of camphor in the corners of the room. After six to eight days the camphor will have evaporated and the room will not be damp any more.

To get rid of dampness in a cupboard in a very short time, place a block of camphor or a box full of quicklime in it.

DECANTER – See also Bottle

To clean decanters and bottles:
1. Put small pieces of potato in them with vinegar and water in equal quantities. Shake for a few minutes. Leave to stand for a few hours if possible before rinsing.
2. Put in some coal dust, add a little warm water, shake well and leave for a

few hours. It will also get rid of any smells in the vessel.

3. Fill it up with water to which household ammonia has been added (three tablespoons ammonia to one litre/two pints of water), leave it to stand at least twelve hours, wash and rinse.

4. Fill up the decanters or bottles with water to which lavatory-pan cleaner has been added (four tablespoons cleaner to one litre/two pints of water), leave it to soak overnight, wash and rinse very thoroughly.

When washing a decanter, do not put it away when still damp or it will get cloudy. Drain it by standing it upside down in a wide necked jug until well dried.

To remove stains from a decanter:

1. Fill it with one pint/half a litre of water in which you have mixed five tablespoons of domestic bleach. Rinse thoroughly.

2. Use powdered denture cleaner (e.g. Steradent). Put two tablets in the decanter, fill up with warm water and leave overnight if necessary.

3. Introduce nettles into the decanter and then fill it up with hot water (taking great care not to crack the glass with water which is too hot). Leave a few hours before rinsing.

To dry the insides of decanters (or bottles), use a hair-dryer. Blow hot air into the decanter, keeping the hair-dryer about two inches/five centimetres from the mouth. You can also dry them by warming them slightly and blowing air into them with a pair of bellows. If you don't have bellows, a piece of rolled-up paper or a tube long enough to reach almost to the bottom of the decanter can be used; but *draw* out the damp air with the mouth, do not blow into the vessel.

Another way to dry decanters or bottles for display is to drain all the water out and then rinse with a tablespoon of methylated spirits. This will quickly evaporate, leaving the glass very clear. If you want to use the decanter later, rinse it with water.

DECKCHAIR
When re-covering a deckchair put some foam rubber over the back and front bars, between the bar and the canvas. It will lessen the wear and tear and also make it more comfortable.

DIAMOND
To test if a diamond is real, drop it in a glass full of water. If the facets are not distinctive and the stones become one, it is false, but if the facets are clearly distinguishable, the diamond is real.

To clean diamonds, place them in a tea-strainer (the closed, egg-shaped sort is ideal), then dip in boiling water to which a few soapsuds and ammonia (one teaspoon) have been added. Dip them for a few seconds, then take them out and let them cool. When cold, dip them in methylated spirit for a few seconds, bring the diamonds out and let them dry on tissue paper. This method is good only for diamonds.

DINING TABLE
For a dinner party, always ensure that your flower arrangement is a sensible height. There is nothing worse than trying to converse with the person

opposite over or round an obstruction of this type. As an alternative, you could use a bowl of fresh fruit.

DIRTY HANDS

The best way to clean very soiled hands is first to rub them generously with vaseline or salad oil before washing them with soap.

DISHWASHER

To refresh the smell in your dishwasher, pour four heaped tablespoons of bicarbonate of soda through the bottom rack and press the rinse-cycle button.

DOLLS

Porcelain dolls can be cleaned with warm soapy water. Bisque dolls (unglazed porcelain) can be cleaned by brushing them with warm soapy water that has had a few drops of ammonia added to it. Use a soft, clean old toothbrush.

Wax dolls can be cleaned if not too dirty, by rubbing the wax with some cold cream. If the wax is dirty, rub it over with cotton wool dampened in turpentine; be very lighthanded, as the turpentine will soften the wax and take some of the colour away. Leave to dry, then polish lightly with a soft cloth. Colouring can be reapplied with watercolours, using your finger to apply the rouge to the cheeks.

DOOR

A quick way to file the bottom of a door which is scratching the floor or the carpet is to put a sheet of sandpaper between the floor and the bottom of the door, then rub the door back and forward over it. Increase the sheets of sandpaper until the door passes smoothly over the surface without rubbing.

To find out where the doors of a cupboard rub when one has difficulty closing it, apply some chalk over the frame of the cupboard; the rubbing will leave a chalk mark on the door's edges when you try to close it, showing you where to sandpaper.

Doors which let draughts in should be dealt with by placing a strip of putty all around the door-frame and by rubbing chalk on the edges of the door so that, when the door closes, the putty will not stick to it. Soon the putty will dry around the door-frame, making it draught-proof.

A creaking door will be silenced at once if soap is applied to the hinges.

DOOR-STOPPER

Stop the door handle from damaging the wall. Take an empty cotton reel, cover it with fabric the same colour as the carpet. Slide a long nail through the middle hole in the cotton reel and fix the whole thing to the floor about four inches from the wall behind the door.

DRAINS

To clear drains, from time to time put a few lumps of washing soda on top of the grid and pour over boiling water.

Do not throw away coffee grounds: pour them down the kitchen sink to keep the drains free of grease.

If a drain becomes blocked with fat, pour one teacup of salt and one teacup of bicarbonate of soda in the drain, then pour two pints/one litre of boiling water down it.

To clear a badly blocked drain when the washing soda method has failed, pour two litres/four pints of boiling water down the drain, then a teacupful of paraffin. Leave for fifteen minutes before pouring another two litres/four pints of boiling water.

If, when trying to clear a clogged drain, you spill some of the drain-cleaner product on your vinyl linoleum or rubber floor, quickly wipe the floor and cover the stained area with vinegar to neutralize the drain-cleaner product, which is caustic. Leave the vinegar a few minutes, then wash and dry. (All this should be done wearing rubber gloves.)

To prevent staining the wall when painting a drainpipe, hold a piece of cardboard or a folded newspaper between the drainpipe and the wall.

DRAWER

For cleaning drawers without removing anything from them, fasten a stocking over the nozzle of the vacuum cleaner with sellotape or a rubber band and suck away the dust and crumbs etc.

Soap or candle wax rubbed along the upper edges of tight-fitting drawers will make them run smoothly.

If a drawer has lost its knobs or handle and cannot be opened without damaging it, open it by suction, using a rubber plunger.

DRAWING PAPER

A roll of wallpaper lining is ideal to give to children for drawing and is very cheap.

DRAWING-PINS

Use a teaspoon to draw out a drawing-pin which is fixed too firmly.

DRILLING

Drilling into metal can be a little tricky sometimes, especially when you want to drill a hole marked at a definite place. To stop the drill skidding cover the mark with a piece of adhesive tape, drill through it, then remove the tape.

To prevent soft and thin metal bending or shredding when drilling, place the metal between two pieces of thin wood and drill through the three thicknesses.

A small torch taped on top of the drill will be very handy when drilling in dark areas.

To prevent bits of plaster going all over the floor when drilling a hole in the wall, tape an open paper bag to the wall beneath the place to be drilled. (Use surgical tape as it does not leave marks when peeled off.)

Some handy jobs need the use of electrical tools for cutting wood, metal etc. A skin-diving mask will protect your eyes perfectly during these operations.

When drilling the ceiling, prevent the chips getting in your eyes by wearing goggles. If you do not have any, take a transparent plastic container (food containers are good), make a hole in the bottom with the drill, rest the container against the ceiling and drill through the hole in the container. Chips etc. will drop into the container.

Protect the floor and the skirting board with newspaper when drilling a wall. Dip one edge of the sheet of newspaper in water and stick it to the wall above the skirting board with the rest of the sheet resting on the floor to collect the falling dust and pieces.

DRIPPING TAP
Until you have time to replace the washer, tie a piece of string around the rim of the tap just long enough to reach the drain; the drops will slide down the string without making a noise.

DRY ROT
To get rid of dry rot on wood, brush the attacked surface with petrol. Wear rubber gloves and do it away from any naked flames and in a well-ventilated room or outside.

DUST
Do not let the dust escape when dusting. Use a duster that you have firstly washed, rinsed and treated by adding a tablespoon of glycerine to the last rinse. Dry before use. The dust will then cling to it.

DUSTBINS
Burn some newspapers in your outside metal dustbin to disinfect it.

DUVET
If you have changed to duvets and your cupboard is full of redundant sheets, make duvet covers with them. You can use different-coloured sheets for the top and underneath of the cover or mix different patterns.

EARTHENWARE (POROUS MATERIALS)
Stains can be removed first by soaking the object in distilled water (obtainable from a chemist) until it cannot absorb any more water. Then coat the stains generously with a thick paste made of French chalk (from a chemist) and distilled water. After about twenty-four hours, when the paste starts to crack, dust it away. Repeat if necessary. If stains persist, rub them with a piece of cotton wool dipped in methylated spirit or white spirit.

Chipped earthenware can be repaired with a paste made of plaster of Paris and white of egg. The chip will be sealed when the plaster dries and becomes hard.

EASTER EGGS
Easter eggs can be dyed with natural products: beetroot juice for red eggs, saffron for yellow and spinach juice for green.

EBONY
For the maintenance of ebony, rub some linseed oil on it from time to time.

To renew the lustre of ebony when the blackness wears off leaving a brown surface, give it the following treatment. Wash with warm soapy water to remove any grease or dirt. Allow to dry and then apply the black dye used for suede shoes. When it is quite dry, polish with a good furniture cream, and it will look as good as new.

EIDERDOWN
Your child's eiderdown won't slip down to the floor during the night if you sew a square piece (four inches/10 centimetres) of fine nylon foam in the middle of the eiderdown – of course the side with the square should be the one placed face down on the bed.

ELECTRIC (CHIMNEY) FIRE
When the artificial coal in an electric fire looks grey, soak a soft cloth in black-currant jelly and rub over the coal. Leave to dry and it will be glossy again.

ELECTRIC FRYING PAN
To clean burns inside the electric frying pan, coat the inside with a thick paste made of a powdered dishwasher detergent and water. Leave for a few hours before scrubbing it.

Another method is to spray the inside of the pan with an oven cleaner. Leave five to ten minutes before scrubbing it.

ELECTRIC HEATER
When storing an electric heater for a long period, cover it to prevent dust covering the motor.

ELECTRIC WIRES
When fitting a plug or something else with electric wire, it is quite difficult to strip the small wires from their rubber covering without cutting some of the tiny copper threads, but if you warm the rubber before with a match, it will strip very easily just by pulling with your fingers.

ENAMEL
To clean small enamel objects (boxes, miniatures etc.) if not too dirty, use warm soapy water. (Do not use detergents.)

If the enamel is cracked and the cracks are penetrated with dirt, cover the enamel with a thick paste made of French chalk (obtainable from a chemist) and water. Leave until it dries and the surface of the paste is cracking. Then brush it off. Repeat the process as many times as necessary.

To clean white enamel, rub the enamel thoroughly with a dry, soft cloth and some bicarbonate of soda. Next wash it off with hot, soapy water.

Do not use coarse cleaning powders on enamel surfaces, as they will scratch.

Stains can be removed by filling the vessel with cold water to which one or two tablespoons of bleach are added. Leave to stand until the stains disappear and rinse well afterwards. To clean the outside of the pan, use a fine abrasive powder (pumice powder) and a strong detergent.

Light stains can be rubbed away with a damp cloth dipped in bicarbonate of soda.

A dirty enamel sink can be cleaned with bleach. Dab the whole sink generously with bleach; leave to take effect on the stains and then rinse.

ENGRAVINGS

Clean soiled engravings by dabbing all over with a piece of cotton wool dipped in a little hydrogen peroxide (10 vol., no more, from your chemist). Wipe with a silk handkerchief or any piece of white silk and leave to dry on a flat surface.

ERASER

Wash a dirty eraser in a little washing-up liquid to get it looking as good as new.

ERMINE

Ermine and other white furs will clean if an equal mixture of dry magnesia and French chalk is rubbed into the fur by hand. The powder should then be well shaken out.

FEATHERS

Feathers can be cleaned in warm soapy water. Hold the feathers by the stem and dip them in and out of the warm soapy water a few times. Rinse in cold water, shake the feathers and leave them to dry, then brush with a soft brush.

FELT-TIPPED PENS

Felt-tipped pens will always be in working order if you store them tip down with their cap on.

If your felt-tipped pen refuses to work, dip the tip in vinegar. This will prolong its life a little.

FILES

Files in the workshop should always be kept clean so they work better. Roll some putty up and down the files; it will gather all the small bits from between the teeth. To prevent this happening in the first place when the file is cleaned, use a piece of dressmaker's marking chalk to rub over the teeth; it will stop particles getting between them.

FIREPLACE

To get the best out of a fireplace which has been unused for a while, before laying the fire, burn a creased sheet of newspaper in the grate to get rid of any dampness in the chimney.

Keep a brick in a permanent position in the fireplace beneath the fire. Build the fire over it and the brick will retain heat long after the fire goes out.

Do not use coloured newspapers or magazines when lighting a fire in the fireplace or a barbecue. The coloured ink gives off some vapour of lead when burning.

Soak old newspapers or any unglazed paper for several days in a bucket of water, then tear up the pulp and squeeze it into hard balls. Place these in a warm place to dry and they will be excellent for lighting fires or for keeping fires burning.

Or soak an unglazed brick or two overnight in paraffin oil and place the bricks under the logs before lighting the fire. The bricks will burn for a long time and keep the fire going.

A fire will burn better if there is a good bed of ashes to hold the heat.

To revive a dying fire, throw two or three handfuls of coarse salt onto it.

Blow hot air over it with a hair-dryer – or use the air pump for party balloons if you don't have a pair of bellows.

When scooping the ashes from the fireplace, light some crumpled newspapers in a corner inside the fireplace; it will draw a lot of the dust up into the chimney.

Stop the dust flying around when emptying the ashes from the fireplace by sprinkling them first with water.

If you burn the vegetable peelings (potatoes, carrots etc.) in the fireplace, it will help to keep the soot from sticking to the inside of the chimney. Alternatively, keep empty tin cans to throw into a new fire.

Throw orange and lemon peels into your fire; the room will smell delicious.

When packing the fire tightly for the night, put a brick on top. The brick will retain and radiate heat for a long time.

To put a fire out in the chimney, lay all the logs in the same direction.

New fireplace tiles should be rubbed with olive oil to avoid cracking before lighting the fire.

FISHING

Marshmallows are the perfect bait for small fishes; they prefer them to worms.

FISH SMELLS – See under **Fish,** p. 138

FLASHLIGHT

One can make a waterproof flashlight by placing the flashlight in a screw-top jar. This is very useful if one is looking for something lost underwater.

FLIES

Get rid of them by putting some balls of cotton wool sprinkled with a few drops of lavender oil on saucers in the invaded room.

To keep flies away, grow basil or mint in pots on your windowsill inside the kitchen or outside in your window box.

FLOOR

A squeaky floor will stop squeaking if talcum powder is sprinkled between the floorboards.

Cement left on floor tiles can be removed with linseed oil.

Heel marks on a vinyl floor can be rubbed off with bicarbonate of soda on a damp cloth.

No more aching knees when scrubbing the floor or steps, if you put a big sponge on each knee as padding. Keep it in place with soft tape, or a rubber band if you wear trousers.

FLUORESCENT LIGHTING

If you are going in and out of a room frequently, do not switch the fluorescent light on and off each time as it will use more electricity. Leave it switched on until you have finished in the room.

FOAM RUBBER

The easiest way to cut foam rubber is to do it with the electric kitchen knife. If you have no electric kitchen knife and you don't mind the smell of burning rubber, heat the blade of an ordinary knife, and do the cutting while the blade is hot.

When filling a cushion with foam crumbs, mix larger pieces of foam with the crumbs to prevent the pieces moving around when the cushion is sat on.

FOIL

Wrap food in kitchen foil tightly for storing, but loosely for cooking in the oven.

FOUNTAIN PEN

To remove dried or clotted ink from a fountain pen which has not been used for a while, flush the pen a few times with ammonia then repeat with warm water, until completely clean. Shake the fountain pen well to get rid of any water left inside before filling it up with ink.

FRAMING

When framing a picture, cover the back of the picture with aluminium foil to prevent damage from damp.

When sealing the back of a picture or a painting with brown paper, before glueing the paper moisten it with water. This way, when glued and dried, the paper will be tightly drawn.

FREEZER
To make defrosting your freezer quick and easy rub inside with glycerine (when it is defrosted). Next time you want to clean it, the ice will come away very easily.

To prevent packages sticking to the shelves after you have defrosted and cleaned your freezer, put the food packets back on the shelves half an hour after you have finished defrosting.

FRENCH POLISH
French polish on wood will come off if rubbed with methylated spirit. Work on a small piece at a time and change your cloth regularly.

FUNNEL
A funnel is the perfect home for a ball of string. Hang the funnel on a hook in the kitchen, or wherever required, and draw the string through the funnel when needed.

FURNITURE POLISH
For a good home-made furniture polish mix equal quantities of linseed oil and vegetable oil and methylated or surgical spirit. Shake well and apply to the furniture.

For another good furniture polish take two teacupfuls of boiled linseed oil, one teacupful of turpentine, one teacupful of vinegar and mix well. Spray onto furniture from a spray bottle, then polish with a clean duster.

FUR RUG
To clean a fur rug, spread some fuller's earth (available at a chemist's) over the rug, brush it well into the fur with your hands, leave for a few hours, then shake it out. Repeat the process several times with new clean powder if the fur is very dirty.

FUSES
When changing fuses, remember to turn off the electricity at the mains before touching the fuse box.

Keep a torch and a card of fuse wire near the fuse box in case of an emergency.

Label all fuses so that you know where they belong when one blows.

To test if a fuse from a plug has blown or not, take a torch, switch it on, remove the battery, then touch one end of the fuse with the head of the battery and the other end of the fuse with the inside of the torch. If the fuse is still good, the bulb from the torch will light up.

FUSE REWIRING

Turn off power supply at main switch. Open the fuse box and pull out the fuses until the one with the broken wire is found.

Fitting a new circuit fuse

When a fuse blows, switch off at the mains and look for and repair loose or bare wires and broken connections. If no fault can be found, replace blown fuse. (If not identified inside fusebox, examine each fuse in turn.)

If a fuse keeps blowing after it has been replaced, do not try to make the equipment work by fitting a fuse of a higher rating; call the local electricity board's emergency service.

Checking fuses

Cartridge fuses Check with a circuit tester (see below) or fit a substitute.

Bridge fuse When it is not blown a thin wire can be seen over the porcelain bridge.

Protected fuse To check, try to prise out wire at one end with small screwdriver.

1. Turn off the power supply at the main switch. Open the fusebox and pull out fuses until the blown one is found.

2. Discard cartridge or wire. Fit new cartridge or wrap new wire clockwise round one screw. Tighten the screw.

3. Draw wire across and wrap it clockwise round other screw. Leave a little slack, then tighten screw. Cut off surplus.

Fitting a plug fuse

Never use a fuse of a higher rating than is needed to safeguard the appliance to which the plug is fitted.

Plug fuses of different ratings from 1 amp upwards are available, but it is recommended officially that only 3 amp or 13 amp fuses need be fitted.

Use a 3 amp fuse for equipment such as blankets, power tools, record players, tape recorders, clocks and lighting up to 700 watts.

Most other domestic equipment requires a 13 amp fuse.

1. Remove plug cover and pull out cartridge fuse.

2. Push new cartridge into holder. Refit cover.

What a fuse does

Every electric cirucit is protected by a fuse, which is designed to melt and break the circuit if too much current is passed through it.

For example, a 3-kW fire used at 240 volts draws current at the rate of $12\frac{1}{2}$ amps. If it is plugged into a circuit with a 5-amp fuse and wiring, the fuse blows to break the circuit and to protect the wiring. A fuse will also blow if a piece of equipment develops a short circuit – for example, if the live wire makes contact with neutral or touches an earthed part of the equipment. Extra heavy current flows through the wiring and the fuse blows.

Identification Some fuses are colour coded white for 5 amp; blue for 15 amp; and red for 30 amp. Or amperage may be stamped on the fuse holder.

Circuit breaker Some fuse boxes have circuit breakers instead of fuses. When the circuit is overloaded, the circuit breaker cuts out. Find and repair the fault, then push in the red button or push up the switch. If it continues to cut out, call the electricity board.

GARBAGE
If you sprinkle pure ammonia over your garbage bags, it will keep the stray cats and dogs away.

GARBAGE-GRINDER
To clean and deodorize a garbage-grinder, grind ten to fifteen ice cubes sprinkled with scouring powder through the grinder, and finish with a few orange or lemon peels. (No water is needed when grinding with ice.)

When the garbage disposal unit stops working it might be the fault of a foreign object that the disposal unit refuses to chew. First switch off the unit, then remove the foreign object. If the unit still won't work insert the end of a broomstick into the drain and push the impeller blades in different places with it. Take the broomstick out, switch on the garbage disposal unit to test.

GARDEN TOOLS
To remove rust from garden tools, rub the stained area with soapy steel wool pads dipped in turpentine.

GAS
Make sure that you know where the main gas tap is, and how to use it, in case of emergency.

GAS BURNER
A toothpick or a pipe-cleaner can be used to unblock a gas burner.

GIFT WRAPPING
An over-sized gift can be wrapped in a pretty paper tablecloth. It's easier than taping small sheets together, and prettier too.

Wallpaper makes a very pretty gift wrap, especially at Christmas time when you need large quantities. It works out much less expensive than wrapping paper.

GILDED BRONZE ORMOLU
To clean, never use metal polish. Wash with vinegar and water, rinse and dry. To remove tarnish, brush gently with soapy water containing a few drops of ammonia and then rinse, dry and polish with a chamois leather. Very dirty gilded bronze will get its shine back if dipped in very hot white wine for a while. Rinse, dry and shine.

GILT
Gilt ornaments can be cleaned with the following mixture: one piece of soft soap the size of an egg, one pint/half a litre of hot water and two tablespoons of ammonia. Mix well and wash the ornament in the mixture. Rinse and dry.

Ornaments can be cleaned with a soft cloth dipped in oil of turpentine (from a chemist). Let the oil dry then buff.

Another method of cleaning gilt is to use four tablespoons of bleach mixed with one egg white: using a soft brush, clean the frame with this mixture and the gilt will brighten straight away. This procedure can be repeated until the gilt looks like new, after which the frame can be sealed with a special varnish to help it keep its appearance.

To clean a gilt frame, use the water in which onions have been boiled, which will greatly improve its appearance.

GLASS

Light scratches on the surface of glass can be treated with a mixture of jeweller's rouge and a few drops of methylated spirit. Rub the paste gently over the scratches until they disappear, then wash and polish the glass with a soft cloth. Or rub the scratches with toothpaste. Leave the toothpaste to dry and wipe away the surplus with a dry cloth.

To frost a piece of glass, lay it over a soft cloth on a flat surface. Sprinkle some fine emery powder (obtainable from an ironmonger) and a little water over the glass and rub a pumice stone all over it. Stop when the frosting effect is produced. Wash well and dry.

GLASS-CUTTING

Always lubricate the tiny wheel on your glass-cutter before starting cutting (paraffin oil or sewing-machine oil will do well). A little oil rubbed over the line where the glass is to be cut will help stop the glass cracking – so will sticky tape. Peel it off when cutting is done.

One way of stopping the ruler moving when cutting a straight line on a piece of glass with a glass-cutter, is to rub the underside of the ruler and the glass where the ruler will be placed with a piece of dry soap.

Make the break as soon as the line is scratched by the cutter or the glass will close up after a while and the break won't be perfect.

GLASSES AND JARS

If drinking glasses stick together, place the bottom glass in hot water and fill up the top one with cold water. They will separate immediately.

New glass tumblers, jugs etc. will be less likely to crack if they are put into cold water and then brought to the boil before being used for the first time.

To prevent jars and other glass vessels from cracking when boiling liquid is poured into them, stand a silver spoon in them before pouring in the liquid. Or stand the glass on a wet cloth.

Another method is to stand the glass with a flat bottom on a marble surface or a china or pottery saucer.

Glasses will sparkle if washed in hot soapy water, rinsed in cold water and then left to dry. (See also **TEA TOWEL**, p. 96).

When clearing broken glass, you will find that any slivers remaining after the large pieces have been swept up can be collected by dabbing them with a damp tissue or paper napkin.

To get rid of small chips around the rim of a drinking class, rub them with fine sandpaper until smooth.

GLASS OVEN DOORS
Stains on glass oven doors will be removed if rubbed with bicarbonate of soda on a damp cloth.

GLASS SHOWER DOORS
Clean by rubbing with white vinegar. Dry and shine.

GLUE
Sometimes the stopper used to close a tube or a bottle of glue gets stuck. To avoid this, submerge the top in glycerine before putting it back on.

If a piece of candle is fitted to the top of a glue bottle and used as a stopper to close the bottle, you will never have any more difficulty in opening the bottle. Glue does not stick to candle wax.

No more half-empty tubes of glue wasted if you take the precaution of applying a little vaseline, or even soap, to the thread before screwing the top on.

A little hot vinegar added to a glue which has become too hard in its jar will soften it immediately.

Hard glue on a wood-joint can be loosened with hot vinegar. Repeat if needed.

Glueing two things can be a messy job. To avoid the glue spreading, put some sellotape along the edges of the objects to be glued. Make sure it is well stuck down. When the glue is nearly hard remove the tape or sellotape and the excess glue at the same time.

An easy way of getting glue into a small crack is to fill a hypodermic syringe with glue and insert it in the cracks.

To make a quick and safe glue for young children, mix flour and water to a thin paste.

For a stronger glue, mix flour and water to a soft paste and bring to the boil while you keep beating it to avoid curdling. This mixture can be used for glueing fabrics and paper.

GOLD – See also **Jewellery**
To clean gold, wash it in hot soapy water to which a little ammonia has been added. For dirty gold, dip it for five to ten minutes in pure household ammonia. Rinse well.

A good cleaner for gold is a paste made of cigar or cigarette ash and water. Rub this solution over the gold with a soft cloth, rinse and shine with a cloth or chamois leather.

GRATER
To sharpen a blunt kitchen grater, rub it over with some coarse sandpaper. Wash the grater afterwards.

GROUT

To clean grout around ceramic tiles, use a solution of bleach and warm water in equal quantities. Scrub the grout with a toothbrush.

Very dirty and black grout will clean with a paste made of bicarbonate of soda and water, which you rub over the grout with a damp cloth.

GUITAR

To get the dirt from the inside of a guitar (or violin), drop two to three heaped tablespoons of rice inside the guitar, shake well, then empty.

GUTTERS

Put a piece of chicken wire over the top of your gutter to stop the falling leaves blocking it.

HAIR BRUSH

To clean a bristle hairbrush, use soda crystals or bicarbonate of soda dissolved in lukewarm water. Stand the brush in the solution so that only the bristles are immersed. They will be clean in a few minutes. Rinse well in salted water to stiffen the bristles. To dry, stand the brush with the bristles pointing downwards. Never use soap and hot water, since they soften the bristles.

To straighten bristles that have been damaged by resting the brush on its head, hold the bristles in the steam of a fast-boiling kettle, then lift the bristles with a comb. Repeat the operation if needed.

Give your hair brushes a dry shampoo from time to time. Spray or sprinkle the bristles with dry shampoo (if there is no dry shampoo, flour will do well). Take a brush in each hand and rub the bristles against each other.

If the bristles become too soft stand them for five to ten minutes in ammonia and leave to dry, or soak in an equal solution of water and white vinegar.

To clean a clothes brush, soak the hair in a solution of ammonia and water (half a teacup of ammonia to $1\frac{1}{2}$ teacups of cold water). Leave for twenty minutes. Rinse in cold water.

HAIR LACQUER – See Mirror

HAMMER

When hammering, stop the head of your hammer slipping over the head of a nail by wrapping or glueing some sandpaper over the head of the hammer.

To remove the broken end of a hammer handle stuck inside the head of the hammer, throw the whole thing in the fire until the broken piece of wood burns itself out of the socket. Then carefully bring the hammer head out of the fire and leave it to cool off and put a new handle onto it.

HANDKERCHIEFS – See also **Tea-towel**
Soak soiled handkerchiefs overnight in cold salted water before washing them.

HANDWRITING
Old handwriting on paper is sometimes so faded that it is difficult to read. It can be deciphered for a short while if brushed over with sulphide of ammonia (obtainable from a chemist).

HANGER
Skirt or trouser hangers often lose their grasp after a while. Stick a piece of the adhesive tape used to prevent window draughts inside each clasp.

Wind a rubber band around each end of a hanger to stop the hanging straps of a skirt from slipping off.

If you are short of hangers for trousers or skirts without loops, put two clothes pegs on an ordinary wire hanger.

For more resistance, tape two or four wire hangers together when hanging heavy clothes on them.

HARD WATER DEPOSITS
To remove hard water deposits from vases, jugs, bottles or glasses etc., use malt vinegar. Fill up the vessel with vinegar and leave for a few hours, or longer if the marks are bad. Then rub off with a fine wire scouring pad. Keep the vinegar, for it can be used again.

HEAT
To increase the heat in a room, aluminium foil taped on the walls behind the radiators will reflect the heat and make quite a difference to the temperature.

Radiators painted in a dark matt colour will radiate more heat.

HIDE
Soiled hide furniture will clean very well if washed with a solution of an equal quantity of vinegar and warm water and a soft cloth. Leave to dry before rubbing with linseed oil. Leave for twelve hours, and then rub the leather with a clean soft duster until the hide doesn't feel sticky any more. Give a finishing touch by polishing it with a white silicone cream.

HOBS AND PANS
To clean sticky hobs and pans soak them overnight in a strong solution of biological washing powder and warm water.

HOOKS – SUCTION GRIP
Suction-grip hooks will hold to the wall and stay there if they are thrown for a few seconds into boiling water before fixing them.

Self-adhesive wall hooks will not come unstuck if you coat the sticky side with clear nail varnish before you put the hooks up.

HORN

To clean horn, wash with soapy water and then wax with a natural-colour wax or a little almond oil. Leave for half an hour before polishing vigorously with a soft cloth.

HOSE

To make the hose fit easily to a tap, rub a piece of wet soap inside the part of the hose to be fitted to the tap or rub your finger – heavily soaped – inside. Once the hose is fixed the soap will quickly dry.

HOSEPIPE

A hosepipe nozzle might be too big to fit the tap. If so use rubber bands to wind around the tap until the hosepipe grips the tap well.

The perfect storage place for the garden hose is inside an old car tyre.

To repair a hole or a tear in a hosepipe, cover the cut part with some strong adhesive glue. Then take some string and wind it, not too tight, around the hose pipe over the glue. Having done this, spread more glue over the string and leave to dry.

HOT-WATER BOTTLES

The safest way to fill a rubber hot-water bottle is to put it flat on the table, holding the neck upright. This will prevent hot water spurting up, which is caused by air in the bottle when it is filled in an upright position. Use a funnel to avoid splashing.

Hot-water bottles will last twice as long if a few drops of glycerine are added to the hot water when they are first filled. The glycerine will prevent the rubber hardening so easily.

When filling up your hot-water bottle add some salt to the water; it will keep the water warm longer.

Sometimes the inside of a hot-water bottle gets stuck together. Submerge the hot-water bottle (without the top on) in hot water and ammonia (two pints/one litre of water to one tablespoon of ammonia), and leave it to soak for at least twelve hours; the bottle will then be ready for use again.

Before storing your hot-water bottle when the warm weather comes, pour some talc inside, close and shake well; this will keep it in perfect condition for future use.

To give a longer life to your hot-water bottle, blow in it when empty before screwing the top on and storing it. This will prevent the insides sticking together.

Of course you can use your hot-water bottle to keep you cool in hot weather, just fill it up with crushed ice cubes.

HUMIDIFIER

To prevent your humidifier smelling musty, add a tablespoon of bleach or vinegar to the water.

ICE-SKATES
When storing ice-skates for a long time rub petroleum jelly over the blades before putting them away.

IMITATION LEATHER (REXINE)
From time to time polish with a little petroleum jelly to prevent cracking.

INK – See also Ink in the STAINS section
To keep ink in good condition inside the bottle and to avoid the formulation of a deposit, place a few cloves inside the bottle or mix a few drops of benzine with the ink.

INSTANT GLUE
If, when using instant glue, your fingers get stuck together and you do not have glue-remover, place your hand in warm soapy water and gradually loosen the skin.

IRONING
To remove starch sticking to the iron, or to remove the sticky patch left after scorching a fabric, sprinkle a piece of paper with fine kitchen salt and rub the iron backwards and forwards over it until the base becomes smooth again. You can also rub the iron with half a lemon dipped in fine kitchen salt.

Residues of burnt man-made fibre left on the iron can be removed by first bringing the temperature of the iron to very hot and scraping as much of the residue as possible off with a wooden spatula. Next let the iron cool off and finish with a fine steel wool pad.

Steam irons can get furred unless you use distilled water (from the chemist) or water which has been boiled for half an hour and left to cool so that the chalk settles at the bottom.

To remove fur, half-fill the iron with vinegar. Warm the iron and press the steam button until all the vinegar has evaporated, then fill the iron with distilled or boiled water and steam it out again until the iron is dry. The iron will be clean inside and ready to be used again.

A few drops of your favourite toilet water mixed with the water inside your steam iron will perfume your linen delicately; or, if you don't have a steam iron, spray your ironing board when you are pressing your clothes.

You will get a better and quicker result when ironing if you put a strip of aluminium foil the length of the ironing board underneath the padded cover. The foil will become hot and your clothes will be heated from both above and below.

If you have to stop ironing before you have ironed all the articles you have dampened, keep the remainder in a plastic bag until you are ready to press them. Don't leave them damp for too long.

Ironing symbols on garments

	Cool iron	For acrylics, triacetate, polyester, nylon and silk
	Warm iron	For wool, wool and nylon mixtures, polyester and cotton mixtures
	Hot iron	For cotton, linen, viscose
	Do not iron	

IRONWARE
Ironware can be protected from rust for a long time if left to soak in a solution of soda for twenty minutes. Remove and leave dry.

IVORY
To clean very dirty ivory, soak for a few hours in milk and then wash with warm soapy water. Hydrogen peroxide is also effective.

To remove marks from ivory, rub on furniture cream and then polish with a clean, soft cloth.

To clean carved ivory, moisten a soft toothbrush in a little warm water and then dip in denture-cleaning powder (obtainable from chemists). Rub the object gently. Rinse with warm water and dry carefully.

Cracked ivory or bone objects can be restored by submerging them in melted candlewax for a few minutes. Take them out, wipe off any surplus wax and leave to set. After this treatment the objects should be kept away from heat.

When an ivory object has been repaired, the new piece of ivory is usually a different colour. You can age the new ivory by dipping the object in cold, wet coffee grounds. Keep watching the progress of the dye. When the colour is the same, dry and polish.

To keep small pieces of ivory white, place them in the sunlight.

To give a patina to a piece of ivory that looks too new, dip it in strong tea or coffee. Do not leave it to soak but keep dipping in and out until you get the required result. Dry and polish.

JADE
Real jade can be recognized from jade substitutes (difficult to identify by looking at them) by scratching a piece of glass with it; only real jade will make a scratch.

Warm, soapy water is the best cleaner for jade. Rinse and dry with a soft cloth.

JAR – See also Bottle
If the rubber ring of a jar becomes dry, soak it for a few hours in a mixture of one pint/half a litre of water and one tablespoon of ammonia. It will then regain its original supple state.

Strong fish or pickle smells in a glass jar can be got rid of by leaving a few drops of bleach in the jar for at least twelve hours.

To sterilize jars, first wash and rinse thoroughly, then place in a cold oven and switch to 140C, 275F, Gas Mark 1. Leave for ten minutes.

JAR LABELS

When making preserves do not put labels on a jar which has just been filled with warm jam. The label will come unstuck. Wait until the jar has cooled off.

JET

Clean jet by rubbing it with a clean chamois leather. Jet can be cleaned with warm soapy water or with soft bread rolled into a ball.

To remove dirt from jet (hair ornaments, bracelet, bangles, beads etc.) take the soft centre of the bread, roll it into a ball and rub the jet with it. It will absorb the dirt, even from the deepest corners and crevices. Brush away any little pieces of bread left after cleaning with a soft toothbrush.

JEWELLERY – See also **Gold** and **Silver**

To clean your gold and silver jewellery, put a few drops of washing-up liquid in a small jar and add one tablespoon of ammonia. Fill up two-fifths of the jar with water, put your jewellery in the mixture and screw the lid on the jar. Shake a little and take out your jewellery. Rinse and dry.

To clean silver jewellery put one teacup of vinegar in a jar with two tablespoons of bicarbonate of soda. Place the jewellery in the jar, screw on the lid and shake a little. Leave to rest for one hour – more if the jewellery is very dirty. Rinse and dry well.

Jeweller's rouge is commonly used for cleaning silver or gold jewellery, but the following will do as well: apply toothpaste on an old toothbrush and rinse well afterwards, or soak in methylated spirit.

To clean very delicate gold or silver jewellery, leave it to soak overnight in ninety per cent alcohol and then dry in some bran.

When stones are set in gold, silver or platignum do not use any chemical to clean the jewellery, use only warm water and soap.

To give a quick shine to your gold jewellery rub with a ball of soft bread.

Rub your silver jewellery with half a lemon for a quick shine; do not forget to rinse before drying.

To loosen and remove a ring stuck on your finger, wash your hands with cold water and soap and try to take off the ring while the soap is still on. Failing that, dry your hands and wrap a narrow ribbon tightly around your finger from the tip of the finger to the ring. Slide the end of the ribbon between the ring and the finger and pull slowly, unwinding the ribbon and pushing the ring up at the same time.

To re-string a bead necklace in record time, glue the end of the old necklace string to the new one with a drop of nail varnish (or glue). Leave it to dry and pull through.

To clean wooden jewellery, rub with a little olive oil, then dry and buff.

KETTLE
A marble in a kettle will prevent furring; so will a clean oyster shell.

To defur a kettle:

1. Pour a small quantity of vinegar (in the case of an electric kettle, the vinegar must cover the element), bring to the boil, shake it and leave to cool. Empty and rinse well. Repeat if necessary.

2. Put a tablespoon of borax in the kettle, fill it up with cold water and bring to the boil. Leave to cool and then rinse thoroughly before using.

3. Fill up a third of the kettle with cold water, bring to the boil, then add one teaspoon of denture powder, leave it to fizz up and to cool, then empty and rinse well. All of these methods might have to be repeated once or twice if the kettle is badly furred.

4. Fill the kettle up with water and place it in the freezer overnight or for at least eight hours. When melting, the ice inside the kettle will pull out the fur stuck inside the kettle.

KEY – See also Locks, p. 57
Rusty keys will shine again if they are left in a bath of turpentine for a few hours, then rubbed and dried.

KITCHEN CLOTH
To clean your kitchen cloth thoroughly, place it in the cutlery compartment of your dishwasher along with your load of dishes.

KITCHEN CUPBOARD DOORS
Use the inside of your kitchen cupboard doors to pin or tape useful telephone numbers (butcher, fishmonger, plumber etc.) or recipes, hints etc.

KITCHEN OR CIGARETTE SMELLS – See Cooking Smells p. 31

KNIVES
To remove fish or onion smells on a knife blade, wash first in cold water, then in hot water.

Alternatively, thrust the blade in the earth a few times before washing in cold water. (Why not have a flower-pot full of earth handy somewhere in the kitchen, near the sink, for this purpose?)

The striking surface of a matchbox is amazingly good for sharpening small knives.

To remove stains from steel knives, rub on a little scouring powder moistened with lemon juice, or rub on a cork dipped in scouring powder.

LABELS
Labels will stick perfectly on glass if their backs are first coated with some white of egg.

Prevent smudging on a medicine label's written instructions by coating it with clear nail varnish.

LACQUER

To clean lacquer, never use a wet cloth as the dampness could make the lacquer peel. Apply a household spot-remover with a dry cloth and then dry the object immediately.

Lacquered papier mâché can be gently cleaned with warm soapy water; dry carefully immediately, then wax with beeswax or furniture polish and shine with a soft rag.

LACQUERED WOOD

Clean with a paste made of white flour and olive oil. Apply the paste gently over the lacquered wood with a soft cloth, then rub it off and shine with a soft clean cloth. Furniture polish or beeswax can also be used to clean lacquered wood.

LAMINATE

To remove a piece of laminate which has been badly stuck to a surface if the glue has already hardened, cover the laminate with some silver foil and run a hot iron over the foil until the laminate becomes hot and the glue underneath softens. It will then be easy to lift off the piece of laminate.

LAMP (ELECTRIC)

When rewiring a lamp, before pulling out the old wire, tie a string to the end of it and pull. The string will take the place of the old wire through the inside of the lampstand. Now untie the string and tie it to the end of the new wire. Pull the string through and the new wire will be in position.

LAMPSHADE

If a fabric lampshade is glued and not sewn on, you should dry-clean it. First remove any grease stains with a fluid stain-remover (such as Beaucaire). Then dip a soft cloth in very fine oatmeal and rub it over the whole shade. Leave it on for ten minutes then rub again lightly with a clean soft cloth, before brushing the oatmeal off.

When the fabric is sewn on, the shade can be held over a bowl of warm soapy water and sponged all over. Rinse with warm water and leave to dry. Replace the shade and switch on the electric light to dry the shade thoroughly. Or use a hair-dryer.

A lace lampshade can be cleaned by rubbing powdered magnesia into the lace with the fingertips, a soft brush or a piece of cotton wool. Leave to stand for two hours before brushing out the powder.

To clean an accordion-pleated lampshade, use a clean, soft paintbrush.

LEAD

When storing lead figures etc., keep them in a polythene bag as lead can be attacked by acidic organic vapours from wood if kept in a wooden cupboard.

To clean lead figures, boil them in two or three changes of water for five minutes at a time and then put them in a container with eight parts of water to one part vinegar. Soak for a short time, then rinse in water containing a small quantity of washing soda. Rinse again in plain water and dry carefully.

LEATHER

Clean light-coloured leather with petroleum jelly.

To keep its natural oils and prevent it cracking clean leather (e.g. chairs, settee etc.) with milk. Dry and buff with a soft cloth.

To give back a shine to old leather, rub it with some beaten up egg white.

LEATHER FURNITURE

A good polish for leather furniture is a mixture of one part white vinegar to two parts linseed oil.

To clean leather furniture, rub it with boiling milk (do not use skimmed milk), then polish with a soft cloth or an old piece of velvet.

LEATHERETTE

On man-made leather fabric, a stain can be treated by covering it with a thick paste made of French chalk and water. Leave on to dry before brushing it off.

LETTERS

Letters or packets cannot be steamed open if sealed with the white of an egg.

LIDS

When a lid sticks and refuses to come off, a rubber band put tightly around it will provide a good grip for the hand and allow the lid to be removed successfully. If all else fails, dip the top of the jar in boiling water for a few minutes and the lid should be loosened. Or put a rubber glove on for a tight grip.

LIFT (ELEVATOR)

The unpleasant feeling some people have inside a lift when it is going down will be greatly diminished by lowering your head sideways or forward.

If you are, unfortunately, inside a lift when it is dropping down very rapidly, try to remember to stand on your tip-toes, legs slightly bent, or, even better, if the inside lift has a ledge to hang on to, hold onto it with your hands.

LIGHT BULBS

Long-life bulbs last for about two thousand hours. They cost more and shed less light than other bulbs.

Normal bulbs have a life expectancy of a thousand hours.

Pearl bulbs cast softer shadows, and throw no shadow on the ceiling.

Clear bulbs do cast shadows.

Pink pearl bulbs give a warm glow without any appreciable loss of light.

A few drops of your favourite perfume rubbed on to a light bulb will fill the room with a delicate scent when the light is on.

To clean light bulbs, take them out of the lamp socket and rub them with methylated spirit.

LILO

When a plastic lilo is leaking, it is not always easy to see where the hole is, even when the lilo is dipped in water. Try this method: when the lilo is dry, fill it with water – straight away drops of water will leak out of the hole. Empty the lilo and patch the hole.

LINEN

Fine linen that is not in constant use should be wrapped in blue tissue paper. This preserves the colour and stops the linen becoming yellow.

To distinguish linen from cotton, wet a fingertip and apply it to the material. If it is cotton the moisture will take some time to show on the other side; if it is linen, this will show immediately.

LINOLEUM

A few layers of newspaper underneath the linoleum will make it last longer and avoid uneven wear. Before sticking or tacking the linoleum around the edge, wait for a few days until it has stretched.

When washing lino, a few drops of paraffin in the washing water will help make it shine.

Black marks on lino disappear by simply using a pencil-eraser. Silver polish will also work.

To renovate lino, beat three eggs into $1\frac{1}{2}$ litres/three pints of water. Rub the mixture over the clean lino with a soft cloth. Leave to dry before buffing.

To repair cracks in lino, use strips of clear adhesive tape (e.g. sellotape) then coat the whole area with some polyurethane clear varnish for a long lasting repair.

LOCKS

When the lock seems to be jammed and the key refuses to turn, coat the key with a little butter or margarine or, even better, vaseline. Put the key back in the lock, pull the door towards you and turn the key, raising it slightly at the same time. Or place a little powdered graphite (from the locksmith) on a piece of paper and blow the powder into the lock through the keyhole.

Soak rusty keys and locks in paraffin oil to loosen the rust so that they can be cleaned easily.

Locks need to be looked after to give long and effective use. A good way to lubricate them is to rub your keys all over with a lead pencil and work the key in the lock a few times.

LOOSE COVERS

Put loose chair or settee covers back on before they are completely dry. They can expand and regain their shape that way. Finish ironing them on the chair or settee. For foam-backed furniture use a cool iron.

MAHOGANY

To clean mahogany wood one of the best cleaners is hot tea or hot beer. Rub the liquid until all signs of grease (fingertips etc.) have disappeared. Dry with a cloth then polish and buff.

MARBLE

To clean marble, use benzine or some copper polish.

To treat dull marble, first wash with soapy water and dry. Then rub with turpentine on a soft cloth. Leave for a few minutes, then polish with a clean, soft cloth.

Yellow stains on white marble can be removed by generously coating the stains with a thick paste of scouring powder and bleach. Cover the stain with a piece of plastic clingfilm to keep the paste from drying out too quickly. Leave overnight. Remove. The bleach will continue to work on the marble for a little while after the paste has been removed.

For slight drink stains (coffee, tea, fruit juice) on a marble tabletop, use pumice powder or powdered chalk, rubbing it firmly over the stains with a strong cloth. Rinse and dry.

Other stains (except grease and oil) should respond to the hydrogen peroxide and ammonia treatment: pour some hydrogen peroxide onto the stain and then sprinkle on a few drops of ammonia. It will bubble slightly. When the bubbling has finished, rinse three or four times with cold water.

Grease or oil stains can be treated by placing a piece of blotting paper dampened with acetone over the stain. Cover it with a piece of cling film to stop the blotting paper drying out too quickly and leave for forty-five minutes. Remove and check. If the stain is old it might be necessary to repeat the treatment a few times.

Another method is to spread a paste made of powdered kaolin and benzine over the stain, cover with cling film and leave for forty-five minutes. Check and repeat the treatment a few times if necessary.

A rust stain on marble will disappear if you dab the stain with a solution of one teaspoonful of oxalic acid (from a chemist) dissolved in a little warm water. (Wear rubber gloves and use the solution carefully).

When ink is spilt on marble, cover the spill immediately with fine salt. When all the ink has been absorbed, wipe it off and cover the stain with *sour milk*. Keep putting more sour milk on as it dries, to keep it always moist. It might take one or two days before the stain clears completely.

MARCASITE

When very dirty, clean marcasite with a soft toothbrush dipped in a soft paste made of French chalk (from a chemist), methylated spirit and a few drops of ammonia.

Keep marcasite in good condition by rubbing it from time to time with an impregnated silver cloth.

MATS
A mat placed inside the house next to each outer door will help to keep the house clean.

To keep the edges of a mat or carpet from curling up, paste some very thick starch along the edge and then iron over some brown paper with a fairly hot iron, or cut a triangle from a rubber tile and glue it at each corner.

MATCH
If you have damp matches that will not light, dip them in nail varnish and strike. You do not have to wait for the varnish to dry.

Or rub them against the bristles of a brush for a minute.

Strike the matches vertically instead of horizontally: they will ignite straight away each time.

MATCHBOXES
Make a miniature chest of drawers by glueing together matchboxes for storing small items in the kitchen, the sewing box or the desk.

MELAMINE
Light stains on plastic tableware will fade away if rubbed with baking soda. Stubborn and heavier stains can be removed with a good rubbing of toothpaste done with a soft brush or a soft cloth.

METAL
When painting galvanized metal you will get a better finish if you first rub the metal with vinegar. Let it dry and then paint.

MELTED PLASTIC BAGS
Pieces of melted plastic bag that get stuck to an electric iron or other electrical appliances can be removed if rubbed with nail-varnish remover or acetone. Unplug the appliance and wait until it has cooled down before cleaning it.

MENDING (china, glass etc.)
A good way to hold two small broken pieces (of china, wood, glass etc.) firmly together after they have been glued, and while they are drying, is to wrap plasticine around the repaired area.

Before mending a broken plate, fill up a container (large enough to hold the width of the plate) with sand or soil. Place the uncracked portion of the plate in the sand or soil with the broken edges sticking out; then it is easy to glue the broken pieces to the broken edges sticking out of the sand or soil. The mended pieces are held by their own weight. This method is good for many broken objects (glasses, cups, teapot etc.).

Clay can also be used to hold small objects that are being mended. Press the object firmly in a block of modelling clay before starting on repairs.

MICA

When dirty, mica responds very well to a rubbing of methylated spirit or vinegar.

MICA ON STOVES

Old stoves have mica openings. To clean the mica, use some metal polish, but do this only when there is no fire in the stove and the stove is cold.

To clean mica on an old stove, wash it first with vinegar, then rub it with vaseline until clean.

MICE BAIT

To catch mice, place a bait of lard, dried fruits, nuts or peanut butter on the trap. Cheese is the last resort.

MICROWAVE OVENS

To clean the inside of a microwave oven, first disconnect the oven from the electricity supply, then rub the interior with a damp cloth sprinkled with some bicarbonate of soda.

To remove any stubborn cooking smells from inside the microwave oven, place a teacup containing water (three parts) and lemon juice or vinegar (one part) inside the oven and cook for eight to ten minutes on lowest setting. Wipe the oven dry after cooking.

MILDEW

To get rid of mildew spots in the kitchen, bathroom or laundry room rub the mildew with household bleach, using a toothbrush for scrubbing stubborn parts. When the mildew is all gone, rinse thoroughly with clean water until no bleach is left, then wash with ammonia. This substance is dangerous, so always wear gloves. Painting over mildew will not get rid of it; it will eventually grow back. So kill the mildew before starting to paint.

The mildew smell in a cupboard can be got rid of by washing the inside of the cupboard with a strong solution of bicarbonate of soda and warm water (one teacup full of bicarbonate of soda to one litre/two pints of warm water).

MILK (SMELLS)

To free a container from the smell of sour milk, fill it with a solution of baking soda and hot water (one teaspoon of baking soda to one pint/half a litre of hot water). Leave to stand until cool, then wash and rinse.

To clean a milk bottle easily, rinse it first in cold water, then in hot water.

MIRROR

Clean mirrors with a solution of equal quantities of water and methylated spirit or water and a little ammonia or white vinegar (three tablespoons of ammonia to four pints/two litres of water). Dry with a chamois leather; if you haven't one, use a crumpled piece of newspaper.

Hair lacquer on a mirror can be rubbed off with methylated spirit or surgical spirit.

For a way to avoid steamed-up mirrors, see **Windows**.

Small scratches on the back of a mirror can be made to disappear if covered with a piece of flattened aluminium foil the size of the scratch. Cover with shellac (obtainable at a hardware store). Leave to dry.

MOROCCO LEATHER

To remove damp stains on morocco leather, rub them with methylated spirit on a soft cloth. Leave to dry and repeat if necessary. Then polish.

MOSQUITOES

To stop mosquitoes coming into the house, hang a mesh bag (from oranges, potatoes, onions) full of cotton wool balls and sprayed with insecticide on open doors and windows.

The mosquitoes won't bite you while you are asleep if you take the precaution before going to bed of placing small saucers filled with turpentine in different parts of the bedroom. The turpentine puts them to sleep and they will fall to the floor.

Another effective way is to dab yourself here and there (face and body) with essence of lavender: the mosquitoes cannot stand the smell, and the lavender fragrance makes you sleep well.

Candles placed on the table during outdoor meals will discourage mosquitoes.

Rub a mosquito bite with vinegar, lemon or ammonia to stop the stinging.

MOSS

Moss often turns a dirty light-green or yellowish colour when dried. To preserve its fresh green colour, dip the moss in a strong solution of washing blue for one minute. Remove it from the solution, squeeze it gently in your hands and leave to dry on newspaper. When completely dry, store in a brown-paper bag until needed.

MOTH

To prevent moths invading your clothes, fill up some small muslin bags with aromatic plants (thyme, mint, rosemary etc.) and place them in your wardrobe and drawers.

Epsom salts are a good deterrent to moths, so sprinkle the crystals amongst clothing, furs etc., in wardrobes and drawers.

Place pieces of soap in a folded blanket before putting it in a polythene bag for storage, and moths will be repelled. This method will also work for clothes etc.

MOTHBALLS (smell)

Powdered charcoal is great for getting rid of the smell of mothballs. Put some in a saucer and place it in a drawer or cupboard; sew the powder into small fine fabric bags and put one in the pocket of a coat.

MOTHER OF PEARL

Mother of pearl needs only to be washed with warm soapy water to keep clean. But do not soak.

Keep it clean by rubbing it from time to time with salad oil.

Dirty mother of pearl can be cleaned with a paste made of whiting (from a paint store or hardware shop) and water. Rub the paste over the mother of pearl and leave to dry before brushing off. Wash in warm soapy water, rinse dry and polish with a soft cloth.

To bleach mother of pearl buttons yellowed with age, boil them in a strong solution of bicarbonate of soda and water (half a teacup of water to two tablespoons of bicarbonate of soda).

MUSLIN

If you have no muslin, use the clean leg of a pair of nylon tights or a stocking.

MUSTINESS

To help eliminate mustiness in a cupboard or a wardrobe, place a saucer full of coffee grounds inside.

Musty odours on old furniture will disappear if an apple stuck with cloves is left inside the piece of furniture.

NAILS

Do not put nails in your mouth when hammering. Get an old rubber glove, cut a fairly wide rubber band out of one finger, then fix the band (which should be tight) around the top of the hammer handle, near the head, and slot the nails into the rubber band.

Protect your fingers when hammering small nails in the wall by using a hairslide as a holder. Alternatively, stick the nail in a small piece of cardboard and hold the cardboard while you hammer. Now tear it away, leaving the nail in place.

Another way is to stick some plasticine on the mark where the nail is to be driven in, then push the nail through the plasticine. It will hold it in place ready to be hammered. Remove the plasticine half-way through the hammering.

When hammering a nail into hard wood, rub it with dry soap and it will go in more easily, or dip it in oil, glycerine, butter or fat.

To avoid making cracks in the plaster when hammering nails into the wall, first cover the spot with a cross of sellotape, then hammer the nail through the tape, or warm the nails in hot water and use them while hot.

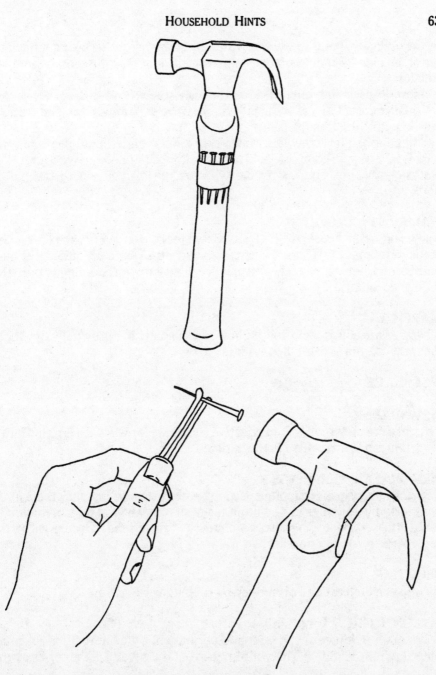

You won't split the wood when hammering a nail in, if you have previously cut the tip of the nail with a pair of pliers.

When the hole becomes too big for the screw pile some small pieces of wet newspaper in the hole before replacing the screw. Cotton wool mixed with plaster of Paris and a drop or two of water is also a good filler.

Alternatively, paint the screw with nail polish before screwing it back or dip it in glue. Winding some steel wool around the threads is another solution.

A few drops of ammonia will loosen a rusty screw.

When you want to remove a nail which has been painted over, first warm it with a match to soften the paint.

To find a nail or screw in a wall when hidden underneath paint or wall-paper, take a small compass, hold it level with the floor and move it along the wall slowly. The compass needle will quickly tell you where the nail is embedded.

NAMES ON WOOD

Names or initials on children's toys, school tools, wooden boxes etc., can be made permanent by using this method: write the name or initials with nail varnish and, before the nail varnish is dry, light a match and slightly burn the varnished initials.

NAPPIES

If nappies are still in good condition when the baby has grown up, dye them different colours and use them as small towels.

NECKLACE – See Jewellery

NEWSPAPER

To light a fire, newspaper is an effective substitute for wood if it is rolled into a long, thin tube and knotted in the middle.

NEWSPAPER CLIPPINGS

To prevent newspaper clippings getting yellow with age, first soak them for at least forty-five minutes in a solution made of one tablet of milk of magnesia and a little soda water in a shallow plate. Next pat off the moisture with a tissue, then leave to dry on a flat surface.

NICOTINE

Nicotine on fingers can be removed by rubbing with acetone.

NYLON CORDS (or Strings)

A knot in a nylon cord can be made permanent by heating it over a small flame (match or lighter). This will also prevent the cut end of the cord fraying.

OAK

To prevent brass screws breaking when being screwed into oak, first use a steel screw to make the hole, then remove it and screw the brass one in. Steel screws should not be used permanently in oak or a rusty bluish stain will appear on the surface of the wood around the screw.

OILCLOTH
Your oil cloth will not get worn through at each corner of the table if an adhesive plaster is stuck on the wrong side of the oilcloth at each corner.

OIL LAMP
To prevent the wick of an oil lamp smoking, dip the wick in vinegar and let it dry well before using it.

A pinch of salt in the oil will give a brighter light.

To make an oil lamp in an emergency, fill a drinking glass two-thirds full with water and pour on some cooking oil to form a layer on top. Cut a thick disc from a cork and make a hole in the centre of it, large enough to hold a wick made from ten to twelve strands of cotton thread knotted together. The wick should stick out one inch/two centimetres on both sides of the disc. Float the disc on the oil, light the wick and you will have a lamp glowing in your hand.

ONYX
To clean stains on onyx rub the area with methylated spirit. Onyx being a porous stone, be sure to wipe up any spills immediately and protect the surface with a good wax polish.

OPEN FIRE
No more black sooty pans to clean after cooking on an open fire when picnicking if you first wrap the outside bottom of your pans in aluminium foil.

ORMOLU (FRENCH GILT)
To clean ormolu, never use metal polish. Wash with vinegar and water, rinse and dry.

To remove tarnish, brush gently with soapy water containing a few drops of ammonia and then rinse and dry.

ORNAMENTS
To keep china ornaments safely on their stand, use a double-sided strong tape stuck to the bases.

OSTRICH FEATHERS
To clean the feathers, put some liquid dishwashing detergent in a large container, pour over four pints/two litres of hot water and beat the solution into a lather. Introduce the feathers, rub them well with your hands then rinse in clean hot water and shake well until dry.

OVEN
Cleaning an oven can be hard work – to keep it clean (if you don't have a self-cleaning oven), rub it all over with a paste made of bicarbonate of soda and water when it is clean and dry. It will then only need a wipe with a cloth next time.

Food spilt in a hot oven will clean off more easily if you cover it immediately with fine salt, then wait until the oven has cooled to wipe up.

To clean a dirty oven: first switch on the oven until very warm, then turn it off. On the top shelf, place a small container filled with ammonia; on the bottom shelf, place a large container filled with boiling water, close the door and leave it for about twelve hours. When the time is up, open the door, wait until the ammonia fumes disappear and wash with soapy water.

To clean burnt-on food stains inside the oven, cover them with dishwasher powder, then place a wet paper towel over it to retain the moisture. Leave overnight and in the morning the stains will come off easily with rubbing.

When an electric oven is switched off it retains the heat for at least twenty minutes. So, to save fuel, switch it off before foods such as biscuits, small cakes and meringues are completely cooked.

After using the oven and when it is still warm, place some orange peel in it; it will absorb all the cooking smells.

PACKING

A small delicate object will travel safely in a hard crusty loaf of bread. Cut the loaf in half, place the object on the dough of one of the halves and cover with the other. Stick the halves back together with sellotape or a strip of adhesive plaster.

Another way is to wrap the object or any china in wet newspaper. When dry, the paper will harden and made a good casing.

PAIL

A hole in a pail can be mended with some putty. Flatten a large piece over the hole outside the pail and a smaller piece inside. Leave to dry before using the pail.

PAINTINGS

Oil paintings which are not of great value can be cleaned at home by rubbing gently with a piece of cotton wool dampened with white spirit. Treat one small area at a time.

Another method is to rub the picture over with a slice of potato dampened in cold water. Wipe off with a damp cloth and finish with clean water. Dry, then polish with a soft cloth or a piece of silk. Then rub the surface with a soft cloth moistened with linseed oil.

PAINT SMELL

One tablespoon of essence of vanilla to two pints/one litre of paint, well mixed, will stop the smell of paint in your house.

One or two shallow containers full of water to which two or three tablespoons of ammonia have been added and placed in the room being painted will stop the smell spreading all over the house.

PAINT TUBES

When a top is stuck on a small tube of artist's paint, it will come off easily if a lighted match is held under the cap for a few seconds.

PAINTWORK

When paintwork gets bleached by the sun, cover the paint with linseed oil. Leave it on for one day. Wipe off any surplus. The colour will then be restored and the paintwork will look sparkling.

PAN

Before using a new pan for the first time, boil some vinegar in it for a few minutes; it will prevent the food sticking.

To remove scaling from a pan, rub with steel wool dipped first in vinegar and then in salt.

To clean burnt food inside a pot, sprinkle the burnt area with bicarbonate of soda and cover with vinegar. Leave to stand (sometimes for a few hours) until the burnt food comes loose easily with the help of a wooden spatula.

Another method is to bring to the boil, in the pan, a very strong solution of salt water. Leave it to cool for at least two hours, for light burns, before rinsing. For badly burnt pans leave at least twelve hours and bring to the boil once or twice during this time.

Very bad burn marks on a pan can be removed with oven-cleaner. Warm the pan up, then spray with the oven-cleaner. Leave it to stand for twenty or thirty minutes before scouring.

To clean a pot that has burnt fat in it, place the pot or pan in a strong plastic rubbish-bag and add a cloth soaked with ammonia; close the bag tightly and leave for a few hours. The fat will then come off easily when rubbed with a plastic scourer.

Do not use this method on an aluminium pan. On aluminium pans use a plastic scourer dipped in a paste made of bicarbonate of soda and vinegar.

To clean pans made of tin, iron or steel (but not aluminium), fill two-thirds full with a solution of washing soda (one tablespoon to one pint/half a litre of water). Bring to the boil and boil slowly for ten minutes. Rinse well.

To clean roasting pans, spray them with an oven-cleaner and leave them overnight in the oven or in a plastic bag. In the morning you can wash and rinse them very easily.

Burnt stains on glass pans can be removed by soaking the pan in cold water to which bicarbonate of soda has been added (two tablespoons of bicarbonate of soda to two pints/one litre of cold water). Leave to stand at least one hour. Make sure the inside of the pan is also filled up with the solution.

PAPER

To cut a long length of paper in a straight line, first roll up the paper evenly. Stick a pin through the rolled paper at the right measurement and unroll the paper; you can then follow the pinhole line to cut the paper (see overleaf).

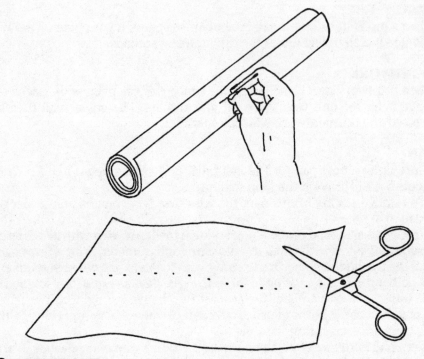

PAPERWEIGHT
Glass paperweights should be cleaned with warm soapy water.

To give back a sheen to a dullish looking glass paperweight, rub it with a silver polish. Leave it to dry, then buff it up with a soft cloth or a chamois leather.

PAPIER MÂCHÉ
Clean papier-mâché with a liquid furniture polish.

To make papier-mâché, tear some cardboard egg cartons into small pieces. put these into a container and cover with cold water. Leave them to get soft and then, with your fingers, work to a smooth mixture. Squeeze out the excess water and add some adhesive (e.g. wallpaper paste) to form about an eighth of the mixture. Mix well and then keep the papier mâché in tied plastic bags. It can be kept for up to two days before use.

PARCELS
When tying up a parcel, first dip the string in warm water and then tie and knot as usual. As the string dries, it will shrink and make the knot very tight.

Also rub a candle over the written label to give it a good coat of wax. The ink will then be waterproof.

PARCHMENT – See also Vellum
To brighten up parchment (e.g. a lampshade) rub it with a cloth dipped in milk. Dry with a soft, clean cloth.

To clean, use half a pint/300 ml of warm water and a tablespoon of soap flakes. Mix well, add two tablespoons of methylated spirit and stir thoroughly. Use a sponge or a soft cloth to rub the parchment, and wipe off the lather. Blot it well and rub with methylated spirit on a soft cloth. Let it dry then polish with a duster.

PARIAN WARE

Clean parian ware with a mixture of half a pint/a quarter of a litre of water and two tablespoons of ammonia. Rinse and dry thoroughly.

PEARLS

Real or cultured pearls can be distinguished by biting them. If they feel gritty to the teeth, they are genuine.

Real or cultured pearls should be worn as often as possible because contact with the skin gives them a brilliance and maintains their natural colour.

Pearls should be stored in a box filled with powdered magnesia to keep them looking their best.

To clean a pearl necklace, leave it submerged overnight in powdered magnesia and gently brush away the powder in the morning. Or rub the pearls with a chamois leather.

To revive discoloured pearls, leave them to soak in a solution of one teacup of water and one teaspoon of ammonia and one teaspoon of whiting (from a paint or hardware shop) for at least six hours.

PENCIL DRAWING

To fix a pencil drawing or pencil writing, brush a little skimmed milk over it.

PENCIL-SHARPENER

To sharpen a pencil-sharpener, wrap a small piece of emery paper around your pencil tip and sharpen the pencil in the normal way.

PERCOLATOR

To clean built-up oil deposits off an electric coffee percolator, fill the percolator up to the full mark with cold water and add five tablespoons of bicarbonate of soda. Plug it in, leave it to run through the full cycle and then allow it to rest for ten minutes, unplugged. Wash in the usual way, rinse and dry.

A pipe-cleaner pushed through the tube of the percolator will clean it perfectly.

PERFUMED WRITING PAPER

Personalize your writing paper by putting a few drops of your favourite fragrance on some blotting-paper sheets and place your writing paper in between.

PEWTER

Pewter is easily dented because it is a soft metal (an alloy of tin and lead), so when cleaning it never use a metal-cleaning powder or liquid. Gently wash it in warm, soapy water and dry and polish with a soft chamois or cloth.

To clean pewter:

1. Use the green part of the leek, or the outer leaves of a cabbage. Just rub over the pewter, then shine with a soft cloth.

2. A piece of newspaper dipped in paraffin oil and rubbed over the pewter will also clean it well.

3. Rub it with a paste made of mild scouring powder and olive oil.

4. The water in which onions have been cooked is also very good to wash pewter in.

5. The stiffly beaten white of an egg mixed with three tablespoons of bleach and rubbed over the pewter is also a good cleaner. Let it dry and wipe with paraffin.

6. Clean with petrol followed by a good rubbing with warm beer. Leave to dry, then shine with a soft cloth.

7. Use a paste made of cigar ash or whiting (Spanish white) and ammonia or linseed oil. Rub the paste over the pewter with a cloth dampened in an equal part of linseed oil and turpentine. Next wash in warm soapy water. Dry and buff with a chamois or soft cloth.

To remove bad stains, rub with the finest steel wool dipped in olive oil. The oil will prevent steel wool making scratches on the surface.

To clean very dirty pewter:

1. First dip the object in a strong solution of warm water and bicarbonate of soda (one litre/two pints of warm water to one teacupful of washing soda). Next rub with a woollen cloth dipped in paraffin oil. Dry with a clean soft cloth.

2. Soak it in a solution of two pints/one litre of water to half a teacup of ammonia for an hour. Rinse and dry and repeat if necessary.

3. Soak the dirty pewter for a few days in paraffin oil, then rub well. Dry with newspaper or absorbent paper and polish with a soft cloth.

4. Clean with a paste made of scouring powder and methylated spirit, then rub with paraffin or vaseline.

Never store pewter in an oak cupboard, as oak gives off fumes which corrode the pewter.

PHOTOGRAPHS

When placing photographs in an album, always put the negative underneath in case it is needed for more printings.

To separate the pages of a photo album which are stuck together, hold the album for a few minutes over the steam from some boiling water. The pages will re-open easily.

To clean photographs, use cotton wool dipped in methylated spirit so as not to damage the surface.

PHOTOGRAPHY

To have nice looking hands (without the veins protruding) when a picture is taken with the hands included in it, hold your hands over your head for a little while just before the picture is taken.

PIANO

An upright piano will sound better if placed about two to three inches/5–8 cm from the wall.

Loading the top of a piano with books and other things will deaden the tone.

When the note of a piano stays down when struck, it is a sign of dampness.

To keep a piano free of dampness, the wires clean, and to prevent the keys sticking, place a shallow container filled with lime inside the piano at the bottom.

Cleaning maintenance of the piano's keys should be done with a chamois leather well wrung out in lukewarm water to which a little white vinegar has been added. Hang a bag of mothballs or crystals inside the piano; this will stop the moths eating the felt.

To clean the ivory notes of a piano, avoid using water. Rub them gently with methylated spirit, lemon juice, eau de Cologne or hydrogen peroxide (20 vol). Keep the keyboard uncovered as ivory gets yellow more quickly in the dark.

To clean very stained piano keys, make a paste with whitening (from iron-mongers) and hydrogen peroxide (20 vol). Apply to the keys; leave to dry overnight before brushing off paste and polishing.

PICNIC

If you do not have a thermos to keep the drink cool when going on a picnic, wrap the bottle in a tea-towel or a newspaper dampened in salted water.

A good tablecloth for a picnic table is a fitted cot sheet. It won't blow away on windy days.

PICTURES

Keep the air circulating behind your pictures hanging on the wall and so stop them marking the wall by sticking a piece of cork on each corner at the back – or stick a small piece of thick emery paper; it will also stop the picture from sliding.

A drawing pin tacked to each corner of the back of the frame of a hanging painting will allow the air to circulate between the painting and the wall.

PILLOW

Real down is the best filling for a pillow as it has the right amount of resistance, moulding comfortably to the head and springing back into shape when the head is removed. It is expensive, but will last for a very long time.

A filling of feathers and down makes the pillow firmer, but is still a very satisfactory mixture and much cheaper than real down.

Goose feathers make the best feather filling as they are not as heavy as hen or duck feathers.

When buying a pillow with a loose filling, shake it from one end. If all the filling drops down to the other end, it means that the pillow will flatten quickly when in use.

When changing the feathers from an old case to a new one, first wash, starch and iron the new case to prevent the feathers working through. Open the old pillowcase half the width of one end, do the same with the new one, then sew the two openings together firmly. Shake and push the feathers from the old case into the new one. This completed, unstitch and discard the old one and sew up the opening of the new one.

PIN BOX

Put a small magnet in your pin box so that the next time you drop the box the pins won't scatter over the floor, but will cling together.

PINGPONG BALLS

If pingpong balls are dented but not cracked, they can be restored by dropping them into boiling water to which a pinch of salt has been added. Stir the balls for a few minutes and the dents will disappear.

PIPES – See also Rubber pipes

Copper, aluminium and other soft metal pipes are hard to cut without the metal bending. Avoid this by introducing a wooden pin of the same diameter into the opening of the pipe, then sawing the pipe and wood together. A stick or a strong wire pushed through the pipe will get rid of the piece of wood left in it. When thawing a frozen pipe, first turn the tap off and start warming (with a hair dryer, or a hot-water bottle) the tap at the side farthest from the water supply, slowly working towards it. This will prevent the pipe bursting.

To prevent your pipes freezing up in cold weather, pour four pints/two litres of water to which two large handfuls of coarse sea salt have been added down the drain.

PLACE CARDS

When using place cards at a table, write the name of the person on both sides – it will be a reminder for the guests sitting across the table.

PLANE (TOOL)

To smooth the surface of woodwork more easily with a plane, rub a piece of candle all the way along the plane first.

PLASTER

To prevent lumps, add the plaster to the water instead of the water to the plaster.

To stop plaster getting hard too quickly, when you are doing a plastering job, mix some vinegar with it (one teaspoon of vinegar for each pint/half a litre of mixture).

To paint on plaster, first cover the plaster with a thin coat of very hot linseed oil. Leave to dry before painting.

To obtain a patina on plaster, brush over the plaster with a solution of warm paraffin to which a little furniture wax or liquid polish has been added. Leave to dry and polish with a soft cloth.

PLASTER CAST

To clean plaster casts, first remove all the dust from the crevices with a brush, then immerse in skimmed milk or apply the milk with a piece of cotton wool until no more liquid can be absorbed by the cast. Next lightly dab any excess liquid with a tissue. Cover the cast with a clean cloth and leave to dry.

PLASTER JEWELLERY

To clean, rub gently with a piece of cotton wool damped in ammonia or alcohol. Do this in a well-ventilated room.

PLASTER OBJECT

To clean plaster make a soft paste with starch powder and water, coat the object, ornament etc. with it and leave it to dry. The paste will become powdery and brush off with a clean soft brush or a cloth. If you don't have starch powder use potato flour. Another way is to spray the object or ornament with starch from a spray bottle or can. Leave to dry and brush or dust gently with a dry, soft cloth.

PLASTIC

Stains on plastic (e.g. coffee, tea) should be rubbed with bicarbonate of soda.

Nail-polish remover or lighter fluid will remove plastic which has melted and stuck to electrical appliances (do not forget to unplug the flex first).

PLASTIC BABY PANTS

One tablespoon of glycerine in the last rinsing water will keep baby's plastic pants soft for a long time.

PLASTIC BOTTLE

Plastic bottles can be made leak-proof for travelling if, after filling them up and while screwing the top in, you press the sides of the bottle gently with your fingers.

For easy disposal, pour a small quantity of boiling water into the bottle. The plastic will become soft and the bottle will collapse – you can then just crush it in your hands.

PLASTIC CONTAINERS

A good way to get rid of persistent odours in a plastic container is to crumble some newspaper (no coloured prints) and place it in the container. Cover tightly and leave for at least twelve hours.

PLASTIC LAMINATED SURFACES

Laminated plastic surfaces are all over the home and are very easy to clean. Wipe with a damp cloth – washing soda with hot soapy water is best for cleaning dusty laminated surface; bicarbonate of soda for obstinate stains and wax or liquid polish for dull surfaces.

PLASTICINE

Plasticine is very useful for fastening slender sprays of foliage to the garden wall; it will last for a long time and is quite waterproof. It can also be used, with or without a stick, to bind up a plant that is bent or partly broken.

A quick substitute for plasticine to give to children is a dough made with flour, water and salt. Add a little paprika or mustard powder for the colour. Store it in a plastic bag.

PLATE-HOLDERS

For a home-made wall plate-holder use four strong sewing hooks placed tightly at equal distances around the edge of the plate and held together by a string going through each hook and forming a square at the back of the plate. Then hold the bottom and top hooks with another string, making a loop for hanging the plate to the nail on the wall.

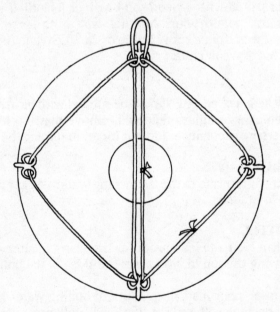

PLATINUM

Clean platinum like gold (see p. 47).

Restore its brightness by rubbing some dry baking soda or flour over it with a chamois leather. Or soak it in a solution of warm water and mild detergent. Rinse and dry before buffing.

PLEXIGLASS
Superficial scratches on plexiglass can be hidden with a little furniture or natural shoe polish rubbed over them. Deep scratches need to be buffed out professionally by a machine.

PLUMB LINE
Make a home-made plumb line by tying a long, thin string to a small heavy object such as a nut.

PLUNGER
To make a small repair to plasterwork on a wall, use the rubber suction cup of a plunger to mix a small amount of plaster. You can then hold it by the handle in one hand and patch with the other.

PORCELAIN (hard paste, non-porous material)
To get rid of stubborn stains, first soak the object in distilled water (obtainable from a chemist) for two hours. The soaking is to prevent the stain retreating inwards. Then cover each stain with a small piece of cotton wool dipped in a solution of hydrogen peroxide (20 vol, from a chemist) and half a coffee-spoon of ammonia. Leave for about two hours. Rinse off and dry. Repeat the process if necessary, but with some time in between to allow it to dry or it may damage the glaze.

Rust stains on porcelain (e.g. porcelain baths or basins) can be removed by applying cream of tartar over it. Leave until the stain has been absorbed before rubbing it off.

PRINTS
When old prints, engravings or etchings are stained by yellowish spots of rust, they can be cleaned by dipping them in a solution of two tablespoons of hydrogen peroxide (20 vol) to six teaspoons of water and a few drops of ammonia. Leave for half an hour and then rinse under running water. Lay the print on blotting paper to dry. To avoid any wrinkling, cover the print with another piece of blotting paper and some heavy books while it is drying.

When a print is wrinkling inside its frame, bring it out of the frame, place it face down on a piece of glass or marble and dab with a sponge moistened with water. Next place the print face up and flat on a table with each corner pinned to the table until it is completely dry.

PROTECTIVE PADS
Use bunion pads as scratch protectors by sticking them to the bottom of furniture legs, small objects (ornaments etc.,).

PUTTY
Keep putty in an airtight plastic bag or aluminium foil.

A piece of cut raw potato is ideal for smoothing down the putty when doing a job.

To keep putty soft longer place it in a container full of cold water, or add a few drops of glycerine or linseed oil to the putty and knead it.

When working with putty, stop it sticking to your hands by dusting them from time to time with flour or talcum powder.

In an emergency, use a home-made putty recipe: take some talcum powder and add linseed oil until you get a dough the consistency of putty.

Old putty around a broken glass window will soften if brushed with varnish-thinner and left for five minutes. Avoid touching the paint during this operation, or the paint will also soften.

To remove old putty from a window frame when replacing a glass, soften the dried putty with a propane torch. If you do not have a torch dab the old putty with linseed oil and leave it to soak in. The oil will soften the putty enough so that it can be scraped away. Remove any traces of left-over putty with a wire brush. Before puting on the new putty, brush the window frame with some linseed oil to stop the wood absorbing oil from the putty.

PYREX DISHES

To clean pyrex dishes that are yellowing, soak them overnight in hot water (four pints/two litres) and one teacupful of household bleach. Alternatively, boil them in one teacupful of vinegar and water (four pints/two litres).

QUARRY TILES

To get white patches out of a quarry-tiled floor, brush the tiles with a solution of vinegar (two teacups) and warm water (four pints/two litres). Repeat if necessary.

QUILTS

The best quilts are those filled with the largest amount of good down as this is light, warm and very resilient. They are expensive, but well worth buying as they will last for a lifetime.

Down quilts contain up to fifteen per cent of their weight of small feathers.

Down and feather quilts must contain at least fifty-one per cent of down.

Feather and down quilts consist mainly of feathers and should contain at least fifteen per cent of down.

RAFFIA

Clean raffia with strongly salted warm water to which a little vinegar has been added.

RAZOR BLADES

To protect your fingers when using a double sided razor blade for handy jobs around the house, slip one edge of the blade into the stub end of a matchbook (after all the matches have been used of course).

To keep razor blades in good condition and prevent them getting a blunt edge too quickly, keep the razor (with the blade on) standing in a solution of water (a glassful) and borax (one tablespoon) between uses.

RECYCLING

Can ring-openers
Use them as tacks to hang light fixtures on the wall. Nail them to the frame on the back or staple to the cardboard.

Cardboard tubes
Cardboard tubes (from aluminium foil, toilet paper, paper towels, cling film) are good for storing pieces of electric wire, extension cord etc. Wind the wire and slide it inside the tube. You will never be faced again with a mass of inter-twined wires.

Tape two cardboard rolls together and slide them inside the leg of your boots to keep the boots in shape. A plastic fruit juice or mineral water bottle will also make a good boot tree.

Tubes are perfect for packaging and sending magazines or papers through the post.

Coffee filter
Re-use your paper coffee filters. Rinse them and place them back in the filter cone to dry.

Coffee grounds
Put them on the soil in your garden or in your plant pots, because they serve the same purpose as tea-leaves; so does an eggshell.

Used and dried coffee grounds make very good and light filling for small do-it-yourself toys.

Coffee tins
Cut a cross in the middle of the plastic lid of a long coffee tin, slide the handle of a heavy paint brush in it, pour some solvent in the tin, put the lid back on and soak the brush in the solvent to the depth required. The brush should not touch the bottom as this could damage the bristles by bending them out of shape.

Containers
Wax-coated cardboard containers (milk, cream, fruit juices etc.) are very good for starting a fire in the grate, or outside in the barbecue, and you don't have to dry them first.

Credit cards
The edges of credit cards are perfect for removing excess plaster when filling a crack in the wall, or removing excess wax or polish when filling a small scratch on furniture.

Egg boxes
Use the plastic egg boxes for making ice. Fill up each half with water and place in the ice compartment of your refrigerator.

Plastic egg cartons make very successful paintboxes for children. Just put a little paint in each hole. They also make ideal seed trays for germination.

Cardboard or fibre egg trays are good to grow seeds. When it is time for planting the young shoots, just bury the cardboard or fibre trays. That way the roots won't be disturbed, and the tray will disintegrate after a while.

Hot water bottle
Do not throw the old covered hot-water bottle away, but fill it up with some old tights or stockings, some foam rubber or tissue paper, and you will have a good kneeling mat.

Jar
Your empty spice jar with a plastic perforated top is ideal for storing your short, thin skewers by pushing them through the holes. You won't have to pour out the whole kitchen drawer to find them next time you need them.

Make some small holes in the lid of a glass screw-topped jar with a nail or a skewer and use it as a water sprinkler when ironing, or as a flour-dredger.

Milk cartons
Milk or fruit juice cartons make perfect moulds for candle-making.

Plastic bottles
Cut a plastic bottle in half and use the bottom part as a container for storing food in the fridge; use the top part as a funnel or as a lid to cover other containers (leave the plastic stopper on).

Plastic squeezy bottles (liquid detergent, for example) are quite good as improvised bellows for a fire. Just press the bottle in and out.

Plastic mesh bags
Plastic mesh bags from oranges, onions etc. can be filled with soap scraps, tied and used for scrubbing pans. Or hang one near an outside tap for rubbing and cleaning dirty hands.

Sardine key openers
Little sardine key openers are perfect as small screwdrivers.

Socks
Old socks can be used as dusters. Slip your hand into them, and the dusting will be done quickly.

Stockings
Save laddered stockings or tights, cut them into shreds and use to stuff cushions and toys.

Suitcases
Half bury an old suitcase in the garden and place your seed trays inside. The seeds will be protected and you simply close the lid when bad weather and frost are predicted.

Tie
Cut the fat end off an old tie, stitch it, slide a piece of cardboard inside to stiffen it, pin it through the point (with a drawing pin) into the inside of your cupboard and use it as a knitting-needle holder.

Toothbrushes
Old toothbrushes are very useful for cleaning around taps.

Watering sprinkler
The washing-up liquid bottle can be filled with water and used for watering your house plants.

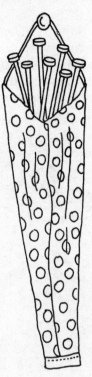

REFRIGERATOR

Test your refrigerator to check if the door seals properly when closed. Close the door on a piece of paper. If you can pull the piece of paper out easily your refrigerator needs to be checked up.

When a refrigerator is noisy, it is usually because it does not stand on a level surface.

When a refrigerator already in use has to be transported from one place to another, and will be unplugged with the doors closed for a while, leave some charcoal bricks inside to absorb the humidity and prevent the fridge smelling of mildew.

When cleaning your refrigerator always add some bicarbonate of soda or vinegar to the warm cleaning water. Rinse well and dry thoroughly.

Eliminate odours in the refrigerator by placing a small open container full of baking soda inside; replace it after a few months. A piece of charcoal placed in your refrigerator will also absorb the smells of cheese, fish, melon etc. Renew the charcoal every five-to-six months.

RESIN

To get rid of resin on your hands when handling a pine tree at Christmas time, wet your hands and rub them with bicarbonate of soda.

RESTRINGING A NECKLACE

When restringing a necklace and a knot is needed between each bead, start the knot by making a loose loop in the thread. Inserting your finger through the loop and bringing the loop near the bead, slide your finger out and replace it with a darning needle. Pull the thread tightly, bringing the knot well against the bead, then remove the needle. Always make sure that each knot is firmly set against the bead.

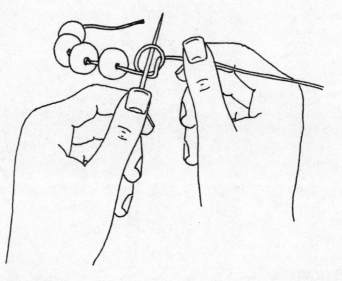

RING – See Jewellery

ROCKING CHAIR

Some rocking chairs have a tendency to move all over the floor when used. A good strong velvet ribbon (nylon velvet will do) glued to the rockers will prevent this.

ROLLER BLIND

To increase tension on a slack roller blind, first unwind it through several revolutions. Next take it down from the brackets and rewind it by hand and put it back on the brackets. Repeat if needed. To decrease tension on a roller blind, bring it down from the brackets. Unwind a little by hand then put it back.

Repair a small tear in the roller blind curtain with some clear nail varnish.

To clean, remove blind from the window, spread it out flat and sprinkle with white flour or cornmeal and rub the surface well with a flannel or terry cloth.

ROOF-RACK

Your empty roof-rack won't make a whistling noise, when you are driving your car, if you wind some thick string very tightly all the way around the loading bars.

ROPE

A stiff rope can become supple if left overnight in a solution of glycerine and water (ten per cent glycerine); then leave to dry.

RUBBER GLOVES

Hands sweat a lot in rubber gloves, so powder the inside with talc when you use them and wash the insides from time to time to avoid an unpleasant smell.

The right hand usually wears out first, so keep the left hand for the next pair: when the right-hand glove goes again, turn the spare left-hand glove inside out and you will have a right-hand glove.

Old rubber gloves can be made into rubber bands of different sizes by cutting across the double thickness over and over again, including the fingers.

Before using rubber gloves for the first time turn them inside out and stick a small piece of adhesive plaster at the tip of each finger. This will help stop your nails from piercing the tips.

If you have long nails, put a piece of cottonwool in each fingertip of the rubber gloves to prevent your nails piercing the rubber.

To stop water going inside the gloves when you are wearing them, hold the opening securely to your wrist with an elastic band.

To store rubber gloves, glue the flat side of two spring clothes pegs inside the cupboard door underneath the sink, then clip the gloves by the cuffs to them. The gloves will dry quicker and without sticking.

RUBBER MAT ·

To get the water deposit off a rubber mat (in the bathroom or kitchen) pour some vinegar over the mat and leave it for at least ten minutes (overnight if it is very badly stained). Brush lightly and rinse.

Another way to clean rubber mats is to soak overnight in a solution of bleach (half a teacup) and warm water (one litre/two pints).

Stains on bath or sink rubber mats will disappear if rubbed with a soap-filled steel-wool Brillo pad, dipped in bicarbonate of soda.

RUBBER PIPES

To fit the end of a rubber pipe to the end of another pipe, coat the inside end with some wet soap.

RUBBER PROTECTORS

Use rubber protectors on top of your draining board and on the end of the tap to save you from cracked and chipped crockery, china and glasses.

RUBBER SHEETS

Rubber sheets used to line a mattress in case of illness or in a baby's cot or small child's bed, when not in use should be rolled around a cardboard tube, a broom handle etc. This will prevent the rubber getting damaged as it would if stored folded.

RUGS

To fix a rug onto a carpet or a shiny floor and prevent it wrinkling or slipping:
1. Sew or glue pieces of carpet, pile downwards, under the corners of the rug at each end.
2. Stick some plastic stick-ons (used for the bath tub) here and there on the wrong side of the rug. You can also use rubber patches used to repair bicycle inner-tubes.
3. Brush the back edges of the rug with some latex adhesive. Leave to dry thoroughly.

To clean a white rug, take it outside and sprinkle generously with talcum powder or white flour. Rub in well and vacuum clean.

The best way to clean a delicate oriental rug is to lay it face down on clean snow. Walk all over it, shake it and bring it back into the house. Lay it on the floor face up. Leave for at least two hours, then vacuum very lightly or, better still, beat it.

A very good result can also be achieved by laying the rug on dewy grass instead of snow.

RULER

A wooden ruler can be kept in place when tracing or cutting a straight line on a slippery surface if you first slightly dampen the underside of the ruler.

RUST

Rust can be prevented inside a metal container if, before filling it up with water, or soil, the inside of the container is rubbed all over with slightly wet soap.

Rust on utensils can be removed by rubbing the stains with a cork dipped in olive oil.

To clean rust off steel or iron, first soften the rust by dipping the object in paraffin for twenty-four hours. Then take it out of the paraffin, wipe it lightly and rub the metal with steel wool until clean. If it is not possible to dip the object, wrap the rusty part with a cloth soaked in paraffin and leave it for twenty-four hours. Then rub the metal with steel wool. Protect non-metal parts with plastic adhesive tape.

To remove rust marks from a steel draining board, rub with lighter fluid or a typewriter eraser.

Rust stains on metal will sometimes disappear if rubbed with half a raw onion.

SAFETY

Pots and pans should have their handles turned towards the back of the cooker to avoid knocking them off.

SALT

To remove salt from windows by the sea-side, use a nylon scouring pad dipped in vinegar.

SANDBOX
To make a cheap, safe sandbox for a child, position a large tyre, lay it on the soil and fill the inside space with sand.

SAP
To get sap off glass windows, rub the glass with baking soda, let it dry and then buff. Baking soda will not scratch glass as a scouring pad would.

SAVING ELECTRICITY OR GAS
Use a plate made of a heat-conducting metal, big enough to hold two saucepans. Put this on the ring of your cooker and you will be able to cook two dishes for the price of one.

SAW
Before storing a saw, rub the blade over with a bar of dry soap. It is a good lubricator and will not stain later on when the saw is used again.

To make your saws sharper, rub a little wax furniture polish on the blade; it will run more freely.

SCISSORS
To sharpen your scissors, take a bottle and act as if you wanted to cut the neck with the scissors – or cut a sheet of emery paper into small pieces.

SCOURING PAD
To prevent a scouring pad from rusting, sprinkle some bicarbonate of soda in the bottom of the container where you store the pad.

SCREWS
To make it easier to insert a screw into hard wood, put wax polish or candle wax on the end of the screw.

To remove a rusty screw if oil has failed, apply a little hot vinegar, or a little hydrogen peroxide (20 vol) or some paraffin oil.

When a screw is loose, because the hole has become too big, take the screw out, wrap some aluminium foil around the thread and replace the screw.

When the hole becomes too big for the screw, pile some small pieces of wet newspaper in the hole before replacing the screw. Cotton wool mixed with plaster of Paris and a drop or two of water is also a good filler.

Alternatively, paint the screw with nail polish before screwing it back or dip it in glue. Winding some steel wool around the threads is another solution.

A few drops of ammonia will loosen a rusty screw.

SEALS
Clean seals with the end of a small wooden stick covered with cotton wool or a cotton bud dipped in a little soft butter.

SEASHELLS

Wash your dusty collection of big seashells in the dishwasher (full cycle); they will come out as clean as china.

SELLOTAPE

Stick a safety pin or a paperclip at the end of a sellotape roll to prevent the end sticking back to the roll.

To peel sellotape off paper (wallpaper, wrapping paper etc.), first warm the sellotape up with a hot iron.

SERVING TROLLEY

Invest in a serving trolley: it will be very useful, not only for serving meals but also for carrying all sorts of things throughout the house, or to stand beside the bed of a sick person.

SETTEE

Settees and chairs covered with chintz, silk, or damask can be dry cleaned by rubbing warm bran over them with a soft cloth. Warm the bran in the oven on a baking tray. (For how to warm bran, see p. 319 (Furs).)

SHARPENER

Use a clay flower pot to sharpen your knives. Do the sharpening under a thin trickle of running water from the tap.

SHAVING FOAM

Keep an aerosol of shaving foam in your office desk drawer. If you cannot leave your desk to go and wash your hands when they are sweaty or dirty following some paperwork, spray them with shaving foam and wipe with a tissue. This will clean and freshen them.

SHEEPSKIN RUG

Sheepskin or lambskin rugs can be cleaned in the bathtub in warm water (enough to cover the rug) to which four tablespoons of glycerine have been added and the following solution: one litre/two pints of boiling water, five tablespoons of olive oil and one teacupful of soap flakes. Mix all the ingredients well and add to the warm water and glycerine in the bath tub. Wash the skin in the solution. Give the skin two rinses. Squeeze the skin to get as much water as possible out. (Do not worry if some soap is left.) Finish off by mopping the wool and skin with towels. Hang it to dry. When the skin feels nearly dry, rub a mixture of flour (one teacup) and oatmeal (one teacup) all over the back and into the fur. Shake well and comb the wool to restore its fluffiness.

Another way to clean a sheepskin is to sprinkle it all over with powdered magnesia. Work it well into the pile with your fingers. Roll up the skin and leave for at least twelve hours. Next take it outdoors and shake it well before vacuum cleaning to remove any powder left in the pile.

Another method would be to use a dry shampoo carpet-cleaner.

SHEETS

To make fitted sheets, tie a knot in each corner of a plain sheet and tuck the knot well under the mattress.

With a laundry marker, write an S or a D in one corner of all your sheets so that you can see at a glance which are single and which are double.

SHINE

Black or dark coloured clothes become shiny with wear. They can be renovated by brushing the shiny part with black coffee (half a teacup of strong black coffee to half a teacup of water). Then press with a wet cloth.

Remove any shininess on black cloth (suits, skirts etc.) by rubbing it with a piece of clean cloth dampened with turpentine or white spirit (the smell will soon disappear).

To remove the shine from dark clothes, especially trousers, take a soft cloth and rub well into the fabric a solution made with laurel leaves and water. Leave to dry before pressing with a damp cloth.

Laurel leaf solution: cut about two dozen laurel leaves into small pieces and boil them slowly with a pint/$\frac{1}{2}$ litre of water in a covered pan for twenty minutes. Use the solution, as hot as possible, to rub over the fabric.

To remove shine marks on clothes brush with a solution of 1 pint/$\frac{1}{2}$ litre water for 1 tablespoon of ammonia.

SHOE BRUSHES

When the brush is caked with hard shoe polish, soak it in a saucer filled with turpentine or white spirit for a few hours. Rub the excess polish on newspaper, and wash in a container lined with a plastic bag filled with warm water and detergent. (The plastic bag is thrown away afterwards and will prevent the unpleasant job of cleaning the greasy container.) This method also applies for floor polishers and brushes.

SHOWER

Use a rubber-bladed window-washing tool to wipe the shower door and tiles dry straight after a shower. This will prevent hard-water spots.

To clear away the steam after having taken a hot shower, run the cold water full blast for a short while.

When a metal shower head is clogged with mineral deposits, boil it for about ten minutes in a solution made of an equal amount of water and vinegar. The shower head must be submerged in the solution.

If the shower head is plastic, do not boil it; let it stand in a solution of equal amounts of hot water and hot vinegar. Try scraping it gently after a few hours soaking. It might need a longer soaking if it is badly clogged.

NB: Take out the rubber washer before boiling or soaking the head, and replace it when the head is cleaned.

SHOWER CURTAIN

To prevent mildew on your cloth shower curtains, soak them for half an hour in a strong solution of salted water. Then hang them up to dry. Sponge shower curtains regularly with some vinegar to prevent hard-water marks or to get rid of the hard-water mark.

Get rid of mould on shower curtains by rubbing with a weak solution of bleach and water. Rinse well.

Rub mildew stains on shower curtains with bicarbonate of soda (which, on a damp cloth, will also get rid of hard-water marks).

Soap deposits on shower curtains will disappear if the curtains are left to soak in warm water to which three to four tablespoons of water-softener have been added.

To prevent shower curtains getting soiled and the pleats sticking together, after washing and drying them, spray them with furniture polish and then rub with a soft, clean cloth before hanging them again.

Add two teacups of vinegar to the last rinse when washing plastic shower curtains; it will keep them supple when dried.

SHREDDED FOAM

Before stuffing a cushion or toy with shredded foam, rub your hands and arms with a fabric-softener and leave it to dry naturally without using a towel. The foam will not stick to your skin then.

SILVER

When storing silver, wrap it in a plastic bag or silver foil; it will keep clean much longer.

Do not let rubber touch your silver, as it will leave ugly black marks.

A piece of camphor in the drawer or cupboard where silver is stored will keep it bright.

Pieces of silver which are stored away unused for a long time will stay bright if buried in flour.

Do not store silver in newspaper. The printing ink would damage the plating.

If your silver salt cellars have no linings, the salt should be removed after use. If they are lined, make sure that no salt is lodged between the silver and the linings. Remove the spoon from the salt cellar after every meal.

To give lustre to new silver, dip it in very hot water to heat the metal, then quickly dip it in bleach, dry it and clean with silver polish to bring out the reliefs.

Table silver should be washed in soapy water with one tablespoon of ammonia (or vinegar). Rinse in hot water and dry. This method will keep the silver in good condition and it will only need occasional treatment with a silver cleaner.

To clean silver in a hurry, apply some methylated spirit with a rag. Leave the silver to dry for a few minutes and then polish with a soft cloth. Tooth-paste will also clean silver.

Table cutlery and table silver should always be washed after cleaning to avoid the cleaning product contaminating the food.

Home dip for silver – an easy and unmessy way to get your silver shining: crumple a piece of aluminium foil in a large container with some washing soda and pour boiling water over it. (Some fumes may be given off but this is a normal electrochemical reaction so do not worry.) Immerse the silver and leave until the tarnish has been removed, then rinse and dry. The solution does not need to be strong – two tablespoons of washing soda to one gallon/four litres of water.

Another equally successful way is to use an aluminium pan, put some bicarbonate of soda or washing soda in it, place the silver in the pan and cover with water. Bring the water to near boiling but do not boil. Take away from the heat and leave the silver until the tarnish has been removed, which takes only a minute or two. The solution should be two tablespoons of bicarbonate of soda or half a teacupful of washing soda to two litres/four pints of water.

Do not wear rubber gloves when cleaning silver as they leave marks all over it.

To clean silver, make a paste with baking soda and water. Rub it gently over the silver and brush away any remnants of the paste. Shine with a soft cloth.

Soot rubbed on the silver is also very good but a little messy.

Lemon juice or methylated spirit mixed to a thick paste with cigar or cigarette ash will clean your silver quite well. Dip a soft cloth in this mixture and rub it on the silver. Polish with a clean, dry cloth.

An equal quantity of ammonia and vinegar is good for dirty pieces of silver; use a toothbrush and brush well over the embossings. Rinse and dry.

A fairly thick paste of powdered chalk and ammonia, when rubbed over silver, will clean it perfectly.

Egg tarnish on silver is quickly removed by rubbing with table salt, wet earth or a cooked potato. Acid stains (e.g. mustard) are difficult to remove but will disappear if rubbed with salt and a few drops of lemon juice, or soak the silver in hot vinegar for fifteen minutes.

To remove a salt stain, rub it with damp salt – this works like magic.

Ink stains on silver – see STAIN section: Ink (fountain pen ink).

SILVER CORD OR BADGES

Clean silver cord or badges on uniforms by using a stiff toothbrush and a generous portion of powdered magnesia or bicarbonate of soda. Brush it into the cord and leave it for forty-five minutes or so. Then brush it off with a clean stiff toothbrush.

SILVERFISH

To get rid of silverfish in cupboards or behind furniture, wipe the floor with a cloth dampened in turpentine or sprinkle epsom salts at the bottom of your walls.

SILVER GILT

Silver gilt is silver coated with gold. It should be cleaned with soapy water. Do not use a silver polish, as this would remove the gold.

SILVER PLATE

Silver plate is either nickel or Britannia metal coated with silver. The best has a nickel base, with the stamp EPNS – electroplated nickel silver. The stamp EPBM means electroplated Britannia metal. Britannia metal is a mixture of tin, copper, zinc and antimony.

Sheffield plate is very valuable because of its rarity. It has a copper base with a silver coating. Clean as for silver.

SINK

To rescue a small object accidentally dropped down the drain of the sink, take a piece of wire, stick some putty or some chewing gum at one end and carefully lower that end of the wire down the drain. With a little luck the small object is lying in the U-bend of the drain and will stick to the gum or putty.

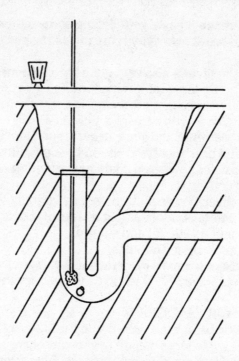

SLATES

To clean slates, rub them with milk or washing soda. Leave to dry, then rub slightly with any salad oil or wax polish.

To restore colour to slates rub them with a cloth dipped in a solution of an equal quantity of white spirit and boiled linseed oil. Polish with a clean cloth.

SMELLS

Unpleasant smells in a cupboard or any piece of furniture can be got rid of by placing a small container filled with boiling milk inside the closed doors until the milk has cooled.

To remove the smell of turpentine from your hands, rinse them with vinegar.

SMOKY ROOM

To prevent a room getting very smoky, when people are smoking, light a few candles. Small containers filled with vinegar will also help to eliminate the smoke.

SMOKY STAINS

Smoky stains on the ceiling or the walls caused by candles or a fireplace will usually clean if sprayed with starch, left to dry and gently brushed with a soft brush.

SNOW

Before starting the shovelling, spray your shovel with some furniture wax and let it dry – that way the snow won't stick to the shovel.

SOAKING

If you do not have a container to soak clothes, linen, socks etc., use a strong plastic bag (bin bag, carrier bag), closing it tightly with a rubber band. Hang it by the carrier-bag handles.

SOAP

To harden and prolong its life, do not use your soap straight after buying it. If you store it in a cupboard in its original packaging for a while, it will harden and last longer when used.

To make a scented soap, save all the small scraps, put them in a jar and stand the jar in boiling water until the scraps melt. Pour in a few drops of your favourite perfume, mix well, and, when it starts to cool remove from the jar and knead into the desired shape.

SOAPSTONE

Clean with soap and water and a soft brush, rinse and dry. You will get a nice sheen on the soapstone by rubbing it gently with jeweller's rouge.

Dirty soapstone can be cleaned with a soft cloth dampened in white spirit. Leave to dry then polish lightly with some liquid furniture polish.

SOFT TOYS

Soft toys can be cleaned by rubbing cornflour generously all over their fur using a soft, clean cloth. Leave the cornflour for at least one hour before brushing it off.

SPECTACLES

To prevent them steaming up when you come in from the cold to the warm, rub both sides lightly with soft soap, then polish until they are crystal clear.

Your spectacle frames will not get stained around the ears when you dye your hair if you wrap these parts with foil.

To keep your spectacles clean, wipe them gently with cottonwool dampened with nail-polish remover.

SPONGES

To clean a sponge:

1. Put your synthetic sponge in the washing machine when you are doing a hot wash.

2. Boil it in an equal quantity of water and vinegar for fifteen minutes; rinse well in water containing a few drops of ammonia.

3. Synthetic sponge can also be cleaned in a solution of warm water and bicarbonate of soda. Rinse well.

4. Clean plastic sponges in a weak solution of water and household ammonia.

5. Very dirty cellulose sponges can be cleaned by being soaked in a mild solution of water and household bleach. Alternatively the sponges can be boiled in a weak solution of water and washing soda. With both methods, rinse well afterwards.

6. To clean a sponge, place it overnight in a bowl of water to which lemon juice or vinegar has been added (half a pint/300 ml of water to five tablespoons of lemon juice or vinegar). Remove the sponge and rinse well; it will be very clean and as good as new.

7. To clean and soften a sponge, soak it in salted water overnight, or soak it for a few hours in buttermilk and then rinse in clean water.

8. Sponges clean well in the dishwasher. Place them with the dishes and give them a full cycle.

9. Another way to clean a sponge is to fill the holes up with powdered borax, and cover the sponge with boiling water. Leave to cool and squeeze a few times under running water, or leave the sponge soaking for at least three hours in a solution of cold water and ammonia (one litre/two pints to two tablespoons of ammonia). Rinse under running water.

10. A sponge soaked in warm water and bicarbonate of soda (one litre/two pints of warm water to two tablespoons of bicarbonate of soda) will be free of dirt in half an hour. Squeeze the sponge from time to time during the soaking. Rinse under running water.

SPOOLS

Paint used spools or leave them their natural colour and use them as knife-holders. Simply insert a screw through the hole of the spool, a little longer than the spool, in order to screw the end in the wall. Put as many as you need touching each other and introduce the knife blades in between the spools.

Wooden spools can become very pretty legs to small pieces of furniture. Paint or stain them the same colour as the furniture.

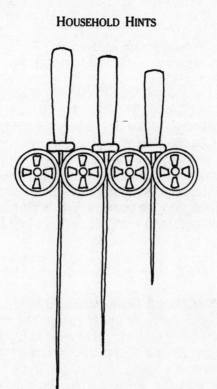

SPRAY CAN

A spray can of paint very often gets clogged when half empty, and becomes unusable. This will be avoided if, before storing it away, you turn it upside down and spray until you have cleared the inside tube of remaining paint.

STAINLESS STEEL

To clean stainless steel:
1. Use bicarbonate of soda on a damp cloth, or a cloth dipped in vinegar. Silver polish is also very good.
2. Rub it with a soft cloth dampened in vinegar. Dry with a soft cloth.
3. Rub with a paste made of ground tailor's chalk and water. Wash and dry.

To get your stainless steel cutlery shiny, soak it for fifteen minutes in an equal solution of vinegar and warm water. Rinse and dry. Soaking it in warm water (one litre/two pints) and ammonia (half a teacup) will also get it sparkling.

Water marks can be removed with methylated spirit applied with a soft cloth.

STAMP

To unstick an unused stamp from an envelope, submerge the corner of the envelope with the stamp on it in boiling water for a few minutes. The stamp will then slip off without difficulty. Leave to dry.

To unstick a wanted stamp from an envelope or a parcel, wet the back of the stamp inside the envelope with lighter fluid.

To unstick stamps which are sticking together, put them in the freezer until they separate.

STARCH

To prevent starch sticking to the iron when pressing, add a few drops of glycerine when making the starch.

To get a greater stiffness and a better gloss when starching, add a tablespoonful of borax to each pint of warm water when making the starch.

Add a pinch of kitchen salt to the starch when mixing it with water. It will give a gloss to the linen, and the starch won't stick to the iron.

When starching clothes, for a really good finish mix milk instead of water with your starch.

STATIC ON CLOTHES – See section on 'Care of fabric'

STATIC ON MAN-MADE FIBRE CARPETS

Static can be greatly reduced, and thereby stop the carpet gathering fluff, if from time to time you spray your carpet all over (using a spray bottle similar to that used when ironing) with a mixture of water (two teacups) and fabric-softener (three-quarters of a teacup).

To free acrylic or perspex surfaces from static, rub the surface with a cloth wrung out in a mixture of water (two teacups) and fabric-softener (three quarters of a teacup).

STEEL

To polish steel, mix the juice of an onion with three times the quantity of vinegar. Keep this in a jar. Dab the steel with the mixture, leave for twenty minutes and then shine with a soft cloth.

Scratches on steel will disappear if liquid polish is used alternately with some fine sandpaper.

To age new steel handles, hinges etc., and give them an antique look, soak them for a few hours in pure bleach. Next rinse, dry and polish.

STEP-LADDER

For safety paint the steps of your step-ladder and, before the paint dries, sprinkle each step with some dry, clean sand to get a non-slippery surface with a firm hold.

STEPS

Keep your outside doorsteps free from ice in the winter by washing them with water (four pints/two litres) to which two teacups of methylated spirit have been added.

Prevent the outside steps becoming slippery when the wet and frosty weather comes by applying some plastic stick-ons over them (those normally used on the bottom of bathtubs).

STICKY BOTTLE TOP

To prevent the tops of bottles of nail varnish, roll-on deodorant and the like from sticking to the bottle, smear the thread of the bottle top with vaseline or petroleum jelly before screwing the top on again.

STICKY LABELS

Sticky label marks on glass or china can be removed with nail-varnish remover, acetone, cooking oil, turpentine or white spirit.

STONE

Oil stains can be removed with clean blotting-paper sheets soaked in hot distilled water, reduced to a pulp and left to dry. Soak in white spirit, place over the stain in a thick coat (1 to $1\frac{1}{2}$ inches/2.5 to 4 cm) and leave to dry. The blotting paper will draw the oil stain out of the stone while drying.

Light oil stains will come off if covered with a thick paste made of water and fuller's earth. Leave to dry.

Mildew on porous stone (sandstone, limestone) can be removed with blotting paper. First soak sheets of clean blotting paper in hot distilled water, then reduce this to a pulp and spread it thickly (at least 1 inch/2.5 cm) over the mildew. As the paper dries, it draws the stain out with the water.

STOPPERS

To loosen glass stoppers, pour on a little vinegar and then turn the stopper sharply.

To loosen the stopper of a perfume bottle, immerse the bottle in a jar of vinegar, leave for a short while and then take it out and stand it in warm water. The stopper will soon loosen.

To insert a glass stopper which is too big to fit the neck of a bottle, wet the stopper and dip it in some fine sand then introduce it to the neck of the bottle with a twisting motion. Repeat the process as many times as needed.

To trim a rubber stopper easily, use the blade of a knife which has been dipped in a solution of caustic soda (use strong gloves).

STORING

A food-processor's cutting discs are a nuisance to store in the cupboard, so keep them out of the way by storing them on a coat hanger that has been bent into a double V. Hang it on a hook inside the cupboard.

Pins, nails, rubber bands, drawing pins, small bits and pieces in the kitchen drawer always look untidy after a while. One remedy is to glue some plastic aerosol spray can lids to a piece of cardboard and place it in the drawer. You then have perfect containers for storing them neatly.

A piece of elastic tacked to the side of a drawer will hold small bottles of nail varnish or perfume, cream jars and other small things in place.

Store screwtop jars underneath the shelves in a pantry or workshop etc. Nail the screw tops to the underneath of the shelves, and screw the jars to their tops (see overleaf).

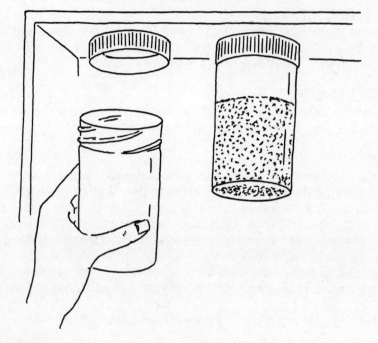

STRAW MAT
Clean a straw mat by rubbing it with a thick cloth dipped in lukewarm water to which a little salt has been added. Rinse well with lukewarm water, adding a little salt to the last rinse. The salt prevents the straw turning yellow.

SUITCASE
Use a dog's collar as an emergency replacement for a broken suitcase handle. Slide the collar through the rings of the handle and fasten the buckle.

Your suitcase will not have musty smells after being stored for a long time when you open it, if before storing you place two or three pieces of sugar inside it.

SIPHON
To ensure a steady stream and prevent any splattering, before using a siphon invert it for a few minutes.

TABLECLOTHS
If a tablecloth is stained during a meal, cover it with a layer of salt. This will remove most of the stain and make it easier to launder.

Press a circular tablecloth starting from the outside and working towards the centre; it will make the job easier.

TABLE FOR FOUR

If you are short of space around the table at a dinner party, use your adjustable ironing board. Cover it with a tablecloth and place in front of the settee. The children will love this kind of arrangement.

TABLE TOP

A natural wood tabletop where not varnished will be protected if, from time to time, it is rubbed with a mixture of equal proportions of linseed oil and turpentine.

Varnished wood loses its gloss after a while, rub it with a solution of turpentine and olive oil in equal quantities to bring back its shine – or mix methylated spirit and linseed oil in equal proportions and apply with a soft cloth (a woollen cloth is best).

To clean gold painted wood use the white of egg treatment. Beat two or three whites of eggs, not too stiff, apply on the gold painted wood with a soft brush, leave to dry and buff with a soft rag.

TAPE

To unstick old messy sticky tape from a surface, cover the tape with foil and apply a hot iron over it. Then peel the tape off and clean away the left-over gum with some lighter fluid, varnish remover or acetone.

Sometimes adhesive tape gets dry and refuses to stick any more. Leave it on top of a warm radiator or in a warm oven for a little while and it will be like new again.

TAPESTRY

To clean a tapestry, sprinkle it generously with powdered magnesia and rub it in well with your fingertips. Leave for at least twelve hours before shaking or brushing it off carefully.

Or sprinkle powdered magnesia, fuller's earth or French chalk over it, then rub it in with a clean cloth. Leave for twelve hours, then brush it off with a soft cloth.

TEAK

To clean natural oil-finished teak rub it three to four times a year with teak oil. (Do not use ordinary furniture polish).

TEAPOT

Clean an aluminium teapot by placing three tablespoons of borax in the teapot, filling it with cold water and bringing the water to the boil. Pour off the boiling water and wash in the normal way.

When a silver teapot is not in use, keep a lump of sugar inside to keep it dry and prevent mustiness. This is also good for coffee-pots.

The inside of a new earthenware teapot sometimes cracks when boiling water is poured in. To prevent this, before using the teapot for the first time, place it in a pan, cover with cold water and bring gently to the boil, then take it out and leave it to cool off.

When a china or earthenware teapot is badly stained, rub it with salt or bicarbonate of soda.

For a badly stained teapot, put one heaped teaspoon of washing soda into the pot and fill it up with warm water. Leave to soak for at least twelve hours before emptying and rinsing.

Another efficient way is to place in the stained teapot some effervescent tablets used for cleaning dentures. Fill it up with boiling water and leave to cool. Rinse well.

A bleach solution (half a teacup of bleach to one pint/half a litre of water) will also clean the inside of a china or earthenware teapot.

TEA TOWEL/HANDKERCHIEF
Press three or four at a time by placing them on top of each other; then press the top and bottom one.

Tea towels will not leave fluff on drinking glasses if a little starch is added to the last rinse when washing the towels.

TEFLON PAN
To scrape a Teflon pan without scratching it, use one of your expired plastic credit cards.

TELEPHONE
The telephone receiver can be left off the hook for hours by small children playing without your realizing. To prevent this, place a wide rubber band over the two contacts and around the telephone. Like this, even if the receiver is off, you will still get calls and the children won't be able to make any.

Clean your telephone with methylated spirit or white spirit to make it look good as new.

TENNIS BALLS
Restore lost bounce to your tennis balls by wrapping them in foil and warming them in the oven at 200°F (approx. 100°C, Gas Mark 'Low') for half an hour.

TERRACOTTA
Clean well with warm soapy water. Rinse and dry. Any left-over marks will disappear if rubbed with one of the following on a cloth or fine steel wool: a piece of fine sandpaper, some powder of pumice, some kitchen scouring powder or some powdered whitening.

THERMOS FLASKS
Thermos flasks become stained after long use. To clean them:
1. Put in half an eggshell and two tablespoons of vinegar. Stand for a few minutes and then shake vigorously, add a glass of warm water and shake well again. The flask should then be quite clean.
2. Fill up the flask with boiling water and add two tablespoons of bicarbonate of soda. Shake well and leave to stand for a few minutes before rinsing.
3. Put three tablespoons of bicarbonate of soda in the thermos flask, fill with warm water, shake and leave to stand for fifteen minutes. Rinse and leave to dry.
   To get rid of the smell of coffee, and coffee stains, pour in a cup of boiling water and one tablespoon of raw rice, shake for a few minutes and rinse.
   Two or three lumps of sugar left in the thermos flask when it is not in use will stop mouldy smells developing.

TICKING CLOCK
If the ticking from your clock on your bedside table prevents you falling asleep, cover the clock with a clear glass bowl, or a drinking glass. That way you will see the time but won't hear the ticking.

TIDEMARKS
Tidemarks on vitreous or porcelain enamelled baths or basins will disappear if rubbed with white spirit. Tidemarks on plastic baths or basins will be removed if rubbed with silver polish on a cloth.

TILE FLOOR – See also **Fireplaces**
When laying a tile floor, instead of emptying one box completely before opening another, open all the boxes and use tiles from each box alternately. That way you will avoid having a floor of different shades of colour, as colour can vary from one box to another.
   Before laying plastic, cork or linoleum tiles, warm them in a cool oven (275°F, 135°C, Gas Mark 1). Tiles are brittle when cold, and easily break or split when being cut to fit.
   The best polish for mosaic or ceramic tiles is to rub them with newspapers.
   The grouting between tiles gets dirty after a while so give it a new clean

look by rubbing it with a round typewriter eraser. Old 'faience' (glazed terracotta) tiles start to yellow with time. To give them back their whiteness, cover them with a thick paste made of starch and hydrogen peroxide (20 vol). Leave on until dry and wipe off.

If a tile loosens in your home and you don't have any glue, place a small amount of flour in a cup and mix to a paste with some white of egg. Put a blot of the paste on each corner of the tile. Set the tile in place and press on it for a little while, then leave it to dry.

Press a rolling pin over a vinyl tile that has just been stuck back in place on the floor to even it out.

When drilling through tiles, cover the spot to be drilled with sticky tape to prevent the drill from slipping.

To replace a damaged vinyl floor tile, cover the tile with aluminium foil. Cover the foil with a clean rag and press over the edges of the tile with a moderately hot iron. Lift the tile off with a putty knife, but if the tile doesn't come loose with the application of heat, then use the cold solution; cover the tile with dry ice or a bag full of ice cubes, leave for 10 minutes. The tile will be very brittle and will break easily under a hammer and chisel. Start in the middle of the tile and work to the edges.

TIN
Tin will clean beautifully if rubbed with half an onion. Wash, dry and polish with a soft cloth.

To clean, rub the tin with methylated spirit.

Clean tin by rubbing with bicarbonate of soda and a damp cloth. Rinse well. For light rusty stains, rub with half a raw potato dipped in some scouring powder.

TINS
To get rid of bad smells in a tin, take the tin outside or, if you cannot, place it in the sink, put a few drops of methylated spirit in it (do not forget to put the bottle of methylated spirit back in the cupboard) then with a match light the tin and put the lid on straight away. Leave it to cool off. Wash and dry the tin. Coffee and other tins are good for storing knives, forks, scissors, spoons etc. Put discs of carpet scraps in the bottom so that the points of the utensils do not get damaged. Paint or cover the tins with attractive contact paper.

TOILET
To get rid of unpleasant smells quickly in the toilet, strike a match or two. You will be surprised how well it works.

TOILET BOWLS
Hard-water marks inside the toilet bowl will easily brush away if you pour three teacupfuls of vinegar in the bowl and allow to soak for a few hours before brushing and flushing.

For a nice clean toilet bowl, drop one or two denture tablets in the bowl. Leave it for at least fifteen minutes before brushing and flushing.

A glassful of coca cola poured down the toilet and left overnight in the bowl before brushing and flushing will give you a sparkling loo.

TOOLBOX
To prevent rusting in a toolbox, place a piece of charcoal or chalk in it to absorb the humidity.

Store your small tools in a bucket of clean dry sand to protect them from rust.

TOOTHBRUSH
The bristles of your toothbrush will become supple again if left to soak for a while in a strong solution of water and salt.

TOOTHPASTE
A tube without its top gets dry quickly, but not if you place it head down in a glass of water.

Toothpaste is good for filling nail-holes in the wall. Fill the holes with the toothpaste, leave to dry, and smooth with fine sandpaper.

TORN FABRIC
Place the torn part flat on a table, spread the wrong side with an egg white, place a piece of the same fabric or a piece of fine linen on top and press with a hot iron. The tear will be almost invisible and the repair will last for quite a time.

TORTOISESHELL
To clean tortoiseshell, moisten a little jeweller's rouge with a few drops of salad oil, rub it gently over the object with cotton wool, then shine with a soft cloth.

To clean imitation tortoiseshell, simply wash it in warm soapy water. Rinse and dry.

When tortoiseshell becomes brittle cover it with petroleum jelly (vaseline) and leave it overnight. Wipe dry and polish with a chamois leather.

TOWEL-SOFTENER
Your towels will feel soft even if you haven't used a softener in the last rinse if, after they are washed and dried, you rub them against each other until they feel soft. It takes a lot of elbow-grease, but it works.

TOYS
Stuffed furry toys can be cleaned by using the lather of a detergent beaten up in warm water. Apply the lather with a small brush. Rinse with a sponge wrung out in warm water and leave to dry, before brushing and fluffing the fur with a clean brush.

Plastic toys will clean perfectly if rubbed with bicarbonate of soda on a damp cloth.

TRANSFERS
One can get rid of a transfer on a surface by dabbing it with warm vinegar until it is soaked up.

TRAYS
Remove heat marks on lacquered Japanese trays by rubbing the marks with vegetable oil until they disappear.

When the children are helping and decide to carry the tray with glasses and plates, cover the tray with a cloth or tea-towel before placing the plates and glasses onto it. This will stop them slipping.

UPHOLSTERY
A loose upholstery button can be put back in place with a long hairpin. Slide the button loop through the hairpin then press the pin into the upholstery.

To clean a small piece of lightly soiled upholstery use shaving cream from an aerosol tin. Spray the foam all over the upholstery and rub it in gently with a clean damp cloth until all the foam disappears. Rinse and wring the cloth out then rub it over the upholstery again. Leave to dry.

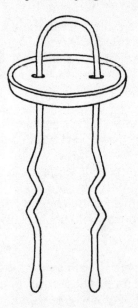

VACUUM CLEANER
To clean the vacuum cleaner brush when hair and threads have gathered on it, use a metal dog brush.

A few little magnets glued to the front of the vacuum cleaner in front of the brush will catch any small, lost, metallic things before they are sucked away. You will be surprised what the magnets can gather.

VACUUM FLASK

A vacuum flask should be kept clean with warm water and a little baking soda or a few drops of detergent. Sterilize the cork stopper from time to time by throwing it for a few minutes into boiling water.

When storing empty leave the top off, to avoid getting a musty smell. If the flask has a musty smell, fill it up with warm water to which two tablespoons of white vinegar have been added. Leave to stand for five minutes, shake well and rinse. If the smell persists, fill up the flask with hot water, into which $1\frac{1}{2}$ tablespoons of bicarbonate of soda have been mixed; leave for at least four hours and rinse well.

VARNISH

Stand the tin of varnish at least half an hour in hot water before using to make it easier to apply.

Always apply varnish with the beam of a torch trained on your working area – straightaway you will notice if your brush has missed any spots.

VARNISH FOR OIL PAINT

This varnish is easily washed off when the oil paint needs cleaning. Take the white of an egg, beat it to a froth and let it settle. Dissolve one piece of sugar with a tablespoon of brandy, remove the egg froth and mix the clear white with the sugar and brandy. Mix well and apply to the picture with a soft brush.

VARNISHED WOOD

To clean varnished wood use ordinary cold tea for the best result.

A dull varnished wood will revive if rubbed with a soft cloth dampened in methylated spirit and linseed oil in equal quantities. Leave to dry for a few minutes, then buff with a dry soft cloth.

VELLUM – See also **Parchment**

To clean stains on vellum, rub the spots with a soft cloth dampened in a little benzine. To remove stains rub with carbon tetrachlora methane on a soft cloth.

To clean vellum (parchment) lampshades, mix half a teacup of warm mild detergent solution with half a teacup of methylated spirit. Sponge the lampshade with the solution, wipe off any lather and next wipe with neat methylated spirit. Allow to dry. Buff with a soft cloth. If the vellum is dull looking, rub over with a cloth moistened with olive oil.

VELVET

Dusty velvet will clean better if rubbed with a piece of coarse black crêpe rather than with a brush.

To clean the seat of a velvet chair, cover the seat with warm bran, leave it on for half an hour, then brush away with a soft brush. Repeat the procedure if necessary.

VENEERS

To get rid of small blisters and swelling in veneers place a piece of cardboard over the blister, press a hot iron back and forth over the cardboard. The heat will soften the glue under the veneer. When it feels soft, put a heavy book or a brick on top of the cardboard and leave for at least twenty-four hours so that the veneer will stick again.

To get rid of small scratches on veneer rub them with an equal solution of turpentine and linseed oil until they disappear. Then polish.

VERDIGRIS – See also **Copper**

Verdigris responds very well to a good rubbing with ammonia and salt.

VINYL FLOOR

Rub black heel-marks on vinyl floors with scouring powder on a damp cloth, or silver polish, or toothpaste on a damp cloth, and they will disappear.

Crayon marks on vinyl surfaces will be removed if rubbed with a silver polish or toothpaste or scouring powder on a damp cloth.

To strip the polish from vinyl tiles when it becomes yellow, use a mixture of cold water (one gallon/four litres) household ammonia (one teacup) and washing-up liquid (one tablespoon). Use a hard brush for scrubbing the tiles. Rinse with a mixture of cold water (one gallon/four litres) and vinegar (one teacup) to counteract the effect of alkali in the ammonia which could be damaging to the vinyl.

To remove a broken or stained vinyl tile on the floor or wall, cover the tile with a piece of silver foil and then run a hot iron over the foil until the tile becomes warm and softens the glue underneath. Then pierce the centre of the tile and lift it off from this point, to avoid damaging the edges of the tiles around it.

WALL

To clean washable painted walls, use the following mixture: – half a pint/a quarter of a litre of vinegar, one teacupful of washing soda, half a pint/a quarter of a litre of ammonia and one gallon/four litres of warm water. The room must be well ventilated when you are applying this mixture and do not forget to wear rubber gloves. Rinse with warm water.

Always start washing a wall at the bottom. If you start at the top, water will run down onto the dirty area, leaving streaks that are very difficult to wash away.

WALL PAINT

To wash the wall paint without getting on a ladder for the higher parts, use a sponge mop on a pole/stick. To dry the walls after washing, wrap an old clean towel around the mop head.

WALLPAPER

Make a dough to clean the wallpaper. Mix eight tablespoons of flour with four tablespoons of white spirit to a thick paste, then add two to three tablespoons of warm water and knead well. Stroke the wallpaper firmly with the dough, turning the dough over frequently so that you are always using a clean area. If not too dirty the dough can be stored in an airtight plastic bag until the next time. Knead well before each use.

When patching wallpaper, you can make it practically invisible by tearing a circular patch, laying it flat, face down, and lightly sandpapering the edges on the wrong side. Coat with glue and stick to the wall, carefully matching the pattern, if any.

To remove sellotape stuck on wallpaper, place a sheet of blotting paper over the sellotape and press with a warm iron until the sellotape peels off.

When stripping wallpaper sometimes small pieces of paper refuse to leave the wall. Soak them with water and apply a hot iron and they will soon come off. Or use vinegar and hot water in equal quantities. Soak twice.

To remove blisters from wallpaper, fill a syringe with paste and inject into the blister. Allow a few minutes for the paper to absorb the paste, and then gently flatten the blister with your fingers. Go over it with a roller to give a good finish.

Another way is to make a very small cut into the blister with a razor blade. Using a wooden toothpick or a matchstick, introduce a little paste in the cut, allow a minute for the paper to absorb the paste then flatten it with your fingers. Go over it with a roller to give a good finish.

WALLPAPERING

Do not store your rolls of wallpaper standing up; lay them down or you might damage the edges.

Grease stains on an old wallpaper will slowly appear on the surface of new wallpaper if the old paper has been left underneath. To prevent this, paint over the grease stains and leave to dry before hanging the new wallpaper.

To strip wallpaper easily, dissolve some alum (three tablespoons, from a chemist) in one litre/two pints of warm water. Soak the wall thoroughly with it – apply with a roller or a large paint brush. When dry, peel the paper off.

When your wallpaper is on the wall, wait until it is dry to cut any excess paper (e.g. around skirting boards, plugs etc.) with a razor blade. When the paper is dry it can be cut neatly.

When wallpapering behind a radiator, use a coat-hanger taped to a wooden stick to smooth the paper down. (Tape a cloth over the hanger to ease the paper down.) See overleaf.

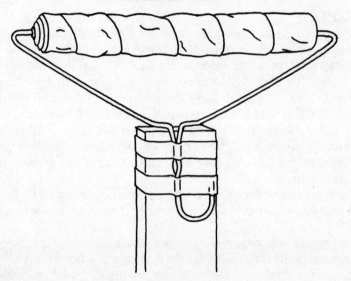

WASHING

To stop coloured linen getting covered with fluff when washed with other garments, add a little starch to the last rinse.

Washing and dry-cleaning symbols on garments

Washing

artwork 16

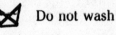 Do not wash

 Hand-wash only

Do not use chlorine bleach

Chlorine bleach can be used

Temperatures given on the international symbols are in degrees centigrade.

100°C Boiling point
  95°C Very hot, boiling point
  60°C Hot: the hand cannot bear the heat
  50°C Medium: the hand can bear the heat
  40°C Warm
  30°C Cool

Textile care
Labelling Code

	Machine	Hand	
1	Very hot	Hand-hot 50°C/120°F	White linen and cotton without special finishes
2	Hot	Hand-hot 50°C/120°F	Colourfast linen and cotton without special finishes
3	Hot	Hand-hot 50°C/120°F	White nylon, white polyester-cotton mixtures
4	Hand-hot	Hand-hot 50°C/120°F	Coloured nylon; polyester; acrylic-cotton mixtures; cotton rayon with special finishes; coloured polyester-cotton mixtures
5	Warm	Warm 40°C/100°F	Non-colourfast linen, cotton or rayon
6	Warm	Warm 40°C/100°F	Acrylics; acetates; blends of these fabrics with wool; mixtures of wool and polyester
7	Warm	Warm 40°C/100°F	Wool; silk; wool mixtures with cotton or rayon
8	Cool	Cool 30°C/85°F	Silk; acetate fabrics with colours not fast at higher temperatures
9	Very hot	Hand-hot 50°C/120°F	Cotton can be boiled but requires drip-drying

WASHING MACHINE

Fasten the cuffs of a shirt to the front buttons before putting it in the washing machine to prevent the sleeves tangling with other articles.

Turn dark-coloured woollens inside out when washing them, to prevent their picking up fluff from other garments.

Instead of buying expensive fabric-softeners, and also to save on washing powder, buy a large bag of washing soda and place one teacupful in the washing machine with the clothes. Use only half the manufacturer's recommended amount of washing powder. The clothes and linen are cleaner, brighter, fresher and softer. This applies for hand washing too.

One teacup of white vinegar added to the last rinse in your washing machine will make sure your clothes are well rinsed. The vinegar also acts as a softener.

If your washing machine overflows because you have put in too much washing powder, or used the wrong powder, sprinkle with salt or add a glassful of vinegar in the soap-powder compartment. The suds will quickly subside (use a low-foam detergent or the overflow of foam can run into the motor or other parts and damage it.)

WASPS
Hair-spray can be used to get rid of a wasp in the house if you have no insect-repellant.

WASTE-DISPOSAL UNIT – See Garbage Grinder

WATCH
When a watch has stopped, the cause is usually dust. Open the watch and place a small piece of blotting paper, dampened in petrol, inside the case next to the works (the blotting paper should be cut a little smaller than the inside of the case). Close the case and leave at least twelve hours. It will generally start again after the blotting paper has been removed.

A watch which is not often used should be wound up fully from time to time to keep it in good working order.

When doing a dirty job, keep your wristwatch clean by wrapping it in transparent plastic cling film before putting it on.

If the glass of your watch gets misted up, turn it over and wear the glass next to your skin for a while. The mist will clear.

WATER
To test if water is safe to drink, the simplest way is to fill a glass with water, put a lump of sugar into it and leave the glass in a warm room either overnight or for twenty-four hours. If the water is clear at the end of the time then it is quite pure, but if it is cloudy or milky then it is unfit to drink.

Make sure that everyone in the family knows where the mains water tap is and how to turn it off in case of emergency.

WATERCOLOUR
Do not throw away watercolour blocks from a paintbox or tube of paint when they get too dry. Split the tube open, put the hard colour in a container and add a few drops of glycerine and a few drops of water. Mix until it becomes a soft thick paste and use again.

WATERPROOF WRITING
Writing on an envelope or a parcel can be made waterproof by rubbing over the writing with a piece of candle.

WATER STAINS ON CEILING
To hide water stains on a ceiling, use a matt oil-based paint. If an emulsion paint is used, the stains will show through.

WAXED PAPER
Put sheets of waxed paper between pieces of meat and fish fillets before freezing. The parcels will then separate easily.

WEATHER PROSPECTS
If a ring encircles the moon, rain will follow – or if the moon looks dim and pale rain is expected. If the moon is red we will have wind, but if the moon is a nice bright colour with a clear sky, fair weather is coming.

If the sun sets into rising clouds on the horizon, bad weather is expected.

Red sky at night, a fair weather day to come.

WEDDING ANNIVERSARY

ANNIVERSARY	WEDDING
1st	cotton
2nd	paper
3rd	leather
4th	woollen
5th	wooden
6th	iron
7th	copper
8th	bronze
9th	pottery
10th	tin
12th	silk and fine linen
15th	crystal
20th	china
25th	silver
30th	pearl
35th	coral
40th	ruby
45th	sapphire
50th	golden
55th	emerald
60th	diamond
65th	ruby

WHITE LEATHER

To clean white leather, use the beaten white of an egg. Apply with a piece of cotton wool and buff with a woollen rag.

WICKER – See also **Basketware** and **Cane**

Do not wash dark brown wicker, as the colour might come out. Give it a good brushing instead, and rub it with vegetable or paraffin oil. To clean light coloured wicker brush it vigorously with a brush dipped in a solution of bicarbonate of soda and warm water (two tablespoons of bicarbonate of soda to one litre/two pints of warm water). Another way is to brush it with a stiff brush and salted water. Use cold water for rinsing as it will harden the wicker. A cloth moistened with a little oil and rubbed over out-of-doors wicker will protect it from the weather.

To stop wicker creaking, brush the joints with paraffin oil.

Do not leave any wicker garden furniture out in very cold weather or it will split and crack. To prevent its drying out apply a wax polish from time to time. Wicker will not turn yellow if washed with very salty warm water.

WICKS

To prevent wicks smoking, soak in vinegar before use.

WINDOW

Do not use soapsuds or detergents to clean windows.

Do not clean windows on a very cold, frosty day because the glass is brittle and might break under pressure.

Do not clean windows when the sun is shining on them as they will look streaky when they dry.

When cleaning both the inside and outside of a window, use horizontal strokes on one side and vertical strokes on the other. In this way you will know on which side any smudges are.

Use a solution of equal parts of water and methylated spirit in a bottle. Shake well, damp a newspaper with the solution and rub on windows or mirrors. Polish with a soft cloth.

For greasy windows one tablespoon of powdered starch diluted in two pints/one litre of water will clean your windows perfectly. But dry straight away.

Bird droppings on windows are hard to remove, especially if left there for a while. Rub with a cloth soaked in vinegar, it will come off easily.

To clean fly-spotted windows and mirrors, use a mixture of warm water (half a litre/one pint) and paraffin (one tablespoon).

When ice is stuck to the windows or windscreens in winter, rub the glass with a cloth dampened with ammonia for quick cleaning.

To prevent frosty or steamy windows and mirrors, clean in the usual way and then apply a small quantity of glycerine with a soft, clean cloth, rubbing lightly but well. Or clean them with strongly salted water. The glass will stay clean for weeks.

Another way is to rub the glass or mirror all over with a piece of moistened soap. Then wipe it off with a clean dry cloth.

When painting window frames, the best way to avoid getting paint on the glass is to use a piece of cardboard laid flat on the glass and held close to the frame. Or use strips of newspapers dampened in warm water – lay the strips on the glass around the window frame, neatly securing the corners. Or take a metal float used for plastering.

Rubbing the glass with a raw onion or vinegar is also good. Rub soap all over the glass (do not miss the corners), and clean your windows when the paint is dry.

To make windows opaque dab them with a paste made with Epsom salts and vinegar.

To make a sash window run smoothly, rub the sash cord thoroughly with soft soap.

WINDOW BOXES

A coating of small pebbles on the soil in your window boxes will prevent the soil splashing your windows when it rains.

Scented herbs such as mint, lovage, thyme, chives, marjoram and rosemary are very good as window-box plants. Keep them well moistened.

An easy way to keep your boxes looking lovely is to fill them with plants in their pots, packing some soil around the pots. This makes it easier either to remove a plant if it is not doing well, or to take all the plants inside during cold weather. (They can be put back later when the weather improves.)

To keep your boxes in bloom all season, remove the dead flower heads as soon as they die. This, of course, also applies to garden flowers.

WIRE

When an electric wire is too long (e.g. a lamp's wire) and lies all over the floor, wind it tightly around a broom handle for twelve hours. The wire will spiral, look shorter and have a neater appearance.

WIRE MESH SCREENING

To clean wire mesh windows and door screens: first dust the mesh with the brush attachment of the vacuum cleaner or a hand brush. Then rub the mesh both sides with a cloth dipped in paraffin oil and wipe off the excess. The paraffin will prevent the mesh getting rusty.

A tiny hole in the screen can be closed in by painting it over with a clear nail varnish or clear wood varnish. Apply as many coats as needed to seal the hole. Leave the varnish to dry between coats.

WOBBLY TABLE

A wobbly table or chair can be corrected quickly by using plastic wood. Place some plastic wood on a piece of greaseproof or foil paper. Put the shorter leg of the table or chair over it. Wait until the plaster wood is dry, take the paper off and smooth the plastic wood by cutting and sanding the surplus.

WOOD – See also **Mahogany**, **Oak** and **Teak**

To get a smooth finish when sanding rough wood, first lightly apply some French polish to it. When the polish is dry, do the sanding.

Strong tea is good for staining natural wood. Cover afterwards with a layer of varnish. When smoothing a furniture surface with fine steel wool, before applying any varnish, get all the tiny pieces of steel wool off the wood by running a magnet over it.

Small scratches can be removed by rubbing with a child's wax crayon or half a brazil nut or walnut. Use white shoe polish to hide scratches on white painted wood.

Rub the scratches with a mixture of an equal quantity of turpentine and linseed oil. Mix well before use.

To fill up a small hole in wood, mix some instant coffee powder with some starch and water to a thick paste, fill the hole with the paste, smooth with a damp finger and wipe with a dry cloth.

WOODEN BLOCKS OR BOARDS

To keep your wooden chopping blocks in good condition, when very dry and clean wipe with a cloth dampened with oil.

To clean a wooden board after rolling out the dough on it, sprinkle the board with salt and rub away the sticky bits of dough with your hand in no time at all.

To clean floury wooden boards and rolling pins, use cold water; hot water makes the flour stick to the wood and it is difficult to wash away.

To clean and get rid of smells on a wooden chopping board, rub it with half a lemon.

To clean and whiten a stained wooden board, first scrub it with warm salted water, next coat the stains with a paste made of fine salt and lemon juice, then place in the sun to dry.

WOODEN FLOORS

Wooden floors will turn yellow after a while if very hot water, strong soaps and soda are used to clean them. Plain wood is absorbent, so never use excessive amounts of water when washing it as the grain will open too much.

A very dirty wooden floor will respond well to a scrubbing of steel wool dipped in turpentine.

Dark marks left by furniture legs on a wooden floor can be removed if rubbed with a damp cloth dipped in paraffin oil.

WOODEN FURNITURE

A good wax for tarnished old wooden furniture is a mixture of equal quantities of linseed oil, vinegar and methylated spirit. Shake well and rub over the wood with a soft cloth. Leave to dry for at least six hours, then buff.

To deal with a dent, soak a piece of cotton fabric in water, wring and place over the dent and hold a hot iron over it. After a few seconds, remove the

iron. Do not keep the iron on for too long or it will damage the polish. Leave
the wood to dry thoroughly then re-polish.

WOODEN SALAD BOWLS

After use, rinse wooden salad bowls in cold water only. From time to time,
clean with warm oil and dry with a paper towel.

Use wooden forks and spoons for mixing a salad, as these do not bruise
the leaves.

WOODEN TABLES

Unvarnished wooden tables should be rubbed frequently with salad oil. Rub
any stains with a very fine steel wool and rinse well afterwards.

Varnished tables should also be rubbed with salad oil from time to time to
avoid the wood becoming dry and brittle-looking.

WOODEN PANELLING

To restore dull-looking wood panelling, rub with an equal amount of linseed
oil and turpentine which has been well mixed in a jar. Pour a small amount
onto a soft cloth and rub the panelling. The surface of the wood will become
oily, but that will soon be absorbed leaving a lovely sheen.

WOODWORM

Put some paraffin in an empty oil can with a pointed nozzle and inject each
woodworm hole with it. Empty the small can if there is any paraffin left, and
fill it with household ammonia and repeat the operation. Leave at least
twenty-four hours then wipe off the excess. It will damage the polished
surface so be very careful not to let any drip.

Or inject each worm hole with turpentine. Keep injecting until no more
wood dust comes out of the holes, then close the holes with furniture polish
or wax. Use a hypodermic syringe for injecting the holes, or a drip-fed
lubricator or a nozzle. Or dip a small brush in paraffin and drop the liquid
into the holes. Wipe off the surplus.

WOK

To stop a wok rusting when not in use, wash and dry it, then warm up one or
two drops of oil in it and rub the oil over the inside of the wok with a clean cloth
or a paper towel. When cool store in a place where the dust won't get to it.

WOOL

To straighten old wool, first wind the unravelled wool round the back of a
chair and tie it in three or four places. Then line a colander with a clean
towel and place it with the wool inside, over a saucepan of boiling water.
The steam will soon straighten the wool which can then be dried, wound up,
and knitted again.

To straighten unravelled wool and take all the twists out, wind it round a
very hot hot-water bottle.

WOOLLENS (sweaters/cardigans) – See also Knitwear

When drying woollens on the line, thread the legs of your nylon tights through the sleeves of the woollen garment and fasten the pegs to the feet of the tights. That way your sweater or cardigan will be free of creases.

To stop woollens being itchy when worn against the skin, add four teaspoons of castor oil to the final rinse water.

Do not press pieces of hand knitting in acrylic before sewing it together, it will lose its bounce. Instead pin each piece flat over a bath towel, cover it with a damp cloth and leave overnight.

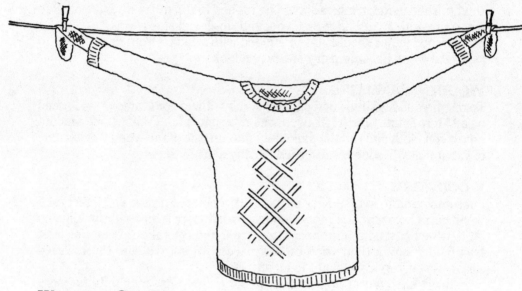

WORKING CLOTHES

These will wash cleaner if one teacupful of ammonia is added to the soapy water.

WRAPPING PAPER

To find out the exact amount of wrapping paper you need to cut for your gift, first go round the present with string.

WRINKLES IN CLOTHES

If you are travelling and are not able to press your clothes, hang them in the bathroom, fill the bath with hot water, close the door and let the steam remove the creases from your garments.

WROUGHT IRON

To keep wrought iron in good condition, brush it with natural wax and then shine.

ZINC

To clean:

1. Wipe with vinegar. Let it stand for a few minutes, rinse well, dry and shine. Bicarbonate of soda rubbed on zinc with a damp cloth will also get rid of the tarnish. Rinse, dry and buff.

2. First wash in warm soapy water, then dry and rub with cloth dipped in paraffin or turpentine.

3. First wash with a solution of washing soda and hot water, then rub with a soft cloth dipped in turpentine.

ZIP

If you have nobody to zip up your dress at the back, tie a ribbon to the cursor (slider) and pull up.

If a zip is not running properly, rub it with a little soft soap, some candlewax or a pencil lead. Do not forget to shut the zip before putting clothes with a zip into the washing machine.

HOUSE AND GARDEN

COOKING

OVEN TEMPERATURE CHART		
°C	*°F*	*GAS MARK*
110	225	$\frac{1}{4}$
130	250	$\frac{1}{2}$
140	275	1
150	300	2
170	325	3
180	350	4
190	375	5
200	400	6
220	425	7
230	450	8
240	475	9

ALMONDS

If almonds in the shells are too hard to break, warm them up in a pan, then break them with the nutcracker.

To skin almonds, pour boiling water over them and allow to stand for three to four minutes. Drain and then rub the almonds between your fingers – the skin will come off very easily.

But skin almonds only when needed, this will keep them fresher much longer.

To give freshness to skinned almonds which have been kept for a long time soak them in hot water for at least twenty minutes.

To cut almonds into strips do this when they are still damp from the skinning. (Use a sharp knife on a wooden board.)

When grilling almonds – to give them a perfect golden look, dust them with powdered sugar before grilling.

ANCHOVIES
To remove excess salt, and to make anchovies moist, soak them in milk for four to five hours or, even better, overnight.

ANGELICA
Hard angelica will soften when soaked in hot water for five minutes.

APPLES
Apples will keep all winter if they are rubbed with glycerine before storing in a cool, ventilated place, stalk end up.

To prevent apples collapsing when baking in the oven, rub them lightly with cooking oil first.

To prevent apples shrinking when you bake them, cut a shallow horizontal line all the way round the middle of the apple.

Apples will peel more easily if you first pour scalding water over them and allow them to stand for a few minutes.

Apple stew will taste and look better if the sugar is added at the end of cooking time with a piece of fresh butter.

To dry apples, first peel, core and cut them into rings ($\frac{1}{4}$ inch/5 mm) and soak in salted water for ten minutes. Put them on a paper towel to remove the excess water, then dry in a cool oven (140°C, 275F, Gas Mark 1) for eight to ten hours until they feel and look rubbery.

If a ripe apple is placed with unripe plums, pears, peaches, tomatoes etc., they will ripen quicker. Place the fruits in a brown paper bag and punch a few holes in the paper.

APRICOTS
To stone apricots take a sharp knife and cut the fruit in half lengthways following the natural line. Get hold of the two halves and twist them in opposite directions. Pull them apart and remove the stone.

ARROWROOT
Use arrowroot instead of flour for thickening sauces and gravies, and making sweet dishes. It is a much finer and more digestible starch than flour, and is particularly suitable as a food for young children and people with delicate stomachs. Blend the arrowroot with a small quantity of cold liquid before adding to the hot soup, sauce etc., and always stir it into the dish off the heat. Arrowroot is good when making clear sauces as it becomes transparent when cooked. Add it at the end of cooking time as it thins if overcooked; so does potato flour.

ARTICHOKES (globe)
A perfect globe artichoke has tight leaves and is heavy and firm. If the leaves are open, the artichoke will be tough and tasteless.

If you intend to keep your artichokes for a few days before cooking them, stand them in a vase with the stems in the water like a bunch of flowers.

Renew the water and cut $\frac{1}{2}$ inch/1 cm off the stem every day. Or store artichokes in the refrigerator up to six days, wrapped in a wet cloth and a plastic bag.

Do not cook artichokes in iron or aluminium pans. The artichokes will lose their colour and look greyish.

When cooking artichokes, put a few drops of lemon juice or vinegar in the cooking water to bring out the flavour.

Never keep a cooked artichoke for more than a day, even in the refrigerator. Because of its iron content it becomes toxic when exposed to the air for a prolonged period.

ASPARAGUS

Fresh asparagus should be firm and should break cleanly when bent. The best time to buy it is in March and April: at the end of the season it becomes bitter, and you should leave the spears in cool water for a few minutes after cooking.

To keep asparagus fresh for a few days, wrap it in a wet cloth and place in the refrigerator.

Revive limp asparagus before cooking by standing it in a jug of cold water to which a few ice cubes have been added. Cover with a plastic bag and put it in the fridge for an hour or two.

For more tenderness peel off the outside of the asparagus stalk with a potato-peeler before cooking.

Cook your fresh asparagus, tips up, in your percolator, on the longest cycle and they will come out perfect.

When opening a tin of asparagus always open the tin at the bottom; that way the asparagus will slip out bottom first, head last, with no risk of damaging the heads.

The bread wrapped round the asparagus for the asparagus rolls will not break when being wrapped if the slices are rolled over with a rolling pin (or a bottle) before buttering.

ASPIC

To prevent bubbles forming when covering food with aspic, do not pour the aspic, spoon it over.

AUBERGINES

Sliced or diced aubergines are best if sprinkled generously with salt and left for thirty minutes. This will remove any excess liquid and any bitterness. Before cooking them, rinse off the salt and dry with a paper towel. Aubergine tends to soak up oil when fried, but you will find it needs less oil after this treatment. Also a dip in a slightly beaten white of egg before cooking will stop them absorbing oil.

AVOCADOS

When buying an avocado which is to be eaten the same day, press the stalk end: if it is soft, the fruit is ripe. Never buy an avocado with dark spots: it is too ripe. To ripen a hard avocado, leave it in the kitchen or a warm place, wrapped in a brown paper bag.

To store a cut avocado, brush the flesh with lemon juice to prevent it going brown. Leave in the stone, and cover tightly with plastic cling film.

To keep avocados fresh for a while, bury them in flour in an earthenware dish.

BACON/GAMMON

Choose bacon in which the lean is a pinky brownish colour and the fat is evenly distributed. The rind should be thin.

To unstick frozen bacon rashers and separate them, straight from the freezer, roll and unroll the packet of bacon a few times before opening it.

To separate frozen bacon rashers, heat a spatula in boiling water before sliding it between them.

To prevent bacon rashers sticking together, roll up the plastic pack of bacon when storing it in the refrigerator.

Dry bacon will soften nicely if soaked in milk for a little while before grilling or frying. It will also make bacon which is too salty, edible.

To get rid of the salt in a piece of bacon or gammon, place it in cold water, bring the water to the boil, throw this water away, replace with cold water, then cook.

When frying bacon it will not curl if it is first passed under cold running water, or if the rind is cut off and notches are made at the edges of the fat.

When frying bacon lay the slices down so that the lean part is resting on the fat one. That way the lean part will baste in the fat. When grilling bacon, reverse the process, overlap the lean part with the fat one for the same self-basting result.

For a different flavour try putting a little honey over some slices of bacon, and grill them. It's delicious.

BAKING POWDER

To test if your tin of baking powder is still fresh, add a teaspoonful to half a pint/a quarter of a litre of hot water. If it bursts into bubbles and gets very effervescent it is still good; if not you need a new tin.

BANANAS

Do not store bananas in the refrigerator as their skins turn black if kept too cold.

You can freeze your overripe bananas. Mash them, add a little lemon juice and keep in the freezer for later use in bread or cakes.

Unripe bananas have a high starch content, the starch content decreases while they are becoming ripe.

BASIL
Grow basil on your kitchen windowsill in pots to keep flies away.

Basil leaves keep their flavour best when preserved in oil. Put cleaned leaves into a container, sprinkle with salt, shake the container and then fill with olive or vegetable oil. Cover the container and leave in the refrigerator, where it will last for months. Remove a few leaves when needed.

BARBECUE
When feeding the fire during barbecues, add the fuel on the edging and push the candescent coals into the centre. Putting new coals in the centre would slow down the cooking.

BAY LEAVES
Bay leaves will stay fresh and keep longer if stored in an air-tight container with a piece of cotton wool dampened in olive oil.

Press bay leaves under a board and then dry them in a dark room, not in the sun. When dry, store them in a dark container such as a cardboard box (not in a glass jar).

BEANS
Dried beans should be soaked before cooking. Newly dried beans will need two hours soaking; older ones will need between six and eight hours. Do not over-soak for this causes the beans to ferment and germinate, making them difficult to digest.

If you don't have time to soak them, use the following method. Put the beans into cold water, bring to the boil, and throw the water away. Repeat this process three times. After the third boiling, keep the water and cook the beans in it.

Do not add salt until the end of the cooking time, or the beans will harden.

Add one teaspoon of bicarbonate of soda to the cooking water of dried beans; this will make them softer and hasten the cooking time.

PULSES' SOAKING AND COOKING TIME		
PULSE	SOAKING	COOKING
Butter beans	10–12 hours	$1\frac{1}{2}$–2 hours
Lima beans	5–6 hours	30–40 minutes
Red kidney beans	3–4 hours	2–3 minutes
White beans (haricots blancs)	3–5 hours	$1\frac{1}{2}$–2 hours
Chick peas	overnight	2–3 hours
Split peas	1 hour	$1\frac{1}{2}$–2 hours
Lentils	$\frac{1}{2}$ hour	20–30 minutes

BEAN SPROUTS

To keep bean sprouts fresh longer, place them in a container (do not squeeze them) and cover with water. Close the container with cling film or a lid. Change the water every other day.

BEEF

Choose meat which is slightly marbled with fat, a sign that the animal has been well fed. The fat should be creamy colour and firm to the touch; the lean should be bright red.

Meat with a marbled effect also indicates that the animal was young. In young animals fat is dispersed through the muscles, in old animals it is massed on the outside of the flesh.

To prevent the raw meat darkening when kept for a few days in the refrigerator, place the meat on a wire grill over a plate and cover the whole thing with cling film. This way the blood dripping from the meat will not be in contact with the meat to darken it.

The perfect way to cook red meat is to grill it until slightly bloody, and then let it rest for a few minutes before serving. This allows the juices which have gathered in the centre of the meat during the cooking to reach the edges, and the meat will be pink throughout. If it is not done, the grilled piece of meat will be flabby and too rare in the middle, the outside having a blackish crust a few millimetres thick.

To test beef, prick with a skewer. If a very light pink juice runs out, the meat is cooked.

Beef to be eaten cold should not be sliced while hot.

When roasting beef the meat should be at room temperature, so bring it out of the refrigerator at least an hour before cooking. The meat should be placed on a rack in the oven, and it should not touch the bottom of the roasting tin. When it is cooked, switch the oven off, half-open the door and let the roast rest for a few minutes to allow the juices gathered in the centre to reach the edges and make it juicy and succulent.

If the roast beef is to be eaten rare, turn it frequently while cooking; the blood will run through the meat evenly, giving perfect red slices. When cooked, take it out of the oven, keep it in a warm place and wait ten minutes before slicing it. If carved at once it will be tough.

See also **Meat** on p. 155.

Beef stew (pot au feu)

When making this dish, line the base of the pan with bones and put the meat on top so it will not stick. Cover with cold water and bring to the boil slowly to keep the meat tender and palatable. (Put a thick slice of carrot at each end of a marrow bone to stop the marrow falling out.) Vegetables do not all have the same consistency, so do not cook them for the same length of time or they will be tasteless. Cook turnips for forty minutes, carrots for thirty, and leeks for ten. This is the way to a successful *pot au feu*.

BEER

When cooking with beer, use it warm; if chilled, it loses most of its flavour.

Left-over beer can be used for cooking if you put a little sugar or a few grains of rice in the bottle before corking it tightly. This stops it going flat.

Do not be afraid of giving food cooked in beer or wine to children. The alcohol evaporates and only the delicious flavour remains.

Instead of red wine in meat dishes, use Guinness: it is cheaper and gives a slightly nutty flavour. Replace white wine with cider. (Reduce the cider by boiling it before adding to the dish).

BEETROOT

If beetroot is bruised, rub the cut or bruised part with salt. This will prevent it bleeding and losing its colour when boiled.

Beetroot has more flavour and is more nutritious if roasted in the oven rather than boiled.

To keep beetroot red when it is being boiled, add a little bicarbonate of soda to the water, or cook them with some of the stem left.

To peel hot beetroot, put it into cold water and the skin will peel off like a glove.

Beetroot in vinegar and oil will taste better if a pinch or two of caster sugar is added to the dressing.

BISCUITS AND CAKES

Do not keep biscuits and cakes in the same tin; your biscuits will become soggy.

Place a lump or two of sugar in the biscuit tin to keep them dry and crispy.

To make it easier to remove home made biscuits from the baking tray, place the baking tray on a wet cloth for a minute or two when taking it out of the oven.

BLACKCURRANTS

These are richer in Vitamin C than any other fruit, and are also very rich in Vitamin A.

Use a fork to strip blackcurrants from their stalks.

BONES

Keep any bones and carcases from chicken, duck, goose, turkey or roast meat and store them in a big plastic bag in the freezer for when you want to make soup. They will keep in the freezer for one month. After using the bones to make stock, give them to chickens to pick as they are helpful in the production of eggshells.

BOUILLON

When making bouillon, always add some minced meat as it gives a better flavour.

Before storing, pour the bouillon through a fine strainer or muslin (the vegetables would ferment very rapidly). Boil the strained bouillon once more and then leave it to cool, uncovered, before pouring into a container.

BOUQUET GARNI

Fresh: Use one bayleaf, two sprigs of parsley and one sprig of thyme, tied together with cotton.

Dried: Use one bayleaf, two pinches of mixed herbs (thyme, marjoram and parsley) five peppercorns and two cloves.

The mixture should be tied in a small square of muslin, with a piece of cotton long enough to tie to the handle of the pan; or put it in a perforated spoon of the sort used for infusing tea.

BRAN

Buy unprocessed bran from a health-food shop or chemist. One teaspoonful before each meal is the best and cheapest way of correcting constipation and diarrhoea. Alternatively, mix two heaped teaspoons of the bran into your breakfast cereal, which makes it easier to swallow.

BRAZIL NUTS

When the shells of Brazil nuts have become very hard, to crack them easily and keep the nut whole, place the shells in a pan of cold water, bring to the boil, then plunge them in cold water again for a few minutes. Drain and leave them to dry before cracking. Or place them in the freezer for a few hours before cracking.

BREAD

To keep bread fresh in the bin, place a well washed and dried potato with it.

Bread will not get mildew if the inside of the bread-bin is wiped with vinegar.

Fresh bread can be a nuisance to cut easily, but if you warm the blade of your breadknife in boiling water beforehand, the cutting will be easier.

To cut very thin slices and to make rolled cocktail sandwiches without breaking the slices, first cut all the crusts from the bread. Then wrap the bread in a damp cloth and leave for several hours before using it.

To re-heat bread, use a lukewarm oven for twenty to thirty minutes rather than a very hot oven. This method allows you to re-heat the bread meal after meal if necessary. But if you are in a hurry to re-heat stale bread, brush it with water and place it in a medium-hot oven until it dries out and becomes crispy again.

To make the dough rise if you haven't got a warm place, rub the inside of a plastic bag with some oil, put the dough inside, close the bag tightly and place it in a container full of warm water. The dough will be ready when it has doubled its size.

To make the dough rise quicker, warm the flour in a low oven for a few minutes before mixing the dough.

To obtain a crisp crust when baking bread, place a roasting pan half filled with water under the bread in the oven and brush the bread with some salted water, half way through the cooking.

Use left-over bread to make French Toast. For one person you need two slices of bread, one egg, a quarter of a pint/150 ml of milk, two level tablespoons of sugar and a walnut-sized knob of butter. Cut the crust from the bread, dip each slice in the milk, (to which the sugar has been added) and then in the beaten egg. Melt the butter in a pan and place the slices in the hot butter. Fry each side until a light golden-brown, and serve hot with brown sugar – a very nourishing and delicious tea snack.

BREADCRUMBS

Make breadcrumbs from left-over bread. Break the bread into small pieces, dry it in the oven or under the grill. When dry and golden put the pieces in a plastic bag and crush them finely with a rolling pin or a glass bottle.

To make fresh breadcrumbs, cut some slices or pieces of fresh or two or three days old bread of any kind into small pieces. Place it in a food processor or a blender and blend until you obtain fine breadcrumbs. Store in a plastic bag or an airtight jar in the refrigerator. It will keep for at least two months.

After your oven has been switched off use the rest of the heat to make breadcrumbs with left-over bread.

Rusks make good instant breadcrumbs.

Most unsweetened breakfast cereals and cornflakes make very good breadcrumbs.

To keep your breadcrumbs fresh for a long time, put them in a plastic bag, squeeze the air out, tie the bag and place it in the refrigerator.

BRIOCHE

To secure the head of a brioche to its base, before cooking, push the handle of a fork in and out once through the middle of the head and the base all the way down until you reach the bottom of the mould.

A brioche will taste fresh again the day after if it is wrapped in tissue paper and placed in a warm oven for five minutes. This applies to croissants also.

BROWNING

You do not have to use browning to colour bouillon. An onion boiled in its skin gives a lovely dark colour.

BROWN SUGAR

Brown sugar won't harden if you store it in the freezer or if you keep it in the refrigerator in its original packaging. Make sure the packaging is always well closed after each time you use it. If you take these precautions, it will always be soft.

To keep brown sugar from becoming dry and hard, put it in a tin. Place three or four marshmallows on top and close the tin tightly with the lid.

A slice of bread or a slice of apple kept on top of the brown sugar will prevent it hardening.

To soften brown sugar which has hardened, when you need it in a hurry, place it in a warm oven until soft. (A microwave oven can also be used.)

Another way is to place the sugar in an airtight container and sprinkle a little water on top, before putting on the lid. It will soften the sugar in twenty-four hours, or a little longer if the sugar is very hard.

But if you need some brown sugar in a hurry and yours has turned hard, grate it on a cheese-grater.

Mix nine level tablespoons of white sugar with one teaspoon of molasses to make brown sugar; add another teaspoon of molasses if you want dark brown sugar.

BRUSSELS SPROUTS

Trim off the damaged outer leaves, but do not cut the ends. Simmer the sprouts uncovered in a little water for ten to twelve minutes, after which they will be crisp and still green.

BUTTER

If you do not have a refrigerator keep your butter in a cool place wrapped in a damp cloth underneath a clay flowerpot – or wrap the butter in a cloth dampened with vinegar and water.

To keep butter firm and fresh when outside in hot weather (e.g. on picnics) wrap it in some fresh cabbage leaves.

Rancid butter can be made perfectly edible and the rancid taste will disappear if the butter is soaked for at least two hours in cold water to which one teaspoon of bicarbonate of soda has been added.

Butter with a rancid taste can be greatly improved if a carrot is planted in it and left there for at least five hours – more if possible.

To make butter go a long way, beat up half a pound with half a teacup of slightly warm milk. Beat just long enough to incorporate all the milk.

To make the butter soft put it through the mixer and gradually add two to three tablespoons of water; it will also make the butter go further.

When a recipe asks for soft creamy butter and you have only a hard block of it, warm a grater and a bowl under hot water and grate the butter into the warm bowl. You can also peel the butter with a potato peeler instead.

When a recipe calls for half a cup of butter the quickest way to measure it is to half fill the measuring cup with cold water and drop pieces of butter in it until the butter reaches the top. Drain the water and you are left with the required amount of butter.

To cut butter into small, even cubes for the table, use some dental floss or a coarse wet thread.

If butter starts to burn during cooking, add a little cooking oil.

To verify the quality of your butter, place a small piece of butter in a spoon over the flame of a gas burner. Good butter will melt and start to boil. Inferior quality butter will crackle and sputter all over.

Clarified butter

When clarified, butter burns less readily. To make clarified butter, melt ordinary butter over a low heat and skim off the foam that rises to the top. A white residue will sink to the bottom. Strain the clear yellow butter and discard the white residue.

A quick and successful way to clarify butter is to melt it and strain it through muslin.

BUTTERMILK

If the recipe calls for buttermilk or sour milk and you have none, add a teaspoon of bicarbonate of soda or lemon juice to half a pint/a quarter of a litre of milk.

CABBAGE

When making stuffed cabbge leaves, you don't have to boil the head of the cabbage in order to separate the leaves. Instead place the cabbage in the freezer a day before needed. When you are ready to use it, thaw and core it, and the leaves will separate very easily, and be soft enough to wrap around the stuffing.

A cabbage salad tastes a lot better if left to marinate for a few hours in its dressing.

When cooking cabbage, to absorb the smell and prevent it spreading all over the house, add a few drops of vinegar or a few drops of lemon juice to the cooking water. A stalk of celery, two or three unshelled walnuts or a small peeled onion will also work wonders.

Some people cannot eat cabbages and other green vegetables because they repeat on them. But if the cabbage or other green vegetable is boiled for a few minutes in water then the water is thrown away and replaced with fresh boiling water to finish the cooking, the problem is solved.

To make cabbage more easily digestible, cook a few carraway seeds with it.

CAKES

When baking a cake (e.g. a fruit cake) which requires long cooking, place the tin containing the cake in another tin a size or two bigger. This will prevent the cake burning. Another method is to place a dish of water in the lower part of the oven, beneath the cake.

To protect a heavy cake from the high temperature in the oven, line the bottom and sides of the tin with greased paper and cover the cake with aluminium foil or greaseproof paper.

To get a lighter short pastry, mix with soda water instead of plain water.

Sugar and fat will cream better when mixed if the mixing bowl is warmed first.

Cream butter and sugar together, and then add part of the flour *before* the liquid to prevent the butter congealing. Add the remaining flour and liquid alternately, beating thoroughly.

When baking a cake without shortening (e.g. a sponge cake), sprinkle the tin with flour but do not grease it.

Use real flowers to decorate your cakes. It is fun, lovely to look at and delicious. Violets, dahlias, lilac, daisies, marigolds, pansies, poppies, geranium, jasmine etc., can be used; add green leaves such as mint, pansy and geranium, and place them on top of the cake. Cover them with a drop or two of warm (not hot) syrup to preserve their freshness. To make the syrup, melt slowly over the heat four tablespoonfuls of sugar with two of water. The syrup is ready when a drop poured onto a cold plate solidifies immediately.

Give a delicious special flavour to your sponge cake by lining the cake tin with clean fresh geranium leaves and pouring the sponge mixture over. Then bake in the usual way.

If a cake recipe asks for dried dry fruits, wash the dry fruits, wipe them in a tea-towel and finish drying with a hair-dryer.

To improvise a cake tin with a detachable base, cut a long band of foil to double the diameter of your cake tin. Fold it in half to make it stronger and place it in the cake tin with the ends sticking out. Pour in the cake mixture and bake. When the cake is ready, get hold of the two ends of foil and gently pull them up to bring your cake out of the tin.

When greasing a cake tin, warm up the tin first, it will make the job much easier, or use melted butter and a brush.

To test a cake, press it with your finger. If it leaves a mark, the cake is not cooked. To make sure, insert a skewer into the centre of the cake: if the skewer comes out clean, the cake is cooked.

When a cake or small cakes come out of the oven and stick to the baking tray, do not force them off or you'll break them. Simply place the hot tray on top of a wet tea-towel and wait for it to cool off. Once cold, the cakes should unstick without difficulty.

When the cake sticks to the baking tin, hold the baking tin for a few seconds over a gas flame or an electric cooker, it will then unstick without further difficulty.

Do not despair if your fruit cake has its top shaped like a dome and is therefore difficult to ice. Cut the top off, making it level, and turn the cake over and ice its base instead.

A pretty and easy decoration on top of a sponge cake is made by laying a doily over it and sprinkling sifted icing sugar through the holes. Then carefully remove the doily.

When icing a cake, first sprinkle a little flour over the top of the cake to stop the icing running over the sides. For a thicker icing, mix the icing sugar with milk instead of water.

A toothpick dipped in food colouring is very good for writing on cake icing.

Avoid cracking the icing when cutting the cake by dipping the blade of the knife in boiling water before slicing.

Before cutting a meringue cake, butter the blade of the knife or dip it in hot water to prevent sticking.

Use dental floss to cut a crumbly fruit cake neatly.

Place an apple in the fruit cake tin; this will keep the cake fresh and moist.

CANDIED PEEL – For hard candied peels, see Angelica

CAPERS (substitute)

Wait until the marigold flowers become seeds, then gather the seeds in a strainer, sprinkle with salt and leave to drain. Next place them in a jar, add a few bay leaves, one or two sprigs of thyme, a few cloves and cover with boiling wine vinegar; leave to cool. Cover and use instead of capers when needed.

CARAMEL

To prevent caramel going hard, add a little lemon juice.

CARROTS

Before storing cut the leaf top off the carrots; the leaves suck the moisture from the carrots, leaving them dry.

When scraping carrots, use a wire pot-scourer: it is quicker and more effective than using a knife.

To skin carrots easily, plunge them in boiling water for five minutes. Next bring the carrots out and drop them in cold water. The skin can then be rubbed off with the fingers.

If you do not have an electric blender or liquidizer, scrub and clean the carrots well; peel them if they are old, scrape them if young. Then put a grater over a clean cloth, grate the carrots, and extract the juice by squeezing the grated carrots through a piece of muslin after blending. Honey can be added for sweetness or parsley for flavour.

Carrot juice contains Vitamins A, B and C, iron, iodine and calcium. Its natural sugar gives energy. It also improves eyesight.

The dressing for raw shredded carrots has to include lemon, not vinegar, to bring the best out of the vegetable.

CAULIFLOWER

Bring the grubs out (if any) by plunging the cauliflower head down in a bowl full of cold water to which a few tablespoons of vinegar have been added. Leave it to soak for five minutes; rinse well under running water before cooking.

To get a snow-white cauliflower, add a few drops of lemon juice or a teacup of milk to the cooking water.

To cook sprigs of cauliflower or broccoli quickly, make an X incision in the stem before cooking. That way the stems will not take longer to cook.

CELERIAC

When grating celeriac in advance for a salad, to stop it getting greyish, sprinkle some milk over it and mix well.

Shredded celeriac eaten raw with a mustard sauce will taste better if dipped in and out of boiling water, and left to drain and cool before adding the seasoning.

CELERY

Wilted celery can often be revived if left to soak in cold water to which a few ice cubes have been added. Place it in the refrigerator for a few hours.

To clean celery stalks, use a clean toothbrush.

Don't discard celery leaves: use them in a salad, or dry them for use in soups, sauces and stews. Add them at the end of the process and do not cook them for more than a few minutes.

CEREALS

Soggy cereals will become crisp again if placed in a warm oven on a tray for a few minutes.

CHAMPAGNE

Your champagne will taste as good and bubble as well tomorrow if, before storing, instead of putting a cork in, you introduce the handle of a teaspoon in the neck opening and leave it hanging there overnight.

To stop champagne bubbling over, dip a wet finger in it.

CHEESE

Cheese is a very important source of protein: 1 lb/about 500g of a hard cheese such as Cheddar provides as much protein as 2 lb/about 1 kg of beef.

The transparent wrapping in which pre-packed cheese is sold causes the cheese to sweat in a warm atmosphere, so remove the plastic, wrap the cheese in aluminium foil and keep it in the refrigerator. If you store it in a cold larder, cover it loosely with a cloth damped in vinegar to protect it from the air. Keep the cloth permanently damp.

Or store wrapped in greaseproof paper or foil underneath an inverted earthenware plant pot (soak the pot thoroughly in cold water first).

Cheese won't harden if the cut end is buttered before storing.

You can stop Camembert cheese from running by storing it in its box, standing up on its side instead of flat on its bottom.

Hard cheese (such as Emmenthal, Gruyère etc.) can get dry very quickly if not stored properly. If this happens, wrap the dry cheese carefully in a cloth dampened in white wine, cover with tinfoil and leave for a few hours.

Cream cheese and cottage cheese in their plastic or carton containers should be stored upside down for a longer conservation.

To keep cheese free of mould, place a lump of sugar on it. This will keep it fresh and absorb the moisture.

Furry cheese is safe to eat: the fur is caused by fermentation and may simply be cut off.

Don't forget that cheese, like red wine, should be served at room temperature, so take it out of the refrigerator at least an hour before it is needed.

The taste of a mild grated Cheddar cheese can be strengthened by mixing a little dry mustard with it.

When cutting hard cheese, dip the knife in very hot water first. This will stop the cheese crumbling.

To spread cottage cheese easily without any crumbs, mix a little skimmed milk into it before spreading. Beat it well.

When shredding soft cheese, it won't stick to the grater too much if you first grate a little butter or margarine.

To grate cheese more easily place it in the refrigerator for at least half an hour before it is needed.

When in a hurry a potato-peeler is useful to grate a piece of cheese.

Cheese for cooking
Gruyère has a strong flavour and is very tasty; it is perfect for soufflés, croquettes and fondues.

Parmesan makes soups velvety and is very good for sauces, soufflés and Italian dishes such as risotto, minestrone and pasta.

Emmenthal is very rich and adds a delicious, mild flavour to a dish.

Tilsit melts quickly; it makes pizza, fondue or topping very smooth.

Cream cheese cannot usually be frozen, but Kraft Philadelphia cream cheese will freeze successfully.

To make use of bits and pieces and left-overs (Cheddar, Stilton, Brie, Camembert), mix them in the blender with two tablespoons of fresh cream. Put this mixture into an earthenware jar and serve like Stilton at the table, or make it a little creamier and serve as a dip or on celery stalks with drinks.

Cheese melts at a fairly low temperature, so if you are browning the top of a savoury cheese dish, place it under a fairly low grill or the cheese will become tough, stringy and indigestible.

When a cheese fondue has curdled, mix one tablespoon of potato flour with some water to make a smooth cream. Whisk this into the fondue and keep whisking until the fondue has regained its normal state.

CHERRY PICKING
After picking the cherries from the tree or stoning the fruits for a recipe, your fingers may be stained. Do not soak your hands or you will fix the stains and make them very difficult to rub off. First dip your hands in vinegar and then wash them.

CHESTNUTS AND WALNUTS
To test whether the chestnuts or walnuts are good, throw them into a container full of water. The good ones will sink to the bottom, the bad ones will float. This also works for dried beans.

Before cooking chestnuts under the grill or in the oven, make a slight incision in the skin to stop them bursting.

To peel the chestnuts without difficulty, first leave them in the refrigerator for at least twelve hours; take them out and put them straight into boiling water. When cooked, take them from the boiling water and straight away rinse under cold running water, then the peeling will be easy.

Chestnuts will peel more easily if you add a tablespoon of cooking oil to the cooking water.

CHICKEN – See also Poultry
Every time you eat a chicken, freeze the liver until you have enough to make a pâté.

Tie your chicken or turkey with unwaxed dental floss before cooking.

When roasting a chicken, for the breast to be juicy and not dry, roast the chicken upside down. The juice will run down to the breast instead of out into the pan.

A good way to avoid basting a roast chicken, turkey etc., is to dip a piece of muslin in melted butter and place it over the bird with the corners inside the dish. The skin will still get brown through the cloth and basting is not needed.

Chicken breasts will be more succulent if soaked for a few hours in milk.

When boiling a chicken, first pour boiling water over it and then the little picks (roots of the feathers) will come out easily when scraped with a knife.

To get the most appetising golden colour when frying chicken, add a few drops of food-colouring to the oil before heating it.

CHICORY
Chicory with green tipped leaves has been exposed to the light and will be very bitter to the taste.

Trim and wash broad-leafed chicory rapidly under cold running water. Do not leave the chicory standing in the water as this makes it bitter.

CHICORY TEST
To find out if there is any chicory in your pure ground coffee sprinkle a teaspoonful into a teacup or a glass full of cold water. If the coffee is pure it will stay floating on the surface, but if there is any chicory it will drop to the bottom and colour the water.

CHIPS – See also Frying
Wash your chips in warm water to eliminate some of the starch and dry well before dipping them in the hot fat. That way they won't stick together and will be nice and crispy.

To find out if the fat is hot enough for the chips drop a small piece of bread in it, if the bread comes to the surface the fat is ready. Also one or two grains of dry corn dropped into the fat will pop when the fat is at the right temperature.

Do not let the fat get too hot; fat that is smoking is too hot. If this happens, turn the heat off before putting the chips in, then turn it on again when it has cooled off a little.

A sprig of fresh parsley placed in the oil or fat when the fat starts to warm up will stop the smell of chips spreading all over the house.

Before frying, dry the potatoes thoroughly to avoid the oil spitting. Very wet chips make the fat bubble and splash which can be a dangerous fire risk.

Chips can be prepared a little while in advance of a meal. Half cook the chips in hot oil or fat, then drain them and keep until they are needed. At this stage, dip them for the second time into hot oil or fat until golden, drain on kitchen paper, sprinkle with salt and serve immediately.

CHIVES

A good replacement for chives can be kept permanently in the kitchen, by placing an onion (Spanish or other) on top of a glass full of water. Soon some sprouts will appear, cut them and use them in salads or sauces. They will soon grow again.

CHOCOLATE

Chocolates become dry and whitish-looking if kept too long in a cupboard. Either eat them quickly or keep them in the refrigerator.

Use the potato peeler for making small flakes of chocolate.

When melting chocolate, if it becomes too dry and sticks to the spoon, add a tablespoon of vegetable oil, butter or margarine to it.

To prevent chocolate sticking to the inside of the pan when melting it, grease the inside of the pan thoroughly before with some butter, margarine or a little oil.

To melt chocolate easily, take a foil container or line a small baking tray with foil, butter the foil lightly, put the chocolate squares in it and place in a pre-heated oven. The chocolate will melt quickly and will not stick to the tin when poured out.

Use red wine instead of milk or water when making chocolate sauce. The wine gives a light, bitter taste, and the sauce is less sweet.

If you have made too much chocolate drink, keep it in the refrigerator and tomorrow you can make yourself a Brazilian chocolate. Reheat the chocolate and add half a cup of strong coffee to it.

CHUTNEY

For a quick chutney, take some smooth apricot jam, add vinegar to taste and a pinch of cayenne pepper.

COCONUT

When choosing a coconut, shake it to find out if it contains any milk. A good coconut should be heavy. Avoid the ones with wet eyes.

To crack a coconut easily, first pierce the eyes with a large nail, drain the juice, and then put the coconut in the oven (325°F, 170°C, Gas Mark 3) for half an hour. When it cools, it will probably crack open by itself; if not, tap it lightly with a hammer.

To shred a coconut: after cracking and lifting the flesh, peel off the brown skin with a peeler, break the flesh in pieces and place in the blender, adding some of the coconut milk.

When coconut flesh has dried out, soak it in milk until it looks and tastes fresh again.

Slightly old shredded coconut can be revived to a fresh and moist taste by steaming it over boiling water for a few minutes.

COFFEE

Beans or ground coffee stay fresh longer if kept in the refrigerator.

Add a pinch of salt to the ground coffee before pouring hot water over it to bring out the aroma.

For good coffee, never boil either the coffee or the milk, but if the coffee has been boiled by mistake, a few drops of cold water added to it before serving will help you to drink it without too much displeasure.

Fill up your ice-cube trays with left-over coffee for iced coffee. Or freeze freshly made coffee of double to treble the normal strength in the ice-cube tray of the refrigerator. Iced coffee will taste better and be stronger if you pour the brew of hot coffee and milk into tall glasses half filled with coffee ice-cubes.

COLD PLATES

Do not spoil your meal by forgetting to heat your dinner plates.

CORN ON THE COB

To find out when the corn on the cob is ready and best to eat, pierce a grain with your thumb-nail. If the liquid which comes out is like water, the corn is not ripe but if the liquid is like milk the corn is ready to be eaten.

To remove any left-over fibres on the corn, brush it lightly downwards with a nailbrush.

To get the corn off the cob, use a metal shoehorn.

Salted cooking water will toughen corn, so do not salt the water.

CRANBERRIES

Do not cook cranberries for too long; just until they burst. Too much cooking will give them a bitter taste.

CREAM

Increase the quantity of whipped cream by adding a stiffly beaten white of egg. Blend lightly and carefully with a fork to aerate the mixture.

Double cream whips best if the cream and the bowl are refrigerated beforehand, and if a tablespoon of milk is added to every quarter pint/ 150 ml of cream.

Single cream will not whip, however hard you try.

Pouring cream cannot be frozen, but whipped cream can. Using a spoon, drop small quantities onto a baking tray and freeze them. When frozen put them in a plastic bag and place in the freezer until needed.

Do not over-beat or the whipped cream will turn into butter. As soon as the cream becomes stiff, stop whipping – it is ready. The mixture can be stored in the refrigerator until needed.

Crème anglaise
To find out if the cream is cooked, plunge a cold spoon into it. After taking it out draw a line on it with your finger; if the two sides stay apart the cream is ready. Always keep a container of cold water on the side so that you can stop the cooking by dipping the pan in it.

Crème brulée
When the sugar has not browned evenly on top of the crème brulée, finish the job by lighting a long match, or a long spaghetti, and holding it over the non-browned areas to melt the sugar.

CUCUMBER
Avoid indigestion when eating fresh cucumber by cutting it a few hours before it is required. Sprinkle it with salt and leave to drain. The drained-off liquid is the cause of the trouble.

CURRANTS
Currants contain iron and provide roughage which helps regularity, and they play an important part in preventing acid conditions of the blood. One pound/about 500 g of dried currants has all the food value of $3\frac{1}{2}$ lb/about $1\frac{3}{4}$ kg of grapes. Currants are a healthy snack for children's school breaks.

Currants should be washed and dried in a cloth before use; if damp, they will make cakes or puddings heavy. A dusting of flour on the currants will make your cakes lighter and stop the fruit sinking to the bottom. Warming them in the oven beforehand will also stop them sinking.

CURRY
If your curry dish is too spicy, add some natural yoghurt to it just before serving. It will cool it down.

CUSTARD
When a custard curdles, to bring it back mix one tablespoon of arrowroot (for every pint/half litre of custard) with one beaten egg and two tablespoons of cold milk. Away from the heat, pour the mixture slowly into the custard, then reheat carefully, stirring constantly.

When a custard has curdled, place the pan in a dish of cold water and beat until smooth, with an egg-beater. Or put it through a liquidizer.

To prevent custard sticking to the bottom of the pan, grease the inside bottom of the pan before pouring in the milk.

Sprinkle a little sugar on top of the custard when it is cooling off – it will stop a skin forming.

DATES
Fresh dates will pop out of their thick skin if you pinch the stem end.

DEFROSTING FOOD
To defrost meat or any other food quickly, place it on a rack or a grill instead of a plate. The air will circulate better around the frozen piece. Place a dish or some paper towels under the grill to collect the liquid as it thaws.

DOUGH
To soften a hard dough, use a glass bottle filled with warm water and sprinkled with flour on the outside instead of a wooden rolling pin.

If you don't want to sprinkle flour over the rolling pin when rolling dough, use a piece of waxed paper between the dough and the rolling pin to prevent the dough from sticking.

To stop the foil or greaseproof paper sliding when you are rolling out dough on it, sprinkle the working surface with water before you smooth the foil or greaseproof paper over it.

To make a dough rise faster, place it in a plastic bag whose inside has been greased with a little oil, so that the dough does not stick to the plastic bag.

DRIED APPLE SLICES
To give extra flavour to dried apple slices, soak them in cider.

DRIED BEANS
Add a pinch of bicarbonate of soda at the beginning of cooking to improve the texture.

DRIED FRUIT – See Fruit

DRINKS MEASURES
One bottle wine serves approx. 6 glasses ($\frac{3}{4}$ full)
One bottle sherry serves approx. 14 glasses
One bottle port serves approx. 12 glasses
One bottle whisky serves approx. 32 mixes
One bottle gin serves approx. 32 mixes
One bottle champagne serves approx. 8 glasses
One bottle liqueur serves approx. 34 glasses

DRIPPING
To separate dripping from fat, put it in a basin and pour boiling water over it. The next day the fat will have formed into a cake on top of the water. Remove the cake, in one piece if possible, and repeat the process three times. You will get beautifully purified dripping.

A delicious way of collecting dripping from grilled steaks, chops, ham and other meat is to place on a sheet of foil underneath them slices of bread which have been well toasted on one side. Place the toasted side down and the dripping will soak into the bread, the toasted lower side preventing the juices from passing through.

DUCK – See also **Poultry**
Stuff duck or goose with two unpeeled apples to soak up the fat. (Do not eat the apples afterwards.)

For very crisp roast duck, the skin must be very dry. In the winter hang the bird for at least four hours in an airy spot, or leave it to dry overnight; or douse the bird with boiling water and dry it thoroughly with a towel or kitchen paper; or try drying the bird with a hair-dryer – the drier the crisper – before putting it in the oven.

EGGS – See also **Easter eggs**
White shell or brown shell? Eggs must be bought clean, as the shell is porous and allows germs to penetrate. Brown shells are thicker and less porous than white shells.

A soiled egg should be wiped with a slightly damp cloth, washing it would take away the natural protecting film which prevents bacteria and odours entering the egg.

Most cooks advocate keeping eggs at low room temperature as temperature variations cause the whites to become thin.

Eggs should be stored big end downward to retain their freshness and quality longer.

To get an egg out when stuck to the cardboard egg carton, wet the box, then it will not stick for long.

Eggs are fresh if, when placed in a bowl of cold water, they sink straight to the bottom and stay there; if they float, they are not fresh. If they tilt between the two they can be used for pastries. To test for freshness you can also place your tongue on the end of the egg: a new egg will feel warm, whereas an old egg will feel quite cold. Or shake the egg by your ear: a fresh egg will not make any noise, an old one will.

To find out if an egg is stale, break it on a plate. If the yolk is flat and the white thin and spreading out then the egg is stale. A fresh egg will have a domed yolk and the white will be thick.

To preserve new-laid eggs, smear the shells with pure glycerine on the day they are laid; at the end of a few weeks they will be just as fresh. If possible, store eggs with the small end upwards. They will keep for a month if you boil them for one minute.

Fresh eggs tend to take a little longer to cook than those that are a few days old, as do eggs coming straight from the refrigerator.

Hens' eggs should be lightly cooked. Prolonged cooking toughens the white and makes it less digestible.

Duck eggs do not keep fresh for very long because they have a very porous shell. They can be contaminated by germs from the duck, so they should be thoroughly cooked to be safe – for at least twelve to fourteen minutes. They should not therefore be used in lightly cooked dishes, but cooked at temperatures high enough to kill any germs that have been present. They should not be preserved.

Goose eggs are larger than hens' eggs, but they are as delicate in flavour and can be cooked in as many different ways. One goose egg is the equivalent of three hens' eggs. Cook seven minutes for a soft-boiled egg, fourteen minutes for a hard-boiled egg.

Gull, plover and pheasant eggs are usually eaten hard-boiled and can be served as an hors-d'oeuvre. (Cook for ten to fifteen minutes.)

Cooking time for hens' eggs varies according to the size of the eggs, but on average the time is as follows:

2 minutes – very soft-boiled egg with creamy white and slightly liquid yolk
3 minutes – soft white, very soft yolk
$3\frac{1}{2}$ minutes – well-done white, soft yolk
5 minutes – very well-done white, well-done yolk
6 minutes – very well-done white, thick yolk
10 minutes – hard-boiled egg

The perfect way to boil an egg is to bring the water to the boil, put the egg in it and then remove the saucepan from the heat. Leave the egg in the water for six minutes. This method prevents the white becoming leathery and is also very economical. Leave the egg for a few minutes longer if you prefer it more cooked.

To distinguish a raw egg from a cooked one, give it a twirl on the table. A raw egg will spin several times; a cooked one will stop spinning immediately.

You can tell when a hard-boiled egg is cooked and ready if you blow on the shell as soon as you take it out of the water. If the shell dries instantly, it is ready; if it stays wet, the yolk is still soft.

When cooking an egg straight from the refrigerator do not place it in boiling water or it will crack. Put it in lukewarm water then bring it to the boil. Time it from the moment the water starts to boil.

An egg will not crack when dipped in boiling water if you previously remove the head from a wooden match, break the match in two and throw it into the boiling water.

To prevent an egg cracking while boiling, prick its pointed end with a needle.

When an egg cracks in boiling water, quickly put in a teaspoon of vinegar to prevent the white running; if the white is already escaping, put a teaspoon of salt in the water.

Before putting a cracked egg into water, wrap it very tightly in tissue paper or silver foil (screw the ends in opposite directions) and it will not boil out of its shell.

To stop the yolk of a hard-boiled egg becoming greyish, plunge the egg in cold water immediately after cooking.

If, when peeling a hard-boiled egg, you realize it is not sufficiently cooked, return it to the boiling water wrapped in aluminium foil and cook it for a few minutes more.

If a hard-boiled egg is cracked at each end, the shell will peel off easily.

When cutting hard-boiled eggs, dip the blade of your knife in hot water beforehand to prevent their breaking.

Peeled hard-boiled eggs will keep fresh longer if placed in a bowl of cold water to which a dash of soda water has been added. Store in the refrigerator.

When poaching an egg, add a little vinegar to the water to prevent the egg breaking.

A delicious way of poaching an egg is to put a small piece of butter into a cup, stand the cup in a little boiling water in a pan, break the egg into it and steam for seven to nine minutes.

Eggs continue to cook in the pan when it is removed from the heat. When making scrambled eggs, fried eggs or omelettes, take the pan off the heat before they are quite ready and let them finish cooking in the pan.

If scrambled eggs have to wait for a little while after being cooked, don't despair, you will still serve them moist and soft if you stir a raw egg into them before putting in a warm serving dish.

When separating an egg, break it into a funnel: the white will run through and the yolk will remain.

When the white only is needed, separate the egg in the usual way and put the yolk into a container. Cover it with cold water and keep in the refrigerator. When needed, drain off the water. The yolk will stay perfectly fresh for several days.

When beating the white of an egg, add a small pinch of salt (not too much as it would make it watery); it will whip better and faster. Do not whip an egg white when the egg is cold from the refrigerator. You do not get the same volume from cold eggs.

To get the most volume out of your whites of egg when whisking them, first rub the inside of the whisking bowl with the cut side of half a lemon, and do not over-beat the egg white, stop when the mixture is firm enough to keep shape. By over-beating the air will escape and make the egg white flat and too stiff.

Stop your whisked egg whites from liquifying if not used immediately by covering the bowl with a plastic wrap or turning the bowl upside down. (If whisked perfectly the whites will not fall.)

When making pastries, sauces etc., use medium eggs. Eggs which are too large could alter the recipe.

When using eggs to thicken a sauce, add a pinch of white flour before pouring into the sauce. This will prevent the eggs curdling in the sauce when it is brought to boiling point.

Do not add milk to the whole beaten raw eggs if you are cooking them with tomatoes. The acid in the tomatoes will curdle the milk.

If you drop a raw egg on the floor, sprinkle a generous amount of fine salt over it to absorb the moisture before wiping it up. It will be much easier to remove.

To avoid breaking the eggs when going camping for the weekend, before leaving break the eggs into a thermos and carry them that way. You will just have to shake the thermos a little before pouring the eggs out as you need them to make scrambled eggs or an omelette.

ESSENCE FLAVOURING

To measure drops of essence flavouring, dip the point of a skewer in the essence bottle: when the skewer is lifted out of the bottle the essence will drip at the point of the skewer drop by drop.

FAT – See also Chips and Frying

When frying fat has burned slightly, a raw peeled potato dropped into the pan for a few minutes and then removed will take all trace of burning away.

Do not pour fat down the sink. If you do, it will solidify and block the drain. If you have done so inadvertently, pour boiling water down the sink immediately.

To stop the smell of fat spreading through the house, place a sprig of parsley in the fat when you start to heat it.

FIGS

When dried figs become too dry, steam them until they soften.

FISH

Fish must be very fresh; this is most important. Gills should be pink or bright red. If there are scales, they should be bright and silvery. Eyes should be clear and prominent, the flesh should be firm, and there should be a pleasantly fresh smell. When cut, the flesh should be creamy and not too transparent. If the scales rub off, the gills are pale, the eyes sunken and the whole fish is flabby then it is stale.

To keep a fish fresh in the refrigerator for a few days before cooking, do the following. Dampen a cloth in vinegar, wring it out and lay it open on the table. Sprinkle with coarse salt, place the fish onto it and sprinkle it also with coarse salt. Wrap the cloth around the fish and place in the refrigerator until needed.

To prevent the fish from becoming dry when being deep-frozen, wrap it in silver foil instead of a plastic bag.

Put small fish in milk or fruit-juice carton containers to freeze them. Place the fish in the carton container, fill it up with water, close the carton with a staple or sellotape, and put in the freezer.

Fish to be thawed in a hurry can be put, sealed in its wrapping, in cold water (not warm). The slower a fish thaws, the less juice it will lose.

Fish thawed in its wrapping in the refrigerator takes about eight hours per pound/about 500g. It takes half as long if thawed at room temperature.

Frozen fish or meat will thaw quicker if a little vinegar is rubbed over it when it is taken out of the freezer.

When handling a fish, prevent it slipping from your hands by dipping your fingers in salt first.

When scaling a fish is difficult, dip it for a few seconds into boiling water.

When scaling a fish, place the fish on a board with the tail to the left for right-handed people and to the right for left-handed people. To hold the fish in position poke a nail through the tail and onto the board. Scale the fish with your own home-made scaler (used by most fishmongers), working from the tail towards the head.

To make your scaler, take two beer-bottle tops and nail them to a small piece of wood with one third sticking out at the top.

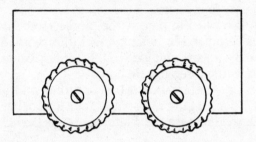

When cleaning a fish, place a sheet of greaseproof paper over your wooden board. That way the board stays clean and free of fish smells.

The many ways of cooking fish

Poaching fish: For fillets, fish steaks and little fish use a shallow baking dish rather than a poacher, or a well-buttered shallow oven-proof dish (avoid aluminium as it discolours the wine or vinegar and may give a disagreeable smell to the fish).

After the fish has been placed on top of the ingredients required in the recipe, it should be moistened (barely covered) with white wine vinegar or fish stock and dotted with butter, placed in a moderate oven and simmered gently, basting frequently.

Do not overcook or the fish becomes tasteless; better undercook than overcook.

Poaching fish in court-bouillon: For big fish use a fish-poacher, on top of the cooker. If it is a fish with large scales, scrape them, but if the fish has small scales (salmon, trout) leave them on as they will hold the fish together during cooking.

Lay the fish on the rack of the fish-kettle or if you do not have a rack wrap the fish in a muslin cloth leaving the end of the cloth hanging out of the pan to avoid spoiling the fish when it is lifted. After the fish is placed on the rack or in muslin cloth, cover it with the cool liquid (salted water, fish stock, court-bouillon); do not use hot liquid as it would contract the flesh of the fish, causing it to break up and cook unevenly. The cool liquid should cover the fish completely. Cover the fish-kettle and quickly bring to the boil, skim as soon as it starts boiling, lower the heat, allowing the fish to simmer gently until cooked, then remove from the cooker. For fish up to 5 lb/$2\frac{1}{4}$ kg, allow 5 minutes per lb/$\frac{1}{2}$ kg, counting from boiling point.

If the fish is served hot it should be left to stand for a few minutes in the liquor then lifted out to drain. Small fish can be served with their skin on; larger fish are skinned, leaving the head and tail. The small bones along the top of the backbone are removed. The fish can be covered with foil and kept warm at the bottom of a warm oven until ready to be served.

A fish to be served cold must be left to cool in the poaching liquor then drained and skinned. It can be cooked in advance and kept in the refrigerator for up to twenty-four hours.

When the fish is cooked in pieces, the pieces should not be cut too thin and they should be dipped in boiling liquid (this method has the effect of concentrating all the juices contained in the fish, a great part would be lost if the pieces of fish were placed in cold liquid).

Note: For certain kinds of fish such as brill or turbot, milk should be added to the liquid ($\frac{1}{8}$ pint/75 ml of milk to $1\frac{1}{4}$ pints/$\frac{3}{4}$ of a litre of liquid required in the recipe). The milk will increase the whiteness of the flesh.

Grilling fish: When the fish is of a medium size and over, some shallow diagonal incisions should be made each side of the body of the fish, this will allow the heat to penetrate easily and facilitate the cooking.

Dry-textured or white-flesh fish will be better off being coated with flour, then brushed with melted butter or oil before grilling (this will prevent the fish from drying out and will give it a golden coat impossible to get otherwise, the golden crust can always be discarded by people on a diet).

Mackerel, sardines, herrings, trout and salmon do not need flour coating, being oily fish; a brushing with oil or melted butter is enough.

The grid of the grill must be hot and oiled before placing the fish on it to prevent the fish sticking. If the heat is too strong a protective envelope will form on the surface of the fish which will burn and stop the heat penetrating inside the flesh. A whole fish, being thinner toward the tail, should have the thin part further away from the heat than the thick part.

Thin fillets of fish do not need turning.

Round fish are grilled on one side then rolled to the other.

Flat fish are grilled first on the white side then on the dark.

Thick steaks or slices should be grilled on one side then the other.

Deep-frying fish: Too large fish or too thick pieces of fish should not be deep-fried, the outside would become dry before the middle is cooked.

If the fish is a little too thick, small incisions into the flesh should be made each side of it to facilitate the cooking.

The smaller the fish the hotter the fat; the quantity of fat should be plenty, the fish must be entirely submerged. The greater the amount of fat, the higher the temperature will reach and the less cooling will occur when the fish is immersed. Only a small quantity of fish should be fried at a time to avoid lowering the temperature, making the fish boil instead of fry.

If, when frying, a basket is used it should be heated in the pan with the oil so that the fish will not stick to it.

The ideal oil for frying is the one which can be brought to a high temperature without burning. Groundnut (peanut) oil will heat to 200°C/390°F without burning, so will olive oil (290°/554°F).

Strain the fat each time after use, to get rid of the coating residue and keep it only for frying fish as the smell would spoil the taste of other food.

Fish cooked in butter (à la meunière): Use butter and oil so that the butter will not brown too rapidly, the fat should be hot, but not boiling. The minimum of fat should be used to allow the fish to retain its natural flavour.

When the fish is cooked and placed on a warm dish, squeeze a few drops of lemon juice onto it. Sprinkle some coarsely chopped, scalded and drained parsley over it, then put a piece of butter in the cooking pan. Heat until slightly brown and pour over the fish; a froth will form on contact with the hot butter on the moist parsley. Serve at once while the bubbling is still going on.

Coating batter: If required for immediate use beat the batter as little as possible; turning it over with a wooden spoon will avoid the development of elasticity which would prevent the batter sticking to the fish to be dipped.

If the batter is to be prepared in advance, it can be well beaten, thus precipitating the fermentation, making a lighter batter (the batter standing will allow the elasticity to disappear). Then before using add the whites of egg whisked to a stiff froth.

Batter: 9 oz/250 g sifted flour, pinch of salt, two tablespoons of olive oil or melted butter, two eggs, one glass (14 fluid oz/400 ml) of water or milk and one glass of beer.

Mix all the ingredients in a bowl, except the whites of egg. If possible leave it to stand for at least two hours in a warm place to allow the fermentation to start. Add the two stiffly beaten egg whites to the batter just before using.

Note: The fermentation can be precipitated by a tiny addition of yeast.

Flour coating: First soak the fish in salted milk, then pass through flour before deep frying (the combination of milk and flour will give a crisp coating to the fish).

Note: Whitebait does not need to be soaked in milk before the flour coating.

Breadcrumb coating: Lightly flour the fish – this helps the mixture (egg and breadcrumbs) adhere better to the fish to make an instant crisp crust when dipped in very hot fat and thus stops the juices escaping.

Fish mousse: Seasoning is very important in cold preparation. Taste very carefully, the seasoning brings out the flavour of the dish. The cream added in the preparation should not be more than half whipped; fluffily whipped the mousse will be drier and less delicate.

Salmon cold: When serving a salmon cold it should be cooked whole, in separate pieces the meat is much drier. Use white wine or lemon juice instead of vinegar when making the court-bouillon for poaching the salmon, as the vinegar might discolour the flesh of the fish.

An excellent way of cooking a salmon for serving it cold: after the fish is covered with the cool court-bouillon, cover and bring slowly to the boil. As soon as the liquid is boiling, skim and remove the pan from the heat. Cover the pan tightly (this can be done by first covering the pan with a tea-towel, then the lid) and leave the fish in the liquid until cold, that way the salmon will never be overcooked. Drain the salmon. It can be kept in the fridge up to twenty-four hours.

Note: A true connoisseur will always prefer the salmon served covered with its own skin to the one skinned and decorated.

If to be served hot, cook the fish by the method given on p. 139.

Salmon trout: A seafish very similar to the salmon, but usually smaller. Almost always served whole and can be prepared in any of the ways given for salmon.

Steam and cook your salmon trout in your dishwasher. Wrap the trout with herbs and seasoning in foil, then wrap it again and seal it well. Place the wrapped trout on the top shelf of your dishwasher and press the full-cycle button. (Do not forget to put some clean plates in the dishwasher at the same time; that way they will be nice and warm to serve the trout on.)

Sole: After the head has been cut off and the black skin removed, when the sole is to be eaten whole, scrape the scales covering the white skin. (To peel the black skin, scrape the extremity of the tail with a knife, catching the thin part of the skin with the corner of a tea-towel and pull quickly.) Then, with a sharp knife, make a cut down the centre of the right and left side of the backbone; this will allow the heat to reach the centre of the fish quicker. Then with the point of the scissors carefully cut the backbone below the tail and below the head; this will make it easier to remove when the fish is cooked. Place the opened side of the sole (where the incision down the backbone has been made) downwards in the dish for cooking.

If the sole is to be eaten in fillets, remove both skins, black and white, using a thin and flexible knife blade to detach the fillets.

Fillet of sole: The thin white skin should be removed to avoid any shrinkage in cooking, the fillet is then flattened slightly with a wet, broad-bladed knife to break the fibres.

In poaching the fillet never allow the liquid to boil; this will prevent the fillet breaking or losing shape.

Fried sole: The black skin is taken off and the white skin is left after having been scraped of the scales.

Grilled sole: Same preparations as for fried sole and some light incisions are made on the white skin with the point of a sharp knife. Place on very hot grill with the white skin underneath.

Sole meunière: Start cooking the sole with the white skin underneath.

Turbot: Poached in court-bouillon (p. 139); served hot. Before cooking the turbot, break the spine in two or three places by folding the fish over on itself and pressing hard with your fingers or hand, to prevent deformation, and help the fish keep its shape during cooking. Also tie the head of the fish in muslin or with a piece of string. Rub a small piece of butter over the fish before serving to give it a shiny look.

Cold turbot: Turbot (especially sliced ones) have a tendency to harden, curl up and become tasteless, so do not cook it too much in advance, not long enough for the cooking liquid to set as jelly.

Young turbot: Before cooking, young turbot is prepared as above.

Fish cooked when still frozen takes longer to cook than if thawed first, and it must be cooked at a lower temperature.

Fish fried in an aromatic beer batter is delicious, as is a beer sauce on plain grilled or boiled fish.

When cooking a fish, the slim part can be protected by sliding a slice of potato under the tail. This should be done when the fish is partly cooked.

For fish without smell, clean the fish but leave on the scales. Bury it without seasoning in 4 lb/about 2 kg of coarse salt and cook for an hour in the oven. Serve with lemony butter — delicious. Cook for only half an hour when using sardines.

When grilling a fish, do not scale it beforehand. The scales protect the fish from the high temperature and keep the flesh soft and tasty. Skin and scales come off easily at the end of cooking.

To test if a fish is cooked, pull out one of the small bones near the head. If it comes out easily, the fish is ready.

When poaching a fish to be eaten cold, leave it to cool in the cooking water.

If you run out of flour to dip the fish in before frying, wipe them dry and dip them in beer instead. The result will be excellent.

FISH SMELL
Cold water instead of hot must be used when cleaning pans and frying pans in which fish has been cooked. The smell will linger in the pan if it is washed with hot water.

To remove fish smells in a pan, put a teaspoon of methylated spirit in the pan, strike a match and burn the spirit. Rinse well afterwards. (Make sure that you put the bottle of methylated spirit back in the cupboard before starting this little operation.)

Another method of getting rid of fish smells is to boil coffee grounds in the pan in which the fish has been cooked.

To remove the smell of fish from silverware, add a spoonful of mustard to the washing-up water.

To remove the smell of fish from your hands, rub them with mustard, bicarbonate of soda or a little earth or beer.

FIZZY DRINKS

Fizzy drinks in bottles lose their fizz very quickly once the bottle is opened. If you have some left and want to keep it, put back the top, seal it with adhesive plaster, and place the bottle upside down in the refrigerator.

To get a fizzy drink that has become flat to fizz again, add bicarbonate of soda to it (one teaspoon of bicarbonate of soda to one pint/half a litre of liquid).

FLAMING DISH

If you have difficulty in making a dish to flame, add a little vodka to it. It will not change the taste but the alcohol content will help the flaming.

FLOUR

When flour is milled, the whole grain is broken up and separated, sifted, blended and ground into flour. Some of the bran is removed, as is the wheatgerm which contains oil and could go rancid. Because the bran and the wheatgerm are left in wholemeal flour it cannot be stored for long (two months). The finer and whiter the flour, the less its food value as more of its nutritious content has been removed.

True wholemeal and whole wheatmeal flours contain 100 per cent of the whole grain. Wheatmeal flour contains 85–90 per cent of the whole grain. White flour contains 72–4 per cent of the whole grain. Self-raising flour contains 72–4 per cent of the whole grain, plus bicarbonate of soda and cream of tartar.

If flour is sifted two or three times before use, cakes will be much lighter.

Flour should always be mixed with *cold* liquid or it will go lumpy.

For dusting flour on food or pastry boards, keep a powder puff inside your flour jar.

FLOURING, BREADCRUMBING

When flouring or breadcrumbing meat or fish, put the flour or the breadcrumbs or both together with the seasoning (salt, pepper, herbs etc.,) in a plastic bag. Place the meat or fish in the bag, hold the top of the bag and shake well to coat the meat or fish evenly. It does the job perfectly and makes no mess in the kitchen.

FOOD BURNING

To prevent food sticking to the pan, sprinkle the inside of the pan with a little salt and heat it for a few seconds before adding the food.

FREEZER

In case of a breakdown or power cut, food will keep for twenty-four hours if the freezer is not opened. Lumps or bags of dry ice (carbon dioxide) put in the top of the freezer will help to keep the food frozen longer, as will layers of newspapers or blankets.

FREEZING LIQUID

To freeze liquid in a plastic bag, first put the bag into a box, then pour the liquid into the bag and place it in the freezer. When frozen, remove the box, and the liquid inside the bag will have taken the shape of the box, making it easier to store in the freezer.

FRENCH BEANS

A French Bean is fresh and good to eat when it snaps in two pieces when bent. If it is soft and pliable, it's an old bean.

FROZEN FOOD

When buying frozen food, always have with you some newspapers in which you can wrap the food to insulate it. Once home, the food should be put straight into the freezer.

If you have other shopping to do after buying frozen food at the supermarket, keep an insulated picnic bag in your car and store the food in it.

Do not re-freeze packets of frozen food once they have thawed.

FRUIT

Fruit such as apples, pears, peaches and pineapples, once cut for fruit salad or other uses, should be covered at once with lemon or lime juice to prevent discolouration.

Fruit will not need so much sugar when stewed if half a teaspoon of bicarbonate of soda is added to them while cooking. (The bicarbonate of soda takes some of the acidity out of the fruit.) Add the sugar at the end of the cooking time, stirring gently with a wooden spoon.

To speed the ripening process, place fruit in closed paper bags in a warm place.

Dried fruits have acid which could corrode tins in which they are kept. Therefore keep dried fruits in glass, plastic or china containers.

Dried fruit should be washed in boiling water. Discard the water, cover again with boiling water and soak overnight. The next day, bring the fruit to the boil in the same water with or without sugar to taste.

DRIED FRUITS

To soak and cook dried fruits in one go: place the dried fruits in a wide necked vacuum flask, fill it up with boiling water or boiling tea (not too strong) put the lid on and leave overnight. In the morning they will be soaked and cooked ready to eat.

FRUIT ICE CUBES
Do not discard left-over syrup from tinned fruit; freeze it in ice-cube trays and use it mixed with drinks (soft or alcoholic).

FRUIT JELLY MAKING
To clarify a fruit jelly, add a few broken eggshells while it is simmering; the impurities will stick to the eggshells. Remove the shell at the end of cooking.

FRUIT JUICE
Fresh fruit juices should always be drunk immediately they are prepared as they lose some of their vitamins and their flavour if exposed to the air for any length of time.

For juices made from soft fruit, lemon should always be added immediately to retain the colour.

Frozen fruit juice can be quickly made drinkable without being thawed by putting it in the blender with the indicated measure of water. Use the low or medium speed.

Frozen orange juice will taste like the fresh one if you add the juice of a lemon to it.

Do not prepare your fresh orange juice in advance, as contact with the air will destroy the Vitamin C.

FRUIT PIE
To thicken the juice in a fruit pie add one or two teaspoons of cornflour or arrowroot to the sugar before mixing it with the rest of the ingredients.

FRYING – See also **Fat** and **Chips**
To prevent any splashing during frying, reverse a colander over the frying pan.

A pinch of salt in the frying pan before putting butter, oil or other fat to melt will prevent any splashing during cooking.

To avoid fat or oil spattering or going over when deep-frying, place a slice of onion or a piece of bread in the hot fat before dipping the chips or any other kind of food.

If fat catches fire in the kitchen turn the heat off, cover the pan with a lid or with a damp cloth spread out. Do not pour water over fat, it would splash flaming hot liquid. Do not try to carry the pan outside as you may burn yourself badly and also spread the fire.

GAME BIRDS
When fresh, game birds should have legs that are pliable and smooth, feet that are supple, and prominent eyes. In young birds, the part under the beak is brittle.

When buying a game bird, ask whether it has been hung. For game to be tender and to develop its distinctive taste it needs to be hung without being plucked or drawn. The length of hanging time is a matter of individual taste and weather – from a week in hot weather to two to three weeks in cold, frosty weather. Hang the bird by the legs in an airy, cold, dry place.

Hang large birds (e.g. geese and turkeys) by their feet; the blood runs into the neck leaving the bird's flesh with a less gamy taste and also whiter. But small birds are hung by their necks – the blood stays in the flesh, giving it a more gamy taste.

To keep flies away while game is hanging, sprinkle the bird with a mixture of ground pepper, ground cloves and flour.

To find out if the bird has been hung long enough, pull out a feather above the tail. If it comes away easily the bird is ready.

To make plucking of poultry and game easier, first plunge them into boiling water for a short while.

GAME GRAVY
Game gravy can be thickened by adding redcurrant jelly or any other jellies to it.

GARDEN PARTY
Use fruit or veg as natural containers for dips at a garden party. Remove the head of the cauliflower and keep the base with the leaves on. Fill it with the cauliflower sprigs, sticks of carrots and cucumber which will be used for dipping. To hold the dips use a melon emptied of its flesh, some large red or green peppers with the ribs and seeds cut out, some large tomatoes with the flesh scooped out, half grapefruits, large oranges, coconuts etc.

GARLIC – See also Salad dressing
Unpeeled garlic cloves give a lighter flavour. Use the whole cloves in soups, stock, stew, sauces etc., but do not forget to remove the clove or cloves before serving.

If you find garlic indigestible, cut the clove in half and remove the germ from the middle before use.

Before peeling a clove of garlic, press it firmly between your fingers or under the flat blade of a knife until you hear a crack. The skin will then come off easily.

One pressed clove of garlic equals three chopped cloves in flavour.

Do not fry garlic for too long as it loses its taste and becomes bitter.

To rub garlic all over the inside of a salad bowl without getting the smell of garlic on your hands, place the peeled garlic in a plastic bag and then crush it with a hammer. When this is completed turn the plastic bag inside out, over the salad bowl, leaving your hand encased in the clean side, and rub the bowl with the crushed garlic. When you have finished, reverse the bag to the right side and throw it away.

Garlic leaves are delicious finely cut in an omelette, mixed with white cheese (e.g. cottage cheese) in a salad etc. Grow some all year round by standing a full garlic head on top of a bottle or a jar full of water (roots touching the water). When the leaves are well developed you can cut a few as needed. They will grow again and again.

To remove the smell of garlic from your hands, rub them with baking soda, and then rinse.

Your breath will not smell of garlic if you use the juice only and discard the fibres.

GERANIUM LEAVES AND FLOWERS

Jams, jellies, sweet stewed fruits and ice-cream will have a more delicate flavour if you add a few geranium leaves, fresh or dried.

Geranium leaves can also be used for infusions: crush a few leaves, place them in a pot and pour boiling water over them.

Geranium flowers are also edible, and can be used to decorate cakes.

GINGER

To keep fresh ginger for a long time, bury it in a box full of sand. Sprinkle the sand with water from time to time to keep it slightly moist.

Another way is to pickle it. Clean it, cut it, put it in a jar and cover with vodka. Secure the lid on the jar and you can keep it in the refrigerator for many months.

Freeze peeled ginger and grate it straight from the freezer when needed.

GINGERBREAD

When mixing all the ingredients to make gingerbread use cold coffee instead of milk, the taste is delicious and the colour a richer brown. This is also good when making chocolate pudding.

GLAZING

To glaze bread, cakes or pies use an egg. Brush on the white of egg for a shiny glaze without colour. Brush on the whole beaten egg for a light-coloured shiny glaze. Brush on a slightly beaten yolk of egg for a dark shiny glaze. One egg will glaze two loaves of bread.

GOOSE – See also Poultry

When choosing a goose, make sure that the feet and bill are yellow; this means it will be young. When the bird is young, the feet are pliable; when old, the feet and bill are red.

GOOSEBERRIES

Use a pair of scissors to top and tail gooseberries.

GRAPES

To peel grapes without difficulty, place them in a strainer and dip them in very hot water for one minute. Then run them under cold water before peeling.

To extract the seeds from the grapes, use a hair-grip. Introduce the folded end through the stalk end of the grape and pull out the seeds.

To keep grapes fresh for months, use bunches which have fully ripened and which are not too tight: remove any bad grapes. In a barrel or wooden box (in preference to plastic or cardboard) lay a coating of very dry bran. Place bunches of grapes on top and cover them with bran, then another layer of grapes and another layer of bran until the barrel or box is full. Close it and keep in a dry, coolish place. When you want grapes in the winter, just dip into the bran.

To freeze grapes, wash them, remove from the stalks and dry them. Place them in a container and freeze. Serve them on a pretty dish after dinner with coffee; they are refreshing and taste like sorbet. The seedless variety is especially delicious. This method also goes for cherries, gooseberries, red- and balckcurrants and small plums.)

GRAPEFRUITS
A heavy grapefruit with a thin skin will be juicier than a light thick-skinned one.
To peel a grapefruit easily, submerge it in boiling water for a few minutes.

GRATIN
To prevent an unpleasant crust forming on the top of a dish *au gratin* in the oven or under the grill, mix the grated cheese with breadcrumbs, sprinkle with a little water and dot with butter. After a few minutes, take out the dish, sprinkle with a little water and finish browning.

GRAVY
To get a fat-free gravy: pour the gravy from the pan into a cup or a wide-mouthed jar. The fat will come to the surface and can be easily removed with a spoon.

GREENS
Many greens and herbs (e.g. mint, parsley, celery and lettuce) will keep fresh and crisp for a week if wrapped in a wet cloth. Keep the cloth wet, and store in the refrigerator or a cool place.

GRIDDLE
To prevent the cake from sticking to the griddle and prevent odours and smoke, rub the griddle with salt instead of fat before cooking.

GRILLING
A small shallow container filled with cold water and placed in the grill pan beneath the grill will stop the kitchen filling with smoke when you grill meat or fish. A little salt sprinkled in the bottom of the tray will also stop the dripping fat burning.

Diagonal incisions when grilling poultry or fish speed up the grilling.

HAM

To find out if a ham is good to eat, insert a steel skewer near the bone. If the skewer comes out clean and smelling good the ham is good to eat. If the skewer has an unpleasant smell and is not clean-looking, discard the ham.

Ham that is too salty will lose some of its salt if soaked in cold milk for a short while.

Sliced ham that has dried out will regain some freshness if soaked briefly in milk.

HAMBURGER

Handle the minced meat gently when shaping a hamburger. The mixture must be loose to leave space for the meat to retain the natural juices. Too firm a mixture will allow the juices to escape, leaving rather dry meat.

A little crushed ice, some stock or water added to the raw meat will also prevent the meat becoming too dry.

To cook hamburgers quickly, before cooking make a hole in their middle, the holes will not be visible when the hamburger is cooked.

To cook hamburgers straight from the freezer without thawing, make a hole in the middle before freezing them. The centre is the part which takes the longest to thaw and does not cook as quickly as the rest.

A hamburger is cooked when small beads of blood begin to ooze through the crust.

HAZELNUTS

Hazelnuts will peel easily if they are first grilled until the skin breaks then rubbed against each other by hand or in a polythene bag.

HEATING UP A COMPLETE DINNER IN ONE PAN

In a large pan place three or four jam jars containing stew, fish, rice etc. Cover each jar with foil and pour boiling water in the pan to come two-thirds of the way up the sides of the jars. Potatoes can be boiled in the water, and in this way a whole meal can be re-heated over one gas or electric ring.

HENS

To make your hens produce more eggs, give them some nettle seeds and dried leaves (chop the leaves before you dry them for the winter)

HERBS

Dry herbs have a much stronger flavour than fresh ones. Half a teaspoon of dried, or a quarter of a teaspoon of powdered, is the equivalent of two level teaspoons of fresh herbs.

To freeze herbs, put the leaves in an ice-cube tray, pour water over, and freeze. When needed, take out one or two cubes, melt the ice and use the herbs as usual.

Never use metal containers for storing herbs as these can easily affect the delicate flavours. Use porcelain, earthenware, china or dark glass containers. The flavour and colour of herbs are affected by the daylight when kept in a transparent jar.

Herbs and garlic lose their flavour when over-cooked, so add them towards the end of the cooking time.

For a herbal infusion made of fresh herbs: use three teaspoons of fresh bruised leaves for each cup. Bruise the leaves by crushing them in a clean linen cloth before use.

With dried herbs use one teaspoon of herbs for each cup and one for the teapot.

HONEY

If honey goes sugary, stand the jar in hot water and it will liquefy again. Or remove the metal cap and heat the jar in a microwave oven for one or two minutes.

HORSERADISH

When horseradish sauce is so strong that it makes your eyes water, quickly sniff a piece of bread.

HOT CHOCOLATE

Before pouring hot chocolate into a cup, beat it to a froth. The froth will prevent a skin forming on the surface of the hot chocolate in the cup.

HOT DRINKS

When hot liquid is poured into a glass it will not crack if the glass is placed on a damp cloth – or if a spoon is put in the glass before pouring.

ICE-CREAM

Make smooth ice-cream or sorbet without an ice-cream maker by adding one tablespoon of melted butter to one pint/half a litre of ice-cream or sorbet. Lemon juice (one tablespoon to one pint/half a litre) is also very good. This will also prevent crystallization.

For a quick ice-cream topping (particularly good with vanilla) melt a few peppermint cream chocolates, stir well and pour over the ice-cream.

Serve ice-cream in chilled glasses or scoops; it won't melt so fast.

At your dinner party serve and keep your ice-cream ice cold by bringing it to the table in a block of ice: take a heat-resistant bowl and weight it down inside a container full of water (the water should come two-thirds of the way up the glass bowl) and put in the freezer (this should be done the day before). When the water has turned to ice take the block of ice with the bowl out of the container and keep it in the freezer until you fill it up with the ice-cream.

ICE-CUBE TRAYS

Coat the bottom of the ice-cub tray with vaseline or rub it with a candle to stop it sticking to the freezer compartment; it will also prevent the ice cubes sticking to the tray. If you line the bottom of the freezer compartment with aluminium foil it will have the same result.

A piece of wax-paper placed underneath the ice-cube trays in the refrigerator will prevent the trays sticking to the freezer compartment.

Ice cubes will not stick to each other in an ice bucket if they are sprinkled with a little tonic or soda water.

The trays are very useful for freezing liquids such as fruit juice, bouillon, stock and tomato juice and tomato sauce. When the liquid is frozen, transfer the cubes to plastic bags. Fruit juices should have a little sugar mixed into them before freezing (except for redcurrant juice, which would become jelly).

ICING
If the cake icing gets too thin, add powdered milk to it or powdered sugar.

JAM
When making jam, coat the inside of the preserving pan with butter or oil to prevent the jam burning.

To stop the jam boiling over while cooking, add a small piece of butter to it.

Some fruits are very watery (peaches, strawberries etc.,) and make jam-making a long operation. Shorten the process by placing a muslin bag filled with two tablespoons of apple pips (gathered and kept in a jar every time you peel and core apples for a recipe) in the preserving pan and cook with the jam.

Pectin is a necessity to set jams and marmalades. Some fruits are very low in pectin (pears, rhubarb, strawberries, cherries) and need to have it added in the form of lemon juice or redcurrant juice. To test the pectin content in jam or marmalade take a tablespoon of the cooked fruit juice, before the sugar is added, and pour into a cup. When cool, add a tablespoon of methylated spirits, mix well and wait a minute or two. If a firm jelly is forming there is enough pectin. If the jelly is very soft boil the fruits a little more and retest before adding the sugar, or the lemon juice ($2\frac{1}{2}$ tablespoons to 4 lbs/2 kg).

To prevent foaming and too much scum forming on the surface of the jam after the sugar has been added and dissolved, add a small piece of butter.

When making syrup for jam, do not stir the sugar and water once they start cooking or the sugar will crystallize.

If jam crystallizes it is due to a lack of acid. To remedy, re-heat the jam with a little lemon juice.

If the jam is too hard and too sweet pour it back into the preserving pan, add a little water, bring to the boil, stir and pour back in the jars.

When making strawberry jam add a few tablespoons of raspberry jelly to help the jam set.

To sterilize and make the jars air-tight first fill the jars (up to half an inch from the top) with the hot jam, carefully screw on the top, then put the jars upside-down and leave them in this position for fifteen minutes, before turning them up again. By this time they will be sterilized and sealed. (See also – **Jar** in 'Household' section.)

The fruit will not rise to the top of the jar when filling with home-made jam, if the jam has been left to cool off beforehand.

To prevent mould, place a lemon-scented geranium leaf on top of each jam jar before sealing them.

If fur forms on the surface, jam is still good to eat. Carefully remove the mould and use the jam as soon as possible.

To seal the jars that have flat rubber bands, rub the top of the jar and the rubber band with salad oil before closing.

JELLY

Fill up the empty halves of an orange or grapefruit with jelly and, when the jelly has set, cut the halves crossways into four sections, making it look like a four-petal flower. It's a big hit at a children's party as they can bite into each portion.

Set your jelly the fast way. Dissolve it in a measuring jug with some boiling water, then add ice cubes until it comes to the full measure.

Your jelly will have a lovely lustre after unmoulding if, before pouring the liquid to set, you rub the inside of the mould all over with a little salad oil.

To unmould a jelly successfully, dip the mould half-way in warm water for a few seconds.

When unmoulding a jelly, wet the serving plate under cold running water. That way if the jelly is not quite in the middle of the plate after unmoulding it will easily slide to it.

KETCHUP

To get ketchup out of the bottle, introduce a drinking straw into the bottle, all the way down. Take the straw out and the ketchup should flow; if not, repeat the operation.

The ketchup will flow easily out of the bottle if you shake it before removing the top.

KIPPERS

When dry, stand them in boiling water for three minutes, drain, dot with butter, and grill gently for five to six minutes.

Or put some water in the tray underneath the grill to moisturize the fish while it is grilling.

Put the kippers in an earthenware pan, cover them with boiling water, put a lid on the pan and leave them for seven to ten minutes. They will swell a little and be cooked perfectly.

LAMB – See also **Meat**

In good-quality lamb, the lean should be pale pink and fine-grained; the fat should be white and firm.

To test lamb, prick it with a skewer. If a colourless juice runs out the meat is cooked.

LEEKS

When making leeks vinaigrette, pour the vinaigrette over the leeks when they are still warm, the leeks will be more savoury.

LEMONS

Fresh lemon or orange juice frozen in ice-cube trays makes an original touch when mixing drinks.

To keep lemons fresh, store them in the refrigerator, or in a bowl of cold water, changing the water frequently. They will stay fresh and juicy for weeks.

To keep half a lemon fresh put some vinegar in a saucer and lay the cut face of the lemon on it – or sprinkle the cut side with fine salt.

To get the most juice out of a lemon pop it in a warm oven for five minutes or leave it in hot water for ten minutes before squeezing. Or roll it on a flat surface back and forward with your hand, pressing on it all the time.

To extract just the juice or a few drops from the lemon, push a knitting needle through from one end of the fruit to the other. Remove the needle and squeeze the lemon with your hand.

When you squeeze a lemon keep the rind and freeze it. When lemon rind is needed in your recipe it will be very handy to grate and you won't have to spoil a new lemon.

Lemon used on cooked ready-to-eat fish, meat and vegetables will kill harmful bacteria, especially in hot countries.

Lemon juice is helpful in cases of jaundice by helping to restore the liver.

Slices of lemon are difficult to squeeze. If lemon is needed for a dish, cut the lemon in wedges.

Frozen lemons are easier and quicker to grate than fresh ones.

A little lemon juice in a fruit salad helps to keep pear or apple slices from discolouring.

Grated lemon peel added to mincemeat improves the flavour.

LIVER

Before cooking liver, soak it for an hour in milk. Dry it before cooking. The soaking will make the liver more tender and succulent.

Do not store liver in its wrapping or it will become dry and will stick to the paper. Brush some oil on the slices and wrap in aluminium foil or put on a covered plate before placing in the refrigerator.

Slicing liver very thin is not easy. Pour boiling water over the liver and leave for a few seconds before slicing.

Another way to slice liver is to place it in the freezer for approximately half an hour or until the thin white transparent skin covering the liver comes off easily when peeled. The liver is then ready to be sliced.

LOBSTERS

The best lobsters are male, which are usually the smaller but do have the best flavour. When boiled, their colour is a deeper red than that of hen lobsters, which are better for sauces. The male lobster can be distinguished from the hen by the narrow back-part of the tail. The two uppermost fins within this section are stiff and hard, whereas those on the hen are soft and the tail is larger.

When buying lobsters, choose the heaviest ones. When lobsters are fresh, the claws will move slightly if you press the eyes with your fingers. When buying them ready-boiled, check whether the tails are stiff: if they are, the lobsters are fresh; if the tails are flabby, don't buy the lobsters.

MARIGOLDS

Marigold petals can be used instead of saffron to colour food. They also have a light, delicate flavour. The petals can be used fresh or dried. Dry them in a cool, dark place in thin layers and they will retain their beautiful colour.

MARSHMALLOWS

To prevent marshmallows from drying, keep them in the freezer. They thaw quickly.

To cut marshmallow easily, first dip the scissors in hot water.

MASHED POTATO

Mashed potato should be served straight away when ready, but if you do have to leave it standing, lightly coat the top with milk and stand the pan in a water bath. When ready to serve, beat the milk into the potato.

If you like to add milk to your mashed potato, keep some of the hot water in which the potatoes were cooked and add some instant dry milk powder to it. You won't have to warm the milk, and your mashed potato will be fluffier.

If your mashed potato is too runny, add a little skimmed milk powder to it.

For deliciously light mashed potato, add the yolk of an egg and, at the last minute, the stiffly beaten white. A touch of garlic also makes a pleasant change.

The best mashed potato in the world (a little extravagant but . . .) is cooked in milk. When the potatoes are cooked, discard the milk (or give it to the cat) and mash the potatoes with butter.

MEAT – See also under individual names

To keep raw meat fresh in hot weather when travelling, wash the meat with weak vinegar and water, then spread with slices of raw onion. In this way it will keep perfectly fresh in the hottest weather. Before cooking, remove the onion and rinse the meat until no trace of onion remains. This method is also excellent for fowl (a raw onion placed inside the bird will prevent any musty flavour).

When keeping meat for a few days in the refrigerator, rub it with a little vinegar or dry mustard; it will keep better and will not alter the flavour.

To slice raw meat very thin, put it in the freezing compartment of the refrigerator until very firm. Use a thin very sharp knife and slice across the grain as thinly as possible.

When thawing meat, *do not* put the meat under a hot tap to thaw it more quickly, as this will make it tough.

Meat should be brushed with oil before being placed on the barbecue grill, and more oil should be applied during cooking. The grill should also be oiled.

Marinate the meat before barbecuing. This will improve and tenderize cheaper cuts of meat.

A tough piece of meat will become tender if you marinate it overnight in beer before cooking. Any meat, including poultry, will improve if cooked in beer.

To prevent meat juices escaping, sear the surface of meat quickly, then finish cooking at a low temperature. Cooking at a high temperature hardens the fibres and toughens meat.

Do not season the meat either before or during cooking as salt makes the juices flow. Season at the end of the process.

Never keep meat stock overnight in copper, brass, tin or iron vessels as it could acquire an unpleasant flavour.

When roasting, do not add water to the meat or it will become tough. The meat should stand on a grill to avoid contact with the fat and juices.

When inserting the thermometer in the centre of the meat before the end of the required cooking time (about thirty minutes), do not touch the bone with the thermometer: it would give wrong information, the bone being a heat-conductor.

To test white meat, prick it with a knife tip. If the juice runs clear and not pink, the meat is cooked. To rest red meat, prick it with a fine skewer. If a light pink juice runs out, the meat is cooked.

When cooking meat, use tongs rather than a fork to turn it. Stabbing with a fork punches holes in the meat which allow the juices and therefore the flavour to drip out.

Tinned meat will slide out of the tin very easily if the tin is dipped in hot water for a few minutes. Or open both ends of the tin, and push the meat out.

MEATBALLS

When shaping meatballs or beefburgers, keep wetting your hands under running water so that the minced meat won't stick to your hands.

To prevent meatballs falling apart when frying, put them in the refrigerator for half an hour before cooking.

MEATLOAF

For a softer and tastier meatloaf add some ketchup (two tablespoons of ketchup to half a kilo/approximately one pound of meat) to the raw minced-meat. Tinned tomatoes are also good (two tomatoes to half a kilo/approximately one pound of raw meat).

MEAT-MINCER

After mincing meat, mince a piece of bread to clean and absorb pieces of meat and blood on the mincer.

MELBA TOAST

A quick way to make Melba toast is to take some ready-cut square slices of white bread, trim off the crust, flatten the slices with a rolling pin, then place them in a low pre-heated oven until they turn light brown.

MELON

Always wrap melon carefully before putting it in the refrigerator or its smell will spread and spoil other food.

A ripe melon should be slightly soft at the top when pressed gently. It should be heavy and have a good strong smell.

Honeydew: Put the melon to your ear and shake it. If it is ripe you can hear the juice rumbling about inside.

Watermelon: Knock it with your knuckle. If it has a hollow sound it is ripe. Try a few to hear the difference.

Melon kept in the refrigerator for too long will lose a lot of its flavour. Melon should only be briefly chilled.

When serving melon whole or portioned, cut off a small piece of the shell at the bottom for the melon to stand securely on the plate.

When serving melon as a starter at a dinner party, make it more interesting by giving each of your guests three or four thin slices of different kinds of melon sprinkled with lemon juice and freshly chopped mint. (Do not forget to cut away the rind from each slice.)

Melon with port, or seasoned with salt and freshly ground pepper, is delicious.

MERINGUE

For a soft consistency, the quantity of sugar must not exceed 1oz/about 30 g for each egg white. Any more will result in hard meringues.

A pinch of baking powder in the egg whites before beating them will make them rise beautifully.

Your meringues will stay white if you cook them with a wooden board under the baking tray.

Your meringues will not collapse while cooking if they are dusted with sifted icing sugar before putting them in the oven.

Do not remove the meringues from the oven as soon as you turn it off. The longer they are left in, the better the result.

MILK

Milk will not stick to the bottom of the pan when being heated if the pan is first rinsed under running water, but not dried.

To test the purity of milk, dip a steel knitting needle into it. If when lifted the milk coats the needle and drips off slowly it is pure. But if it runs off fast, leaving the needle clean, it is adulterated.

Milk and butter can be kept cool without a fridge by using the following method. Up-turn a bowl in a container, stand the milk bottle and butter on top of the upturned bowl, fill the container with water up to two-thirds of the bowl, cover the bottle and butter with a tea-towel and let the edges of the tea-towel soak in the water. The water evaporating from the wet tea-towel will keep the milk and butter cool.

Milk will keep fresh and good in hot weather (when no fridge is available) if the bottle is wrapped in wet newspaper. Keep the newspaper always wet.

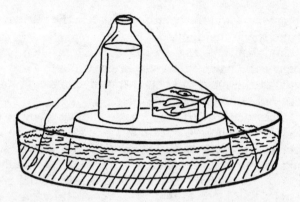

If your milk is beginning to go sour, add a small pinch of bicarbonate of soda to it (one pinch to a pint/half a litre) and bring to the boil. Your milk will be as fresh as new.

To stop boiling milk going over when you catch it rising in the pan, quickly take the pan away from the heat and bang it on the table as you put it down.

A wooden spoon or a clean marble slab standing on the saucepan will prevent milk or custard boiling over; so will a little butter smeared around the edge of the saucepan, or a small saucer upside down at the bottom of the pan.

Never add milk to the tea in a thermos flask as it could curdle if left for any length of time.

MILKSHAKE

Produce a delicious milkshake in a minute by blending or whisking a small carton of flavoured yoghurt with half a glass of cold milk.

MINCED MEAT

Minced meat should be eaten straight after being minced, or as soon as possible. Mince your own meat when needed; it does not take long and is well worth the effort. Do not mince it too finely.

To make mincemeat go further, add some bread soaked in water and lightly squeezed out, some porridge oats or some breadcrumbs.

Minced meat will defrost quickly if sprinkled with a little salt. (But do not add any more salt when cooking.)

Minced meat left wrapped in its greaseproof wrapping paper for a while will stick to it and is a nuisance to unstick. Run the wrapped meat under cold running water for a few seconds.

MINT
Sprinkle a little salt or sugar on the mint that you are chopping; it will make the cutting easier by drawing out the juices.

To keep mint green when dry, first wash it in water to which bicarbonate of soda has been added: two level tablespoons of bicarbonate of soda to half a pint/300 ml of water.

To preserve mint for sauce, pick the mint when dry, choosing the most tender leaves. After chopping it finely, put it in a jar. Do not press the mint down tightly or it will spoil the colour. Fill the jar with cold boiled vinegar, cover with a lid and leave. When you need mint sauce, take out a few spoonfuls and add sugar and vinegar to taste. Using this method, the mint will keep for months.

MIXER
When using a hand electric mixer for mixing something small in a small container, use only one beater.

MIXING BOWL
Prevent the bowl from sliding when mixing mincemeat and ingredients or kneading pastries or bread dough, by placing the bowl on a wet cloth.

MORNING TEA/COFFEE
If you like to have a cup of tea or coffee first thing in the morning but are too lazy to get out of bed, fill up a vacuum flask with hot coffee or tea the night before and keep it on your bedside table for your morning treat.

MUSLIN BAGS
When you have a little spare time, make a few muslin bags of different sizes. You will find them very convenient when you are using herbs in dishes where only the flavour is required.

MUSHROOMS
Mushrooms stored in a brown paper bag in the refrigerator will last for a week. Never keep mushrooms in a plastic bag; the mushrooms cannot 'breathe' and quickly become covered with slime.

If you have bought too many mushrooms and don't know what to do with them here's a suggestion: wash them, dry them and put them through the mincer; add a little stock or water, pour into ice-cube trays and freeze. When frozen, place the cubes in a plastic bag, put them back in the freezer and use them for sauces, stews or soups.

When cleaning mushrooms, do not peel them as the skin has a very good flavour. Trim the sandy part and put the mushrooms in cold water with a few drops of vinegar (this will bring out any little insects hidden in the head). Wipe gently and then rapidly wash again twice. Dry carefully in a tea-towel.

Your mushrooms will not produce a lot of water while cooking if you have previously dried them for a little while in a warm oven.

MUSSELS
When buying mussels, do not choose ones with the shell open.

Do not eat any mussels which are still closed at the end of the cooking process, as they could be bad.

MUSTARD
A crushed clove of garlic added to mustard is very tasty.

To obtain the full flavour of mustard, mix the powder with salad oil, not water.

When mixing mustard add a pinch of salt to it to keep it fresher longer and also prevent hardening.

Avoid the mustard turning dark by mixing it with milk instead of water. It will also keep it fresh much longer.

MUSTARD SEEDS
Grow mustard seeds for sandwiches or salad on a piece of wet blotting paper or paper towel. Sprinkle the wet paper generously with the seeds. Keep the paper thoroughly wet all the time. The sprouting seeds will be ready to eat in a few days. The above method is good for Chinese beansprouts, alfalfa salad, etc.

MUTTON – See also MEAT
In good-quality mutton, the lean should be dark red and fine-grained; the fat should be creamy-coloured and firm.

NUTS – See also Hazelnuts and Walnuts
To keep their freshness and to stop their fat content getting rancid, store nuts in a container and keep it in the refrigerator.

Pecan nuts can be difficult to remove from their shells but if they are soaked overnight in cold water the kernel will come out whole when they are cracked.

Brazil nuts will be easy to crack if you freeze them first. To crack and shell Brazil nuts easily, put them in a warm oven for ten to fifteen minutes.

OCTOPUS
When cooking octopus, throw a few corks into the water; they will make the octopus more tender.

OIL
Some oils are refined for consumption and others are not. The unrefined oils include olive oil, sunflower oil, corn oil, groundnut (peanut) oil, sesame oil and walnut oil. Ideally these have been cool-pressed, and have undergone

very little more in the way of processing. Those oils that are refined have free fatty acids removed as well as particles of seed and juice. They lose some vitamins and minerals in the process, but their tendency to go rancid is reduced. Refined oils are useful for frying, but are a poor substitute for unrefined oils in dishes where the flavour of the oil is important.

Polyunsaturated oils have a high calorie content and provide energy. They also contain fatty acids essential to our diet. They can reduce blood cholesterol levels and so lessen the risk of coronary disease. The best poly-unsaturated oils are cold-pressed (extra-virgin) olive oil, sunflower oil, soya bean oil, safflower oil, groundnut oil and corn oil.

The best olive oil is cold-pressed oil that has not been heated or rectified. Its flavour is excellent; it is very pure, and contains many vitamins and minerals which are removed by heating and rectifying. It is expensive, and thus best kept for dishes where its distinctive flavour is important.

Sunflower and corn oils are very good for salad dressing and mayonnaise. They have no appreciable flavour. Sunflower oil is also a very good cooking oil.

Soya bean oil can only be used cold (e.g. for salads and mayonnaise). It takes on an unpleasant flavour at high temperature, but it is much cheaper than other oils used for both frying and seasoning.

Groundnut oil is the best oil for frying as it will heat to a temperature of 390°F/200°C. Strain often and keep it in a dark container.

Make your own mock olive oil by filling up a quarter of a bottle with plain green olives. Pour over them a light, tasteless vegetable oil to fill the bottle, and then cork it. After two or three days your oil will have a delicious light olive flavour, lighter on the digestion than the real thing.

To preserve cooking oil for longer, add half a teaspoon of sugar to two pints/one litre of oil, and keep it in a dark place.

OMELETTES

Two eggs for each person is the quantity usually required.

Slow cooking and over-cooking make the eggs tough, so never make an omelette with more than eight. A few little omelettes are tastier than one big one.

A dash of soda water in the beaten eggs will make the omelette much lighter.

Increase the volume by adding one tablespoon of milk or water for each egg used.

A few strokes with the fork will be enough to mix the eggs. Too much beating liquefies the eggs, which means that they will not swell when poured into the hot butter and the omelette will become heavy and not so tasty. If the eggs are beaten too far in advance they will take on a brownish colour.

ONIONS

Peel onions under running water. In this way they will not irritate the eyes and will not leave any smell on knife or hands.

Put onions in the freezer for fifteen minutes before peeling. It fixes the volatile oil which would otherwise escape and which is the substance causing tears.

If the root end is held over a flame for a few moments or singed with a hot iron, the onion will not sprout when stored. Or wrap the onions singly in foil.

To peel small onions, immerse them in boiling water for one minute, then in cold water before peeling.

Strong onions can be made less strong by slicing and soaking them in cold water for half an hour or a little longer if necessary. Dry before using.

To get very crisp onion rings for salad, drop the rings in cold water and put in the refrigerator for one hour, drain and dry well.

To remove the smell of onion from a wooden chopping board, rub it with salt or celery leaves.

To get rid of the strong smell when boiling onions, add a few drops of vinegar or lemon juice to the water. Another way is to throw the cooking water away when it starts boiling, replace it with fresh water and finish cooking the onions in the second water.

To keep an onion whole while cooking, peel it and make a cross with a small, sharp knife at the base.

Small onions will fry to a golden colour, without breaking, if before cooking they are sprinkled with flour.

Add a little sugar to the pan when frying onions; they will brown faster.

To fry sliced or chopped onions in butter without burning them, put them in a small frying pan with the butter, cover with water and cook over medium heat until the water evaporates and the onions are a nice golden colour. If the water evaporates too quickly before the onions are tender, add a little more water. This way the onions do not need stirring.

To make onion juice, proceed in the same way you would for an orange – cut the onion in two and squeeze.

To get rid of the smell of onions on your hands rub them with vinegar, mustard or raw potato or some lemon juice. Or rub them with some soil, then wash them.

ORANGE

The juiciest oranges are those with a thin skin. Do not go by the colour for an indicator of ripeness as they are often dyed to improve their colour.

If you put an orange in the oven for a few minutes before peeling, the white fibres will come away easily with the rind.

You will get more juice from an orange if you first press on it with both hands, rolling it over a flat surface at the same time.

ORANGE PEEL

Don't throw orange peel away. Scrape off the pith, then cook the skin in a syrup of sugar and water for twenty minutes. Allow it to cool, cut into small pieces, keep them in a jar and use them to flavour your pastries.

OYSTERS

Use a hand can-opener to open an oyster.

A healthy oyster should be very difficult to open. If the shell opens very easily just by touching it, the oyster is dead and not good for eating.

PANCAKES

When making pancakes, use only the yolk of an egg to begin with. If you add the lightly beaten white at the end, when the batter is ready for use, the pancakes will be much lighter.

Batter should be the consistency of thin cream, the thinner the better for light pancakes.

Half a pint/300 ml of batter will make seven to eight pancakes.

When making pancakes fill up a bottle or a jug with your pancake mixture, then you will just have to pour from the bottle straight to the pan – much easier than a dripping ladle.

To keep your pancakes warm while you are making others, put them one on top of the other on a plate which has been placed over a pan of boiling water, and cover the pancakes with a tea-towel.

To re-heat pancakes, overlap them on a buttered baking sheet, brushing them lightly with melted butter as you do so. Place in a warm oven for about fifteen to thirty minutes, until hot enough to serve. They taste exactly like freshly made pancakes even if they have been made the day before.

Pancakes can be frozen. For quick thawing, interleave them with grease-proof paper before freezing. To re-heat pancakes once thawed, wrap them in foil and place in a moderate oven for about thirty minutes.

PARSLEY

Parsley contains a lot of calcium and Vitamin C. Do use plenty of it – it stimulates the appetite and aids digestion.

Wash and drain the fresh parsley well. Cut off the stem and store in a jar with a tight lid. It will keep well over a week that way.

Fried parsley is good, healthy and decorative. Tie it in a bunch with a long string and dip into the deep-fryer, holding the string.

Scissors are useful for chopping parsley into a cup.

To keep parsley, chop it finely and work it into butter. Store in the freezer – the butter will thaw very quickly when needed.

PASTA

To stop pasta boiling over, put a few drops of oil in the water, or leave a wooden spoon standing in the saucepan during cooking.

To find out if the spaghetti is cooked, bring one strand out of the boiling water and throw it against the wall. If it sticks to the wall it's cooked; if it falls down, it needs to cook a little more.

To cook spaghetti, noodles and other pasta in an economical way, throw the pasta into boiling water and allow to come to the boil again. Turn off the heat and cover the pan with a thin tea-towel and then the lid; leave for fifteen minutes. The pasta will be cooked, will not stick and will never be over-cooked.

Run the cold water tap when draining pasta or vegetables from boiling water to prevent the steam burning your hands or face.

Keep left-over pasta in the refrigerator. When needed throw the pasta in boiling water to reheat for a few minutes, drain, season and eat immediately.

PASTRY

After lining the mould with pastry, run your rolling pin across the top of the pastry mould to get rid of the surplus overhanging the edge.

Cracked flan pastry cases will be sealed and leakproof if the crack is covered with some egg white and the case is then rebaked for a very short time.

Get a crisp well-risen puff pastry by placing a roasting pan half filled with hot water on the bottom of the oven while baking the pastry.

PÂTÉ

Make pâté go a long way when you do not have enough meat (or if the terrine is too big) by adding hard-boiled eggs: after peeling them cut them lengthways, place half the pâté preparation in the terrine, cover tightly with the halves of hard-boiled egg and then cover with the rest of the preparation.

PEACHES

To peel peaches, immerse them in boiling water for a few seconds, then dip into cold water and the skin should come off easily.

PEANUTS

Peanuts have a high protein content and a large amount of minerals and B-complex vitamins which are necessary for growth and tissue building. They have a high calorie content and are very good for children's snacks.

PEARS

Use a teaspoon to scoop out the cores of half pears when cooking in wine or for bottling.

When eating very juicy pears, cut in half and eat with a spoon as you would an avocado.

PEAS

Do not use any water when cooking fresh or frozen peas. Line the bottom of the pan with lettuce leaves, place the peas on top and cover them with more leaves. Cook slowly.

PEPPER

Pepper will stay dry in a wooden container, as the wood absorbs dampness.

PEPPERS (green, red and yellow)

To peel peppers, put them in a hot oven for five to ten minutes, turning from time to time; this will loosen the skin. You can also char the skin over the gas burner of your cooker.

Hot peppers can be dried and stored in the kitchen. Uproot them at the end of the season and hang the whole plant with the peppers on it in the kitchen. They will keep for well over a year.

To skin a large green, yellow or red pepper, place it under a hot grill, turning it frequently, or spear it on a fork and hold it over a gas flame until the skin starts breaking. Then dip it in cold water. The skin will rub off easily.

PIES

Sometimes the fruit filling for a pie is too juicy. Add a heaped tablespoon of tapioca to the filling to absorb the excess juice.

A good substitute for a pie funnel is a thick macaroni. Push the macaroni through the centre of the pie crust to allow the juices and steam to escape while cooking.

If your pie does not brown nicely on top, a little sugar and water mixed together and brushed lightly on the crust will brown quickly when the pie is put back in the oven. It should be watched carefully at this stage.

A little white vinegar brushed over the crust five minutes before the end of cooking gives a lovely sheen to the crust.

PINEAPPLE

A fresh, ripe pineapple should be heavy and have a strong, sweet smell. Its scales should be reddish yellow, plump and shiny. When pulled, the leaves from the tuft should come off easily. A pineapple with brown spots is over-ripe.

Pineapple helps the digestion and is recommended after a rich dinner. It also acts as a laxative.

A pinch of salt sprinkled on fresh pineapple will neutralize the acidity of the fruit.

Fresh pineapple should not be used in jelly, unless it has been boiled for a few minutes first as it will not set properly. You can use canned pineapple.

PIPING BAG

In an emergency a piping bag can be made by cutting off one small piece of a corner of a polythene bag.

PLUCKING

To make plucking a bird a little easier, plunge it into boiling water for a few minutes before you start pulling off the feathers.

POTATOES See also Chips and Mashed potato

Baked potatoes retain virtually all their Vitamin C, whereas more than two-thirds is lost if they are peeled and boiled. You lose less by boiling them in their skins.

Germinating potatoes provoke the birth and development of toxic alka-loids which are harmful to health. Always cut off the germinating part before cooking the potatoes. Also cut out any green patches as they are also harmful.

To stop the potatoes sprouting roots when stored, place some apples with them.

To scrape the skin off new potatoes, first give them a little soaking in hot water. As soon as the water gets cooler scrape them with a nylon pan-scourer.

Add some salt to the water if the scraped potatoes have to stand for a while before cooking, it will prevent discolouration.

If you have peeled too many potatoes, put them in a bowl of cold water with a few drops of vinegar. They will keep in the fridge for up to four days.

For a crisp skin on baked potatoes, rub with a little butter or oil and sprinkle with salt before baking. If you push a skewer through the potato it will conduct the heat to the centre and help it to cook much more quickly.

Before baking potatoes, stand them in hot water for fifteen minutes. The cooking time will be halved and the potatoes will be mealy and more tasty.

Left-over baked potatoes can be reheated for eating by dipping them in boiling water and placing them in a hot oven for twenty to thirty minutes.

To get the crispiest, golden-looking oven-cooked roast potatoes: rub them all over with cooking oil before putting them in the oven.

Old potatoes will taste as good as new if, before cooking, you stand them for two or three hours in cold water. Then plunge them into boiling salted water. When cooked, pour off the water and put the pan of potatoes back on a low heat for five minutes, shaking from time to time.

When boiling peeled old potatoes, add a few drops of vinegar to the water near the end of the cooking time to prevent the flesh becoming dark.

Do not put potatoes in a stew to be frozen; they become soggy and spoil the stew.

POTATO CRISPS
To keep potato crisps crisp, place them in the freezer. To bring back some crispness to your potato crisps, spread them on a baking tray and put the tray in a moderately warm oven for a few minutes.

PORK – See also Meat
In good-quality pork the flesh should be lean and pink with a fine grain; the rind should be thin and smooth, and firm to the touch; the fat should be white and firm.

Remove any hairs left on the skin of pork loin with a disposable razor before cooking it. This method also applies for poultry instead of the sing-eing method over a flame.

To get a good crackling, rub the skin with highly salted olive oil before placing on a rack in the oven.

Cook pork slowly at first. Near the end of the cooking time, finish off quickly at a higher temperature to make the crackling crisp.

To test pork, prick it with a skewer. If a colourless juice runs out, the meat is cooked.

Pork cutlets will be tastier if, before frying or grilling, you soak them in boiling water for two or three minutes.

Apple sauce is eaten with pork because it is slightly laxative. The apple counteracts the effects of this rich meat. Also the acid of the apple prevents biliousness by neutralizing the oily nature of the fat. For those reasons apple sauce is also eaten with goose.

POULTRY – See also under individual names

When you are buying poultry for roasting, the breast-bone should be elastic and crisp, the breast plump, the neck and legs fat. The skin should be white and clear.

Old birds for boiling should have a plump appearance, clear skin and a firm breast-bone.

Before cooking older birds, the sinews (pieces of tough, fibrous tissue uniting the muscles and the bone) should be removed; this will relax the muscles and make the meat tender. To remove the sinews, take a sharp knife and make a slit in the leg above the claw to reveal the sinews. Draw out each sinew from the flesh, using a skewer slipped under the sinew and holding the foot tightly as you pull.

If you have a tough bird, soak it in cold water overnight before boiling and it will be beautifully tender.

To test poultry, prick with a skewer. If a colourless juice runs out, the bird is cooked.

Carving a cooked bird (chicken, duck, turkey) will be made much easier if the wishbone has been removed before cooking.

To remove a wishbone, cut through the skin and flesh at the neck. When the wishbone is exposed scrape it out with a sharp knife.

PRAWNS AND SHRIMPS

To moisten dry prawns or shrimps, soak them in milk before cooking.

PRESERVES

A good way to cover the preserve jar before storing is with white tissue paper which has been brushed with the white of an egg. No tying is then needed. When dry, the tissue paper will become hard and protect the preserve from air contact and mould.

PRUNES

To save fuel, cook prunes in a vacuum flask. First heat the flask with hot water, throw the water away, fill up the flask with prunes, then pour hot water or hot weak tea over them. Add a little lemon or orange juice, close the flask and leave overnight. In the morning the prunes are ready to heat.

PUDDINGS

When baking milk puddings, custards, etc. in the oven, place the dish in a tin of water to prevent the pudding burning.

PUFF PASTRY

To prevent puff pastry getting hard when cooked in the oven, place a tray of cold water on the underneath shelf, under the pastry mould. Do not oil the mould before lining with the puff pastry.

PUMPKIN

To remove the strings from a cooked, mashed pumpkin, run the electric whisker through it. The strings will collect around the beaters.

QUAIL

Your quail will have more flavour if they are wrapped in vine leaves, then in fatty bacon before being cooked.

RABBIT AND HARE

When fresh, these have smooth, sharp claws, bright eyes, and unbroken ears that are smooth, tender and easily torn.

When skinning and then emptying a rabbit or a hare, inspect the liver carefully. If it is covered with dark marks, discard the animal – it is a diseased one.

RADISHES

To keep them fresh and crisp for a few days, stand the leaves in the water with the roots up (the roots must not be in contact with the water). Change the water every day.

To get rid of the sharpness of black radishes sprinkle with salt when you are slicing or shredding them. Leave for at least one hour, drain or squeeze, and season.

It is easy to make pretty radish flowers. Trim off the root end and leaves of the radish and cut lengthwise six or eight times without severing the base. Put the cut radishes into a bowl of cold water in the refrigerator and leave them to stand for an hour or so. The sections will open up and curl like a flower. This can also be done with celery: cut the sticks (3 inches/8 cm long) into fine strips to within 1 inch/2 cm of one end and put in cold water for a while.

RAISINS

To separate raisins stuck together, steam them for a short time over boiling water.

Raisins which are too dry will become soft if they stand in hot water for a few minutes. Dry them well in a tea-towel afterwards.

To stone raisins, pour boiling water over them and leave for a few minutes before draining. Rub each raisin between the thumb and finger to bring out the seeds. Dry the raisins before use.

To chop raisins, freeze them or soak them in cold water for ten minutes before, to stop them sticking to the blades, and put them in the blender. That way you can get coarse or finely chopped raisins. If you have no blender, coat the raisins with a little salad oil, this will stop them sticking to the scissors while being cut.

To stop raisins falling to the bottom of the cake, roll them in flour or sugar before adding to the mixture.

RASPBERRIES
Raspberries have more flavour if served at room temperature.

RAVIOLI
To get ravioli out of their tin without damaging them, first open the tin with a tin-opener, then reverse the tin in a pan, open end down, and perforate the other end with the tin-opener, then lift the tin out.

RECIPES
When cooking with a recipe written on a piece of paper, slide the paper through the prongs of a fork and stand the fork up in a jar. It makes it much easier to read.

REDCURRANTS
Use a fork to strip redcurrants from their stalks.

RHUBARB
Do not eat rhubarb leaves – they are poisonous.

Young and tender rhubarb does not need to be peeled.

Before cooking rhubarb, cut it up and soak it for forty-five minutes in cold water with a teaspoon of bicarbonate of soda. The water will become dark, which means that the acidity has been drawn out. Less sugar will be needed, too.

If you are not sugar-conscious, a few jelly cubes (raspberry, strawberry) added to the stewed rhubarb will make it thicken and improve its colour.

Cooking rhubarb in cold, medium-strong tea will also reduce the acidity.

RICE
One cup of raw rice yields three cups of cooked rice.

Do not wash long grain rice before cooking. This rice is perfectly clean and by washing it will lose some of its nutritional value.

Use it to thicken the soup, by grinding it to a powder in a grinder and adding it to the soup near the end of cooking.

A teaspoon or two of lemon juice in the cooking water helps to keep the rice white and the grains separate. A few drops of oil in the boiling water will also keep the grains separate.

Do not stir rice during cooking; it will damage the grains and make them sticky.

If the rice has to stand for a while, add a small piece of butter to it, stir lightly and cover. The butter will stop the rice drying up.

If you have scorched the rice: turn off the heat, place a slice of bread on top of the rice in the pan, cover with a lid and leave for five minutes or a little longer if you can. The bread will absorb most of the burnt taste.

If the rice is to be eaten cold, cool it quickly by spreading it on a flat dish so that the grains are well separated.

If eaten with vinaigrette (oil and vinegar) season when still a little warm as this will improve the flavour. Cover and place in the refrigerator to prevent the rice getting dry.

To reheat left-over rice without burning it or getting it dry, place it in a plastic cooking bag (used for roasting poultry in), close the bag tightly and place in a pan full of cold water. Heat slowly.

When re-heating rice, do not put the container directly over the heat. Stand it in another pan of lightly boiling water and cover the container with a clean tea-towel instead of a lid, to absorb the steam and prevent the condensation falling back into the rice and making it sticky.

ROLLING DOUGH
It can sometimes be a little tricky transferring a thin pastry dough from the table where it is lying flat to the mould or dish for cooking. Roll the dough around the rolling-pin or a glass bottle and transport it this way.

RUSKS
To butter rusks, French *biscottes* and other crumbly biscuits without breaking them, stack them in a pile, butter the top one and put it at the bottom of the pile. Repeat until all the biscuits are buttered; none will break.

SAFFRON
Saffron threads can give a bitter taste to food if put straight into it. Lightly pound the threads, then pour two to four tablespoons of liquid (boiling water or cooking liquid) over them. Leave to infuse until the liquid becomes a bright orange (but not dark orange or the bitter taste will appear again) and strain before adding to the dish.

SALADS
Fresh lettuces straight from the garden or grower will keep for over a week if wrapped in newspaper and stored in a dark, cool corner before being washed or trimmed.

Lettuce should be washed by dunking it up and down, head first, in a container of cold water. The suction draws out the dirt. To prevent the leaves going brown, they should be separated carefully by pulling them apart and tearing them with the fingers, *not* cutting them with a knife.

Lettuces are very delicate and cannot be drained thoroughly, so invert a saucer at the bottom of the salad bowl before placing the lettuce leaves in.

The excess water will drain off under the saucer and can be poured out before adding the seasoning.

Add salt to a lettuce salad just before serving; if added too long in advance, it will make the leaves drop.

For a very crisp green salad, pour the dressing into the salad bowl and set aside. After washing and draining the salad, put it in a plastic bag in the refrigerator for at least half an hour before it is required and it will be lovely and crisp. Don't wash salad that you want to store in the refrigerator.

For quick crispy salad: put the cut-up salad in a container (a metal bowl is best as it becomes cold very fast) and place it in the freezer for five minutes.

When mixing salad always use a large bowl; it is then much easier to toss the leaves.

To spin salad (lettuce, chicory etc.) in big quantities (e.g. for a party) put the leaves in a clean pillow case, fasten the opening tightly with safety pins or similar, and spin in the washing machine (light spinning).

A good way of tossing salad for a picnic is in a transparent polythene bag. Carry the salad in it and when ready to eat, pour the dressing into the bag, close tightly and shake.

Left over salad makes a very tasty soup. Mix the salad in the blender with some bouillon or tomato juice.

For potato salad with oil and vinegar, the potatoes must be dressed while still hot.

For potato salad with mayonnaise, the potatoes must be dressed when cold.

SALAD DRESSING
Make up a quantity of oil and vinegar dressing in a jar so that it can be stored in the refrigerator for a week to ten days. The dressing has a better flavour this way, and is ready when you need it.

Remember the salt must always go in first when making a dressing. The vinegar goes in second and the oil last because salt does not dissolve in oil.

Use corn oil or olive oil and wine vinegar (this has a more delicate flavour than malt vinegar), a teaspoon of mustard and a pinch of sugar to give the dressing a pleasant bite.

A pinch of curry powder in the dressing will give it a walnut taste.

Use a baby's feeding bottle to make and store your salad dressing. Once you have found the right proportions of oil and vinegar by using the measures on the feeding bottle, you can make the perfect dressing in no time.

The mixer makes the creamiest salad dressing. Pour the oil over the other ingredients (vinegar, salt, pepper, mustard etc.) slowly as for mayonnaise.

If you don't like garlic in your salad, try a grated onion – it gives a delicious flavour. If you do like garlic in your salad but do not like pieces of it, rub the inside of the salad bowl with a cut glove of garlic.

If the dressing has too much vinegar and the salad is already tossed, add a few pieces of bread to it and toss it again so that the bread absorbs the dressing. Remove the bread and add a few drops of oil to the salad.

SALAMI

Salami skin is sometimes hard to peel off. Wrap the salami in a wet cloth for fifteen minutes before peeling it.

SALT

Salt stays dry in wooden and porous stoneware containers as they absorb dampness.

To prevent salt becoming damp, put a piece of blotting paper at the bottom of its container. A few grains of rice mixed with the salt will also stop it becoming damp.

Coarse salt or sea salt ground in a salt mill will give a better flavour to food.

To extract water from vegetables such as cucumber and tomatoes before adding them to a salad, sprinkle them with a little salt after slicing and leave for fifteen minutes. Drain off the liquid before putting the vegetables into the salad.

SALT AND PEPPER – Seasoning

To save time, fill a salt container with a mixture of salt and pepper ready and handy. Mixture: three tablespoons of salt to one of ground pepper.

SALTY FOOD

A raw potato added to a soup or stew that has become too salty will take much of the saltiness away.

SANDWICHES

When making sandwiches containing mustard, mix the mustard and butter together before spreading. The mustard will be evenly distributed and the sandwich-making will be much quicker.

Put mayonnaise between two lettuce leaves in a sandwich so that it will not soak into the bread if the sandwich is left to stand.

SARDINE TINS

If you have a wheel tin-opener, open the tin from the bottom, cutting the whole base out; this is much easier than using a sardine key.

SAUCES

Roux

A roux is made of equal quantities of melted butter and flour. Use a heavy pan, (a thin-based pan very often scorches the sauce) of stainless steel, heavy bottom enamel or aluminium (although aluminium might discolour the white sauce if egg yolk or wine is added). Stainless steel or tin-lined copper is the best for making sauces.

White roux is for béchamel (white sauce) and soups.

Blond roux for cream sauces and velouté soups.

Brown roux for brown sauces.

A roux must be cooked slowly and carefully; if it is cooked quickly the heat will harden the starch in the flour and it will not combine with the liquid later to make the sauce.

Melt the butter in the pan to its point of clarification (when all the white sediment has evaporated) then add the flour with the wooden spoon or a whisk; stirring constantly to avoid scorching, slowly cook the roux to its colour required in the recipe but bear in mind that a roux must cook not less than fifteen minutes to eliminate the raw taste of uncooked flour.

Note: A roux can be prepared in advance and kept in a cool place as it is always used cool when mixed with hot liquid for making the sauce.

To avoid having a lumpy sauce allow the roux to cool off, then add a small quantity of boiling liquid (bouillon, milk, chicken stock, beef stock, etc,) whisking constantly to obtain a soft paste. When the paste is smooth bring the mixture to the heat and slowly to the boil.

To prevent curdling when making sauces always strain the whole beaten raw eggs before adding them to the sauces or custard.

Do not go on cooking a lumpy sauce, take it off the heat and whisk it thoroughly. If it is still lumpy after this, pass it through a very fine sieve or, if you have an electric blender, you can blend the sauce for a few seconds.

When making a sauce with alcohol, never add the alcohol before cooking. The sauce would lose its flavour. The alcohol should be added at the end of cooking.

If a sauce is not used immediately (veloutés, béchamel, brown sauces) it can be kept in a refrigerator for three to four days; rub the surface when the sauce is still warm with a piece of butter speared on a fork, or pour a thin layer of milk or stock on the surface to avoid a skin forming. If egg yolk, butter or cream is used to enrich the sauce, it should be added only when the sauce is reheated for serving.

Béchamel sauce

To obtain a sauce of great savouriness, lean veal (cut into dice, cooked in butter without colouring it, with chopped onion, a sprig of thyme, a fragment of bay leaf, a pinch of nutmeg, salt and pepper) should be added: one small onion for 4 oz/100 g of roux and 2 oz/50 g of lean veal.

Warm the roux and hot milk after the milk has been brought to the boil, to obtain a smooth sauce. Add it to the cooked diced veal, onions and seasoning and simmer for one hour. Then, pass through a fine strainer and coat the surface of the sauce with melted butter or a thin film of milk to prevent the formation of a skin on the surface.

A good way to prevent curdling when making a béchamel sauce, is to stir the sauce with half a peeled raw potato stuck on the end of a fork.

Note: Béchamel sauce can be kept in the fridge for three to four days, and it does freeze well. Veal can be replaced by white-fleshed fish.

Béarnaise sauce

Proceed as for Hollandaise sauce (see p. 175), but after adding the yolks of egg to the reduction (vinegar, shallots, pepper, herbs) the consistency should be heavier than of the Hollandaise and more piquant. Add the rest of the boiling liquid in a steady stream, whisking constantly, and season. The sauce will be quite heavy to start, getting lighter as it cooks.

Too thin sauce: If a sauce is too thin, a little potato flour or arrowroot (for one pint/600 ml liquid, two or three level teaspoons of flour or arrowroot mixed with cold water, stock or white wine) should be added gradually to the boiling sauce, stirring constantly; this should be done no more than five minutes before the end of cooking time.

Another way of thickening the sauce is to add a liaison of '*beurre manié*' (a mixture of butter or cream with uncooked flour in equal quantities). Away from the heat mix well the butter or cream with the flour using a fork to make a smooth paste. Add small bits at a time to the simmering sauce, whisking constantly, until the sauce thickens to the required consistency; this will happen very quickly. Then let it simmer for five minutes to allow the flour to cook. This method adds flavour to the sauce and gives it a perfect consistency.

Another way of thickening the sauce is with an egg yolk and cream liaison but this should be added just before serving to avoid any curdling. Mix the yolk or yolks with equal volume of cream then add some of the hot liquid (used for making the sauce), whisking constantly. Take it off the heat, add the liaison to the sauce, then return the sauce to a moderate heat, whisking non-stop until the sauce thickens. Do not let it boil or it will curdle.

Too thick sauce: Whisk a tablespoon at a time of milk or stock into the simmering sauce until it gets to the right texture.

Butter sauce

The saucepan must be heavy, of the right size, with sloping sides. Too big and the sauce will separate because the whisking wouldn't be fast enough and the eggs will curdle. Too small and the sauce will splash when whisked. Be sure to reach all the corners of the saucepan when whisking.

The butter sauce is very delicate, in both texture and flavour, so not too much heat and not too much seasoning. The liquid base (wine or vinegar) must be well reduced to avoid acidity. The shallots must be well cooked. By the end of the reduction most of the liquid should be evaporated. For a richer sauce the butter is increased, but for one yolk of egg not less than 6 oz/175 g must be used. The butter is clarified (melted, skimmed of any scum from the surface) and allowed to cool to tepid (hot butter added to the egg yolk would make the egg curdle).

If you did not make a success of your sauce, start again. Whisk one yolk of egg with a tablespoon of water to a creamy, fluffy liaison then gradually whisk in the curdled mixture, using very small quantities at a time.

Lemon juice is added to the sauce just before serving; it might cause a fermentation if added when the sauce is waiting in a 'bain-marie' (water bath).

Hollandaise sauce

For a safer result the mixture (vinegar, water, egg yolk) should be whisked in a pan placed in a 'bain marie' (water bath) over a gentle heat. Too much heat and the yolk will coagulate like scrambled egg. The idea is to make a creamy liaison, for the butter to be added when the liaison gets to a light, fresh, creamy consistency or when a stroke of the whisk leaves a clear line at the bottom of the pan. The clarified butter can be added a little at a time, and also a pinch of salt, whisking constantly. Then keep warm but not hot in a water bath of lukewarm water.

If during the making of the sauce the egg yolk becomes too thick, add a few drops of cold water and lower the heat.

If on the contrary the egg yolk makes a froth and does not thicken, the heat is too low.

Too much heat would make the eggs and butter separate; if this happens put a tablespoon of hot water in a warm bowl and whisk in the sauce a small quantity at a time. Or put a tablespoon of lemon juice in a warm bowl, add in a tablespoon of the sauce, whisk until it becomes creamy then add the rest of the sauce gradually.

Curdled sauce: Hollandaise will re-emulsify if poured slowly drop by drop into a warm bowl where a soupspoon full of hot vinegar has been placed. Or a soupspoon full of hot water.

When a Hollandaise sauce curdles, mix an egg yolk with two teaspoons of melted butter. Stir it into the sauce, then add one or two tablespoons of hot water.

Marinades

The purpose of the marinade is to enable the meat or fish to be kept longer than is normally possible, to impregnate the food with the flavour of the condiments, and also to tenderize the flesh by softening the fibres. The length of time during which the food should be kept depends on its size and texture, and on the temperature of the surrounding area. In summer, large pieces of meat will need to marinate twenty-four to forty-eight hours, in winter five to six days, turning the pieces of meat or fish frequently.

Never salt the marinade. The salt would drain the blood out of the meat. Salt the meat after it has been marinated.

An efficient way to marinate meat is to place the meat in a plastic bag, pour in the marinade and fasten the bag tightly after pressing the air out. Put the bag on a plate and refrigerate, turning the bag over from time to time for the marinade to penetrate the meat all over.

Do not use only pure vinegar in a marinade (it would destroy the flavour of the meat); use white or red wine, vinegar and oil. The oil in the marinade, by staying on the surface, prevents air contact with the meat which would cause it to decompose and decay.

Note: The marinade can be preserved quite a long time if brought to the boil every three to four days; each time the marinade is reboiled one glass of wine or a half glass of vinegar should be added to replace the alcohol evaporated during the process.

Mayonnaise

One egg yolk without germ to $\frac{1}{3}$ pint/200 ml of oil. Bowl, eggs and oil should be at room temperature; use a wooden spoon for best results. Beat eggs, adding oil slowly until all added. When mayonnaise is ready, incorporate the beaten white of an egg; this will make it light and more digestible.

If the consistency becomes too thick during the process, add a teaspoon of vinegar or lemon juice.

If the mayonnaise separates, the reason may be too cold oil – adding it too quickly at the beginning, or using too much oil in proportion to the yolks.

If the mayonnaise curdles, place a teaspoon of mustard in a warm bowl then add a tablespoon of the curdled mayonnaise to it. Whisk until a smooth consistency – add the rest of the curdled mayonnaise spoon by spoon, whisking each time to a smooth texture. Or put a fresh yolk in a warm bowl and slowly beat in the curdled mayonnaise. Whisk to a smooth texture.

Mayonnaise can be kept in the refrigerator. If so, one tablespoon of boiling water is to be added at the end of the making to ensure that the emulsion holds. When the mayonnaise has been in the refrigerator for a few days, remove and wait until it is back at room temperature before stirring it. If the mayonnaise has thinned out, use the same method as for curdled mayonnaise to bring it back to normal consistency.

SAUCEPANS

When buying a new saucepan, at the same time buy an enamel dish which fits on top. When you use the saucepan you can place the dish on top of it and steam left-over food to re-heat it without using extra fuel.

SAUSAGE

To peel the skin easily from a dry sausage, wrap the sausage in a wet cloth for at least half an hour first.

For cocktail parties small sausages are more expensive than the big sausages, so make your own by squeezing and twisting the big ones in the middle, making two small sausages out of one (four can also be made out of one).

Prick the skin before cooking to prevent the sausage bursting, or dip it for a few minutes in boiling water before adding it to other ingredients for a slow-cooking dish.

When grilling sausages, put them on a wooden skewer. It will make it easier to turn them over (a steel knitting needle will also do the trick).

SCISSORS

Scissors are useful for snipping dried fruit or peel (for cakes, puddings or mincemeat) instead of chopping them.

Use scissors for cutting fresh herbs, removing stalks and veins from cabbage leaves and cutting off cress roots and radish leaves.

Scissors can also be used to cut meat for stews, to trim fish or to cut a pizza.

SCONES
To make scones lighter use yoghurt instead of milk when making the dough.

SCRAMBLED EGGS
Enhance the flavour of your scrambled eggs. Before cooking, beat the eggs with a fork on which a peeled clove of garlic has been speared.

SELF-RAISING FLOUR
To make your own self-raising flour, take 2 lbs/one kilogram of plain flour, add four level tablespoons of baking powder and mix well.

SERVINGS
Servings, of course, vary with appetite, but on average the following quantities are sufficient for one person. Weights are for uncooked food. (Metric equivalents are approximate only.)

FISH	Headless, cleaned and skinned, with bones	8 oz (225 g)
	Whole, with head, bones skin and tail	1 lb (450 g)
	Fillets	6 oz (175 g)
	Steaks, with bone and skin	7 oz (200 g)
	Smoked, with bones	8 oz (225 g)
	Smoked, filleted	6 oz (175 g)
GAME	Hare	10 oz (275 g)
	Rabbit	10 oz (275 g)
	Venison, with bone	8 oz (225 g)
	*Grouse	1 portion
	*Partridge (young)	1–1½ portions
	*Pheasant	2–3 portions
	*Pigeon	1 portion
	*Quail	½–1 portion
	*Snipe	1 portion
	*Woodcock	1 portion
MEAT	Beef, pork, veal, lamb, with bone	12 oz (350 g)
	Beef, pork, veal, lamb, without bone	8 oz (225 g)
	Minced meat	6 oz (175 g)
POULTRY, PLUCKED AND DRAWN	Chicken, turkey	1 lb (450 g)
	Poussin	1 portion
	Duck	1½ lb (675 g)
	Goose	2 lb (1 kg)
	Guinea fowl	12 oz (350 g)

*One bird

PULSES, RICE, PASTA (UNCOOKED)	Beans	2 oz (60 g)
	Lentils	2 oz (60 g)
	Pasta	3 oz (90 g)
	Peas	2 oz (60 g)
	Rice	2½ oz (75 g)
SHELLFISH	Crab, in shell	12 oz (350 g)
	Lobster, in shell	8 oz (225 g)
	Scallops (depending on dish served)	1 or 2 per portion
	Oysters, fresh, as starter	at least 6 per portion
	Mussels	¾ pint (450 ml)
	Shrimps, peeled	4 oz (100 g)
VEGETABLES	Asparagus	12 oz (350 g)
	Cabbage	6–8 oz (175–225 g)
	Carrots, old	8 oz (225 g)
	Carrots, new	6 oz (175 g)
	Green beans	10 oz (275 g)
	Peas, in pod	8 oz (225 g)
	Potatoes, old	1 lb (450 g)
	Potatoes, new	8 oz (225 g)
	Spinach	1 lb (450 g)

SHALLOTS
To peel shallots easily, plunge them in boiling water for one minute then in cold water, before peeling.

SHELLFISH
Wash the shellfish in very salty water to get all the sand out of them.

Shellfish poached in vinegar and water do not give nettle rash.

Shellfish which is to be eaten cold should always be left to cool off in the court-bouillon in which it was cooked. Drain only when completely cold.

Shellfish (lobster, crab etc.) are difficult to digest, they have long and firm fibres.

SHRIMPS
Your peeled shrimps bought at the supermarket will taste better if you bathe them for twenty minutes in a little vinegar, or better still a little port.

SIFTING
Do not forget that sifting when specified in a recipe is very important. It not only removes lumps in the flour, but brings air to it making it lighter.

SORBET
A quick fruit sorbet, and very delicious too, is made by putting tinned fruit through the blender, syrup included. Put this light purée into the freezer to set.

SORREL

Sorrel is a delicious vegetable to serve with fish (e.g. salmon), not only for its taste but also because its acidity content dissolves the tiny bones in the fish.

SOUFFLÉ

When making the mixture, do not forget to use a large saucepan, so it will be easy to add in the egg yolks and the beaten white of egg. The eggs have to be very fresh or the soufflé will not rise properly, but sometimes with fresh eggs the white, when beaten and starting to stiffen, might separate; if this happens add a level soupspoon of caster sugar for four eggs, or a pinch of salt. Do not add the beaten egg white all at once; using a spatula stir a large spoonful of it into the mixture, using an under and over cutting rotation (or motion) rather than a stirring one, in order not to get rid of the tiny air bubbles in the egg white. Those bubbles will expand with the heat and make your soufflé rise. Then add the remaining egg white as delicately as before. After smoothing the surface of the soufflé with the blade of a knife, push the mixture away from the edge of the dish with your finger; it will help the soufflé to rise.

Small soufflés are easier to make than large ones, so use two dishes instead of one. Fill the dishes no more than three-quarters full. Start the cooking on a hotplate for two minutes and warm the dish first. If the mixture is already warm, a savoury soufflé will cook much more quickly.

A soufflé ready to cook in the soufflé dish can be kept covered in the refrigerator up to four hours before baking.

To make a soufflé rise quicker, place a flat baking tray in the oven on the middle rack before pre-heating the oven. When the right temperature is reached, place the soufflé dish on top of the baking tray.

When it is in the oven, from time to time give a half swirl to the soufflé dish, quickly so as not to keep the oven open for too long.

A soufflé is ready when it has increased by half, or sometimes two-thirds, in volume, above the rim of the dish. (A thick soufflé made of vegetable purée will never rise as much as a light one, e.g. cheese soufflé.) When the top surface is brown, when shaken it should not quake all over. If it still wobbles in the middle it is cooked for those who like a soft soufflé; for a firm one leave it in the oven for another two or three minutes. A soufflé should be served straight away from the oven – no waiting; it should be served with two spoons to break the crust and reach the centre to get some of the soft part.

Cheese soufflé

The best cheese to use is Parmesan or gruyère. After greasing the bottom and side of your soufflé dish with butter, sprinkle some grated cheese (one tablespoon) evenly on the bottom and side of the dish. Do not make a 'roux' (butter and flour mixture) but boil the milk then cool it off slightly. When cool, add small quantities at a time to the flour in a pan until you get a smooth mixture without curds; season (salt, pepper, nutmeg) and heat until the sauce comes to the boil, stirring constantly. When slightly bubbling remove from the heat and add cheese, butter and yolks (the yolks previously diluted with a tablespoon of cold milk).

Ham soufflé
Pound the ham in a mortar then pass it through a fine sieve before using it for the mixture.

Fish soufflé/Shellfish soufflé/Chicken soufflé: As for **Ham soufflé.**

Fruit soufflé
The best fruits for this kind of soufflé are: apricots, pineapple, strawberries, melon and redcurrants (raw and well ripened). For the fruit soufflé, cook the sugar syrup to the soft crack, 138°C/280°F. To recognize this, stop the cooking then drop a little syrup into iced water. Next remove it and stretch it gently between your fingers. If the syrup separates into strands which are hard but elastic, then it has reached the soft-crack stage. When the sugar is ready, add the fruit purée. It might get the sugar back below the hard ball stage, so it must be recooked to the soft crack again. It is important to use some lumps of sugar which have been rubbed against the skin of an orange or a lemon to bring out the flavour of the fruits used.

You could add to the soufflé two coffeespoons of your favourite alcohol (rum, Kirsch, etc.); this should be added to the whites of eggs.

SOUR CREAM
Mix half a small carton of natural yoghurt with the same quantity of single or double fresh cream, then add four drops of lemon juice and mix again.

SOUP – See Stocks

SMOKED SALMON
Smoked salmon should be pale orange and translucent. An opaque pink salmon has been frozen too long.

SPAGHETTI SAUCE
The spaghetti sauce will not splash on your stove when you are cooking or reheating it if you smear some oil or butter around the inside edge of the pan, down to the sauce line, before cooking.

SPINACH
Spinach shrinks when cooking. To obtain 1 lb/about 500 g of cooked spinach, you will need about 3 lb/about 1½ kg of raw spinach.

To retain its goodness, cook spinach without water over a low heat. Use a heavy saucepan. Avoid aluminium or iron, which give a metallic taste to the spinach.

STEAK PIE

When making a beefsteak pie, ask your butcher for a piece of marrowbone the depth of your pie dish, and use the bone in place of a funnel. It gives a fine flavour to the pie and the marrow helps to make a good gravy.

STEAMING

To warn you when the level of the water is getting too low in the pan beneath a steamer, place one or two small marbles or stones inside the pan before you start cooking. They will start to rattle if the water has evaporated too much.

STEW

To rescue a stew which is burning, dip the pan quickly into cold water. The effect of the cold water will make the stew leave the bottom of the pan. Turn into another pan and continue cooking, adding more liquid if necessary.

STILTON CHEESE

To keep a whole uncut Stilton cheese in good condition, turn it upside down every five or six days. This will keep the moisture well distributed. It should then be kept in your cellar or larder.

STOCK

A tall, deep pot is the best to use for making stock, as it doesn't evaporate too quickly. All the flavour should be extracted from the bones so break them small; all the flavour should be extracted from the vegetables so cut them in small pieces. Do not salt the liquid when making the stock, it would become too concentrated when it has been reduced. Only salt when the stock is used for different purposes. Skim carefully and often, to keep the stock clear. Let it simmer, never boil. At the end of the cooking, strain the liquid through muslin or a clean nylon stocking. Let it cool uncovered or it might turn sour, then place it in the refrigerator until the fat on the surface is solid. Then discard the fat. You may keep the stock in the refrigerator for a few weeks, if you bring it to the boil for ten to fifteen minutes every four or five days to keep it fresh. Stock can also be kept in the freezer. First reduce the strained de-fatted stock until very concentrated, then let it cool, pour it in ice cube trays and freeze it. When frozen, the stock cubes, taken out of the trays, can be put in plastic bags which are easier to store in the freezer. When needed, melt the cube or cubes in the pan over the heat, with some water.

Brown stock

To give colour to the stock, roast the bones without fat, place them on a roasting tin in a very hot oven and turn them often until they are evenly roasted, and of a lovely brown colour. Then they are ready for making stock.

White stock

Do not roast the bones in the oven, or boil the stock during cooking, but simmer and skim often, to get the transparent consistency of the white stock.

Fish stock

The best fish stock is made with bones and trimmings of sole, but any white flesh fish such as whiting, brill and turbot will do well (avoid oily fish). Never boil a fish stock; simmer for no more than thirty minutes or it will turn bitter. If you use wine (which is optional) use good dry white wine, a low quality will give the stock an unattractive greyish colour.

Consommé

To clarify: the clarity is obtained by the albumin in the blood of the meat and the white of egg. It acts as a magnet to the cloudy particles in the stock, and rises to the surface, leaving the liquid perfectly clear underneath. For the best result all meat added to the stock should be free of fat, chopped and minced, the vegetables finely cut. Meat, vegetables and egg white should be well mixed before adding the warm but not hot stock (too hot stock would coagulate the white too quickly, and not give time to attract all the particles clouding the stock). Return all the mixture to a moderate heat, stirring continuously, until it comes to boiling point then allow to simmer gently for the time indicated in the recipe. When cooking time is over, scald a clean cloth, wring it out and pass the consommé through. If the consommé is not transparently clear, pass through the cloth again.

Cold consommé

A cold consommé should be lightly jellied, with a mellow texture. To obtain this texture, the consommé needs to have been cooked with a lot of meat to extract the juices, which makes it quite an expensive dish. To compensate for the lack of juices, when not using much meat add a small quantity of tapioca (or arrowroot or gelatine, but tapioca is more tasty). Cold food always needs extra flavouring so more salt and pepper should be added. Do not forget to chill the cups in which the consommé will be served (one to two hours in the bottom of the fridge).

Velouté soup

Make a white roux (p. 172) and wait for it to cool, to avoid lumps when the boiling liquid (specified in the recipe) is added to it small quantities at a time, whisking constantly. Cook slowly for thirty-five minutes. A skin will form on the surface of the velouté, skim it from time to time. This will get rid of any impurities in the flour. After the thirty-five minutes, sieve the velouté before adding the purée (again, as specified in the recipe). At the last moment the liaison (yolk and cream previously diluted with a small quantity of velouté) should be added to the pre-heated but not boiled velouté. This should be done away from the heat, whisking constantly. Then the final touch is made by adding the butter in small pieces.

Note: After sieving the velouté, if it is not to be used immediately spread a little butter over the surface to avoid the formation of skin.

Cream soups
The preparation is very similar to that for the velouté except the liquid added to the soup (which should be even lighter in colour than the one for velouté) is always milk, sometimes mixed with bouillon, making a very thin béchamel sauce. After adding with purée when the final consistency is achieved, reheat for only a few seconds and place in a bain-marie, rub the surface of the preparation with a small piece of butter to prevent a skin forming. The finishing touch of adding the fresh cream should be done at the last moment, when ready to serve. If the cream soup is a little too thick, add some boiling milk. Butter or yolk of egg should not be added to cream soup.

Purée soup
Usual preparations: $3\frac{1}{2}$ pints/2 litres liquid to $1\frac{3}{4}$ pints/1 litre purée. A good purée is velouté of smooth texture. Sometimes in pea, lentil, fresh pea and bean purée soups, the purée separates from the cooking liquid and deposits at the bottom of the plate can occur: to avoid this, a liaison of 'beurre-manié' (a paste of butter and flour in equal proportions) should be added in small quantities at a time to the purée soup. Also, a few bread croûtons fried in butter are a very good addition. For extra interest, try herb croûtons: simply mix chopped parsley or other green herbs into the butter before frying the croûtons.

Note: After a soup has been buttered and creamed, it must not be reboiled or it will lose its fresh flavour.

When making tomato soup with cream or milk, prevent curdling by adding the tomato soup to the cream or milk instead of the other way round.

A few lettuce leaves placed in the soup will absorb most of the fat (discard the leaves before using the soup).

To make an instant, delicate, delicious soup follow this recipe: in a soup tureen or a large bowl, grate one carrot, and two spring onions finely cut, half a cucumber thinly sliced, a few lettuce or chinese cabbage leaves finely chopped and some chopped parsley, and pour over this 3 pints/$1\frac{1}{3}$ litres of boiling stock made with concentrated stock cubes. Serve immediately.

STORING FOOD
IN THE CUPBOARD
These foods should be stored in airtight containers in a cool, dry place. The storage times given overleaf are the minimum: some food may last longer and might still be edible after a few years. The times refer to unopened packages.

FOOD		STORAGE TIME
Cereals	Oatmeal (its high fat content can cause it to become rancid, do not store for too long.)	Up to 2 months
	Breakfast cereals	Buy in small amounts
Coffee	Vacuum-packed	1 year
	Ground, gas-packed	3 months
	Beans, gas-packed	6 months
	Instant	3–5 months
Cornflour		Up to 1 year
Custard Powder		Up to 3 months
Dried Fruits	Need dry, cool storage. They can shrink if kept too warm, or ferment if too damp.	6 months to 1 year
Dried Herbs, Spices, Seasonings		6 months
Flavourings		Indefinitely
Flour	Flour and semolina keep well in suitable conditions, but can be affected by insects, so be watchful and throw away any that becomes contaminated. Check in case the damage has spread.	
	Self-raising	Up to 2 years
	Plain white	Up to 2 years
	Wholemeal (Its high fat contents can turn it rancid. Do not store too long.)	Up to 3 months
Fruit	In glass	4–6 months

Fruit Drink	In glass	1 year
	In plastic	4–6 months
Mayonnaise (*BOUGHT*)		6–8 months
Mint Sauce		1 year
Nuts	Their fat content can cause them to become rancid.	
	Almonds	
	Coconut (shredded)	Buy in small
	Peanuts	amounts
	Walnuts	
Oil	Olive or other cooking oil, in glass or plastic	1 year
Pasta		2–3 years
Pickles		2 years
Pulses	Beans	
	Dried peas	1–2 years
	Lentils	
Rice	Ground rice	
	Semolina	1–2 years
	Tapioca	
Salad Cream		6–8 months
Sauces	Bottled, unopened	2 years
Sugar	Brown	
	Caster	
	Granulated	Up to 3 years
	Icing	
	Demerara goes lumpy if kept for too long.	Buy small amounts
Syrups	Golden syrup	1–2 years
	Treacle	
Tea	Tea bags	6 months
	Packet tea	4–6 months

Tinned Food

Tinned food should be stored in a cool, dry place. When kept too long, tinned food first loses most of its colour, and then its flavour and smell. If the top of a tin is no longer flat, but raised, the tin should be discarded as it means that the food is fermenting inside (unless it is a fizzy drink, beer or ground coffee), Leaky tins are usually caused by rust and should not be used as the food inside has probably been contaminated. Food should never be stored in an opened tin: transfer it to another container.

Fish (sardines, mackerel, pilchards, herrings, etc.) in brine	3 years
Fish, in tomato sauce	1 year
Fruits (soft, stoned)	1 year
Fruit juice	6–9 months
Meat	2–3 years
Milk (dried) will keep well although it might lose some of its flavour after 3 months.	3 years
Milk (sweetened, condensed)	6–10 months
Pasta, in tomato sauce	8–12 months
Soup	1–2 years
Tomato purée	1 year
Vegetables (baked beans, broad beans, carrots, etc.)	Up to 2 years

Vegetables	In glass	4–6 months
Vinegar		3 years

IN THE REFRIGERATOR:

Cheese	In original pack or foil	1–3 weeks
	Cream cheese in covered container or foil	1 week
Eggs	Hard-boiled, in shell	5–6 days
	Yolks, covered with water	2 days
	Whites, separated, in covered container	2 days

Fish	Raw, loosely covered in foil	1–2 days
	Cooked, loosely covered in foil or in a covered container	1–2 days
Fruits	Stone and hard fruits, lightly wrapped	4–8 days
	Soft fruits, cleaned, in covered container or in the crisper	2–3 days
Meat, Raw	Rinse under clear water, wipe dry, wrap loosely in foil and refrigerate straight away	
Chops		3–4 days
Roasts		3–5 days
Steaks		3–4 days
Stewing		2–3 days
Offal		1 day
Bacon		8–10 days
Smoked Ham		1 week
Meat, Cooked	Joint, in a covered container or wrapped in foil	4–5 days
	Casseroles	2–3 days
Milk	Fresh, in bottle or covered container	4 days
	Cultured, in original container	8–10 days
	Custard, milk sweets, in dishes	2 days
Poultry, Raw	Washed, dried, wrapped in aluminium foil	2–3 days
Poultry, Cooked	Refrigerated as soon as cool (stuffing removed), wrapped in foil	3–4 days
	Dishes, cooled and refrigerated in covered container	1–2 days
Vegetables	Greens, loosely wrapped or in crisper	4–5 days
	Salad, loosely wrapped or in crisper	4–7 days

Strawberries

Wash strawberries *before* hulling them, or they will absorb the water.

Store the strawberries in a colander or a basket in the refrigerator for longer conservation.

Frozen strawberries will keep their fresh strawberry look if you keep them lightly coated in sugar while thawing in your refrigerator.

To bring out their flavour, pour a glassful of orange juice (fresh or from a carton) over your fresh strawberries and toss them lightly before serving.

A little wine vinegar sprinkled over the fresh strawberries will also bring out their flavour. Toss and serve.

Another way to bring out the flavour is to marinate the strawberries in a glass or two of red wine for an hour before serving.

Stuffing

Cool off the stuffing before filling poultry. Warm stuffing could help the growth of micro-organisms in the bird. Stuffed birds should be kept in the fridge until cooking time.

Sugar

If you do not have icing sugar you can make some by crushing granulated or caster sugar in an electric blender.

Sweets

To stop sweets sticking together, sprinkle them with powdered sugar.

Sweet Potatoes

Sweet potatoes will peel in no time if, when taken from the boiling water, they are dipped in cold water straight away.

Syrup

To make a successful syrup (sugar and water), the sugar must be perfectly melted before it starts boiling. The syrup appears on the surface and a wooden spoon dipped in the syrup comes out covered with a glossy film. The syrup will be better if still mineral water is used instead of the hard, chlorinated tap-water.

Syrup And Treacle

To weigh golden syrup or treacle, flour the scales well and then pour in the syrup. You will find it will leave the scales easily. The same applies if you are measuring with spoons.

GLASS

1.
2.
3.

1. WINE DECANTER   2. SPIRIT DECANTER   3. WATER JUG

4.   **5.**   **6.**   **7.**   **8.**   **9.**   **10.**   **11.**

4. WHITE WINE   7. RED WINE   10. SHERRY
5. BRANDY   8. WATER   11. LIQUEUR
6. CHAMPAGNE   9. PORT

TABLE SETTING

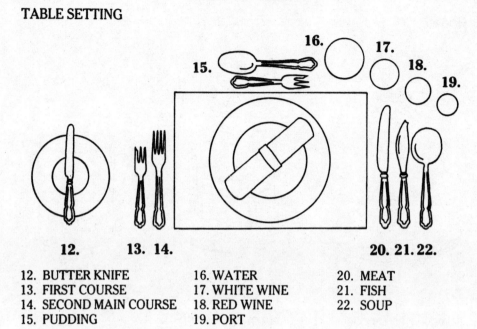

12. BUTTER KNIFE
13. FIRST COURSE
14. SECOND MAIN COURSE
15. PUDDING

16. WATER
17. WHITE WINE
18. RED WINE
19. PORT

20. MEAT
21. FISH
22. SOUP

When dressing a table, the blades of the knives go inward. The heads of the fork point upwards, so do the spoons.

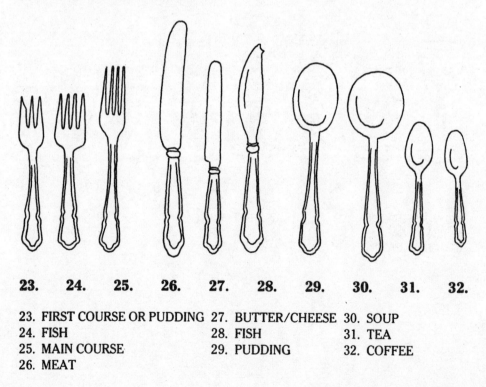

23. FIRST COURSE OR PUDDING
24. FISH
25. MAIN COURSE
26. MEAT

27. BUTTER/CHEESE
28. FISH
29. PUDDING

30. SOUP
31. TEA
32. COFFEE

TARTS

To avoid soggy pastry in fruit tarts, sprinkle the bottom and sides of the pastry case with a mixture of flour and sugar, some semolina or ground almonds before putting in the fruit. This only applies to tarts which are to be cooked.

Another way is to brush the pastry with a light coating of white of egg. Leave to dry before filling.

When cooking the pastry for a tart cover the bottom of the tart with dried beans or macaroni to prevent it swelling. Place a container with water in the oven to moisturize the atmosphere and make the dough softer. Place the tin with the dough on a tray during cooking.

To prevent the tart sticking to the bottom of the mould or tin when baking, dip the bottom of the mould in a little cold water as soon as you take it out of the oven.

TEA

To verify the quality of your tea, place one small teaspoonful of tea in a glass. Fill up one third of the glass with cold water. Stir once or twice. If the tea is pure the water is hardly coloured. If the tea is mixed with some other vegetable leaves, the water gets rapidly tainted.

TIN

To get solid food out of a tin without damaging the food (e.g. pâté, corned beef, fish etc.,) open both ends of the tin with an electric tin-opener, remove one end and gently push out the food with the other.

A good way to slice a tinned pâté, fish etc., without breaking it is to push it out of the tin a little at a time (using the above method) and cut along the rim of the tin with a sharp knife. Push and cut until the bottom of the tin has been pushed through to the top.

TOAST

When toasting small slices of bread in a toaster, to stop them from falling to the bottom push a skewer or toothpick through the top of the slices and lay them across the toaster. When ready, just lift up the skewer or toothpick to remove the slices.

TOMATOES

Ripen green tomatoes by placing them, stem up, out of direct sunlight. Sunlight softens instead of ripening them. They will also ripen if wrapped in newspaper or brown paper.

Green tomatoes will ripen best in a dark warm place with a red tomato for company and encouragement.

To make a too soft tomato more firm, place it in a container of salted water (one heaped tablespoonful of salt for three teacupfuls of water) and place the container in the refrigerator for at least an hour.

To get firm slices, stand the tomato on its base and cut vertically.

To skin raw tomatoes easily, cover them with boiling water for a few minutes, then run the cold water tap over them. The skin will come off practically by itself.

Or prick the tomato with a fork and hold it over the gas flame for a few minutes until the skin starts splitting.

Tomatoes are acid. A pinch of sugar in your tomato sauce will improve the taste.

Left-over tomato paste will keep perfectly in the refrigerator if you coat it with a thin layer of oil or freeze it.

TREACLE – See also **Syrup**
To pour treacle more easily when measuring, first warm the jar for a few minutes in a warm oven or place the jar in hot water for a little while.

TURKEY – See also **Poultry**
When cooking a turkey start breast side down for the juices to drain down to the white meat, keeping it moist. Forty-five minutes before the end of cooking time turn it over, breast up.

The turkey will be juicier if an equal mixture of stock and oil is injected with a syringe to a few different parts of the raw turkey (breasts and thighs).

After cooking a turkey, take it out of the oven at least forty-five minutes before carving. Keep it in a warm place, covered with a warm cloth. This will allow the fibres to settle and the turkey will be more tender.

To get the stuffing out of a cooked turkey easily, make a cheesecloth bag big enough to fit inside the turkey. Before cooking, place the bag inside the bird, leaving the open end of the bag hanging out. Fill the bag loosely with stuffing and close the cavity with some small skewers. When the turkey is cooked remove the skewers and pull out the bag.

VANILLA CREAM
When making a vanilla cream, add a pinch of salt to it; it will increase its flavour.

VANILLA SUGAR
To make your own vanilla sugar, place a vanilla pod in a jar of caster sugar. After a few days the sugar will be impregnated with the vanilla aroma. Keep topping up the sugar in the jar when the stock gets low.

VEAL – See also **Meat**
This is looser in texture than any other meat. The best veal should have pale pink flesh which is dry to the touch, and white fat which is firm and fairly transparent.

To test veal, prick it with a skewer. If a colourless juice runs out, the meat is cooked.

VEGETABLES

Most of the nutritive value of vegetables is in the outer leaves or just under the skin, so the mineral salts can easily be lost if the vegetables are carelessly prepared. Where possible, cook vegetables in their skins; if you must peel them, do so thinly.

Your vegetables will last longer in the refrigerator if you line the bottom compartment with an absorbent paper towel to absorb any excess moisture. If you haven't a vegetable compartment in your fridge wrap your vegetables in paper bags rather than plastic.

To absorb the moisture in the vegetable drawer of the refrigerator, place a dry sponge inside it.

Vegetables which have become frozen in the garden in winter will regain some of their freshness if soaked in cold, salted water for approximately two hours. Cook immediately.

Bring the insects out of cabbage, Brussels sprouts, cauliflowers etc., by soaking the vegetables for a little while in cold water to which a little vinegar has been added.

When washing fresh vegetables, do not leave them too long in the water as this dilutes the mineral salts. For the same reason, never cut them into small pieces.

Frozen vegetables will taste better if, before cooking, you pour boiling water over them to get rid of the taste of frozen water.

Tired vegetables will get a lift if soaked for an hour in cold water to which a little vinegar has been added.

To tenderize fibrous vegetables (e.g. celery), cut them in diagonal slices before cooking; that way a larger area of the slice will be exposed to the heat, much more than if cut straight across.

When boiling vegetables a lid should be put on the saucepan for all vegetables grown underground. The lid should be off the saucepan for all vegetables grown above the ground.

To cook several vegetables separately in one pan of water, pack each one (carrots, string beans, cabbage, etc.) in foil. Take account of the different cooking times: put the ones which need most cooking in first, and then those that cook more quickly, so that they are ready together. Each vegetable will retain its flavour, and you will save fuel.

Never throw away the water in which your vegetables have been cooked. Use it for making gravy, soups etc.

Green vegetables cooked in copper utensils keep their colour better, as copper has properties which preserve the chlorophyll.

Do not store carrots and apples together, the carrots would gain a bitter taste.

VINEGAR

Do not keep vinegar in a stone jar; its acidity will affect the glazing, and the vinegar will taste bad.

To strengthen vinegar, freeze it repeatedly and remove the ice from the surface.

Herb vinegar can easily be made at home by putting fresh sprigs of your favourite herbs in a bottle of vinegar.

VODKA

Vodka should be drunk very cold. The best place to keep it is in the freezer, and the best way to serve it is to have the bottle wrapped in a block of ice. This effect is easy to achieve: before putting the bottle of vodka in the freezer, place it in a cylindrical container long enough and large enough for the bottle with at least $1\frac{1}{2}$ inches/3 cm of space all around. Fill the container with water three-quarters of the way up the bottle, and place in the freezer. When you need it, run warm water over the container – the bottle, in its block of ice, will slide out easily. A pretty touch can be added if half-way through freezing, when the water around the bottle is still at the icicle stage, you slide some flowers or leaves into it.

To flavour vodka with lemon, place the skin of half a lemon in the bottle of vodka and leave to macerate for twenty-four hours. Strain before use.

To flavour vodka with red pepper, place one red pepper in the bottle of vodka and leave to macerate for one hour only before straining.

WALNUTS

When walnuts are hard to break, pop them in a hot oven for five minutes or in a saucepan on a fairly high heat for five minutes.

Old dried walnuts will regain some of their freshness and peel off very easily if left to soak in lightly salted water for two or three days.

WATERCRESS

Watercress should be thoroughly washed before being eaten as it often grows in water where it can be contaminated by animals.

Watercress leaves will not yellow and will last much longer if kept in the refrigerator wrapped in damp newspaper.

WATERMELON

To have fresh melons all year round, buy them when they are sweet and juicy and coat them thoroughly with plaster of Paris or, better still, plaster of Paris bandages (obtainable from chemists). Store in a cool, dark place. When you want to use one, break the plaster cast and you will find the melon as fresh as if newly bought. Try this method with other varieties of melon, too.

WEDDING CAKE

Give the fruit wedding cake a lavish taste by piercing a few small holes on the top of the cake and pouring over some rum or brandy. Leave it to soak in for a while.

WHIPPED CREAM

If your whipped cream does not stiffen enough, add an unbeaten egg white to the cream, then put it in a cool place for a short time or in the refrigerator for five minutes, after which it can be whisked again.

Two or three drops of lemon juice added to whipped cream will make the cream whip quicker.

To increase the quantity of whipped cream when the cream is needed for making a dish or a sauce but you are on a 'semi-diet' or don't want the dish to be too rich, whip a little cream to a thick custard consistency, then add a teaspoonful of cold water and go on whipping. Keep addding a teaspoonful of cold water between whipping until the cream can absorb no more water.

WHITE SAUCE

For a smoother white sauce, heat the milk before making the sauce.

WINE

Never store bottled wine upright, as the cork will become dry and the wine might become tainted. Bottles should be stored on their side.

Some cooking wine left in a bottle will keep for a long time if a few drops of olive oil are added to it.

Left-over red or white wine will keep well in the bottle if, before putting the cork back on, you push a match into the base of the cork, light the match and quickly cork the bottle with the match inside the neck. The flame will use up some of the air inside the bottle and preserve the wine.

If white wine is needed for making a sauce or any other dish and you don't have the real thing, use one tablespoon of white wine vinegar mixed with two tablespoons of water and half a tablespoon of sugar.

YEAST

Fresh yeast will keep for a few days if immediately covered with cold water.

If frozen, yeast will stay effective and in good condition for at least three months. Before freezing, cut it in small pieces of 1 oz/about 30 g, which is the usual amount required for bread making. Wrap in foil and place in a labelled and dated plastic bag. Thawing can be hastened by placing the yeast in cold water.

YOGHURT

Yoghurt does not freeze well as it separates when frozen, although this can sometimes be corrected by whisking. Sweetened fruit yoghurt does freeze quite well.

People with delicate digestions find yoghurt easier to digest than milk.

When yoghurt is added to a dish, beat it well first, then add a little at a time.

To prevent yoghurt getting lumpy when added to a sauce, mix cornflour into it first.

Mix one teaspoon of cornflour with two teaspoons of cold water, add this to the yoghurt and heat the mixture slowly, stirring constantly, for a good five minutes. The yoghurt is now ready to be used in your recipe.

A simple recipe to make yoghurt
1 Bring the milk to the boil.
2 Then leave the hot milk to cool off.
3 Add one level tablespoon per pint/approx ½litre of commercial yoghurt. Mix well.
4 Put in a closed container and place the container in a warm place.
5 It will set after a few hours (depending how warm the place is) to a smooth firmness. Keep looking as it must not be left in the warm after reaching this state as the yoghurt will start to separate.
6 When the yoghurt looks nice and firm place it in the refrigerator to cool off, then it will be ready to eat.

Microwave

APPLES
A delicious way to bake apples is to add beer or cider instead of water to the dish when cooking them.

BISCUITS
Small biscuits get dry and hard in a microwave and they cook unevenly.

BRANDY
Heat the brandy for your Christmas pudding or other flaming desserts in your microwave for a few seconds, then pour over the dessert and ignite.

BREAD
Bread with yeast in it does not bake successfully. It is tough and does not rise.

BUTTER AND OTHER FATS
Soften or melt your butter in the microwave for spreading or working. Melt fat the same way for making cakes, sauces or brushing pastries.

CAKES
Angel, meringue or sponge cakes are not a success in the microwave – the eggs do not leaven well.
Other cakes do well in a microwave, they rise high and are fluffier than those baked in a conventional oven.

CHEESE
Soften your cold cream cheese taken out of the fridge, by placing it in the microwave oven on low for a very short time.

CHICKEN

When defrosting poultry or pieces of poultry wrapped on a foam tray, remove the tray as soon as possible. The foam tray slows down the defrosting process.

CHOCOLATE

Melt the chocolate in the microwave without added liquid, just put the chocolate in a container and place it in the oven.

COOKING CONTAINERS

The rounder the dish the more evenly cooked the food will be. Sharp corners can cause the food to dry out by allowing more exposure to the microwaves in those areas before the centre is cooked.

Ring moulds are excellent for cooking or heating the food (not the metal ones) and one does not have to stir the food that way during cooking or heating. Make your own ring mould by placing a glass tumbler in the centre of a round dish.

TEST FOR COOKING CONTAINERS

Place a glass half full with cold water beside the dish you want to test. Switch on the microwave oven at full power for one minutes. At the end of this check:
– If the water in the glass is warm and the dish cool, the container is suitable.
– If the dish is warm, it will take longer for the food to cook in it.
– If the dish is hot and the water cool, the container is not suitable as it absorbs all the microwave energy.

EGGS

Do not cook an egg in its shell, it might blow up and cause damage to the microwave. To prevent the yolk from breaking when cooking a fried or poached egg, pierce the yolk a few times with a needle or a toothpick before cooking.

HERBS

Cooking herbs will dry quickly and perfectly in the microwave between two sheets of kitchen paper.

JACKET POTATO

To keep the jacket potatoes hot after being cooked in the microwave and while you are cooking something else, wrap them in foil after cooking. They will keep the heat for 30 minutes.

JELLY

Melt your jelly in no time in the microwave without any added liquid.

MEAT, TO DEFROST

Always defrost meat on a microwave rack to keep the meat from standing in its own juice and stew in the juice while defrosting. Cover the meat loosely with waxed paper while it defrosts to keep it from drying out. Cover all edges of chops, steaks or roasts with strips of foil (secure the strips with a wooden toothpick) to stop them from starting to cook while defrosting. (Foil slows down cooking by reflecting the microwaves from these areas. The foil must never touch the interior of the oven)

A meat is completely defrosted when a metal skewer (with a little pressure) slides into the meat easily.

MEAT, TO COOK

When cooking meat in a browning dish use only vegetable oil. Butter or margarine would burn.

Meat on the bone will cook quicker than boned meat because bones conduct heat. But boned meat will cook more evenly.

Meat marbled with fat will cook more evenly than meat with lean areas and fat areas, because fat heats quicker than lean meat.

ORANGES, LEMONS

To get more juice, place them for a short while in the microwave oven before squeezing.

SALT

Do not sprinkle salt directly onto vegetables or meat when cooking in the microwave. Salt absorbs moisture, and as a result toughens the food.

SOUPS

When reheating soup you will see the soup bubbling around the edges long before the centre is hot. Stir the soup once or twice during reheating.

STEWED DRIED FRUITS

Add the sugar during the last few minutes of the cooking time, when making stewed dried fruits; adding the sugar earlier would stop the fruits from becoming tender.

STAMP

To unstick a stamp from its envelope, place it in the microwave for a minute or two.

STRONG SMELLS

Strong smells in the microwave can be removed by boiling, for one or two minutes, some water and lemon juice half-and-half in a teacup in the oven.

INTERIOR DECORATIONS

BATHROOM

For extra storage space in the family bathroom, hang a fabric or plastic utensil holder (from department stores) on the wall or on the back of the bathroom door.

BEDHEAD

An inexpensive, attractive bedhead can easily be made by hanging one long or two small rectangles of fabric (matching the bedspread) from a pole. Place a fairly thin layer of foam between the lining and the fabric when making the bedhead. *See illustration overleaf.*

CARPET

When choosing a carpet ask to see it flat on the floor. The colour might look quite different when the carpet is displayed rolled vertically.

A patterned or dark-coloured carpet will make a room look smaller.

CEILING

To whiten a ceiling which is not soiled enough to need repainting, wash it with a solution of one ounce/about 30 g of alum (obtainable from a chemist) to two pints/one litre of water.

To make a high ceiling look lower, bring the paint down to the height of the picture moulding, or paint it dark.

To make a ceiling look higher, paint it in a lighter shade than the walls – or the same colour.

COLLAGES

When covering a screen or other things with collages, do not cut the edges of the picture to be glued on with scissors, tear them; the final effect will be much smoother where the pictures overlap.

COLOUR CHOICE

When choosing a single colour to decorate the walls of a room, settle for a shade slightly lighter than the one you want, as a colour seems to look more intense when the room is painted.

Use red in a dining-room, it incites appetite and conversation. In a dark, north-facing room, use glowing, strong, brilliant colours for a warm atmosphere.

In a bright, sunny room use pale delicate colours for peaceful, relaxed, airy surroundings.

Dark blue on the walls of a small room will give a feeling of being boxed in.

Use a light chalky blue on the walls to give a room an airy peaceful, cool feeling, but avoid using blues in a room facing away from the sun; it can give it a chilly atmosphere.

A fundamental rule when decorating a room is to choose three colours; two colours can be very dull, and it is only when a third colour is introduced that the room comes alive.

CURTAINS

To make curtains for your windows, quickly and well finished, use bedspreads. They are already hemmed and sometimes lined. All you have to do is pleat the top and sew the rings or hooks on.

When making velvet curtains, for dark colours, have the pile running upwards to give a deeper effect. But for light colours have the pile running downwards for a softer, more delicate appearance.

A simple, elegant idea, and a very quickly accomplished way of hanging curtains to a window, is to take a long length of fabric and drape it over a pole (wooden or brass). A roller blind fixed behind the curtain can be pulled down when needed.

If curtain sashes are hard to pull, rub them with a piece of candle or a piece of soap.

You must place a piece of black fabric between the lining and curtains if you don't want any daylight to come through.

If your curtains have shrunk after being cleaned, a long fringe sewn to the bottom edge might look very nice and solve the problem. Or if the curtains hang with rings on a pole, add another ring into each one already there to give the curtain the extra length lost when being cleaned.

CUSHION

Feather cushions can be made very cheaply from an inexpensive feather pillow. Push the feathers equally to either end of the pillow then sew the middle twice with two parallel seams before cutting to make two cushions.

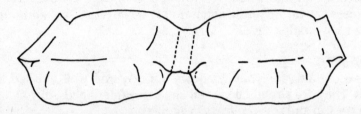

To re-fluff feather cushions make a small opening in one of the seams, introduce a piece of rubber tube and blow air into the cushion. One can also use the tube of a bicycle pump, introduced through the opening in the seam to pump some air in. Then sew the seam back and fluff the cushion.

An embroidered cushion, if made of dark colours, will dry-clean when brushed over with hot bran on a soft cloth. Light colours will dry-clean if an equal mixture of borax and magnesia is rubbed over it with a soft cloth. For very soiled embroidery, rub the mixture over and leave it to stand overnight before shaking it off.

DECKCHAIR

An inexpensive deckchair can become a very comfortable, attractive chair to have anywhere in the house. Paint the frame with red or black lacquer or gold paint. Remove the canvas and replace it with some upholstery fabric (velvet, brocade etc.,) of your choice and nail the fabric with brass studs. Add even more comfort by making a head-rest matching the upholstery fabric.

DECORATING

When decorating a room write in a small hidden corner on the wall the quantity of wallpaper rolls, paint etc., that you have used so that next time you will know what you need to redecorate the place.

DINING-ROOM

If your dining room is very small, place the dining table and the chairs in the centre of the room and do not infringe on floor space further. Use the walls for wall-hung pieces of furniture such as cupboards, shelves etc. A shelf attached to the wall with hinges and dropped down when needed will serve as a sideboard.

DINING TABLE

A very pretty dining-room table can be made easily, cheaply and of the size you need by making a square base to the right height (approx. 29–30 inches/74–76 cm) and fixing a circle on top, cut in chipboard or blockboard. To seat four people the diameter should be between 36–39 inches/90–100 cm. For five or six people it should be between 45–50 inches/125–127 cm, for eight people a diameter of between 55–59 inches/140–150 cm will do. Cover the table permanently with a heavy cloth draped to the floor, and cover the cloth with a matching small square tablecloth when dining.

DOUBLE GLAZING

In an emergency, to break a double glazed window attack the corner of the glass with a sharp weapon.

FIREPLACE

An unused fireplace can become a bookcase or a cupboard. First remove all fittings from the fire recess then block the flue. Clean and paint the inside of the fireplace then fit it with shelves. Add doors for the cupboard.

FLOOR

A dark floor will make a room look smaller and bring the eyes down to it. A plain, light carpet will give it a spacious effect.

FRAMING

An original way of framing a print, a watercolour or even a photograph is to place it between two pieces of glass instead of glass and a background. When the frame is put on and it is hung on the wall, the picture will look as if it is floating in the air and the transparent glass will let the wall colour appear through.

FRINGE

To make a fringe on the edge of a piece of fabric, first draw a line near the edge of the fabric to indicate how long the fringe should be, then snip from the edge up to the line at intervals. Draw out the threads a short length at a time, and you have your fringe.

FURNISHING A HOUSE

When furnishing a house or a flat do not buy everything at once, but just enough to get along with at first, even if you see bargains, and remember, 'Nothing is cheap that you do not need.'

Use transparent furniture (chairs, tables etc.) made of perspex or glass to give a sense of space and lightness to a room.

FURNITURE

Do not leave varnished furniture exposed to sunlight: the wood becomes discoloured and it is impossible to restore its veneer.

Make your furniture shine by rubbing it with a soft cloth dipped in vinegar, before waxing.

To remove paper stuck to furniture (because of moisture or stuck to the wood's varnish), moisten it with linseed oil, wait until the paper soaks the oil and it can be removed easily with the fingers.

HALL

Make a narrow hall look bigger by decorating the walls with a light colour. Alternatively, cover an entire wall with mirrors or place a mirror facing the front door.

CHANGING PICTURES

Do not hang a small picture over a large piece of furniture, the picture will look lost. Also, do not hang a large picture over a small piece of furniture or the furniture will look lost.

KITCHEN STORAGE

For more storage space, screw a pegboard to one of your kitchen walls or the side of a cupboard to hang kitchen utensils (pans, pots, etc.).

LAMPSHADES

A lampshade should spread out and soften the light (e.g. very light colour shades: white, off-white etc.). Patterned or coloured shades stop the light flowing and obscure the room.

NET CURTAINS

Buy $1\frac{1}{2}$ times or twice the length of the track if you want full curtains.

PAINTBRUSHES

To soften the bristles of a paintbrush, leave to soak overnight in two parts water to one part ammonia, or in a solution of one tablespoon of washing soda to two teacupfuls of warm water. Leave to soak overnight, then wash in warm soapy water, rinse and let dry.

To soften brushes which have hardened, immerse them in hot vinegar.

For very neglected paintbrushes, immerse them in hot vinegar (bristles only) and simmer for half an hour. Wash in warm soapy water, rinse and let dry.

Undisciplined bristles on a paintbrush can be corrected by spraying them generously with hair lacquer, putting them back into shape with hands and finally letting them dry.

Shave the bristles of your old paintbrush with an electric razor to give it back its original lost shape. If you are using a small paintbrush and you need a finer tip for the job, wrap some tape around the bristles at the head of the brush. Take the tape off when the job is finished.

Wrap the paintbrush you will be using again in foil instead of washing or cleaning them, or if you have no time straight away, smother them with vaseline.

Use a piece of cardboard when soaking light brushes in solvent. Put the handle through the cardboard, put the cardboard over the opening of the jar and the brushes are held in the liquid with no risk of damage. A clothes–peg can be used to hold small artist's brushes over the narrow opening of a jar filled with solvent. For heavy brushes, see p. 77 ('Coffee tins'). A tap washer slipped up the handle of the paintbrush near the ferrule (metal band) is ideal as support when you want to rest the paintbrush.

PAINTING

Place a paper plate, from which the middle part has been cut away, round the top of your tin. The drips will collect in the brim. When the job is finished, throw the paper brim away.

Or stretch a thin piece of wire across the top of your tin of paint, so that you can wipe your brush against it after dipping into the paint.

To protect your hair when painting a ceiling, wear a shower cap or an old scarf.

To prevent the legs of a table or a chair sticking to the floor when being painted, hammer a nail to the base of each leg before you start painting.

A plastic lid from a yoghurt carton is useful for putting underneath the legs of any furniture to be painted; it will collect all the surplus paint and completely protect the floor.

If paint needs to be strained, place a stocking over the tin of paint and pour through the stocking into a clean empty tin.

Line your paint-roller tray with aluminium foil when you are painting. When the job is finished just throw the foil away and your roller tray will be clean and ready for the next painting job.

If lacquered or enamelled paint is being applied in cold weather, stand the tin for twenty minutes in hot water before using it. The paint will get thinner and will be easier to brush on.

A stroke of coloured paint on a blotter will give a good idea of how the colour will look on the wall when decorating.

To paint wire-mesh fence fast and successfully, put on rubber gloves and use a sponge instead of a paintbrush.

To remove fresh splashes of paint from a window, use hot vinegar; for old splashes use a razor blade.

Splashed paint on cork tiles will go if rubbed gently with a cloth dampened in acetone or nail-varnish remover.

A skin won't form on top of the gloss paint if, before closing the tin, you coat the surface of the paint with a thin layer of white spirit. When next using the paint, discard the white spirit or mix it into the paint.

A little water covering the top of a half used oil-based paint will also stop a skin forming. When ready to use the paint again, pour the water away.

Yet another way is simply to store the tin upside down; this will stop the skin forming by excluding the air.

To remove paint from your hands, rub them with some salad oil. This method will be gentle on your skin, too. Sawdust is also good for removing paint from hands. Take a handful of sawdust and rub your hands with it, using soap and water at the same time.

For a paint-shade sample, dip a lolly stick into the paint and leave to dry – very useful when you want to buy curtains, bedspreads etc., to match the walls.

PAINTINGS

Do not hang an oil painting over the mantelpiece: the heat will make it crack.

Do not hang a small picture over a large piece of furniture, the picture will look lost. Also, do not hang a large picture over a small piece of furniture: the furniture will look lost.

A general rule, when hanging a picture on the wall, is to place it at eye level for the best result, not higher or lower. Judge while seated or standing up.

PAINT SMELL – See p. 66

PAPER HANGING

Paste the wall instead of the wallpaper – you will find the paper much easier to hang.

To get rid of creases on a wall covered with fabric, spray the creases with water.

RADIATOR MESH

Use chicken wire instead of mesh to hide radiators or to net cupboard doors. It is very much cheaper and the effect is perfect. Spray the chicken wire with gold or bronze paint before fixing it.

Another idea to hide radiators is to use garden trellis in the same way as chicken wire. The trellis can be painted the shade of the wall or given a mahogany finish.

ROOMS

Make a big long room look shorter by covering one end of the room with bookcases.

To make a large room look more closed in, bring the walls 'together' by using matt paint on the walls and a continuous frieze (border) or a band of contrasting colour all the way round the room. Patterned wallpaper with a dark background will also help the room seem more compact.

Make a room seem larger by covering wall, ceiling and floor in a light colour. Use glossy paint on the walls to give an even greater sense of space or patterned wallpaper with a light background.

Create an illusion of space in a small room by using pale colour on walls and floor coverings. Transparent furniture (glass, plexiglass) and mirrored walls will also help push out the walls. Light-proportioned antique and reproduction furniture with simple lines can also be utilized most success-fully.

ROOM SCENT

A bunch of fresh or dried mint leaves thrown in the fireplace will diffuse a beautiful fragrance in the room.

SCREEN

Make your own screen by using three or four shutters hinged together with some decorative brass hinges. Or use three or four louvred doors for a larger screen.

SHOE STORAGE

Here is an extra shoe-storage idea which is quickly and cheaply made to nail inside a cupboard door in the garage, the hall etc. Take some wire hangers and secure them to the back of the door. Add some loops of cord or rubber at regular intervals and hang the shoes. *See illustration overleaf.*

SPOOL

Use empty thread spools to raise a chair or table that is too low. Screw or glue them to the end of the existing legs and paint or stain them to match.

STAIRS

Hide the threadbare areas on the stair carpet by rubbing it with ink the same colour as the carpet.

When stairs have to be painted or stained, but will still be in use during this operation, paint every other stair first. The unpainted ones will be used while the other ones are drying, then paint the remaining stairs and use the drypaint stairs to go up and down. (Make no mistake!)

STORAGE

Use the inside of a cloakroom door for storing shoes and handbags by fixing some box shelves and hanging plastic shoe-bags.

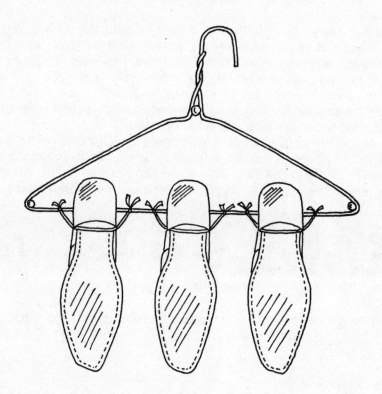

A trunk placed at the foot of the bed is perfect for storing blankets, quilts, pillows etc., when one needs extra storage.

Make more storage space in a child's room by fastening a bookshelf to the foot of the bunk bed.

WINDOWS

A good way to dress a window with an uninteresting view outside is to fix some glass shelves across the window where pots of plants and herbs (if the window is in the kitchen) will make a very attractive display.

Make a small window look bigger by extending the curtain rails or pole further than the window frame each side. When the curtains are drawn back the whole window should be visible.

To bring more daylight into your room if your windows have wide embrasures, mirror the embrasures (use mirror tiles, which are cheaper than full-length mirrors).

To curtain a window in an obliquely inclined position (e.g. a window in an attic in a sloping roof) use this method: the left-side cord goes through a hook then down the pole, through the rings and is secured to the bottom ring. The right-side cord goes through a hook then down the pole, through the rings and is secured to the bottom ring. Both poles are fastened to the wall at the top and bottom.

PLANTS

Gardening

ANTS
To kill ants make a mixture of one part sugar to two parts powdered borax and sprinkle around the house, or outside. But this is not recommended if you have small children or pets who could get to it.

Another way to get rid of ants is to make a hole with a stick in the centre of an anthill and pour $\frac{1}{2}$pint/$\frac{1}{4}$litre of household ammonia into it.

To prevent ants climbing, rub a good thick coating of chalk around the plant or object to be protected (walls, pipes, wooden posts etc.) – ants cannot walk on chalk. Renew every few weeks. Salt can be used instead of chalk.

ARTICHOKES
The head of the artichoke will grow larger if, when the stalk is fully grown, two incisions are made in the stalk just underneath the head and two matchsticks are introduced, crossing each other.

BEANS
To prepare a good crop of beans when seeding, soak some newspapers for three to four hours, then squeeze them lightly and place them at the bottom of the seeding trench. Cover thinly with soil, lay the seeds and finish covering with more soil. This method applies to peas also.

BEETLES
To exterminate beetles put some honey or treacle in a soup plate and place strips of cardboard (with the end bent into the plate) from the floor to the top of the plate to make a kind of gangway for the beetles to climb up. Rub the cardboard with a cut onion. If there are lots of beetles, set some saucers with a mixture of plaster of Paris and flour on the floor with saucers of water next to them; the plaster will make the beetles drink, and this will destroy them.

BIRCH LEAVES
Birch leaves added to the compost will disinfect the soil from fly diseases.

210

BULBS

To prevent flower bulbs drying in the winter, wrap them in aluminium foil and store them in empty suitcases.

Nylon stockings are ideal for storing bulbs. Fill up the stockings with the bulbs and hang them so that the air can circulate through them.

CABBAGE – See also **Natural insecticides**

To stop the head of a cabbage or cauliflower cracking open, make an incision in the stalk on one side, beneath the head, and insert a small piece of wood into the cut.

Bury your stock of cabbage, carrots, turnips and celery in sand for use throughout the winter. Store in your cellar or shed; lay the cabbages with the roots up.

CATERPILLARS

To get rid of the caterpillars in your garden, place some small branches of elder in a container, cover with water and boil for twenty minutes. Leave to cool and water your invaded plants with the mixture.

CAULIFLOWER

Frost can blacken the white head of the cauliflower, and bright sunlight will make it yellow. To avoid this, snap a few leaves of the cauliflower and cover the head with them.

CELERY – See **Cabbage**

CROCKERY

Use broken crockery to line plantpots.

CUTTINGS

To grow roots quickly and successfully on plant cuttings, use a large transparent plastic bag. Fill up one third with moist compost and plant the cutting. Next blow air into the bag and close it hermetically to keep it blown up. Soon the roots will grow.

DEER

Deer won't chew the plants and trees in your garden if the latter have pieces of cloth dipped in creosote fastened to them.

EARWIGS

Catch the earwigs which are eating your plant by placing an upside-down flowerpot filled with hay or straw near the plant.

To stop earwigs going on the blossoms of the dahlias and the tender tops of the stems to eat them, tie a piece of cotton wool dipped in salad oil to the stalk and another to the stake of the plant about a foot from the ground.

To trap earwigs stuff a flowerpot with moss, invert the pot on the top of a stake near the infected plant and inspect morning and night. Destroy the earwigs by throwing the contents of the pot into boiling water. Refill with fresh moss each time.

FROZEN PLANTS
To revive greenhouse plants which have become frozen, make it as dark as possible in the greenhouse and thaw the plants with cold water. If watered in the light, the plants would die.

GARLIC
To grow one big, round clove of garlic instead of several small ones, plant the cloves in the second week of March. Garlic planted between October and February will produce a head of several smaller cloves.

Garlic planted near beans, lettuces, tomatoes, roses etc will discourage greenfly; so will basil.

GERMINATION
To get good outside summer sowing germination, first make the holes in the soil and then water each until they are very moist. Let the water sink in and then sow the seeds, covering them with dry soil and giving it a firm pat. The dry soil will prevent the moisture evaporating in the hot weather.

GRASS
Do not walk over your frosted lawn or you will have an unpleasant surprise when the spring comes; the grass won't grow where it has been walked on.

To stop grass growing between the stone slabs of a footpath in the garden, sprinkle salt in the interstices, or pour on very salted boiling water or some pure bleach.

HANGING PLANTS BASKET
When watering plants in a hanging basket avoid dripping by slipping a shower cap over the bottom of the hanging basket before watering.

HERBS – See also Window boxes
Herbs can be grown together, except for fennel and dill. Mint develops its roots so quickly that there is no room left for other herbs, unless you restrain it by planting it in a large tin (e.g. a paint tin). Cut the top and bottom off the tin, and sink it into the soil.

To make herb plants thick and bushy, and to stop them growing too tall, pinch out the centre stem to encourage the side shoots to develop.

Dry seedheads by placing them in a paper bag and hanging them in a dry, warm place.

INSECTS
To stop insects (wasps, flies etc.) coming into the house, tie a fresh bunch of stinging nettles in front of your open doors and windows.

INSECTICIDE – See also **Natural insecticides**

A cheap insecticide can be made at home by mixing equal quantities of milk, paraffin and water. It is impossible to mix paraffin and water, but if you mix the milk and paraffin first the water will then blend easily into the solution.

IVY

To make ivy climb a wall, without the help of trellis or wire, use some plasticine to stick the ivy against the wall from time to time.

LADYBIRDS

An adult ladybird eats about a hundred greenflies a day, so leave ladybirds on your roses or fruit trees and do not use insecticide on them.

LEEKS – See also **Natural insecticides**

To discourage maggots, from time to time place some eggshells on small sticks between the leeks – butterflies will lay their eggs on or inside the shells instead of the leeks.

Leeks can be left in the ground all winter. Cover one row at a time with straw or peat to enable the leeks to be dug out when needed, even if the soil is frozen.

MAPLE LEAVES

Apples and root vegetables will keep much longer if they are stored on a bed of maple leaves and covered with maple leaves too.

MINT

Mint planted with cabbage and broccoli will discourage cabbage moths; so will thyme or dill.

MISTLETOE

Mistletoe is a parasite and weakens the tree it grows on. Remove it as soon as possible in November when the leaves of the tree have fallen. Cover the wood with a mixture of clay and cow-dung to stop it growing again.

But if you want to grow mistletoe on a tree (e.g. apple, poplar) make a few slits on branches and insert a squashed berry into each slit. This should be done in the spring so in the winter store some mistletoe and keep it in a cool place until the spring.

MARIGOLDS

Marigold petals can be used instead of saffron to colour food. They also have a light, delicate flavour. The petals can be used fresh or dried. Dry them in a cool, dark place in thin layers and they will retain their beautiful colour.

MOLES

Moles hate mothballs. If you want to get rid of a mole in the garden, drop a few mothballs in the molehill and it will soon move away.

MANURE FOR PLANTS
Do not throw away soapsuds and ashes – they are both very good as manure for young plants and bushes.

MULCH
Pine needles are perfect to mulch the strawberries – and oak leaves are best to mulch plants and protect them against snails and slugs.

NATURAL INSECTICIDES
Broccoli
Thyme or mint planted near broccoli will discourage cabbage moths.
Cabbage
Thyme or mint planted near cabbages will discourage cabbage moths.
   Radishes planted near cabbages discourage maggots.
Carrots
To discourage the carrot fly, plant onions next to carrots. Both carrot fly and onion fly will avoid the plot. Radishes also fight the carrot fly.
Onions
To avoid onion fly, plant onions next to carrot (or better still *with* the carrots). Both types of fly will avoid the plot.
Potatoes
Plant horseradish near potatoes; beetles hate horseradish and will avoid both.
Radishes
Radishes planted near cabbages will discourage maggots.
Thyme
Thyme planted near cabbages and broccoli will discourage cabbage moths.
Tomatoes
Grow tomatoes between leeks as butterflies are repelled by their smell.
   Do not plant cabbage near strawberries, or garlic near peas; they do not like each other's company.

NETTLES
Where you see nettles growing, this is a sign of a very fertile soil.

ONIONS
To prevent onions sprouting wrap them individually in silver foil.
   Nylon stockings or tights are perfect to store your reserve of onions for the winter. Hang them up so the air can go through to keep the onions dry.

PARSNIPS
Parsnips become sweeter if left in the ground until they are needed. Cover the soil with mulch to prevent freezing as frost will make the lifting of the parsnips impossible in the winter.

PESTS AND DISEASES

Greenfly

Greenfly accumulates on the underneath of the leaves and young shoots, making them look distorted and sticky. To get rid of greenfly, spray the whole plant (particularly the undersides of the leaves) twice a week with a weak soap-flake solution.

To discourage greenfly, plant garlic amongst the plants that attract it and keep cutting the shoots when the garlic starts sprouting.

Mealy bugs

Mealy bugs attack both the undersides of leaves and the joints in the stem; they look like dots of cotton wool. Rub them off the plant with a cotton wool bud dipped in methylated spirit or white spirit.

Red spider mites

Red spider mites cause leaves to become yellow-brown and brittle, and a white webbing can be seen on the underside of the leaves of afflicted plants. To get rid of the mites, spray the plant with water, which is their worst enemy.

Scale insects

Scale insects attack both leaves and stems, making them very weak, but are very difficult to detect because of their brownish colour and their stillness. Rub or knock them off the plant with a cotton wool bud dipped in methylated spirit or white spirit.

POISONOUS PLANTS – See also p. 220

Anemone: the sap can provoke intense itching.
Buttercup: provokes inflammation of the kidneys and cardiac disorder if eaten.
Conker: the fruit is highly toxic and provokes strong digestive disorders if eaten.
Daffodil: lowers the blood pressure and provokes drowsiness.
Honeysuckle: the berries can be deadly.
Lily of the valley: provokes cardiac disorders and convulsions.
Mistletoe: provokes diarrhoea and cardiac disorders.
Narcissus: the bulb contains poisons.
Snowdrop: the bulb is dangerous, lowers blood pressure and provokes cardiac disorders.
Tulip: the bulb is dangerous, provokes convulsions and cardiac disorders.
Wistaria: the pods are very toxic, and can provoke drowsiness, colic and digestive disorders.

POTATOES

When planting potatoes make them go a long way by cutting them in two. Make sure that each half has healthy shoots, and each half will give you a plant.

To stop your winter stock of potatoes starting to germinate, sprinkle them generously with powdered charcoal.

RABBITS

Keep rabbits away by throwing mothballs here and there around the garden. Sprinkle talcum powder on and around the plants; this will also keep them away.

ROSE TREES

When planting rose trees, take a patch of grass and place it face downwards at the bottom of the prepared hole. Spread the roots of the rose tree out on it and plant in the usual way. This seems to make the rose trees grow much healthier.

Fertilize your roses by burying chopped banana skins in the rose beds.

To revive tired roses, take soot from a chimney or stove where wood has been used as a fuel. Put it into a container, pour boiling water over it and when cold use every day to water the roses. The effect is remarkable: it deepens the colour and produces the rapid growth of shoots. Try with other plants as well.

SALSIFY AND SCORZONERA

For long, straight, healthy-looking salsify, the soil needs to be dug deeply before planting. With only a superficial digging, the salsify will grow forked.

SEEDING

To make your seeds grow quicker, soak them in water for forty-eight hours before planting.

If you line the seed tray with newspaper it will hold the moisture.

Very tiny seeds are difficult to sow. Mix the seeds with a small quantity of dry sand and then you will be able to sow them evenly.

When putting tiny seeds in seed trays for germination, put them in a salt cellar before scattering them. It will ensure a better distribution.

A broom handle is ideal for making a shallow trench in the garden soil for seeds. Just lay the broom handle on the earth, press it down with your feet, dig it out and you have a perfect straight trench of about $\frac{3}{4}$–1 in/1–2 cm deep.

SLUGS

An equal mixture of wood ash and soot will make the slugs run away in disgust.

A small amount of bran placed around the garden will attract slugs and kill them very quickly.

After squeezing oranges, keep the empty halves and put them in your garden, face down, along a flower bed containing seedlings. Slugs will crawl underneath and can easily be removed each day.

Fill a container with beer and leave it in the garden overnight. In the morning it will be full of slugs.

SNAILS

To catch the snails which are eating the flowers and vegetables in your garden, sprinkle some bran on the ground and cover it with cabbage leaves. The snails are very fond of bran and will soon assemble under the leaves where you can collect them every morning.

SOIL QUALITY

A quick way to find out the acidity of the soil when acquiring a new piece of land for a garden is to look at the weeds growing in it:

Chickweed, groundsel: the soil is rich with good drainage.

Poppies, sorrel, dock: the soil is acid.

Moss covering a wet soil: the drainage is not good and should be treated with lime or given an artificial drainage before starting to cultivate. (Seek professional advice.)

STOCKINGS – See also Bulbs and Onions

Cut nylon stockings into narrow strips and use them in the garden to tie trees and shrubs to their stakes.

TOADS

Toads are the gardener's best friend for they feed on destructive vermin. If you have none in your garden, try to catch one, but handle it with care for it is very delicate.

TREE

When planting a new tree, avoid damaging the roots by putting the supporting stake in place before putting the tree in the ground.

VEGETABLE STORING

Do not store apples and carrots next to each other; the carrots will give the apples a bitter taste.

A bed of maple leaves is a very good preservative to store apples or root vegetables for the winter.

HOUSE PLANTS

BUYING PLANTS

When buying a houseplant during the cold months of winter, insist on a good wrapping to protect it from the cold when taking it home from the shop.

Do not buy a houseplant from a pavement display outside a shop.

Azalea: When buying an azalea, make sure it is properly moist; at no time should it be allowed to dry out. This can be easily detected by looking at the short woody stem between the soil and the foliage. There should be a dark water mark about half-way up the stem – if the mark is up where the branches begin, it is too wet; if there is no mark at all, it is too dry and you should not buy the plant.

Chrysanthemum: When buying a chrysanthemum, choose it when most of the buds are just opening, never when the buds are tight. A well-looked-after plant will last for five or six weeks.

CLEANING LEAVES

Houseplants with hard green leaves (rubber plant, fig tree, philodendron etc.) should be sponged every two or three weeks with a piece of cotton wool dipped in milk or flat beer. This will get rid of dust, allow the leaves to breathe more freely and make them look glossy and green.

The use of oil is not recommended, as it clogs the pores of the leaves and makes it harder for them to breathe.

COLOUR

Houseplant flowers will have a deeper colour if the plant is watered with sooty water from time to time. This also applies to garden flowers.

FEEDING

Plants have a dormant period (September to April or May) so do not feed them during that time as they are practically inactive. Also, do not water them as often as during the summer months.

Do not feed plants when they are in full bloom.

Most plants develop their new growth in the spring, so feeding should start in spring and continue until early autumn.

Grind some egg shells, mix them with some caster sugar and add to your houseplants' soil; they will quickly show you their gratitude.

Of course a can of beer or a glass of red wine mixed with water is fully appreciated too but much more expensive.

A few pieces of coal mixed with your houseplants' soil will help them stay green.

To improve the growth and the foliage of your houseplants add a table-spoon of ammonia to one litre/two pints of watering water.

HERBS

A most attractive gift to give to an invalid is a large bowl filled with several small pots of aromatic herbs to keep by the bedside.

HOME-GROWN PLANTS

Children enjoy growing their own houseplants, so let them experiment with the following. Cut the tops off fresh carrots, beetroots, turnips, parsnips etc. and stand them on a dinner plate with enough water to cover the bottom section. Put the plate in a light place and keep the base moist. Shoots will appear after a few days, and leaves after about a week. The carrots will have feathery leaves, and the beetroots and turnips will have red-veined leaves.

Plants from seeds

Avocado: An avocado makes a lovely leathery-leafed plant. Put an avocado stone, pointed end uppermost, in a glass filled with water or a pot filled with compost, leaving half the stone above the surface. If using water, push three or four toothpicks into the side of the stone and rest them on the rim of the glass as a support. Keep in a warm place which is not too light until shoots appear, and then move to a lighter place. Transplant into sandy soil when the roots become strong.

Citrus fruit: Orange, lemon, grapefruit, tangerine and lime all form plants with small, shiny, dark-green leaves. Plant a few pips to germinate together in moist compost about half an inch/1 cm deep. Keep in a warm dark place until shoots appear, then re-pot singly when they are about three or four inches/about seven to ten centimetres long.

Date: A date can make a strong and most attractive plant. Take some fresh date stones and put them to germinate in moist compost about half an inch/1 cm deep, with the pointed end uppermost. Keep in a warm, dark place with constantly damp soil until shoots appear, then bring the pot into the light, keeping the soil moist.

Pineapple: For a hardy and very attractive green plant, cut off the top of a pineapple at the base of the tuft. Scoop out the flesh and put the base in a vase containing water, or in a pot of moist, sandy compost. Leave in a light, warm place. Roots will develop at the base, the leaves will grow longer and stronger every day, and new leaves will appear. For the best results, choose a pineapple with healthy leaves.

Plants from leaves

African violet: This can be propagated by cutting a leaf with its stem and planting it in a pot of compost. Mother-in-law's tongue, dragon plant and pepper elder can also be propagated in this way.

Begonia: This can be propagated by leaf planting or vein cutting. Take a fully grown leaf with very prominent veins and make a few small incisions in the biggest veins on the underside. Place the leaf, shiny side up, on damp compost. Weight it with small stones, cover the pot with a piece of transparent plastic and place in indirect sunlight. Roots will form where the incisions were made; shoots will grow from them, and when they are big enough they can be potted separately.

Sansevieria: This can be propagated simply by cutting the leaves into sections (use a sharp knife) and planting each section in a pot. Do not water too much or the plant will rot.

HOUSEPLANTS

African violets

Water them with warm water to get the best out of them. They like warmth but a gas-heated room won't suit them. Gas is harmful to African violets.

Cyclamen

If your cyclamen hangs limply, you might have been too cautious and not watered it enough. Stand it on an upturned teacup in a container and fill the container with boiling water. In a short time the steam will have revived the cyclamen.

Ferns

Vivify your ferns by watering them once a week with tea.

Poinsettia

If your poinsettia from last Christmas is doing fine but shows no sign of red leaves, place it in a dark cupboard every night for fifteen hours. That amount of darkness is necessary for it to regain its colour. If you don't want to move the plant, cover it with an upturned box or plastic bucket.

To stop the sticky white sap flow of a poinsettia, dust the cut with cigar or cigarette ash or powdered charcoal.

A plant leans towards the daylight, so do not forget to rotate the pot if you don't want a crooked plant.

PESTS

To get rid of pests in houseplants' soil, water the plants with a decoction of tobacco made by slowly boiling old cigarette ends in water for ten minutes. Strain, leave to cool and water the houseplants.

POISONOUS PLANTS – See also p. 215

Some common houseplants are poisonous if eaten. Be particularly careful when there are children and animals around.

Azalea: the whole plant is toxic and provokes colic.

Cyclamen: the whole plant is toxic and causes violent headaches and convulsions.

Dieffenbachia: the whole plant is venomous and the sap is toxic.

Philodendron: the plant can provoke intoxication.

Poinsettia: the corrosive sap can provoke diarrhoea, cramp and delirium.

Primrose: the plant can provoke curious allergies.

Solanum (pommes d'amour): the whole plant is toxic.

POTS

Plastic pots may be less attractive than clay pots, but they do have advantages: plants in clay pots need more watering, because the clay absorbs the moisture. Plants are as happy in one as in the other.

If you put a plant in a decorative pot, do not forget to place a deep layer of gravel at the bottom to provide drainage, before putting in the compost.

POTTING

When potting plants, add a small quantity of charcoal dust to the compost; it will take away the acidity in the soil.

Some used tea leaves mixed with the compost when potting plants will help retain the moisture in the soil.

To dig a small plant out of a pot if you don't want to turn the pot upside down for some reason, use a shoe horn.

When transferring a plant from outside to inside the house, put the plant and pot in a polythene bag for a few days to protect it.

SCENT
To give a lovely smell to a plant, soak some flower seeds for two days in some rose water in which you have infused a small quantity of musk. Leave the seeds to dry a little and then plant them. Water with the same mixture in which they were soaked.

WATERING
Growth takes place in spring and summer, and plants need a lot of watering during this time.

Growth is slow in winter and plants need less water, but a certain amount of watering is still necessary, particularly if you have central heating.

If a plant is absorbing water very quickly, it probably needs a larger pot. Check the roots: if they are compressed, the pot is too small.

A plant with yellow, falling leaves has been over-watered; allow it to dry out for a few days.

If your plant has brown-tipped leaves, it might be the chlorine in the tap water so let the water stand overnight before watering your plant.

A plant with a limp stem and dropping leaves needs watering badly. Plunge the whole pot into a container of water and leave it submerged until the last bubble comes to the surface, then drain.

To test if a plant needs watering, leave a pebble on top of the soil: if the underside is still damp when you turn the pebble over, the plant does not need water; if it is dry, it does. Alternatively, insert a skewer or pencil in the soil: if it comes out with damp soil attached to it, it still does not need watering; if it comes out clean, it does. (Soil can appear dry on the surface but be moist underneath.)

To keep soil moist longer and to avoid evaporation, cover the surface of the pot with pebbles, gravel or moss.

Your plants will soon show their gratitude if you put a little vinegar in their watering container, as vinegar neutralizes the chalk and makes the water much softer.

Snow is very good for watering houseplants because it's full of minerals. Place some clean snow in a bucket, let it melt and get to room temperature, then water your houseplants.

Cooking water from hard-boiled eggs is good for watering the house plants when it has cooled.

A little watering from time to time is not enough, and will make the roots turn upwards to reach the water. A successful method with most plants is to plunge them into a bucket of water (the whole pot must be submerged) until bubbles of air stop coming to the surface. Drain carefully.

Do not leave pots standing in a saucer of water as this causes the roots to rot.

Most plants can be watered from the top, except for cyclamen, African violets and peperomia – if these corms were submerged under water, the buds or young leaves could be damaged. Stand the pot in 2 inches/5 cm of water for half an hour or until the surface of the soil shows moisture. This method of watering should also be used for plants with delicate leaves and flowers.

All plants like to have their foliage sprayed, except for furry-leafed plants like African violets. Spray plants often as this keeps humidity in the air, which is perfect for the plants to thrive in.

When you are planning to go away and there is nobody to water your plants, soak the soil thoroughly and, while still dripping, put the plant and pot in a polythene bag. Close the bag and put the wrapped plant in a good position where it will get indirect daylight. When you come home after three or four weeks, the plant will be as happy as when you left it and still quite damp.

Another method of long-term watering is to take a piece of bandage, put one end in a bowl of water and tuck the other end into the soil. The bandage will draw water from the bowl into the soil. Or place some bricks in your bathtub, submerge with water and place the houseplants on top.

If a philodendron develops aerial roots instead of winding them around on top of the soil in the pot, direct the roots into a container of water. The plant will take moisture from this source and the soil in the pot will need very little watering.

WORMS IN HOUSEPLANTS

Stick the sulphur end of matches in the soil of a diseased houseplant to get rid of worms.

To catch any worms in your potted plants, bury a slice of raw potato under the surface of the soil. Leave it for a few days and it will entice the worms to it.

Cut Flowers

FLOWERS

The best time to pick flowers from the garden is in the early morning or early evening. Do not pick them during the warmest part of the day, because this is when the plant is at its lowest sweating point and the flowers would not last very long.

Do not pick flowers in full bloom as the petals will fall very quickly. Choose half-opened blooms, and always leave your freshly picked or bought flowers standing in a deep container full of water in a cool place for at least three hours, more if possible, standing up to their necks in water.

When buying flowers, avoid any that have been standing in the sun, or any from which the pollen is dropping.

Arranging flowers: To arrange cut flowers in a bowl, fill the bowl with sand to within an inch/2 cm of the top and soak with water. The flowers will stay fresh and upright twice as long.

Flower holder: Cut a slice from the base of a potato and make it sit squarely and then make holes to take the stems. The moisture from the potato will keep foliage fresh for many days without water in a shallow arrangement.

If some of the flowers are too short to make a flower arrangement, slide their stems in drinking straws and cut the straw to the required length.

To keep the water pure in a vase, put a piece of charcoal at the bottom, or add a few drops of bleach to the water, or a tablespoon of sugar.

Some flowers such as roses, lily of the valley, irises, cherry blossom, apple blossom and primroses, will last longer when cut if, before putting them in a vase, the stems are dipped in boiling water for two minutes to open their pores.

To keep flowers fresh, add a pinch of nitrate of soda every time the water is changed.

To make flowers last longer, put their stems into lukewarm water to which a spoonful of salt has been added.

To revive limp flowers, cut half an inch/1 cm from the stems and plunge the freshly trimmed ends into boiling water at once. The flowers will resume their beauty in a surprisingly short time.

Cyclamen, tulips and other similar flowers are very decorative, but tend to droop. A little starch in the water will keep them upright for several days.

Flowers such as daffodils and narcissi exude a sticky substance when cut, which makes drinking difficult for them. Before arranging them, hold the ends of the stems under warm running water to remove this juice. Place a copper coin in the vase.

Flowers with milky stems (e.g. dahlias, poinsettias and poppies) cannot absorb water until the milky juice has coagulated. To prevent bleeding, singe the end of the stem with a match just after cutting, or dip 2 inches/5 cm of the stem in boiling water for thirty seconds.

Carnations: Carnation stems should be broken between the joints to allow the flowers to drink more freely.

Chrysanthemum: The leaves of the cut chrysanthemums in a vase will not droop so quickly if some sugar, first melted in warm water, is added to the water in the vase.

Gladioli: Your gladioli will live longer if you pinch the head off and place the gladiola in a vase with very little water.

Heather: The heather will not drop its bells at once if cut and put in a vase containing a potato instead of water. Push the stems into the potato, making holes in the potato first if necessary.

Hydrangeas: The flowerhead of a hydrangea absorbs water, so when arranging hydrangeas in a pot or vase spray the flowerhead or first soak it in cool water for a few seconds.

Lilac: The bark should be peeled off the stem below water-level or it will poison the water; the bottom inch/2 cm of the stem should be hammered or split to allow the lilac to drink more freely and so last longer.

Lupins: Lupins have hollow stems which after being cut should be filled with sugared water (one tablespoon of sugar, two pints/one litre of warm water) and then blocked with a piece of cotton wool. Afterward place them in deep water up to their bottom blooms for a few hours.

Marigolds: Marigolds and flowers of the same family give off an unpleasant odour in a room when placed in a vase. To eliminate the smell add one tablespoon of bleach to the water or one tablespoon of sugar.

Mimosa: Place mimosa in hot water and spray two or three times a day to keep its fluffy look.

Poppies: To prevent poppies drooping almost straight away after being cut, singe the end of the stalk with a candle or a match immediately after cutting. If it is necessary to cut the stems later when making an arrangement singe them again before placing them in water.

Roses: The stalks should be well bruised to make them last longer, or split with a knife about 1 inch/2 cm up the stem.

Tulips: To allow cut tulips to drink freely and so live longer in a vase, pierce the stalk right through with a needle at half-inch/1-cm intervals from the head to the stem before putting the flowers in water.

Tulips have juicy stems and do not last as long as they should if mixed with other flowers in a vase.

A little table salt in the water will stop tulips opening fully in a vase and so make them last longer.

Wallflowers: Being bushy, wallflowers are excellent for arrangements, but if they are to last their stems should be cut short.

To intensify the colours in a flower arrangement, include a touch of white (this applies to flowers in a garden, too).

Drying flowers: A warm dry day is the best time to cut flowers for drying.

To dry flowers, cut them when in full bloom and dip the ends of the stalks in candlewax. Dry them, hanging upside down, in a gentle heat.

FOLIAGE

To preserve foliage, cut sprays and take them home before they wilt. Peel off a few inches of the bark at the stem ends and make a split in them. Place the sprays in a container into which a solution of equal parts of glycerine (cheap crude glycerine will do, or car anti-freeze liquid is equally suitable) and hot water has been poured. Shake well and mix. The stems should be well immersed. Leave the foliage in a cool dark place until the leaves become slightly greasy and wet underneath; they are then ready to be used in an arrangement. This method will preserve the foliage for many months.

PRESSED FLOWERS

When pressing flowers to make pictures, greeting cards etc., make and press a supply of daisy stalks. Daisy stalks do not become brittle and hard, and are ideal to use for other flowers.

An old telephone directory with its absorbent pages is perfect as a pressed flower retainer.

A quick way to press flowers is to iron them: place the flowers between two sheets of blotting paper or toilet tissue. Place the whole thing between newspaper, then press firmly with the iron (set to heat mark 'wool'). Next remove from the newspaper and put the blotting paper with the flowers inside a book with a weight on top. Keep in a warm place for twelve hours.

ROSES

To preserve roses for winter, select rosebuds, snip the stem ends and drop the stems into cool melted candlewax or melted sealing wax to cover the end. As soon as the wax is set, wrap each rosebud separately in aluminium foil or greaseproof paper and pack loosely in an airtight box. After sealing the box, store it in a cool place. When the roses are required, unpack them, cut off the waxed end of the stem, stand them in water overnight and they will look as if they have just bloomed.

VASES

When you want to make an arrangement of flowers in a wide-mouthed vase and you have no chicken wire, criss-cross sellotape across the mouth of the vase and slide the stems through it.

PETS

BIRD (to get back in the cage)

If you want your bird to go back to its cage when it has escaped in the room, take a feather duster and place it nearby; the bird will soon settle down cosily next to it. Then place the feather duster at the entrance of the cage. Your bird will fly willingly into its cage.

BIRD–BATHS

When putting water out for the birds in winter, (for drinks or baths), add a little sugar to the water to stop it freezing.

BIRDCAGE

Aluminium foil is good for protecting the tray of a birdcage. Do not forget to sprinkle the foil with clean sand; your bird will love it.

BUDGIE

Your budgie will not sing if it has another bird in the cage or a mirror.

CANARY

A few drops of brandy in a little water will act as a pick-me-up for a sick canary, especially if the bird is cold.

CAT

Stop your cat (or dog) digging the garden up by scattering some holly leaves over the place where they usually do it.

To keep your cat healthy dilute his milk with warm water and do not give him the cream from the top of the milk.

Cats love the smell of bleach so clean the place reserved for his necessities with it and he won't go anywhere else in the house.

A hairball in a cat's stomach can cause vomiting, bad breath, coughing and loss of appetite; this happens during the moulting season. To prevent or to cure hairballs give the cat one tablespoon of salad oil to lap once a week or add half a teaspoon of oil to its food every day.

DOG

Do not give chicken or lamb bones to your dog. They can splinter and perforate the intestines. Knuckle of beef is the best bone for a dog.

Do not feed your dog lettuce as it will give him gripe. Other grated or shredded raw vegetables, like carrots, tomatoes, cabbage etc., are very good for him.

A dog with a constipation problem will make frequent attempts to defecate. To help get rid of the problem, give the dog some liquid paraffin by mouth: four dessertspoonfuls for a large dog, and one dessertspoonful for a small dog.

For simple diarrhoea give the dog plain boiled rice flavoured with a little beef or chicken stock. Remove all other food and drink and frequently give him glucose and water in equal quantities, a small amount at a time.

Rub your dog's teeth with half a lemon, he will like it (we hope!) and it will keep his teeth clean; or clean your dog's teeth once a week with bicarbonate of soda on a wet cloth or a toothbrush to keep his teeth healthy and his breath fresh.

If your dog has a very itchy skin and doesn't stop scratching itself, sprinkle its fur with baby's talcum powder. Work the powder in with your fingertips. Repeat the treatment a few times; your dog will soon stop scratching itself.

Do not forget to put cotton wool in his ears when you give him a bath to stop the water going inside.

If your dog is licking his paws after walking in the street in the melting snow it might be because the chemical used to melt the snow in the street is burning his feet. To soothe the burning feeling wash his paws in a strong solution of warm water and bicarbonate of soda.

You can remove tangles from a dog's fur by working salad oil into the tangles.

Give your dog a dry shampoo. Warm some towels in a pre-heated oven (switch the oven off before placing the towels inside) and vigorously rub the dog. You will be surprised how your dog likes it – and how dirty the towels will be. . . .!

Add a little vinegar to the last rinse when washing your dog – it will prevent his fur tangling. If your dog has white fur a few drops of washing blue in the rinse will make his fur look whiter.

To make your dog's coat shine, spend a few minutes rubbing it all over with a piece of clean silk. (Do this after his usual brush and comb session.)

Tar on a dog's paws can be removed gently with oil of eucalyptus.

Glue a pickle jar rubber ring underneath your dog's feeding dish; it will stop the dish slipping about the floor when your pet is eating his meal.

A few handfuls of fresh pine needles under his cushion or in his dog kennel where he sleeps will keep away the fleas (if any). Renew the pine needles regularly.

To stop a fight between dogs sprinkle pepper over their heads.

Bury a few mothballs in your garden in places where your dog is not allowed to lift his leg! (For example, near sensitive plants or flowers.) He will carefully avoid these areas.

To remove a tick from a dog's fur, cover the tick with a thick coat of vaseline and wait for at least half an hour before pulling it out. Or hold the end of a burning cigarette on it. Yet another way is to soak it with methylated spirits until it lets go. Simply pulling it without using one of these methods would remove the tick's body, leaving the head firmly stuck to the dog's skin causing great discomfort.

FISH BOWL

There is a lack of oxygen in a fish bowl or a tank when too many fishes are in it, when they keep near the surface of the bowl and gulp for air, or if the water is dirty and so becomes poisonous.

FISH POND

Do not alarm your fish by noisily breaking the frozen surface of the garden pond. Instead melt it gently with boiling water.

GUINEA-PIG

Do not place two male guinea-pigs in the same cage, because they will fight all the time. Two females can live happily together.

PUPPY

Keep your new puppy happy and silent at night by placing a hot water bottle (not too hot) in his bed under the blanket and a ticking clock near his bed. He won't feel so lonely.

Or oil his paws with some oil from a sardine tin or give him some warm milk, and leave a radio playing soft music, your puppy will soon settle down.

STAINS AND CLEANING
AGENTS

STAINS ON FABRIC

Some fabrics and colours can be damaged by certain solvents or spirits, so always test a small corner of the fabric first (leave for twenty minutes).

When removing stains from fabrics, start from the edge of the stain and work towards the centre. This will prevent the stain spreading.

A simple rule for unknown stains on fabric: first rub the stain with cold water. If the stain persists, rub on a mixture of lemon juice and salt. If this has no effect, rub on bicarbonate of soda. If this also fails, dab the area with methylated spirit.

Always rinse the fabric after removing a stain, or rub it with a piece of cottonwool dampened in cold water, to remove all traces of spirit or solvent.

Liquid detergents are best to remove stains. When they are used on washable fabrics just dampen the stain, then work the pure liquid detergent well into the stain. Next wash the usual way.

When liquid detergent is used on non-washable fabrics dilute the detergent with an equal quantity of water and work it in using a very small amount. If too much is used, rinse by sponging the stain with cold water, or by using a syringe or a medicine-dropper to force the water through.

Another way for rinsing the stain is to dab it with alcohol, as it dries faster (for material not damaged by alcohol of course).

Many small stains on fabrics will disappear simply by rubbing them gently with the same fabric (hem, small end of the tie etc). Persevere.

Sponging: When the directions say to 'sponge' the stain proceed in the following manner:

Fold a clean cloth. Place the stained material over it, wrong side up if possible, so that the stain can be melted away without having to go through the material. With a moistened white fleece of cotton wool or a white cloth, gently wipe the solvent into the stain. Change the pad underneath frequently (as soon as some of the stain has been absorbed). **Do not** rub hard or the stain might spread and the surface of the fabric be damaged. Blot dry.

On fabrics likely to form a ring, sponge with a pad hardly moistened and start from the edges of the stain, going to the centre. Blot dry, place the fabric on the palm of one hand and rub over the area with the other; this will prevent a ring forming. Repeat the whole process if needed.

Rings on fast-coloured fabrics can also be removed by holding the area over some boiling water.

ACIDS
On all fabrics: First wash or sponge at once with running cold water; then dip or sponge the stain in, or with, a solution of one tablespoon of ammonia to half a pint/a quarter of a litre of cold water.

One tablespoon of bicarbonate of soda diluted in half a pint/a quarter of a litre of water can be used instead of the ammonia-water solution.

On all carpets: Proceed as above.

ADHESIVE
On all fabrics, washable and non-washable: Place a piece of cotton wool or any absorbent cloth on the right side of the stain. Then dab the wrong side with a piece of cotton wool dampened with some non-oily nail-varnish remover.

On man-made fibres: Do not use non-oily nail-varnish remover. Use pure amyl acetate (obtainable from a chemist).

On carpets: If the carpet is wool, dab the stain with non-oily nail-varnish remover. If the carpet is synthetic, or if in doubt, dab the stain with amyl acetate.

Epoxy resin (e.g. Araldite)
On fabrics: Only fresh stains can be removed. Place a piece of cotton wool or an absorbent cloth on the right side of the stain, then dab the wrong side with some cotton wool dampened with cellulose thinners or methylated spirit.

On man-made fibres: Dab the stain as above, using lighter fuel instead.

On carpet: If the carpet is wool, dab the stain with non-oily nail-varnish remover. If the carpet is synthetic, or if in doubt, dab the stain with amyl acetate.

Model-making cement
On fabrics: With a knife, carefully scrape off as much cement as possible, so as not to spread the adhesive. Then dab the stain with a piece of cotton wool dampened with acetone or some liquid stain-remover (e.g. Beaucaire).

On man-made fibres: Use some pure amyl acetate (from a chemist) to remove the stain.

On carpet: Proceed as for fabric. On synthetic, or if in doubt, dab with amyl acetate.

Copydex (Latex adhesive)
On any fabric: If the stain is still not dried, wipe it off with a damp sponge or cloth. If dry, scrape off the surface carefully with some liquid stain-remover.

On carpet: proceed as above.

ALCOHOLIC BEVERAGES – See also **Beer** and **Wine**

On fabrics: Blot spilled drinks straight away and sponge the fabric with cold water. If the stain persists, work a little liquid detergent into it, then rinse. Next sponge with some methylated or surgical spirit to remove any traces of detergent.

Another way is to rub the stain straight away with a sponge dampened in methylated or surgical spirit.

On man-made fibres: Rub the stains with a solution of methylated or surgical spirit (one tablespoon) and cold water (two tablespoons). If the stains persist, rub with an equal mixture of hydrogen peroxide and cold water.

On carpets: On a fresh stain, flush some soda from the siphon and blot well. Or sponge with cold water, blot well and shampoo if needed. On a dried stain, follow the fabric instructions above.

On synthetic carpet: Follow the instructions for man-made fibre.

On wood: When the stain is dealt with immediately, first wipe up the spilled drink, then rub the stain with a soft cloth slightly dampened with ammonia or methylated spirit. For an old stain, rub it with a paste made of cigar or cigarette ash and salad oil (or better still, linseed oil). Rub over gently until it disappears. Then wax and polish with a soft cloth. If any faint white marks are left, rub them with the raw edge of a cut Brazil nut or a walnut.

Metal polish rubbed over the stain will also remove it. Work in the direction of the grain.

Sweet sticky marks on varnished wood will disappear if rubbed gently with some used coffee grounds, slightly warm. Wipe and polish.

ALKALI

On all fabrics: First wash or sponge at once with running cold water. Then dip or sponge with some white vinegar or lemon juice. Lastly rinse or sponge wtih cold water.

On carpets: Proceed as above.

ANIMAL STAINS (Excreta, urine, vomit)

On all washable fabrics: Scrape any surface deposit. Sponge with cold water, then soak in a biological detergent or a solution of borax (one tablespoon) and warm water (one pint/½ litre) for more delicate fabrics. Leave to soak for an hour before washing.

On non-washable fabrics: Scrape any surface deposit. Blot dry with absorbent paper. Sponge with a solution of powdered borax (one tablespoon) and warm water (one pint/half a litre). Then sponge with clear water. Blot dry. Clear any remaining trace with some methylated spirit on a damp cloth.

On all carpets: Scrape any surface deposit. Blot dry with absorbent paper. Rub with a mixture of warm soapy water (one pint/half a litre) and vinegar (two tablespoons). Blot dry, then flush some soda water from the siphon. Blot dry again, and rub with a cloth dampened with ammonia. Leave to dry.

Another way to remove urine stains is to blot-dry them, and pour methylated spirit on to it. Rub well. Then pour a little more methylated spirit and dab gently. Raise the pile and leave to dry.

ANTI-PERSPIRANTS, DEODORANTS
On all fabrics: For light stains rub with an equal solution of vinegar and water.

Or wash or sponge the stains with warm water to which a little liquid detergent has been added. Rinse well with cold water.

For more persistent stains rub with methylated spirit or liquid stain-remover. Next, sponge first with ammonia, then with cold water.

Or rub it with some hydrogen peroxide. Then rinse.

On carpet: Proceed as above.

APPLE STAINS
To remove stains from your hands after peeling a large quantity of apples, just rub the stains with apple peel and then wash your hands.

BALL-POINT – See **Ink**.

BEER
On washable fabrics and table linen: For fresh stains rinse through under cold water before washing as usual.

For dried stains on table linen or white cotton, soak for a few minutes in a weak solution of warm water and bleach. Then put straight into cold water to which a few drops of ammonia have been added. Next rinse well.

Non-washable fabrics and coloured fabrics: Sponge with a solution of hydrogen peroxide (20 vol) (one tablespoon) and warm water (five tablespoons), or with a solution of vinegar (one tablespoon) and warm water (two tablespoons). Then sponge with clear water or launder.

On man-made fibres: Sponge with a solution of borax (one tablespoon) and warm water (one tea cup). Launder, or sponge with clear water.

On all carpets: Treat fresh stains with a spray from the soda siphon. Then blot well. But fresh stains should respond very well to simple clear, warm water if there is no siphon. Treat old stains by rubbing them with methylated spirit or a solution of hydrogen peroxide (one tablespoon) (20 vol) and water (four tablespoons). Next sponge with warm water to which a few drops of ammonia have been added.

On wood: See **Alcohol**.

BEESWAX
On all fabrics: Dab the stain with turpentine, soaking it well. Then rinse well and wash, or sponge well.

Man-made fibres: Dab the stains with a solution of methylated or surgical spirit (one tablespoon) and cold water (two tablespoons) rinse well and wash.

On carpets: For wool carpet proceed as for fabric. For synthetic carpet, or if in any doubt, proceed as for man-made fibres. Sponge well with clear water to finish.

BEETROOT
On all washable fabrics: Follow the directions for *Fruits, fruit juices*, but sprinkle some powdered borax over the stain before pouring the boiling water.

Another way to remove fresh beetroot stains is: first, rinse out under cold running water; then dab the stain with methylated spirit; next, wash in the usual way.

For coloured fabric: Soak in a solution of borax (two tablespoons) and warm water (two pints/one litre) until the stain disappears. Then launder.

On non-washable fabrics: Follow the directions for *Fruits, fruit juices* on non-washable fabric.

On all carpets: For fresh stains first blot up any liquid with a sponge or paper towel. Then sponge the area with lukewarm water or spray it with the soda siphon, leave for a minute, then blot up the liquid.

For old stains work undiluted liquid detergent into them. Then rinse well; or dab the stain with an equal mixture of water and methylated spirit; or soak the stain with an equal mixture of water and hydrogen peroxide (20 vol). Rinse well.

BERRIES, Blackberry, blackcurrants etc. – See **Fruits, Fruit juices**

BIRD DROPPINGS

On all washable fabrics: A good soaking in some biological detergent before washing should remove the stain. If the stain persists, dab with hydrogen peroxide (20 vol), (one tablespoon) diluted in water (four tablespoons). White cotton can be soaked in a solution of bleach (two tablespoons) and warm water (one gallon/four litres).

Non-washable fabrics: First wipe or brush any deposit, then sponge with a mixture of ammonia (one tablespoon) and water (one tea-cup). Next sponge with white vinegar and rinse.

On carpets: Follow the non-washable fabrics directions.

On canvas garden furniture: Wipe or brush any deposit, then rub the stain over with household soap and sprinkle with washing soda. Leave for half an hour. Rinse well. Repeat if necessary.

BLOOD

On washable fabrics: Fresh bloodstains should always be cleaned with cold water, as hot water makes the mark permanent. Soak in cool water for a while and then wash in warm soapy water. If the stain still persists, soak the material in a solution of warm water (one gallon/four litres) and bleach (two tablespoons) or soak the stained area in a solution of water (seven tablespoons), ammonia (half a tablespoon) and hydrogen peroxide (one tablespoon) (20 vol). Rinse well.

On non-washable fabrics: Sponge with a mixture of cold water (half a pint/a quarter of a litre) and ammonia (one teaspoon). Rinse and blot well.

For dried stains place a clean pad underneath the stain and sponge lightly with hydrogen peroxide or ammonia. Rinse well and blot.

Another way is to spray some starch on the stain and leave it on for a few hours. Then brush it off and wipe it with warm soapy water. Rinse well. If any brown mark is left, dab some hydrogen peroxide (20 vol) over it until it disappears. Rinse well again.

On silk, satin or crêpe de chine: Make a thick paste of starch or talcum powder and water, or spray some starch over the stain. Leave it to dry completely. Brush the starch off with a soft brush. The stain will have disappeared and no harm will have been done to the fabric.

A paste made of a crushed aspirin tablet and water instead of starch or talcum powder will also work. Leave long enough for the paste to dry.

On all carpets: Sponge the fresh stain immediately with cold water, or better still, flush some soda water from the siphon over it. Blot well afterwards and shampoo if needed.

Cover dried stains with a paste made of starch or talcum powder and then brush or vacuum clean. Repeat if necessary.

On wood: Sand the stained area with some very fine steel wool (0000 grade). Then rub with a cloth or apply some hydrogen peroxide (20 vol) with a fine brush until the stain disappears.

BOTTLED SAUCES (ketchup, HP, etc.)

On washable fabrics: Rinse the stain immediately under cold running water. Work some liquid detergent into the stain. Then rinse. If any traces remain, soak in a biological washing powder solution for a while. Then launder in the usual way. *Do not* soak silk or wool in biological detergent; dab any remaining traces with diluted methylated or surgical spirit (one part) and water (two parts). Rinse well.

Dried stains can be softened first with an equal solution of glycerine and warm water. Leave for an hour before treating with one of the above methods.

On non-washable fabrics and man-made fibres: First, sponge the stain with cold water; then work some liquid detergent into the stain and rinse it well; next wipe with methylated or surgical spirit or ammonia on a damp sponge. Rinse. If any traces remain, dab the stain with an equal solution of hydrogen peroxide (20 vol) and water. Rinse.

On all carpets: Scrape the excess and wipe with a damp cloth. Sponge with some warm water, then blot. Next sponge with a solution of water (half a pint/a quarter of a litre), liquid detergent (one tablespoon) and white vinegar (two tablespoons). Rinse and blot. Raise the damp pile. Leave to dry, or dry with a hair-dryer. If any traces remain, wipe with some methylated or surgical spirit. Rinse.

BRANDY – Follow instructions for **Alcoholic beverages**.

BUTTER – Follow instructions for **Grease, oils, fats**

CANDLE WAX

On all fabrics: First remove as much as possible with the blade of a blunt knife, or if possible put the garment in the freezer for an hour. You can then break the frozen pieces off. Next place the stain between two sheets of blotting paper and press with a warm iron, moving the paper frequently until no more grease appears on it. Sponge any remaining traces with some dry-cleaning fluid, some methylated or white spirit (but not on acetate fabric). Sponge with clear water.

For heavy fabrics another method is to stretch the stained fabric over a container and pour boiling water through the stain. Dry, and remove any remaining marks with some dry-cleaning fluid, methylated or white spirit.

On all carpets: Scrape off the wax as much as you can with a spoon. Then place a sheet of blotting paper or a few layers of tissue paper over the stain. Apply the pointed end only of a warm iron. Keep moving the paper frequently until no more grease appears on it. Remove any remaining traces with some dry-cleaning fluid, methylated or white spirit on a soft dry cloth. Sponge with clear water.

On polished wood: Hold a plastic bag with some ice cubes in it over the wax to harden it. Next, with a plastic spatula, your fingernail or a stiff card, scrape away as much of the wax as you can. Then wash off any remaining film with some warm soapy water to which a little vinegar has been added. Dry and polish. If any traces remain, rub gently with lighter fuel. Dry and polish.

Wallpaper: Do not scrape the wax for fear of tearing the wallpaper. Place a sheet of blotting paper over the stain and press with a warm iron, moving the paper frequently. Remove any remaining traces by covering the stain with a paste made of french chalk or talcum powder and methylated spirit. Leave to dry. Brush off.

On vinyl wall-covering: Leave the wax to harden entirely before lifting it off with your fingernail, a plastic spatula or a thick card. Remove any remaining colour from the wax by dabbing lightly with methylated spirit or surgical spirit.

CAR OIL – Follow instructions for **Grease, oils, fats**

CAR POLISH
On all fabrics: Remove with a dry-cleaning fluid or methylated spirit. Next sponge with some liquid detergent, then rinse.

CARAMEL
On all fabrics: Sponge with cool water and a little detergent. Rinse. Let it dry. If any grease traces remain, sponge with a solution of ammonia or hydrogen peroxide (20 vol) or methylated spirit and water in equal quantities.

CARBON PAPER
On washable fabrics: Use undiluted liquid detergent and work it into the stain. Rinse well. If any traces remain, apply a few drops of ammonia or methylated spirit. Rinse well. Repeat if needed.

Non-washable fabrics and man-made fibres: Dab the stain with methylated or surgical spirit (one part) and water (two parts). If any traces remain, rub with a little liquid detergent and rinse. Repeat if needed.
On carpets: On wool carpet use the method for washable fabrics. On synthetic, or if in doubt, use the man-made fibres method.

CARROT JUICE – Follow instructions for Grass

CAT'S PUDDLE – See Animal stains

CHERRIES – See Fruits, Fruit juices

CHEWING GUM
On all fabrics: Place the garment in the freezer for an hour; the chewing gum will then crack and can be picked off easily. Treat any remaining traces with methylated spirit or white spirit. If it cannot be put in the freezer, hold a plastic bag with a few ice cubes in it over the chewing gum to harden it, then pick it off.

Another method is to saturate the stain with a liquid stain-remover. Repeat if needed. Sponge with cold water.

Yet another method is to hold the back of the stained fabric over the steam from a kettle. The gum will become soft and can be pulled off easily by hand or with tweezers.
On all carpets: Use one of the above methods.
On hair: Rub a plastic bag with some ice cubes in it over the gum until it becomes hard and can be picked off easily.

Another effective method is to rub the gum with some paintbrush cleaning solvent or peanut butter.
On vinyl upholstery: Scrape as much as possible. Then rub with some lighter fuel or kerosene.

CHOCOLATE
On washable fabrics: Soak and wash in a biological detergent. If any of the stain remains, stretch the strained fabric over a container, sprinkle the stain with powdered borax and pour boiling water through the stain. Rinse or dab any remaining stain with a liquid stain-remover.
On non-washable fabrics and man-made fibres: Sponge with lukewarm water, then with a solution of powdered borax (one teaspoon) and warm water (one teacup). Rinse and blot dry. Clear any remaining traces with a pad of cotton wool which has been first dampened with water then squeezed and dipped in methylated or surgical spirit or ammonia.
On non-washable fabric: Old stains should be loosened first by dabbing an equal solution of glycerine and warm water over the stain. Leave it for at least one hour. Rub with a sponge wrung out in warm water. Blot dry.
On all carpets: Blot up as much as possible. Flush some soda from a siphon

over the stain. Blot up when dry, remove any remaining traces with some liquid stain-remover or some methylated or surgical spirit. Shampoo if needed.

Or blot the stain with absorbent paper first. Then dab with an equal mixture of white vinegar and methylated spirit. Sponge with clear water. Blot dry.

CHUTNEY
On all washable fabrics: Sponge the stain with clear water. Then launder.

Old stains will need to be soaked in a borax (one tablespoon) and warm water (one pint/half a litre) solution for one hour before laundering, or soaked in some biological detergent for an hour before laundering. This treatment is for stronger fabrics.
On non-washable fabrics: Scrape any surface deposit. Sponge the stain with clear water. Rub with a pad of cotton wool which has been first dampened in water, then squeezed and dipped in methylated spirit or ammonia.
On all carpets: Scrape off any surface deposit. Sponge with warm water. Wash with carpet shampoo or a liquid detergent. Blot off. Then dab with some methylated spirit if any coloured stain remains.

COCA-COLA
On all fabrics: Sponge with cold water. Rub with a little liquid detergent. Rinse well. If any traces remain, treat with a solution of methylated spirit (two tablespoons) and white vinegar (one teaspoon). Rinse well.

COCOA – Follow instructions for **Chocolate**

COD LIVER OIL
On all washable fabrics: Treat the stain immediately before it dries. Sponge the stain with some liquid stain-remover or methylated or surgical spirit. Then wash in the usual way.

Dried stains are difficult to remove. First remove as much as you can with some liquid stain-remover. Then loosen any remaining traces with a solution of an equal quantity of glycerine and warm water. Leave for at least one hour. Rinse and wash in the usual way. Bleach stubborn marks by dabbing them with a solution of hydrogen peroxide (20 vol) (one tablespoon) and cold water (four tablespoons). Rinse.
On non-washable fabrics: Sponge the stain with liquid stain-remover.
On woollen garments: Put liquid detergent on the fresh stain. Rub lightly between the hands. Rinse well and wash as usual.
On all carpets: Blot the excess and sponge with a liquid stain-remover. Then wash with a dry-foam carpet shampoo. If a lot of cod liver oil has been spilled, it may be necessary to repeat this treatment after a few days.

COFFEE – Follow instructions for **Chocolate**
Stain inside coffee-pots or tea-pots/porcelain, earthenware. Rub it with salt or bicarbonate of soda.

For a badly stained tea-pot put one heaped teaspoon of washing soda into the pot and fill it up with warm water. Leave to soak for at least twelve hours before emptying and rinsing.

Another efficient way is to place some effervescent tablets used for cleaning dentures into the stained pot. Fill it up with boiling water and leave to cool. Rinse well.

A bleach solution ($\frac{1}{2}$ teacup of bleach to 1 pint/$\frac{1}{2}$ litre of water) will also clean the inside of a china or earthenware tea-pot.

On chromium: To take the tannin out of your chromium tea-or coffee-pot, rub it with a cloth dampened with vinegar and dipped in salt. Rinse well, as salt left on chromium will damage it after a while.

On glass: To clean a glass coffee-pot, first wet the inside of the pot, sprinkle it with salt, then place 10–20 ice cubes in the pot and swirl them around for a few minutes. Rinse and dry.

On marble: For slight drink stains (coffee, tea, fruit juice) on a marble table-top, use pumice powder or powdered chalk, rubbing it firmly over with a strong cloth. Rinse and dry.

On plastic: Coffee or tea stains on plastic will disappear if rubbed with nail-polish remover.

CORRECTION FLUID (Tippex)

On fabrics: Dab the stain with acetone or nail-varnish remover.

On man-made fibres: Dab the stain with amyl acetate (obtainable from a chemist).

On carpets: Follow the above instructions. On synthetic carpet, or if in doubt, follow man-made fibres instructions.

COSMETICS (all types)

On washable fabrics: Work liquid detergent into the stain. Rinse well. Repeat if needed. Wash in the usual way – or blot the stain, then soak for a few minutes in a solution of ammonia (one tablespoon) and warm water (one pint/half a litre). Rinse and wash.

Treat dried stain before washing by dabbing it with an equal solution of glycerine and warm water. Leave for an hour. Wash in the usual way.

On non-washable fabrics: Blot up any excess. Sponge with liquid stain-remover – eucalyptus oil, ether or methylated spirit. For man-made fibres dilute the methylated spirit with an equal proportion of water. If any traces remain, work some powdered detergent into them. Rinse and blot dry.

On silk: Blot up any excess. Rub some French chalk or talcum powder into the stain. Leave for two to three hours. Brush off. If any traces remain, spray with an aerosol stain-remover.

On all carpets: Follow the instructions for non-washable fabrics.

On wood: For lipstick on light wood, rub the stain with toothpaste.

COUGH MIXTURE – See Medicines.

CRAYON
On fabrics: Follow the directions for **Cosmetics**.
On wallpapers: First make a test on a hidden corner. Sponge gently with some fluid stain-remover. Leave to dry. Repeat if needed. If a ring appears after the cleaning fluid has dried, cover it with a paste made of French chalk or talcum powder with some liquid stain-remover. Leave to dry. Brush off.

Another way is to rub the stain with some bicarbonate of soda on a damp cloth.
On vinyl wallpapers: Rub the stain with some silver polish.
On lino and vinyl floors: Rub with silver polish.

CREAM SAUCE
On all washable fabrics: Follow instructions for **Grease, oils, fats**.
On non-washable fabrics: Scrape the excess. Sponge with warm water. Leave to dry, then sponge with a fluid stain-remover.
On all carpets: Follow the treatment for non-washable fabrics. Then wash with a dry-foam carpet shampoo.

CREAM SOUP – Follow **Cream Sauce** directions.

CREOSOTE
On all washable fabrics: First dab the stain with eucalyptus oil or liquid lighter fuel. Then wash as usual.

Dried stains should be loosened up before washing by rubbing in an equal solution of glycerine and warm water. Leave on for at least one hour before washing.
Non-washable fabrics: It is advisable to send the garment to a professional cleaner.

CURRY
On all washable fabrics: On white material the fresh stains should be soaked for at least an hour in an equal solution of methylated spirit and water or ammonia and water, before being laundered in a biological detergent.

Another method is to rinse the stain in lukewarm water, then rub an equal solution of glycerine and water into the stain. Leave for at least an hour. Rinse, then soak the garment for another hour in some biological detergent before washing. If any traces remain dab the stain with some diluted hydrogen peroxide (20 vol) (one tablespoon) and water (four tablespoons).
On non-washable fabrics: Dab the stains with some ammonia or methylated spirit on a piece of cotton wool. Test coloured material first to make sure the alcohol does not affect the colour.
On man-made fibres: Dab the stain with an equal solution of methylated spirit or ammonia and water. Rinse.
On carpets: Blot up, then rub the stain with some methylated spirit or ammonia. Test the colour first in an inconspicuous place.

Another method is to blot up, then dab the stain with a solution of borax (one tablespoon) and warm water (one pint/half a litre). If any traces remain, work some glycerine into the stain. Leave for fifteen minutes. Sponge with warm water. Blot dry. Restore the pile by combing it with a fine, clean comb.

CYCLE OIL – Follow instructions for **Grease, oils, fats**.

DANDELION – Follow instructions for **Grass**.

DEODORANTS – Follow instructions for **Anti-perspirants**

DRINKS – Follow instructions for **Alcoholic beverages** or individual entries

DUPLICATING INK AND POWDER – See **Ink**.

DYES

On washable fabrics: Rinse immediately under cold water. Then work undiluted liquid detergent into the stain, then rinse. Repeat if needed and dab with some ammonia. Rinse and sponge with some methylated spirit.

For natural fibres (white or fast dye) soak the stained fabric in a solution of water (1 litre/2 pints) and bleach (4 tablespoons). Stir well before immersing the fabric.

On silk and wool: Dab or soak with, or in, a solution of hydrogen peroxide (20 vol) (one tablespoon) and cold water (five tablespoons). Rinse well and wash.

On non-washable fabrics: Sponge with a solution of methylated spirit (two tablespoons) and ammonia (one teaspoon).

On man-made fibres: Follow the washable fabrics instructions. If any traces remain after washing, dab with a solution of methylated spirit (one tablespoon) and water (two tablespoons).

EGG

On all washable fabrics: Scrape off any deposit. Then wipe the stain with cold salted water. Then wash in the usual way. Do not use hot water to wipe the stain as it would set it.

Soak a dry stain in a biological detergent before washing.

On non-washable fabrics: Scrape off any deposit. Sponge the stain with some cold salted water. Rinse with clear, cold water. Leave to dry, or dry with the hair-dryer. If any traces remain, sponge with some liquid stain-remover.

On all carpets: Scrape any deposit. Sponge with some liquid stain-remover. Then shampoo if needed.

Egg stains on cutlery: Egg stains on cutlery can be removed by soaking the spoon or fork in the water the egg has been boiled in.

Electrical appliances
Nail-polish remover or liquid lighter fuel will remove plastic which has melted and stuck to electrical appliances. (Do not forget to unplug first.)

EMBROIDERY TRANSFER
On all fabrics: Dab gently with methylated spirit before washing.
Man-made fibres: Dab gently with an equal solution of methylated spirit and water, then wash.

ENGINE OIL – Follow instructions for **Grease, oils, fats**.

EPOXY RESIN – See **Adhesives**.

EYE MAKE-UP – Follow **Cosmetics** instructions.

EYEBROW PENCIL
On all fabrics: Rub with some fluid stain-remover on a cotton-bud or some cotton wool wrapped round an orange stick. Then dab with ammonia. Next sponge with water.

FAT – Follow instructions for **Grease, oils, fats**.

FELT-TIP PEN – See **Ink**.

FISH OIL – Follow **Cod liver oil** instructions.

FLOWER STAINS – Follow **Grass** instructions.

FLY PAPER
Washable fabrics: Launder.
On non-washable fabrics: Wipe with fluid stain-remover.

FLY STAINS
On all fabrics: Sponge with some methylated spirit or some liquid stain-remover.
Man-made fibres: Sponge with an equal solution of methylated spirit and cold water. Or dab with some stain-remover.
On light shades: Rub inside and outside with a sponge squeezed in some warm biological detergent solution. Sponge with clear water. Blot well and leave to dry away from heat.

FOLIAGE – Follow **Grass** instructions.

FOOD COLOURING
On all fabrics: Sponge fresh stains immediately with cool water. Then work some undiluted liquid detergent into the stain and rinse. Next sponge with some methylated spirit.

On man-made fibres: Dilute the methylated spirit (one part) with water (two parts). If any traces remain, dab with some hydrogen peroxide (20 vol). Then rinse.
On all carpets: Follow the above instructions.

FOUNDATION CREAM – Follow **Cosmetics** instructions.

FOUNTAIN PEN INK – See **Ink**.

FRENCH POLISH (Shellac)
On all fabrics: Dab with methylated spirit.
On man-made fibres: Dilute the methylated spirit in equal quantities of water.
On all carpets: Follow the above instructions.

FRUITS, FRUIT JUICES
On all washable fabrics: Do not use soap and water or it will set the stain. Rinse with cold water, then stretch the stained fabric over a container and pour boiling water through the stain. If any traces remain, rub with some ammonia followed by diluted hydrogen peroxide (20 vol) (one part hydrogen peroxide, five parts water), or work an equal solution of glycerine and warm water into the stain. Leave for at least an hour and wash in the usual way.

If the above method of stretching the fabric over a container is not possible, then rinse with cold water, work some liquid detergent into the stain, leave the garment to soak for a few hours and then wash.

If the stain is old, cover it with powdered borax before pouring boiling water; or soften the stain first with an equal solution of glycerine and warm water. Leave for at least an hour. Then treat with boiling water.
On non-washable fabric: Sponge with cold water, work some liquid detergent into the stain and rinse. If any traces remain, dab with ammonia and then with some diluted hydrogen peroxide (20 vol) (one part hydrogen peroxide, five parts water). Rinse and blot dry.

Another method is to dab the stain with white vinegar, and sponge with cold water. Another method is to dab the stain with cold water and then cover with bicarbonate of soda. Leave for fifteen minutes. Brush off and leave it to dry.
On all carpets: Blot up with paper towel, then shampoo. If any traces remain, dab with some methylated spirit.
On your hands: To remove stains from your hands after peeling a large quantity of apples, just rub the stains with apple peel and then wash your hands.
On marble: See under **Coffee**.

FURNITURE POLISH – Follow instructions for **Grease, oils, fats**.

GIN – Follow **Alcoholic beverages** instructions.

GLUE (animal and fish glues – for any other glue, see **Adhesives**)
On all fabrics: Soak or dab the stain with warm white vinegar. Rinse and wash in the usual way, or rinse and blot dry or dry with a hair-dryer.

Another method is to sponge with cold water and treat with ammonia. Rinse and blot dry or dry with a hair-dryer.
On all carpets: Follow the above methods, or dab the stain with some non-oily nail-varnish remover.

GRAPE – Follow instructions for **Fruits, fruit juices**.

GRASS
On all washable fabrics: Dab some methylated spirit on the stain, then rinse and wash in the usual way.

Another way is to work some liquid detergent into the stain. Then rinse. If any traces remain, treat with some hydrogen peroxide (20 vol), then rinse.
On non-washable fibres: Sponge with diluted methylated spirit (one part methylated spirit, two parts water). Test colours first on an inconspicuous area of the garment.
On all carpets: Foliage or flower stains will be removed if dabbed with methylated spirit.

GRAVY
On all washable fabrics: Soak in cold water for half an hour, then wash in the usual way. If any traces remain, treat with a stain-remover or a dry stain-remover.

Dried stains on table linen should be soaked in a biological detergent solution (follow instructions on the packet). Then wash.
On non-washable fabrics: Sponge with cold water, then sponge with some liquid stain-remover.
On all carpets: Scrape and blot up any excess. Treat with some liquid stain-remover. Then shampoo.

GREASE, OILS, FATS
Eucalyptus oil will remove grease spots on any fabric, even the most delicate, without leaving any traces. Sponge lightly with water.
On all washable fabrics: First treat with some dry-cleaning fluid or methylated spirit. Then wash in warm soapy water.

Or rub the stain with some dry household soap or some pure liquid detergent before washing. If any traces remain after laundering, rub with some dry-cleaning fluid, or methylated spirit, surgical spirit or ammonia.
On non-washable fabrics: If the stain is fresh, spread a layer of talcum powder over it and gently press with your fingers. When the talcum becomes caked, brush it off. Then spread another layer and leave it overnight. Or spray with a dry-clean stain-remover before leaving overnight.

A quicker way is to place blotting paper underneath the stain, sprinkle the stain with talcum powder, cover it with another sheet of blotting paper, then press with a hot iron. Do not use this method for velvet.

On velvet: Drop a little turpentine over the stain, then rub with a soft cloth until dry. Repeat if needed, then brush the pile well and air it for a while.

On silk: A small, fresh stain can be removed if gently rubbed with a piece of the same fabric (the hem of dress or blouse, the narrow end of a tie). Persevere as this takes time. The soft part of a piece of bread rubbed over the stain is also good, or rub a lump of magnesia (powdered magnesia and water) over the stain. Leave to dry and then brush off. For older stains use the non-washable fabrics method above.

On all carpets: Follow the non-washable fabric instructions. Shampooing might be necessary afterwards.

On leather: Rub the stain with dry-cleaning fluid, or cover the stain with some rubber adhesive, e.g. bicycle puncture repair adhesive. Leave for at least twenty-four hours, then roll it off under your fingers. On light-coloured leather, test the rubber adhesive over a small surface first, as it may stain. Polish and buff. Another way is to make a paste with some pounded chalk and methylated spirit. Apply to the stain, leave to dry and then brush off.

Yet another method is to cover the stain with some white of egg. Leave it to dry in the sun, then brush it off.

On vinyl upholstery: Remove immediately with lighter fuel or turpentine to prevent a permanent stain,

On suede: Rub the stain lightly with liquid lighter fluid.

On suede shoes: Grease or oil on suede can be difficult to remove. Cover the stain with a paste made of cleaning fluid and salt and leave for a few hours. Repeat if the stain is stubborn.

On wallpaper: Spray or paste the stain with starch or corn starch. Leave to dry, then brush off. Repeat if needed.

Or place some blotting paper over the stain and press with a warm iron. If any marks remain, apply a paste made of talcum powder and methylated spirit. Leave to dry, then brush of.

Another way is to make a thick paste with talcum powder and a little liquid soap. Cover the stain and leave to dry. Then brush off.

On tile floors: To remove very dirty dark grease marks on floors, first scrape as much as possible with a knife, then rub some fat (butter, lard, salad oil) into the stain to soften it. Rub with methylated spirit or paraffin or white spirit. Lastly wash with warm soapy water.

On wooden floors: Dab the stain with methylated spirit. Next coat with talcum powder, cover with some blotting paper and press with a warm iron. If the stain is old, repeating the operation might be necessary.

On wood: Sprinkle salt as soon as the stain appears, to prevent the grease sinking into the wood.

Thickly coat the stain with some talcum powder or fuller's earth. Cover it with some blotting paper or many layers of tissue paper, then press with a warm iron. Move the paper in such a way that there is always some clean part over the stain and use large enough paper not to touch the wood with the iron. Repeat until the heat has drawn all the grease out of the wood, on to the paper.

Another method is to rub the stain first with turpentine for a few seconds. Next cover with talcum powder. Then take a hot iron and hold it over the stain as near as possible without touching it, for a few minutes. Wipe away the talcum powder. Repeat if needed. If not, wax and buff.

On polished wood: First rub the stain with some hot milk. Wait a few minutes, then rub with a soft cloth dampened in a little vegetable oil or, even better, linseed oil. Then wash and buff.

On oak: Rub the stain with beer.

On marble: The stain is dark grey in the centre, getting lighter around the edges. To remove it apply over the stain a thick paste made of whiting (Spanish white is obtainable from hardware stores) or powdered chalk and benzine or acetone, methylated spirit, white spirit or lighter fuel. Cover with a plastic film to hold in the moisture, then leave until it starts getting dry. Rinse and repeat if needed. If no whiting or chalk is available, use a piece of blotting paper.

On paper: First dab the stain with ether, then place the stained paper immediately between two sheets of blotting paper. Leave to dry.

On stone : See *Stone.*

On wicker: Grease stains on wicker will be removed if rubbed with methylated spirit.

HAIR DYE

On all washable fabrics: Treat immediately, as most hair dye will be difficult to remove when dried. First sponge, then work liquid detergent into the stain; next dab with white vinegar, then more liquid detergent before washing in the usual way.

On non-washable fabrics: Sponge off any excess, then dab with some methylated spirit followed by hydrogen peroxide diluted in an equal part of water. Blot dry.

HAIR OIL

On wallpaper: Follow instructions for **Grease, oils, fats** on wallpaper.

On vinyl: First wash with warm, soapy water. If any traces remain, rub gently with white spirit.

On fabric-covered headboards: Rub gently with some liquid stain-remover.

On wooden board: Wipe with a cloth moistened with liquid stain-remover or white spirit. Then polish.

HAIR LACQUER

On all fabrics: Dab first with some amyl acetate (from a chemist), then with some methylated or surgical spirit.

On a mirror: Rub with a soft cloth dampened with methylated spirit.

HAND CREAM
On all washable fabrics: Rub in some liquid detergent, then rinse or wash in the usual way.
Non-washable fabrics: Treat with a stain-remover.

HONEY
On all washable fabrics: Sponge with cold water, rub in some liquid detergent, then rinse.
On non-washable fabrics: Sponge lightly with cold water, then sponge with some hydrogen peroxide (20 vol). Then wipe with a cloth wrung out in cold water.
On all carpets: Wipe with cold water first, then shampoo.

ICE-CREAM
On all washable fabrics: Scrape and wipe off excess, then soak in a warm biological detergent. If any grease traces remain, treat with a liquid stain-remover. For final traces use hydrogen peroxide (20 vol). Rinse.
On silk and wool: Do not soak. Sponge the stain with a solution of borax (one teaspoon) and warm water (half a pint/a quarter of a litre). Next wash as usual. Treat any remaining grease traces with liquid stain-remover. For final traces use hydrogen peroxide (20 vol) (one part) diluted in water (two parts).
On non-washable fabrics: Scrape and wipe the excess. Sponge with luke-warm water, leave to dry. Remove any remaining stain with a liquid stain-remover. For final traces use some hydrogen peroxide (20 vol) (one part) diluted in water (two parts).
On all carpets: Scrape and wipe off any surface deposit, then shampoo. Treat any remaining stain with a liquid stain-remover.

INK
Ball-point ink
On fabrics: Dab with methylated spirit on a cotton wool bud. Rinse. Wash the fabric if possible. Seek professional treatment for delicate fabrics.
On polyester (dacron, diolene, linelle, terylene, trevira): Spray some hair lacquer generously on the stain. Leave for a minute, then rub well with a clean cloth. Repeat if necessary.
On all carpets: Dab with methylated spirit. Rinse and blot dry. On all synthetic carpets spray the stain generously with some hair lacquer. Leave to dry. Then brush lightly with a soft brush and a solution of water and white vinegar in equal quantities. Blot dry. Raise the nap.
On leather: Dab the stain with some methylated spirit or an 'EFFLAX' pen used by schoolchildren.
On suede: Rub the stain with some fine sandpaper or a typewriter-ink eraser.
On wall covering and vinyl surfaces: Do not wait as the stain would become permanent. Brush the mark with a soft nailbrush or a toothbrush and some warm soapy water.
On oilcloth: Rub the stain with a solution of vinegar and methylated spirit in equal proportions.

Duplicating ink
On all fabrics: Dab with white spirit. Next rub in some liquid detergent or neat washing-up liquid. Rinse. Repeat if needed. Wash if possible.

Duplicating powder
On all washable fabrics: Brush with a soft brush or vacuum. If any stain remains, wash in lukewarm soapy water. Do not use hot water or any solvent.
On non-washable fabrics: Brush off with a soft brush or vacuum. If any stain remains, seek professional advice.
On all carpets: Follow the non-washable instructions above.

Felt-tip ink
On all fabrics: Dab the stain with methylated spirit on a cotton wool bud. (Do not use on acetate fabric and triacetate.) Then rinse or wash if possible.
Another way is to work some glycerine into the stain before washing in the usual way. If any stain remains, sponge with some methylated spirit. For acetate and triacetate use an equal part of methylated spirit and water.
On all carpets: Follow the above instructions.
On wall coverings and Vinyl surfaces: Rub with some neat washing-up liquid, then rinse. Or dab with methylated spirit or lighter fuel.

Fountain-pen ink
On all washable fabrics: Rub the stain off under cold water as much as you can. Next stretch the stained fabric over a bowl, cover the stain with a good layer of salt and pour the juice of a lemon over it. Leave for at least two hours. Then launder.
Another way is first to blot the stain. Next soak it in some lukewarm salted milk until the stain disappears. Then wash.
On linen: Cover the stain with some tomato juice or a ripe tomato until the stain disappears. Then wash in lukewarm mild detergent solution.
Another method is to spread freshly made mustard over the stain. Leave for half an hour. Rinse and wash.
On wool: Place a pad underneath the stain and rub the spot with turpentine.
On non-washable fabrics: Blot up the stain. Dab the stain with a solution of hydrogen peroxide (20 vol) in equal proportions with water or ammonia (one tablespoon) and water (half a pint/a quarter of a litre).
Another way is to blot up the stain, then sprinkle with some talcum powder, removing the powder as soon as it is stained; repeat until the powder remains clear. Next make a paste wtih the talcum powder and some methylated or white spirit. Cover the stain and leave to dry. Brush it off. Repeat as many times as necessary.
On silk and wool: Stretch the stained area over a small container and put a drop of turpentine on the stain. Repeat from time to time until the ink disappears.
On all carpets: On fresh stains use the talcum powder method as above. Or

flush the stain with soda water from a siphon, then blot with some absorbent paper. Next sponge with warm water and blot again. Dry-foam shampoo the stained area and blot dry. Repeat if needed. If any traces remain, sponge with liquid stain-remover or methylated or white spirit.

Another method is first to blot up the stains as much as possible and then rub plenty of warm milk into it. Blot again then sponge with warm water to which a little ammonia has been added. Blot dry. Repeat if needed, and shampoo.

Old stains will respond if sprinkled with salt and rubbed with half a lemon. Or pour some lemon juice over it and rub with a cloth. Shampoo. Or rub the old stain with some methylated or surgical spirit. Shampoo.

Ink on your fingers: A little tomato sauce will remove it. Also toothpaste rubbed in with a soft brush.

Ink on paper: Place a blotting paper underneath the stain and pour a few drops of hydrogen peroxide over it. Move the blotting paper a little to get a dry part under the stain, then dab the stain with a damp piece of cotton wool to rinse it. Next place the wet paper between two layers of blotting paper to dry it.

Ink on silver: To remove ink-stains from silver, make a paste with some chloride of lime (from a chemist) and water. Rub the paste over the stain with a soft cloth until the stain disappears. Wipe the silver with a damp cloth (or wash if possible), dry and polish in the usual way.

On wood: See **Red ink**.

Indian ink
On marble: See **Marble**, p. 58
On all fabrics: Dab the stain with some liquid stain-remover followed by some methylated spirit (dilute the methylated spirit for man-made fibres: one part of methylated spirit to two parts water). Then work a little liquid detergent into the stain. Sponge and blot dry.
On all carpets: Follow the above directions.

Marking ink
On all fabrics: Treat at once or it is practically impossible to remove. Dab with a liquid stain-remover. Repeat several times.
On all carpets: Follow the above instructions.

Printing ink
On all fabrics: Dab with methylated spirit (dilute the methylated spirits for man-made fibres (one part methylated spirits/two parts water). Next work some liquid detergent or washing-up liquid into the stain, then rinse.
On all carpets: Follow the above directions.

Red ink
Red ink is more difficult to remove, but try rubbing the stain with a paste made of borax and water. Rub any remaining traces with methylated or

surgical spirit. Shampoo.

On lino/rubber/vinyl floors: Cover the stain for a few minutes with a cloth dampened in methylated spirit or white spirit. Then wipe with a soft cloth dampened with ammonia. Do not use ammonia on lino.

Another way is to cover the stain with a cloth dampened in hydrogen peroxide (20 vol) and leave it on until the stain disappears.

On leather: Rub some lemon juice over the stain. It will take some of the colour away, so use shoe polish to bring the colour back.

On wood: Rub the stains with a cloth dampened in vinegar and methylated spirit in equal quantities.

Another method is to apply a solution of oxalic acid (chemist) (one tablespoon) and warm water (one teacup) over the stain with a brush. Wipe with a damp cloth, blot dry and polish.

Old stains are very difficult to remove. Dab the stain with a piece of cotton wool or a cotton wool bud and some household bleach. Then blot up with some absorbent paper. Repeat as many times as necessary, blotting up each time.

Another method is to rub the stain with some powdered pumice or rotten stone (from an ironmonger) mixed to a paste with some linseed oil. Rub in the direction of the grain. Then wipe with some linseed oil. Repeat if needed, then polish.

On marble: See under '**Fountain-pen ink**'.

On silver: Rub the stain with some chloride of lime (from a chemist) mixed with water to a thick paste. (See also **Fountain-pen ink**.)

On wallpaper: Blot up the stain immediately and carefully, so as not to spread it, put some talcum powder or French chalk or fuller's earth on a clean cloth and dab the stain with it. Brush off the absorbent powder as soon as it absorbs the ink and apply some more. Next make a paste with hydrogen peroxide (20 vol) and some talcum powder, French chalk or fuller's earth. Cover the remaining stain with it. Leave to dry before brushing it off. This might take some of the colour too.

Typewriter ribbon

On all fabrics: Dab with methylated spirit (dilute the meths with its equal quantity of water for man-made fibres) or a liquid stain-remover. Next work some liquid detergent to which a drop or two of ammonia has been added into the stain. Rinse. If any traces remain, sponge with some hydrogen peroxide (20 vol), then rinse.

On all carpets: Follow the above instructions.

IODINE

On washable fabrics: Treat the stain immediately. Moisten the stain with water and place over the radiator, the steam from a boiling kettle or in the sun. Or soak in soapy water (four pints/two litres) to which two tablespoons of ammonia have been added. Then wash in the usual way. Or rub the fresh stain with a freshly cut lemon. Then wash.

On non-washable fabrics: Dab with methylated spirit. Rinse with methylated spirit, then in water.

Or place a piece of cotton wool dampened in methylated or white spirit over the stain and leave for several hours. Moisten the pad with the alcohol from time to time.

On man-made fibres: Dab the stain with some methylated or white spirit diluted in water (one part meths and two parts water).

On carpets: On wool use the non-washable fabrics method above, then shampoo.

For synthetics: Follow the man-made fibres instructions, then shampoo.

JAM

On all washable fabrics: Fresh stains will wash out. Soak old stains in a borax solution (one teaspoon of borax, one pint/half a litre of warm water). Then wash in the usual way.

Or work some liquid detergent into the old stain before laundering in the usual way.

On non-washable fabrics: Scrape off any excess, then sponge with some liquid detergent diluted in warm water. Rinse. If any traces remain, sponge with some hydrogen peroxide (20 vol) diluted in its equal quantity of water and rinse.

Or rub a little powdered borax over the remaining stain. Leave for a few minutes, then rinse. Blot dry.

On all carpets: Scrape any excess. Wipe with a damp cloth. Then shampoo. If any traces remain, dab with methylated spirit. For synthetic carpets dilute the meths (one part meths, two parts water).

KETCHUP – Follow **Bottled sauces** instruction

LACQUER (nail varnish, transparent lacquers)

On all washable and non-washable fabrics: Blot up immediately with absorbent paper, place a pad underneath the stain, then dab the stain with acetone, amyl acetate (chemist) or non-oily varnish remover. If any traces remain, dab with some methylated spirit or liquid stain-remover.

On man-made fibres: Dab the stain with amyl acetate (from a chemist). Nail-varnish remover might be used, if it does not contain acetone, so test before in an inconspicuous place.

On carpets: On wool use the washable and non-washable fabrics treatment. Then shampoo.

For synthetics: Use the man-made fibres treatment. Then shampoo.

LEAD PENCIL

On all fabrics: Rub with an eraser or dab with a liquid spot-remover. If any traces remain, soften with a solution of glycerine and warm water in equal quantities. Sponge with some liquid stain-remover. Blot dry.

On all carpets: Follow the above instructions.

LEATHER MARKS

Leather rubbing against fabric can make marks very difficult to remove because of the tannin in the leather dye.

On all fabrics: Work some liquid detergent into the stain. Sponge and blot dry. Repeat if needed. If any traces remain, dab with some hydrogen peroxide (20 vol).

LINSEED OIL

On all fabrics: Blot up any excess, then dab the stain with liquid stain-remover. Then work some liquid detergent into the stain. Sponge and blot dry or wash the article if possible.

LIPSTICK – Follow **Cosmetics** instructions.

LIQUORS – Follow **Alcoholic beverages** instructions.

MACHINE OIL

On all fabrics and carpets: Rub with eucalyptus oil.

MAKE-UP – Follow **Cosmetics** instructions.

MAYONNAISE

On all washable fabrics: Scrape off the excess. Soak in a biological detergent following the instructions on the packet. Launder.

On non-washable fabrics: Scrape off the excess and then treat with a liquid stain-remover or an aerosol stain-remover.

On all carpets: Scrape off any excess, then shampoo. If any traces remain, dab with some liquid stain-remover or methylated spirit (dilute the meths for synthetic carpets: one part meths to two parts water).

MEAT JUICES

On all washable fabrics: Soak in biological detergent before washing.

On non-washable fabrics: Work some liquid detergent into the stain. Rinse and blot dry. If any traces remain, sponge with some liquid stain-remover.

On all carpets: Shampoo. If any traces remain, sponge with some liquid stain-remover.

MEDICINES

On all fabrics: If the medicine has a base of sugar syrup (e.g. cough medicine), wash out with soap and water if the fabric is washable. If it is non-washable, sponge it off. Remove any remaining traces with methylated spirit, diluted with two parts water for man-made fibres.

If it is a *gummy* medicine, loosen the stain by rubbing some vaseline, lard or butter into it, then sponge with a liquid stain-remover. Rinse and blot dry, or launder if the fabric is washable.

On all carpets: Follow the above instructions.

MERCURO CHROME

On all washable fabrics: Soak the fabric in a warm detergent solution to which some ammonia has been added (ten tablespoons of ammonia, four pints/two litres of water) for at least twelve hours. If any traces remain, place a pad of cotton wool dampened in methylated spirit or white spirit over the stain. Keep the pad moist with the methylated or white spirit and leave it on until the stain disappears. Dilute the alcohol with two parts of water for man-made fibres.

On non-washable fabrics: Sponge the stains with methylated or white spirit. Dilute the alcohol (one part alcohol, two parts water) for use on man-made fibres.

On coloured fabrics: Where alcohol cannot be used, rub some liquid detergent on the stain; next, dampen a pad of cotton wool with ammonia and dab it over the stain. Rinse with cold water. Repeat if needed.

On all carpets: Follow the above instructions.

METAL POLISH

On all fabrics: Wipe any excess. Next sponge off with water, work some liquid detergent into the stain, sponge with water again. If any traces remain, sponge with methylated spirit (diluted in two parts of water for man-made fibres). Rinse and blot dry.

On all carpets: Wipe any excess. Dab with methylated or white spirit. Leave to dry. Brush the powdery deposit. Shampoo if needed. On dried stains brush off any powdery deposit before treating it.

METAL STAINS

Stains caused by tarnished silver, copper, brass etc. rubbing against fabrics.

On all fabrics: Wet the stain with lemon juice or white vinegar. Sponge with water. Blot dry. Bad stains can be removed by treating them with oxalic acid (from a chemist).

MILDEW

On all washable fabrics: Fresh stains can be removed by laundering and if possible drying in the sun. If not, treat any remaining traces by dabbing them with a solution of hydrogen peroxide (20 vol) (one part) and cold water (three parts). Diluted bleach (one tablespoon bleach to one teacupful of water) can be used to dab the remaining traces on cottons or linens.

Another way is to soak the stain with buttermilk and leave in the sun to dry. Repeat until the mark disappears.

On coloured fabrics: Slightly wet the stain with cold water, then rub some household soap over it. Dry in the sun. Repeat until the mark disappears.

Small stains on any fabrics can be removed by rubbing them with half a lemon dipped in salt. Then sponge with lukewarm water. Dry in the sun.

On non-washable fabrics: Seek professional advice.

Mildew on linen: This can be removed by rubbing the stains with a bar of soap when the linen is damp, then covering the soapy stains with powdered chalk. Rub the powder in well; wet it a little as it gets dry. Leave for twelve hours. Repeat the whole process if necessary.

On all carpets: Sponge with a carpet shampoo. Rinse with a clean, damp cloth. Next rub the carpet with a mild bleach solution (one tablespoon of bleach to one pint/half a litre of water). Dry with an electric fan.

On tiled walls, cement floors, tiled floors: Wash with a bleach solution (two teacups of bleach to four pints/two litres of water). Rinse with water and dry as much as possible.

On vinyl wall-covers: Soak the stains with a solution of ammonia (one teaspoon), hydrogen peroxide (20 vol) (half a teacup) and water (one teacup). Leave it on for fifteen minutes. Rinse with water and blot dry.

On plastic shower curtains: Sponge the curtains with a bleach solution (two tablespoons bleach to one pint/half a litre of water). Rinse and dry.

On mattresses and upholstery: Take the article outside if possible and brush off the mould. Leave the article in the sun until thoroughly dry. If this treatment is not possible, sponge the stains with an equal solution of methylated or white spirit and water. Then dry throughly using an electric fan.

On leather: Rub the stains with petroleum jelly. Then polish.

Another way is to wipe the stains with some undiluted antiseptic mouthwash. Wipe dry, then wax and polish.

Yet another way is to rub the stains with an equal solution of methylated spirit and water. Dry well, then wax and polish. If the mildew is still remaining, wash it with some thick sud detergent. Rinse by wiping with a damp cloth and dry well. Wax and polish.

Or scrape the stain with very fine sandpaper, then rub with shoe polish the same colour as the leather.

On paper: Sprinkle the stain with talcum powder if it is damp. Leave it overnight, then brush off. Erase the stains by dabbing them with a small pad of cotton wool dampened with a solution of household bleach (one teaspoon of bleach, three teaspoons of water) or with an ink-eradicator. Blot dry.

On stone: see **stone**.

MILK

On all washable fabrics: Soak for a while in lukewarm water, then wash in the usual way. If any traces remain, sponge with a liquid stain-remover.

Non-washable fabrics: Sponge the stain with dry-cleaning fluid then sponge with lukewarm water.

Or soak the stain in methylated spirit in a saucer. Then sponge with lukewarm water. Do not use this method for man-made fibres.

On all carpets: Shampoo. If any traces remain, sponge with dry-cleaning fluid or methylated spirit.

Another way is to blot the milk as much as possible. Next flush the stain with soda water from a siphon, then sponge with lukewarm water. Blot dry. If any traces remain, rub in a little solution of carpet shampoo. Leave to dry.

MUD

On all washable fabrics: Wait until the mud is dry, then brush off as much as you can before laundering. If any traces remain, treat with a liquid stain-remover.

On coloured fabrics: If, after washing, the colour has faded, dip the stained part in a solution of ammonia (one tablespoon) and water (six tablespoons) for a little while. Rinse well.

On non-washable fabrics and upholstery: Wait until the mud is dry, then brush it off. Sponge the stain with a mild detergent solution. Wipe with a sponge squeezed out in cold water, and blot dry. If any traces remain, treat with a liquid stain-remover.

Another way is to wait until the mud is dry, then brush off. Next sponge the stain with a solution of methylated or surgical spirit and water in equal quantities. Or wipe the mark with water to which some bicarbonate of soda has been added (water one teacup, bicarbonate of soda one tablespoon).

On raincoats: Wait until the mud has dried, then brush it off. Next sponge with water to which some vinegar has been added (water one teacup, vinegar three tablespoons).

On all carpets: Wait until the mud is dry, then brush it off and vacuum. If the stain remains, use a carpet shampoo. Leave to dry. Treat any remaining traces by dabbing them lightly with a cloth dipped in methylated spirit.

MUSTARD

On all washable fabrics: Laundering in a warm detergent solution should remove the stain. If any traces remain, sponge with an ammonia solution (ammonia three tablespoons, water half a pint/a quarter of a litre).

Dried stains should be loosened up before laundering by rubbing some glycerine solution (water and glycerine in equal quantities) into the stain. Leave for at least an hour, then launder.

On non-washable fabrics: Wipe with a cloth wrung out in water. Next sponge with a mild detergent solution and rinse. If any traces remain, wipe with an ammonia solution (ammonia three tablespoons, water half a pint/a quarter of a litre). Blot dry.

On all carpets: Scrape any excess, then shampoo. If any traces remain, dab with an ammonia solution (ammonia three tablespoons, water half a pint/a quarter of a litre)

NAIL VARNISH

On all fabrics: Blot up the excess with some absorbent paper. Then place a pad underneath the stain and dab with cotton wool dampened with non-oily nail-varnish remover or acetone. (Do not use non-oily nail-varnish remover on man-made fibres.) If any traces remain, sponge with methylated spirit.

On man-made fibres: Blot up the excess with some absorbent paper, then place a pad underneath the stain and dab with cotton wool dampened with amyl acetate (from a chemist).

On all carpets: Blot up the excess with some absorbent paper, then dab the stain with cotton wool dampened with amyl acetate (from a chemist). Non-oily nail-varnish remover can be used on some carpets, but make a test first. If any traces remain, sponge with methylated or white spirit. Finish the whole treatment by shampooing the area.

NICOTINE

On all fabrics: Sponge the stain with some methylated or white spirit (dilute the alcohol with two parts of water for man-made fibres).

Another way is to sponge with cold water and work a little liquid detergent into the stain. Rinse and blot dry. If any traces remain, dab with some hydrogen peroxide (20 vol) and water mixed in equal proportions.

On fingers: Rub your fingers with a quarter of a lemon or with cotton wool dipped in hydrogen peroxide (20 vol). Rinse your fingers immediately.

On china: Rub the stain with a slightly damp cork dipped in salt.

OIL – See Car oil, Cycle oil, Grease, Hair oil, Paraffin oil

OINTMENT

On all fabrics: Dab with a liquid stain-remover. Rinse with cold water. If any traces remain, work some liquid detergent into the stain, then rinse and blot dry.

ORANGE JUICE – Follow Fruits, Fruit juices instructions.

PAINT, VARNISH

Clean fresh stains immediately as it is very difficult to remove dried stains.

Oil paints, gloss, enamel paints, oil-based undercoat, varnish

On all washable fabrics: Dab with white spirit, a liquid stain-remover or commercial paintbrush cleaner. Rinse. Repeat if needed. Wash the garment if possible.

Another way is to rub the stain with a solution of turpentine and ammonia in equal quantities until the stain disappears. Next launder.

Treat dried stains with a special paint-remover. Test man-made fibres in an inconspicuous area first. Then wash.

On non-washable fabrics: Dab with turpentine, then sponge with methylated or white spirit to remove the turpentine stain. Sponge with cold water and blot dry.

Dried stains should be loosened up by placing a pad dampened with turpentine over it for half an hour. Rinse. If any traces remain, work a little liquid detergent into the stain, then rinse. Repeat if needed by using the turpentine and liquid detergent alternately until the stain disappears. Dab with methylated or white spirit (dilute the alcohol for man-made fibres: one part alcohol, two parts water). Rinse and blot dry.

On all carpets: Dab with white spirit, liquid stain-remover or commercial paintbrush cleaner. Sponge with cold water. Repeat if needed, then shampoo.

Emulsion and water-based undercoat and paints

On all fabrics: fresh stains can be washed off with cold water, then laundered if possible.

Dried stains need to be loosened up with methylated spirit (dilute the alcohol in equal parts with water to use on man-made fibres). Next wash in the usual way or sponge with warm water. If any traces remain, dab the wet stain with ammonia. Rinse well.

On all carpets: Follow the above instructions.

Cellulose paint

On all fabrics and carpets: Treat with acetone but not on man-made fibres. Instead use a liquid stain-remover or an appropriate thinner.

Acrylic paint

On all fabrics and carpets: Sponge with water then work some liquid detergent into the stain. Rinse. If any traces remain, dab with a liquid stain-remover or methylated spirit (do not use methylated spirit on man-made fibres).

PARAFFIN OIL – Follow instructions for **Grease, oils, fats**.

PENCIL, black and coloured

On all fabrics: Try to rub the mark with a pencil-eraser first. If it is not possible, rub with a liquid stain-remover. Sponge with a mixture of water and ammonia, half and half. Repeat the treatment if needed.

PERFUME

On all washable fabrics: Gently rub the stain with white spirit. Then wash in warm soapy water.

Another way is to loosen the stain with a solution of glycerine and water in equal quantities. Leave for at least an hour, then wash.

On non-washable fabrics: Gently rub the stain with white spirit. Use diluted white spirit on man-made fibres (one part white spirit, two parts water). If the stain persists, rub with hydrogen peroxide (20 vol) and sponge with cold water immediately.

Another way is to loosen the stain with a solution of glycerine and water in equal quantities. Leave it on the stain for at least one hour. Wipe with a sponge squeezed in warm water. Blot dry.

On all carpets: Blot up as much as you can. Next dab with white spirit, then shampoo.

PERSPIRATION

On all washable fabrics: Do not wash the garment until the stain has been treated. Soak the affected part in cold, very salty water for half an hour, then rub half a juicy lemon on it and let it soak in for a minute or two. Rinse and wash as usual.

If the colour has been changed by the perspiration, try to restore it by holding the fabric, first dampened with water, over the fumes of an open bottle of ammonia.

If it is a fresh stain, apply ammonia and white vinegar. For an old stain, methylated spirit can also be used to restore colour, but do not use it on man-made fibres.

White cotton and linen: Bleach in a solution of methylated spirit and ammonia (half a teacup of methylated spirit, one teaspoon of ammonia). Soak until the stain disappears.

Or soak in a solution of hydrogen peroxide (20 vol) and water (hydrogen peroxide one part, cold water five parts).

On silk and wool: Dab or soak with a diluted solution of hydrogen peroxide (20 vol) and water in equal quantities. Dab or soak for at least ten minutes before washing.

Non-washable fabrics: Sponge the stain with a solution of ammonia and water in equal quantities.

PITCH – Follow **Tar** instructions.

PLASTICINE

On all fabrics and carpets: Scrape off any surface residue. Place an absorbent pad under the stain and dab the stain with some liquid stain-remover or lighter fuel (on man-made fibres test over an inconspicuous area first). Next wash washable fabrics or sponge non-washable fabrics with warm water and blot dry. Shampoo the carpet.

PLUM – Follow instructions for **Fruits, fruit juices**.

PRINTER'S INK – See **Ink**

RAIN SPOTS

On leather handbags: Hold the handbag over a container full of boiling water, not too close, for one or two minutes. Wipe well. Wait until well dry and then polish with natural-colour wax.

Another way is to rub the leather with a cloth dampened in cold soapy water. Rinse. Blot well, then polish.

On a felt hat: Rub the spots with crumpled tissue paper.

RASPBERRY – Follow instructions for **Fruits, fruit juices**.

RESIN

On all fabrics and carpets: Dab with one of the following products: liquid stain-remover, methylated or white spirit (dilute the alcohol with two parts water for man-made fibres), eucalyptus oil (for more delicate fabrics), liquid lighter fuel or ether. Dab the liquid on the wrong side to push the stain out, if possible. Rinse by sponging with cold water or launder. Old stains can be loosened up with a glycerine solution (half warm water, half glycerine) before washing.

On woollens: Place the stain over some talcum powder (the talc is then underneath the stain). Next dab with turpentine.

On fast-colour fabrics: Dab the stain with turpentine. Next sponge with methylated or white spirit (diluted in two parts water for man-made fibres).

RIBENA – Follow instructions for **Fruits, fruit juices**.

RUM – Follow instructions for **Alcoholic beverages**.

RUST
On bath: See under **Baths** in 'General Hints' section.

On iron or steel: A small stain on a delicate object can be removed with an ink-eraser. For more persistent stains on tougher objects, first soften the rust by dipping the object in paraffin for 24 hours. Then take it out of the paraffin, wipe it lightly and rub the metal with steel wool until clean. If it is not possible to dip the object, wrap the rusty part with a cloth soaked in paraffin and leave it for 24 hours. Then rub the metal with steel wool. Protect non-metal parts with plastic adhesive tape.

On vinyl floor tiles: Wearing rubber gloves, rub in a weak solution of oxalic acid (one tablespoon of oxalic acid to one pint/half a litre of warm water).

On linen: Place a little oxalic acid (obtainable from a chemist) on a piece of white material. Knot the material into a small bag. Dip the bag in hot water and dab it on the stain. The mark will disappear immediately. Rinse in clean water.

SALAD DRESSING – Follow instructions for **Grease, oils, fats**.

SAUCE – See also under different headings for **Bottled sauces etc., Gravy, Mayonnaise, Mustard**.

On all fabrics and carpets: When in doubt about the origins of the sauce, sponge with cold water. Work some liquid detergent or washing-up liquid into the stain. Sponge with cold water. Dab with methylated spirit (dilute the alcohol in two parts of water for man-made fibres). Sponge with cold water. Blot dry or wash.

SCENT – Follow **Perfume** instructions.

SCORCH MARKS
When the fibres have been badly burnt, scorch marks cannot be removed.

On all washable fabrics: Light scorch marks can be removed by sponging with hydrogen peroxide (20 vol) or by rubbing the marks with a piece of sugar moistened with water. In both treatments sponge with cold water afterwards.

Another method for light scorch marks is to dampen the area with a glycerine solution (half warm water, half glycerine) and rub it fabric to fabric. Next soak in a solution of borax (two tablespoons) and warm water (one pint/ half a litre). Leave until the scorch mark clears up. Rinse, then launder.

Another method is to place the stained fabric over a small container of boiling water. Make a paste with two teaspoons of fine salt and two teaspoons of lemon juice. Spread over the stain. Leave for a short while. Rinse with water. Repeat if necessary.

Another method is to cover the stain with a paste made of fine salt and lemon juice and leave it to dry in the sun, or hold it over the steam from a boiling kettle. Rinse well.

Yet another way is to boil the stained fabric or garment in a solution of water (four pints/two litres) and cream of tartar (four tablespoons). Boil under the stain has disappeared. Rinse well.

On white cotton and linen: Stretch the stained fabric over a container and pour boiling water through the mark (from as high as possible without splashing). Next cover the stain with a paste made of white vinegar and cream of tartar or powdered borax. Leave for two minutes, then rinse in warm water to which a little ammonia has been added. Repeat if needed before laundering.

Very light, fresh marks will respond well if dabbed with hydrogen peroxide (20 vol) or lemon juice. Rinse immediately.

On non-washable fabrics: Follow the hydrogen peroxide (20 vol) or sugar treatment above – or seek professional advice from a dry-cleaning specialist.

On all carpets: If the burn is small and light, rub it out with hydrogen peroxide (20 vol) and leave it to dry. Any burned tips left can be trimmed with nail scissors.

For a small but deeper burn, cut as much as you can of the burnt part with small scissors, then cover the burn with a light coat of glue, and patiently, with the help of tweezers, cover the glue with some pile of the same carpet cut from an inconspicuous corner of the room. Leave to dry.

On wool: Light marks can be rubbed with very fine sandpaper or an emery board.

SEA-WATER MARKS

On all fabrics: Sponge with a solution of vinegar (one part) and water (two parts). Launder if possible.

On leather shoes: Dissolve a small piece of washing soda in four tablespoons of hot milk. While the mixture is warm, apply it to the stain with a cloth, rubbing well. When dry, clean the shoe with your usual polish.

Another way is to rub white vinegar and warm water in equal proportions over the stain, then polish.

SEALING WAX

On all fabrics and carpets: Dissolve the wax by dabbing it with methylated spirit or white spirit (dilute in two parts water for man-made fibres). Rinse and blot dry. Repeat if necessary.

SEWING-MACHINE OIL
On all fabrics and carpets: Rub the spot with ammonia. Next wash or sponge with warm water and blot dry.

SHELLAC – Follow **Resin** instructions.

SHOE POLISH
On all fabrics and carpets: Scrape off the surface residue and dab with a liquid stain-remover. If any traces remain, dab with methylated or white spirit (diluted in two parts of water for man-made fibres). If after this treatment any stain remains, wipe with hydrogen peroxide (20 vol). Sponge with cold water afterwards. Blot dry, or wash if possible.

Dried, difficult stains should be loosened first with a glycerine solution (half glycerine, half warm water). Work it well into the stain. Next dab with a liquid stain-remover. If any traces remain, sponge with methylated or white spirit (diluted in two parts of water for man-made fibres). Rinse and blot dry, or wash if possible.

On vinyl upholstery: Wipe away any excess, then rub with turpentine.

SOFT DRINKS – Follow instructions for **Fruits, fruit juices**.

SOOT
On all washable fabrics: Soak in cold water, then launder.

On non-washable fabrics: Shake or vacuum the stain. Do not brush, to prevent spreading the soot. If any traces remain, dab with a liquid stain-remover or use an aerosol stain-remover.

On all carpets: Never wet a soot stain.

On light-coloured carpets: Cover the stain with salt, French chalk or fuller's earth and vacuum. Repeat the process until the stain has disappeared.

On darker-coloured carpets: Vacuum the stain first and sponge away any remaining traces with a liquid stain-remover.

SPIRITS – See **Alcoholic beverages**.

STOVE POLISH
On all washable fabrics: Work liquid detergent into the stain, then launder.

On non-washable fabrics: Apply salt or talcum powder over the stain. Work it into the fabric, then brush it off. Repeat until the stain has almost gone, then wipe with a liquid stain-remover.

STRAWBERRY – See instructions for **Fruit, fruit juices**.

SUN TAN LOTION – Follow instructions for **Grease, oils, fats**.

SYRUP – Follow **Jam** or **Medicine** instructions.

TAR

On all washable fabrics: Small stains on fabrics will be removed if dabbed with non-oily nail-varnish remover or acetone. Do not use these on man-made fibres. For larger stains work some butter, margarine, lard or glycerine into the stain with your fingertips. Leave on for a good hour. Next sponge with a liquid stain-remover, then launder.

Another way is carefully to scrape as much as possible, then dab with eucalyptus oil (from a chemist). Leave to dry before laundering.

On wool and silk: Scrape as much as you can, then treat with eucalyptus oil (from a chemist) or ether. Next launder as usual.

On non-washable fabrics: Scrape as much as possible and treat with eucalyptus oil.

Another way is to loosen the stain with a glycerine solution (half glycerine, half warm water). Leave for one hour, then sponge with cold water. Blot well and dab with a liquid stain-remover.

On all carpets: Scrape as much as possible. Loosen the stain with a glycerine solution (half glycerine, half warm water). Leave on for an hour. Rinse with water and blot well. When dry, use a liquid stain-remover or an aerosol stain-remover on any remaining traces.

Another way is to scrape any excess, then cover the stain with a thick paste made of fuller's earth and turpentine. Rub it well into the stain. Leave to dry, then brush it off.

On feet and hands: Rub the stain with paraffin or with the outside of a lemon or orange peel, or with oil or butter.

On leather: Dab the stain with liquid lighter fuel.

On dogs' paws: See p. 227

TEA – See **Chocolate** instructions.

TOBACCO – See **Nicotine** instructions.

TOMATO JUICE, PURÉE – See **Fruit, Fruit juices**.

TREACLE – See **Jam**.

TURMERIC

This is a spice used in curry powder, mustard and pickles. Follow **Curry** instructions.

TYPEWRITER RIBBON – See **Ink**

URINE – See also **Animal stains**

On all washable fabrics: Rinse in cold water to which ammonia has been added (two pints/one litre of water, one tablespoon of ammonia), then launder in the usual way.

Soak dried stains in a biological detergent before laundering, (follow instructions on the packet). Any yellow marks on cotton or linen can be bleached out by dabbing with a hydrogen peroxide (20 vol) solution (one part hydrogen peroxide/five parts cold water) to which a few drops of ammonia have been added.

On non-washable fabrics: Sponge with cold water. Blot dry. Then sponge with a vinegar solution (three tablespoons of vinegar, one pint/half a litre of warm water). You might have to repeat the process for dried stains as they are difficult to remove.

On all carpets: Flush soda water from the siphon over the stain or sponge with an ammonia solution (two tablespoons of ammonia to one pint/half a litre of warm water). If the colour has been changed and the ammonia solution does not help, sponge with white vinegar and blot dry.

On mattresses: Sponge with cold washing-up liquid solution. Wipe with cold water to which a dash of white vinegar has been added or a few drops of antiseptic (e.g. Dettol). Blot well and leave to dry in an airy place.

VARNISH – See **Paint**.

VASELINE
On all fabrics and carpets: Sponge with turpentine or a liquid stain-remover. Then wash or sponge with warm water.

VEGETABLE STAINS – See **Grass**.

VINEGAR – See **Acids**.

VODKA – See **Alcoholic beverages**.

VOMIT – See also **Animal stains**
On all washable fabrics: Scrape any surface deposit and rinse under cold running water. Soak in a biological detergent solution (following the instructions on the packet), then wash.

On non-washable fabrics: Scrape any surface deposit. Sponge with warm water to which a few drops of ammonia have been added. Blot dry.

Another way is to scrape off excess, sponge with warm water, then blot dry. Next sponge with a liquid stain-remover.

On all carpets: Scrape any excess, then flush some soda water from a siphon. Blot well. If you have no siphon water, sponge the stain with a borax solution (three tablespoons of borax, one pint/half a litre of warm water). Shampoo, rubbing well until the stain has gone. Rinse with warm water to which a few drops of antiseptic have been added.

On mattresses: Remove any surface deposit. Sponge with a warm washing-up liquid solution. Sponge with cold water to which a few drops of ammonia have been added. Blot well and leave to dry in an airy place.

WALNUT

Dark brown stains are very difficult to remove, so try to deal with them when freshly done.

On all fabrics: Work some glycerine into the stain, then apply a pad of cotton wool dampened with white vinegar over it. Let it stand for five minutes. Next work a little liquid detergent into the stain with your fingertips, then sponge with cold water. Blot dry. Repeat the treatment as many times as necessary.

Another way is to sponge the stain with methylated or white spirit (dilute the alcohol in two parts of water for man-made fibres).

If any traces remain, wipe with hydrogen peroxide (20 vol). Sponge with water and blot dry.

WATER SPOTS AND RINGS – See also **Rain spots**

Water spots, rain spots on fabrics such as velvet, felt, taffeta, silk, moiré can be removed by holding the fabric in the steam from a boiling kettle (not too near the spout). Press while damp.

Methylated spirit on a clean cloth dabbed over the mark will also remove water stains. Next dab with a clean, soft, dry cloth.

On satin: Rub gently with tissue paper in a circular motion.

On French-polished wood: If the mark is slight, rub it with metal polish, then wax and shine.

Or rub it with some cigar or cigarette ash mixed to a paste with some salad oil. On light french-polished wood rub the mark with an oily Brazil nut. Or rub the mark with ammonia then polish.

If water has penetrated the wood, mix equal parts of linseed oil and turpentine and rub into the mark with a soft cloth.

Or rub over the mark with vaseline, coat it and leave overnight. If the next day it is not completely removed, repeat the process.

WATERCOLOUR PAINT – See **Paint**.

WAX

On all fabrics and carpets: Dab with liquid stain-remover. Next work some liquid detergent into the stain. Rinse and blot dry.

WHISKY – See **Alcoholic beverages**.

WINE

On all washable fabrics: Rinse in warm water, soak in biological detergent solution (follow the packet instructions) or in borax solution (three tablespoons of borax to one pint/half a litre of warm water) or cover the stain with lemon juice and salt for ten minutes before laundering.

Red wine stains will disappear if white wine is poured over them. Or cover with salt until the wine is absorbed. Afterwards stretch the stained fabric over a container and pour boiling water through the stain, then launder in the usual way.

On linen: Red wine stains will quickly disappear if they are dipped in boiling milk while the milk is boiling in a pan over the cooker.

Old stains: treat white cotton and linen with household chlorine bleach, as directed on bottle, then rinse thoroughly and wash.

Do not use bleach on fabrics with special finishes, e.g. drip-dry. Do not soak coloureds for longer than fifteen minutes otherwise slight bleaching may occur.

On non-washable fabrics and upholstery: Blot up as much as possible and sponge with a solution of hydrogen peroxide (20 vol) (half hydrogen peroxide, half water). Blot dry.

Another way is to blot up as much as possible, then sponge with warm water. Blot well. If any traces remain, sprinkle the stain with talcum powder while still damp. Wait ten minutes. Brush off. Repeat until clear.

On all carpets: Flush the stain with some soda water from the siphon and blot well. Shampoo. Sponge with cold water. Blot well. Repeat if needed.

Old stains can be loosened up with a glycerine solution (half glycerine, half warm water). Leave it on for half an hour to an hour, then shampoo. Any remaining traces can be removed with methylated spirit or a solution of hydrogen peroxide (20 vol) – half and half with water.

On leather: First wet the stain with warm water. Next rub it with turpentine. Leave to dry, then polish in the normal way.

XEROX INK – See **Ink** (duplicating ink).

Cleaning Agents

ACETIC ACID (from chemists)
A colourless liquid which neutralizes any alkaline effects on fabrics. (Alkaline residue comes from hard water calcium soap deposits and takes the brightness out of colour.) Dilute two teaspoons of acetic acid with two pints/one litre of water for the last rinse. As a stain-remover, dilute one teaspoon of acetic acid in ten teaspoons of water. If the dye changes colour when using acetic acid, sponge the fabric with ammonia. Vinegar is a form of acetic acid and a good substitute for it.

ACETONE (from chemists)
A highly flammable solvent. Good to remove nail varnish, paint and oils (animal and vegetable) – **do not use** on acetate fabrics.

ALCOHOL (from chemists and hardware shops)
Organic chemicals, methylated spirit and surgical spirit are forms of ordinary rubbing alcohol. These solvents are good for removing stains on

fabrics. First test if dyes are affected by the alcohol. Dilute the alcohol in two parts of water for man-made fabrics.

ALKALI
As opposed to acids (ammonia, washing soda and other soda compounds). They neutralize acids and change colours in some dyes.

AMMONIA (from hardware shops)
Alkali and grease solvent. Gives off strong fumes, so use in a well-ventilated room and wear rubber gloves to avoid skin contact. Keep in a cool, dark place. Buy cloudy household ammonia as it has a little soap added to it. It removes stains such as grass, chocolate and blood from fabrics. For household purposes use a solution of one part ammonia to ten parts water. **Do not use** ammonia and bleach together: the combination releases a dangerous gas.

AMYL ACETATE (from chemists)
Useful solvent to remove stains such as lacquers, cellulose paint, nail varnish etc. It is poisonous and flammable. It can be used on fabrics that cannot be treated with acetone.

BENZINE (from chemists)
Inflammable liquid, distilled from crude petroleum. Used as a solvent and in dry cleaning.

BICARBONATE OF SODA (baking powder) (from chemists and supermarkets)
Useful for removing stains from fabrics, cleaning chrome, paint, ovens, china, glass, refrigerators. Cleans teeth. Softens water. Appeases tummy aches. Cleans jewellery etc., etc. It is a *must* in the house.

BLEACH (household bleach) (from hardware shops and supermarkets)
Useful to bleach white cotton and linen. Soak in a mild bleach solution (one tablespoon to two pints/one litre water) for ten minutes, rinse thoroughly. **Do not use** on wool or silk. Bleach can be used as a lavatory cleaner, but **do not** mix it with vinegar, ammonia or any other household product; it will produce a highly irritating gas which can cause serious injury. Bleach can lose its effectiveness if stored for too long.

BLUE/WASHING BLUE (from supermarkets)
Makes white look whiter.

BORAX (laundry and domestic) (from chemists and supermarkets)
It is a compound of mineral salt, which is a combination of boracic acid and soda. It loosens grease and dirt, and is also an antiseptic. Some old stains on fabrics, such as jam, ice-cream, coffee etc., will loosen off if just soaked in a

borax solution (one tablespoon to one pint/half a litre of warm water).

BRAN (from chemists and health food shops)
The husk of grain sifted from the flour, after grinding. Used hot or warm as an absorbent to clean velvet upholstery, felt hats and furs.

CASTOR OIL (from chemists)
Obtained from the seeds of the castor-oil plant. A very good leather-conditioner. First clean the leather; next with a soft cloth apply a small amount of oil, rub it well into the leather and wipe off the excess.

CHLORINE BLEACH – See under **Bleach**

CHLORINE LIME (from hardware shops)
A combination of lime and chlorine gas. A good disinfectant for outside dust-bins and damp basements.

DETERGENTS (synthetic detergents) (from supermarkets)
Made from petroleum, natural fats and oils, used to clean around the house and for dish-washing and laundry. Available in liquids and powders. Laundry detergents are in two types: light duty for delicate fabrics and heavy-duty biological (enzyme) detergents for more heavily soiled fabrics. Always follow instructions on the packet. Liquid detergent is a very good stain-remover.

EMERY CLOTH/SANDPAPER (from hardware shops)
Use as an abrasive to polish metal, hard stones and wood. It can be bought in varying degrees of roughness, graded from coarse to fine.

ENZYMES See Detergents

ETHER (from chemists)
Dissolves animal fats and oils. A powerful anaesthetic liquid. Use carefully, in a well-ventilated room.

EUCALYPTUS OIL (from chemists)
A volatile, aromatic straw-coloured oil. It will remove grease stains on any fabric, even the most delicate, without leaving a trace. Also used in medicine as an inhalant.

FRENCH CHALK (from chemists)
Powdered, a kind of talc. Tailors use it to mark cloth; often used as an absolvent on fresh grease stains on fabrics, wood, paper etc. It is completely harmless and does not leave a ring.

FULLER'S EARTH (from chemists)

It is composed of a variety of clays and is used as an absolvent to remove grease and oil stains from non-washable fabrics (suede, fur, tapestry etc).

GILDER'S WHITE – See Whiting

GLYCERINE (from chemists)

A colourless, odourless liquid which is a useful solvent to loosen many kinds of stains on fabrics. Use neat or as a solution with equal quantities of warm water, following instructions.

HYDROGEN PEROXIDE (20 Vol) (from chemists)

A colourless liquid. Buy it in 20 volume strength. Keep it in a cool, dark place. It is used for delicate treatments such as cleaning marble and ivory and removing light scorch marks or stains such as blood, ink, perfume etc. from fabrics. **Do not use** on pure nylon. Hydrogen peroxide will work better if kept in the refrigerator.

IODINE (from chemists)

A volatile chemical element used as an antiseptic in medicine and also used in photography. It is also used to remove silver nitrate stains.

JEWELLER'S ROUGE (from hardware shops)

An abrasive red powder, used as a paste with methylated spirit or water for cleaning and polishing glass, jewellery, silver etc.

KEROSENE (from hardware shops)

A volatile oil. Highly flammable. Kerosene is used to remove rust on metals, and stains on vinyl upholstery.

LANOLIN (from chemists)

A waxy yellow substance which is obtained from wool grease. Used in cosmetics, and can also be used as a leather-conditioner.

LINSEED OIL (from chemists or hardware shops)

Comes from the common flax seeds. Highly flammable. Used in oil paints, varnishes and furniture polishes. It can be bought 'raw' or 'boiled'. Boiled linseed oil can be used to darken wood and to rub off water marks on furniture (mixed with equal proportions of turpentine or mixed to a paste with cigar or cigarette ash).

METHYLATED SPIRIT (from chemists and hardware shops)

A volatile and inflammable liquid. It should be handled with care. A grease solvent, good for cleaning mirrors, glass, jewellery and ivory, and for removing grease stains from fabrics. It will also remove ballpoint or felt-pen ink stains, chocolate, coffee or mud stains from non-washable fabrics. For man-made fabrics, dilute one part of methylated spirit to two parts of water.

Do not use on French polished wood surfaces: it will dissolve the polish.

OXALIC ACID (from chemists)

Used as a bleach or stain-remover (ink, rust). Always wear gloves when using oxalic acid. Dissolve in warm water (one tablespoon of oxalic acid crystals to one pint/half a litre of warm water), in a glass container as it may damage a metal one. Poisonous. Keep in a safe place and labelled.

PARAFFIN (from ironmongers or petrol stations)

Colourless, odourless, useful as a solvent for grease. Paraffin wax can be used as a substitute for bees wax. Paraffin oil is poisonous and is used to get rid of rust on metal.

Liquid Paraffin (from chemists) is not poisonous and is used as a laxative. It is also a good substitute for face cream.

PARIS WHITE – See **Whiting**

PEROXIDE – See **Hydrogen peroxide**

PETROLEUM JELLY – See **Vaseline**

PUMICE (from chemists or hardware shops)

A piece of lava useful for smoothing rough skin.

Powdered Pumice is used as an abrasive; it is a good polisher and scourer. Many commercial scouring powders include pumice powder.

ROTTEN STONE (from hardware shops)

A soft stone used for polishing metals. Powdered rotten stone mixed with linseed oil will remove white spots from furniture. Apply lightly with a soft cloth. Follow the grain of the wood.

ROUGE – See **Jeweller's rouge**

SADDLE SOAP (from hardware shops)

A special soap for cleaning leather. Good on all polished leather.

SANDPAPER – See **Emery cloth**.

SILVER SAND (from ironmongers and domestic stores)

A clean, very fine sand, used as an abrasive and absolvent.

SOLVENT

A liquid used to dissolve grease stains from fabric and other materials. Water, acetone, ammonia, amyl acetate, glycerine, methylated, surgical and white spirit, paraffin and turpentine are all solvents.

SPANISH WHITE – See **Whiting**

SURGICAL SPIRIT (from chemists)
Use as a solvent to remove grease stains on fabric. Flammable.

TEAK OIL (from ironmongers)
Use on teak wood to clean and polish.

TURPENTINE (from chemists)
Use as a solvent for varnish, wax, paint, etc. Flammable. It is quite expensive. White spirit will sometimes be as effective and is much cheaper.

VASELINE (petroleum jelly) (from chemists)
A soft greasy substance, used as a soothing ointment. It is also used to loosen heavy grease and tar stains on fabric, before using a solvent. Used also on metal as a rust-preventative, and for conditioning leather.

VINEGAR
White vinegar is a mild acid and a most useful cleaning agent around the house. Few other products have as many culinary and chemical virtues. It dissolves dirt deposits, diminishes scum and film from soap, and softens water. It is used in stain removal to counteract alkalis and to restore colours altered by it. Hot vinegar will soften paint brushes.

WASHING SODA (from some domestic stores, chemists or ironmongers)
This is a very strong concentrated alkali, and can be injurious to the skin, so wear rubber gloves when using it. It cleans grease from waterpipes, is used for cleaning silver and copper, and softens water for cleaning purposes.

WHITE SPIRIT (from chemists and hardware shops)
A good turpentine substitute. It is used as a solvent or thinner for paint. It removes grease and stains from fabric and leather. Dilute in two parts of water for man-made fibres. Flammable and toxic.

WHITING (from hardware shops)
A fine powdered chalk, used as an abrasive.
  Whiting is known by different names, depending how fine and free from grit it is. The Spanish white and the gilder's white are used to polish silver; Paris white is the finest of the whiting powders.

CARE OF FABRICS

ANTISTATIC
Static in washable fabrics can be got rid of by adding a little fabric-softener in the rinse. Dry cleaning can give an antistatic finish to non-washable fabrics.

If your skirt clings to your slip or your legs while you are getting dressed, take a wire coat hanger and run it between the slip or between your legs and the skirt to absorb some of the static.

Clothes made from synthetic fibre retain static electricity; a fabric-conditioner in the last rinse will reduce the effect. A tumble-drier makes static electricity worse. This effect will be lessened if, after drying, you allow the dryer to cool off and then cold-tumble clothes for five to ten minutes.

To get rid of static electricity, add two tablespoons of white vinegar to a gallon/four litres of water in the final rinse.

BLEACH
The damage caused by a little spill of bleach on fabric can be greatly diminished if the spot is immediately impregnated with hydrogen peroxide (20 vol). Leave for one minute before rinsing well.

To get the smell of bleach out of linen, add a small quantity (one teaspoonful to one pint/half a litre) of distilled malt vinegar to the last rinse. Always dilute the bleach in cold water, for if hot water is used it will act too quickly and may ruin the fabric. It is better to soak the fabric in a weaker solution for longer.

COLOUR FASTNESS
Test your clothes for colour fastness before washing with other items for the first time. Dampen a small area with water and press it between two pieces of white cloth. If the white cloth gets stained with the colour, the item should be washed separately.

When washing coloured fabrics add half a teacup of salt to the water to prevent the colour running.

DYEING
To dye a garment black successfully, use an equal quantity of navy blue dye with the black dye. This will prevent the fabric taking on a greenish tinge.

FROSTY WASHING

To prevent linen or clothes getting frosty on the line in the winter, add half a teacup of salt to the last rinse.

SHINE ON FABRIC

Black or dark-coloured clothes become shiny with wear. They can be renovated by:

1. Brushing the shiny part with black coffee (half a teacup of strong black coffee to half a teacup of water). Then press with a wet cloth.
2. Rubbing with a piece of clean cloth dampened with turpentine or white spirit (the smell will soon disappear).
3. Rubbing the fabric with a soft cloth soaked in a solution made with laurel leaves and water. Leave to dry before pressing with a damp cloth. Laurel leaf solution: cut about two dozen laurel leaves into small pieces and boil them slowly with a pint/half a litre of water in a covered pan for twenty minutes. Use the solution as hot as possible to rub over the fabric.
4. Brushing with a solution of one pint/half a litre of water for one tablespoon of ammonia.

SCORCHES ON FABRIC

Dab the scorch mark with a piece of cotton wool dampened in hydrogen peroxide and then sponge with water. If the fabric is cotton, put a cloth dampened in hydrogen peroxide over the scorched area and press with a warm iron.

To remove scorch marks on fabric, providing they are not too firmly set or too old, cut an onion in half and rub the scorched part with a circular motion. Then soak in cold water until the stain disappears.

If a scorch mark on fabric is very obstinate, wet the mark with hot water and sprinkle with powdered borax, then expose to strong sunlight for a few hours. A bad scorch mark can be generally improved that way, if this method is repeated with each washing.

ACETATE

Silk-like fabric. Wash by hand in warm soapy water; do not spin unless mentioned on label and do not wring as tiny creases will appear in the fabric. Get rid of excess water by rolling in a towel or leaving to drip-dry. Press while still damp with a warm iron.

For knitwear the last rinse should be cold; the cold water cools the fibres so that the garment will not crease when wrung out or spun.

ACRYLIC (Acrilan, Courtelle, Orlon, Dralon, Nylon)

Acrylic knitwear: to get rid of little fluffy balls forming on the knitwear, brush the dry garment with a hard nylon brush – or shave it with an electric razor. Always rinse an acrylic garment in cold water; the cold water cools the fibres so that the garment will not crease when wrung out or spun. Before ironing, do not sprinkle water on an acrylic garment which has dried out because the water will not be evenly spread and it will leave marks. Wet the entire garment and press with a cool iron.

Do not forget that acrylic fabrics do not dye successfully.

ANGORA

Fabric made from the wool of an Asiatic goat; also made with the fine hair of a white rabbit with pink eyes. Wash as for wool – use lukewarm water and special wool detergents. Handle gently. Rinse in lukewarm water. Roll in a towel to absorb excess water, then shake the garment out gently to fluff the yarn up, before shaping and putting it flat to dry.

If angora knitwear loses its hair, put it in a plastic bag in the refrigerator for a few days.

BATISTE

A very light fabric made of cotton or linen, so it must be washed accordingly. (Follow **Cotton** or **Linen** instructions).

BROCADE

Heavy silk or velvet fabric threaded with silver or gold thread, often raised with designs of flowers, leaves etc. It should be dry-cleaned. Press the material on the wrong side with a warm (not hot) iron over a piece of thin cloth.

A little dry powdered magnesia rubbed on and left for an hour or two will also clean lamé fabric. Brush away the powder with a soft brush.

Gold or silver lamé fabric can be kept shiny if it is regularly rubbed gently with a chamois skin. If the fabric is dull-looking, rub with a very warm piece of crustless bread. Repeat the operation until the lamé shines again, or rub the fabric with warm bran and then finish shining with the chamois skin.

CALICO

Made from fine cotton. Follow instructions for **Cotton**.

CANDLEWICK

Bedspreads and dressing-gowns are sometimes made of candlewick. It may be pure cotton or cotton mixed with synthetics (see label). Clean according to the type of fabric. Shake well after washing and when dry shake again to fluff up the pile.

CANVAS

Wash in warm water and detergent. Scrub with a brush if very dirty. Rinse well.

CASHMERE

Made from soft hair of certain goats. Cashmere fabric must be dry-cleaned. Wash cashmere sweaters very carefully, following instructions for **Wool**, using the finest wool detergent.

CHEESECLOTH

A very light, loosely woven cotton fabric. It should be hand-washed to keep its shape. Do not wring. Roll in a towel to absorb excess water. Iron while damp. Put back into shape while ironing.

CHENILLE

Clean according to the type of fabric, for the material could have been made from silk or a synthetic (see label). Shake from time to time while drying to fluff the pile. When dry, brush up the tufts gently with a dry, clean, soft brush. Do not iron.

CHIFFON

Very soft, gauze-like fabric made of silk or synthetic (viscose) fibres (see label). Clean according to the type of fabric. Dresses or blouses should be dry-cleaned.

Flimsy chiffon or similar materials should be placed in a jar with warm water and some borax. Screw the top on and shake the jar to clean the chiffon without rubbing. Rinse in clear water and pat it dry in a towel. Avoid ironing when it is too wet or it will stiffen. Do not sprinkle dry chiffon with water to dampen as the spots will mark.

CHINTZ

Cotton cloth printed in colourful designs with a glazed finish on the right side. If the glaze wears off after many washes, it can be restored professionally. Old chintz should be dry-cleaned. New chintz can be washed very carefully in lukewarm water with a mild detergent. Do not rub or twist. Rinse in lukewarm water and then give a final rinse in cold water. Pat it in a towel to absorb excess water. Iron while still damp.

To prevent fading when washing chintz, wash it in bran water instead of soapy water. Dry in the shade and iron when still damp.
(To make bran water, use 1 teacup of bran to 6 pints/3 litres of water; bring to the boil and simmer for half an hour, then strain and throw away the bran. When bran water is used no detergent is necessary. Bran water is perfect for washing delicate fabrics; i.e., chintzes, muslins, etc.)

CORDUROY

Made from cotton, a hard-wearing velvety fabric, completely washable. For the best results wash by hand. Do not wring or twist. Shake well and smooth the pile in the right direction while still damp. Iron on the wrong side when still damp.

COTTON

A cloth woven from cotton threads can be washed in very hot water. White cotton can be boiled to make it whiter. Wash coloured and white materials separately. Most colourfast cottons will stand hot water but they might 'bleed' slightly for the first two or three washes. Some cottons will shrink when washed for the first time. Most cottons can be ironed with a hot iron. Starching cotton will help keep it clean longer and make it look crisper.

Cotton sometimes gets yellowed by chlorine bleach. To make it look snow-white again, soak the cotton for a few hours in a solution of white vinegar (one part) and cold water (eight parts).

Half a teacup of beer added to the last rinse will cheer up your black cotton garment and make it look like new.

CRÊPE AND CRÊPE DE CHINE
Crêpe is a thin cloth with a wrinkled surface. To clean, follow the label instructions. If it is washable, wash by hand in warm soapy water. Rinse well and iron on the wrong side, while still damp.

Crêpe de chine is a lighter fabric made of silk or synthetic fibres. Clean according to the type of fabric. Iron on the wrong side while still damp.
Some crêpe fabric shrinks after washing. To get it back to normal, press it very wet.

DACRON – See Synthetic fabrics

DAMASK
Reversible fabric made of linen, silk or synthetic fibres (see label). Shiny threads are woven into the fabric to make wavy designs. Clean according to the type of fabric.

DENIM
Denim is usually made of cotton. Wash on its own as the colour never becomes fast. Press while still damp.

FELT
A matted fabric made out of compressed fur, hair or wool. It cannot be washed as it would shrink terribly. Dry clean.

To clean felt, make a paste with French chalk and white spirit. Lightly rub it into the felt. Leave to dry, then brush it out.

Use hot bran to clean felt. Heat the bran in the oven and then rub over the felt; it will absorb any grease. Brush thoroughly.

White felt can be cleaned by rubbing powdered magnesia into the felt with a clean cloth. Leave the powder on for twelve hours, then shake off the excess and brush with a clean, stiff brush.

To clean white felt, make a paste with some arrowroot and cold water. With your fingers, carefully coat the felt with the paste and allow it to dry thoroughly before brushing it off.

Marks on light felt can be dealt with sometimes by gently rubbing with fine, clean sandpaper.

FINE LINGERIE
Do not wring out your lingerie after washing; get the excess water out by putting it in your salad-spinner!

FLANNEL

A loosely woven woollen fabric. It should be dry-cleaned for best results. Small items can be washed by hand following instructions for **Wool**.

GABARDINE

A finely ribbed woollen fabric. It should only be dry-cleaned.

HESSIAN

A coarse sackcloth made from natural fibres. Should be dry-cleaned.

JERSEY

Fine woollen jersey should be dry-cleaned. The viscose version should also be dry-cleaned.

Other synthetic jerseys can be washed following the label instructions. Do not twist. Roll in a towel to absorb excess water. Can also be lightly spun.

LACE

Delicate old lace should be placed inside a pillowcase to be washed. Place the pillowcase in warm soapy water, press gently, do not wring or squeeze. Rinse carefully and iron the lace under a cloth in order not to catch it and tear it. Synthetic lace should be washed and pressed following the instructions for the type of fibre it is made of.

To clean delicate old lace, spread it on a piece of white blotting paper. In a saucepan gently heat some potato flour until quite hot and then spread a thick layer of the hot flour over the lace, pressing it down with your fingers. Leave until cool and then remove with a soft brush. Repeat the operation if necessary.

To clean very delicate black lace, fold the lace to a square and place it inside a container. Cover it with beer and leave to soak for twenty minutes. Knead the square of lace with your fingers without rubbing. Rinse in lukewarm water.

To dye white lace, dip the lace in a saucepan filled with a weak, strained brew of tea or coffee. Simmer, stirring until the desired colour is obtained.

LINEN

A fine cloth made from flax. Treat as cotton. Iron on the wrong side with a hot iron when still very damp. Creases in dry linen are practically impossible to get rid of.

New linen is sometimes very stiff; to get rid of the stiffness, soak the material in warm water to which a few soda crystals and some salt have been added.

MOHAIR

A fabric made from the angora goat. Follow label instructions. After many washes mohair woollens have a tendency to fur.

MOIRÉ
Made of silk or synthetic fibres, moiré has an appearance like the surface of water. It should be dry-cleaned only.

MUSLIN
Very fine thin cotton fabric with large open weave. Hand-wash only as for cheesecloth.

NET
Most net curtains are now made of synthetic fabrics. Do not machine wash them; the treatment is too harsh. Do not wring. Instead, fill up one third of your bathtub with lukewarm water, add two teacupfuls of ammonia and mix well. Take your net curtains, shake out the dust, fold them lengthwise, then across, and lay them in the bathtub keeping them under water. Leave to soak for half an hour. Next run out the dirty water without moving the net curtains and replace with lukewarm water. Add some synthetic detergent and squeeze the water through the material, but do not rub or twist. Leave to soak for ten minutes. Rinse several times by running out the dirty water and replacing it with lukewarm water, without moving the folded net curtains.

After the last rinse, lift the folded net curtains out of the water and hang them on a rack placed across the bathtub. Leave to dry for half an hour before laying them folded on a towel. Roll them up lightly to absorb moisture and hang them at the window, where they will finish drying. This way the net curtains do not need ironing. If you have to iron them, do it when they are still damp, with the iron on synthetic setting.

NYLON – See also **Synthetic fabrics**
To prevent white nylon becoming yellow, soak it first in a strong solution of warm water and bicarbonate of soda. Leave to soak for at least two hours.

OILCLOTH
A cotton material made waterproof with oil. Clean by wiping with a damp cloth. Do not fold when wet as it would crack at the corners. Acetone and alcohol are very damaging to its shiny surface.

To make oilcloth as new again, lightly beat the white of an egg and rub it over the oilcloth with a soft cloth. Leave it to dry and then polish with a dry cloth. Pure vinegar will also bring back colours to an oilcloth.

To remove marks left by hot plates, rub the marks with a cloth dipped in camphor oil.

ORGANDIE
Transparent cotton muslin. Hand-wash gently in warm soapy water. Do not wring. Roll in a towel to absorb moisture and iron while still damp. After many washings organdie might need to be slightly starched.

For embroidered organdie, iron on the wrong side.

ORGANZA
Dress material made of various fibres – nylon, silk, rayon etc. Dry-clean or wash according to the type of fabric. Follow label instructions.

ORLON – See **Synthetic fabrics**

PIQUÉ
A ribbed cotton. Wash like any cotton fabric. Iron on the wrong side.

POLYESTER
A man-made fibre. It dries quickly and normally requires no ironing; but if a little ironing should be needed, use a cool iron on the dry fabric.
   See under **Synthetic fabrics** for washing instructions.

POPLIN
Can be made of cotton or synthetic fibres. Wash accordingly.

RAYON
A silk-like man-made fibre. Can be hand-washed or dry-cleaned following label instructions. When in doubt about washing follow the directions for **Acetate**.

SATIN
Glossy fabric made of silk or synthetic fibres. Clean accordingly.
   A delicate fabric to wash – add a little sugar and some vinegar to the last rinse. Always press damp.

SERGE
Strong twilled woollen fabric made from pure wool mixed with cotton or synthetic fabric. Dry-clean.

SHANTUNG
A coarse silk fabric. It is also made of synthetic fibres nowadays. Wash according to the fibre it is made of.

SILK
To distinguish pure silk from artificial silk, pull a few threads from the fabric, double it and roll it between your fingers to make a double thread of two to three inches/approx. 8 cm. Take a match and light one end of the thread. If the thread burns a little, then dies out, forming a small ball of charcoal, it is pure silk. If the thread burns easily to the end, it is not pure silk.
   A lustrous soft fabric, which should be dry-cleaned. If the silk is washable, handle with care using a mild synthetic detergent in lukewarm water. Do not rub or wring. Add a little vinegar and sugar to the last rinse. Roll in a towel to absorb moisture.

Iron while still damp on the wrong side. If allowed to dry, wet it again entirely and roll it in a towel to absorb moisture. Slight dampening would cause water marks.

Another way is to let the silk dry completely and then place it in a plastic bag to which three to four tablespoons of water have been added. Close the bag and leave overnight. In the morning you will find the silk evenly damp and ready to be pressed.

White silk which has become yellowish with age can be brought back to its original whiteness if soaked in a bath of water, hydrogen peroxide and ammonia (two pints/one litre of water to $\frac{1}{4}$ pint/125 ml hydrogen peroxide and one tablespoon of ammonia). Check the progress from time to time.

To renovate black silk, slice some raw potatoes and pour boiling water over them. When cold, sponge the right side of the silk with this liquid and iron on the wrong side. Stale beer is also good.

Another method of renovating silk is to sponge it with a weak solution of household ammonia and water (two tablespoons ammonia to half a litre/-one pint of cold water) and press it on the wrong side.

A shine on silk will disappear if rubbed along the weave of material (not across) with a solution of one teaspoonful of borax to a teacupful of water.

Scorch marks on silk can be removed by applying a paste made of bicarbonate of soda and water to the mark. Leave to stand for at least two hours. Next brush off the bicarbonate of soda, stretch the affected part over a basin and pour cold water over it a few times.

Raw silk should be dry-cleaned.

Pongee is soft, unbleached silk. To wash, follow instructions for silk above. Do not iron pongee too wet or it will stiffen.

SUEDE
Natural untreated leather should only be dry-cleaned. It can be washed by hand in soap flakes sometimes, following label instructions.

SYNTHETIC FABRICS (Dacron, Nylon, Orlon, Polyester) – Man-made fibres.
If instructions are given by the manufacturer, follow them.

Always wash white and coloured garments separately. If no washing instructions, proceed as follows:

Machine wash: Use the special synthetic setting on your washing machine (if there is no special setting, use warm water) and a biological detergent.

At the end of the rinsing cycle stop the washing machine; do not spin the garments. Take them out of the machine soaking wet, place them on hangers, put them back into shape and drip-dry.

The garments can also be tumble-dried but the result is not as good.

When tumble-drying, use the spinning cycle of the washing machine, then tumble-dry on low or medium heat. When dried remove immediately, place on hangers and put back into shape. Leave to cool off.

Hand wash: in lukewarm water and biological detergent. Do not wring or rub. Squeeze the water through the fabric. Rinse in lukewarm water. Squeeze out the excess water gently. Place the garments on hangers (or roll in a towel to absorb moisture and then place on hangers), put back into shape and leave to dry.

Synthetic-fibre sweaters can be machine-washed (following label care instructions) but turn them inside out to avoid fuzzy balls collecting.

TAFFETA
Made of silk or synthetic fibres. If made of silk, it should be dry-cleaned.

Synthetic taffeta can be washed gently in warm water and a mild detergent. Do not rub or wring.

Hang up to drip-dry. Iron while still damp on the wrong side.

TOWELLING
Made of cotton fibres, it can be machine- or hand-washed following label instructions.

After washing shake the towelling out lightly before hanging it to dry. Ironing is not needed.

Terry towelling is used for nappies. Machine wash on a hot setting and use fabric-softener.

VELVET
Cotton and silk velvet should be dry-cleaned. If washable as indicated on the label, follow instructions for **Corduroy**.

Iron velvet face down on a very, very thick bath towel and press over the wrong side.

To clean velvet, gently rub it with a cloth dipped in powdered magnesia. Then brush with a soft brush. Or brush it with a solution of water (one teacup) and ammonia (half a teacup). To keep a velvet collar clean, after wearing it, rub it with a synthetic foam brush or a piece of synthetic foam.

To restore the flattened pile of velvet, cover a hot iron with a wet cloth and hold the velvet firmly over it. Or hold the velvet, stretched tight, over boiling water, or iron velvet face down on a bath towel.

Methylated spirit or surgical spirit on a clothes brush will remove fluff and hairs and give a new look to dusty, tired velvet.

VISCOSE
Man-made fibre. Follow label instructions. When in doubt follow instructions for **Acetate**.

VIYELLA
A mixture of wool and cotton. Wash by hand in warm water and mild synthetic detergent or on the woollen programme of a machine. It does not shrink.

Iron while still damp, preferably on the wrong side.

VOILE

Very thin cotton or synthetic fabric. Wash according to instructions for the type of fibre.

Do not wring. Roll in a towel to get rid of moisture. Iron while still damp.

WOOL

Careful treatment must be given to wool. Wool can be damaged when washed in water that is too hot, by sudden changes in water temperature, by alkalis in soap, by household bleach and by rubbing or wringing.

Some wools are machine-washable. Look for washing and drying instructions on the label when buying woollen or wool by the metre (directions are written on the end of the roll of fabric).

Hand-wash woollens in lukewarm water using a special wool detergent or a soapless detergent. Squeeze the water through the fabric gently. Rinse well again using lukewarm water. Squeeze out the water, roll in a towel to absorb moisture. Shake the garment a little to restore the pile. Dry flat, on a towel, away from sunlight or artificial heat.

A little ammonia added to the soapy water when washing woollens will help to clean them thoroughly.

Two tablespoons of vinegar in the last rinse will keep your woollens soft. This applies to silk garments also.

Woollens will feel wonderfully soft if you add two teaspoonsful of cream hair rinse to the final rinse.

Woollens can be ironed while still slightly damp using a dry cloth between the woollen and the hot iron. Do not press heavily on the iron or it will mark.

White wool getting yellowish can be bleached by soaking it in a solution of hydrogen peroxide and lukewarm water until it is white again (four tablespoons of hydrogen peroxide to two pints/one litre of lukewarm water). Strengthen the solution if the wool is very yellow, and rinse.

When your woollen garments have been washed in water that is too hot and they have become hard and 'felted' wash them in warm water to which glycerine has been added ($1\frac{1}{2}$ tablespoons to $1\frac{1}{4}$ pints/about one litre). Then rinse very thoroughly in warm water.

Oily wool should be washed in soap flakes only to prevent the oil escaping from the fibres.

The best softener for wool blankets is two tablespoons of olive oil or glycerine added to the last warm rinse.

PERSONAL CARE

Health

This section is not intended to suggest that all complaints can or should be treated in the home. Any acute or recurrent ailments should, of course, be treated by a doctor. The following hints are for minor aches and pains, or for times when you cannot see the doctor immediately and want some temporary relief.

ADHESIVE PLASTER

Tearing adhesive plaster from the skin won't be agony any more if you first rub oil, baby oil or salad oil over the plaster.

Marks left on the skin by adhesive plaster can be removed with nail-varnish remover.

ANKLES

To relieve swollen ankles, chop some ivy leaves and secure round the ankles with a bandage, leaving for a few hours. If the swelling persists or recurs, consult a doctor.

Sprained ankle must be kept elevated. Do not put any pressure on it. Apply ice packs frequently during the next twenty-four hours. After this, strap the ankle with a bandage and get it back to normal by making little circles with the foot to begin with. The next exercise is to place your foot against the wall and press lightly. Strap your ankle well before trying to walk.

ARTIFICIAL RESPIRATION

If the patient is not breathing, put him on his back, support the nape of his neck, tilt his head back and press his chin up to stop his tongue blocking the air in the throat.

Mouth-to-mouth respiration

The previous procedure should start the patient breathing again – if not, start mouth-to-mouth resuscitation: pinch his nostrils with your fingers, open your mouth, take a deep breath and seal your lips around the patient's mouth. Blow into the lungs until his chest rises, then remove your mouth and watch his chest falling. Continue doing this twelve times each minute until professional help arrives. When the patient is a child, mouth-to-mouth resuscitation should be done by sealing your lips around his nose and mouth and blowing gently into his mouth sixteen to eighteen times a minute.

Heart massage

If, despite mouth-to-mouth resuscitation, the patient starts turning a blue-grey colour, start heart massage. The patient should be on his back: place yourself on one side, and put the heel of your hand on the lower half of the breastbone with the palm and fingers off the chest. Cover this hand with the heel of your other hand and, with straight arms, press down on the lower half of the breastbone in a rocking motion. For an adult do fifteen heart

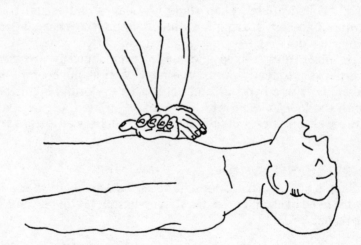

compressions, followed by two lung inflations; for children do ten compressions, applying much lighter pressure with only one hand, about seventy times a minute. Every twenty compressions do two inflations, being careful not to be too violent in case you break a rib.

BABY
While feeding baby at night, put a hot-water bottle in his empty cot. Take the hot-water bottle away when you put him back: the warmth will help him go back to sleep.

If a baby dribbles over his clothes, wipe them with a wet cloth dipped in bicarbonate of soda and he will always smell fresh.

BABY'S BATH
For a safe feeling, place the baby in a loose-mesh plastic laundry basket in the tub when he is having a bath. He will hang onto the sides of the basket and feel much more secure.

BABY'S BOTTLE
To avoid going to the kitchen in the middle of the night to warm baby's bottle for his nightly feed, get it ready and warm before you go to bed. For this get a wide thermos and fill it up with hot water to warm it up. Leave the hot water for a few minutes, then pour it out and place the feeding bottle (which has already been made and is at the correct temperature) in the thermos and screw the lid on. Place it next to the baby's bed, and it will be nice and warm when needed.

BABY'S COT
Baby will stop slipping to the bottom of his bed if a cushion is placed at his feet on the mattress underneath the bottom sheet.

BABY'S DUMMY
To help your child outgrow the habit of sucking his dummy, make a cross with a needle and some thread through the top of the teat. Knot the thread carefully and give the baby the dummy to suck. He will soon reject it.

BABY'S NAILS
Cut your baby's nails when he is asleep. It will simplify the exercise.

BACK
When picking things up from the floor, do not bend over from the waist only. Bend at the knees, keeping the body straight, as this will prevent back troubles.

BEDSORES
To prevent bedsores, rub the pressure points (shoulders, buttocks, elbows, knees, heels, toes) with surgical spirit.

BEE/WASP STING

For a bee or wasp sting, wash the area with a mixture of one tablespoon of vinegar and half a glass of water. Then apply a slice of raw onion, which will ease the pain and reduce the swelling.

The sting of a bee is barbed at the end (unlike that of a wasp which is pointed) so is always left in the wound with the poison flowing through it. The first thing to do after a person has been stung by a bee is to extract the sting with tweezers, being careful not to squeeze the tiny poison sac at the end of the sting. Next rub with ammonia, garlic or a leaf of a leek.

To relieve a bee sting, apply a thick paste of salt and water over it and keep it in place with a bandage. A paste made of bicarbonate of soda and water will also relieve the pain and swelling of a bee sting.

As soon as you feel the sting of a wasp, rub the sting quickly with any aromatic herbs (e.g. parsley, thyme, basil, mint etc.) or some grass or any soft green leaves. If the sting is still in the skin, get it out with tweezers, then rub the skin with some ammonia.

For a wasp sting apply a paste of bicarbonate of soda and vinegar or lemon juice. Another method is to bathe the wasp sting with vinegar. Yet another method is to apply a slice of raw onion on the wasp sting after having cleaned it with vinegar. It will ease the pain and reduce the swelling.

To stop the poison spreading, apply a piece of ice to the bee or wasp sting. If the sting is in the mouth, suck a piece of ice.

If the swelling gets larger and the person has difficulty breathing, call a doctor immediately.

BLACK EYE

To treat a black eye, make a solution of hot water (one teacup) and bicarbonate of soda (one heaped tablespoon) and bathe the black eye with the help of a small piece of cotton wool. Bathe frequently. The solution can be reheated.

BLEEDING

The most important thing to know about bleeding is that most of the time it can be stopped by direct pressure to the damaged part. Place a clean piece of linen or a pad of clean gauze over the cut and press very strongly with your hand for at least three minutes, then check if the bleeding has stopped. If not, apply pressure again until the doctor arrives. (A tourniquet is not recommended for fear of damaging a vein or a nerve.)

To stop bleeding, lay a handful of flour on the cut or dredge it with some freshly ground pepper. This will also act as a disinfectant. So will the fine dust of tea.

BLISTER

To prevent a blister bursting and to get it to dry quickly, take a fine sewing needle and thread it with some fine cotton. Disinfect the needle by passing it quickly through the flame of a match. Pierce through the blister with the needle from one side to the other (it does not hurt), leaving the thread in the blister. The fluid will come out drop by drop, and the top skin will dry very fast. Cover with adhesive plaster or a sterile dressing.

If your skin blisters easily, rub it for at least five or six days with surgical spirit to harden it.

BLOATED BODY
If you feel bloated, boil 2 lb/1 kg of leeks in 3 pints/1½ litres of water for thirty minutes. Strain. Fast for a day and drink the leek water, hot or cold.

BOILS
To make an ointment for boils, mix together one dessertspoon each of honey, olive oil and flour. Beat the yolk of an egg and mix it with the other ingredients. Spread this on gauze and put it on the boil. Renew the application every six hours: it will draw out the core after the boil has broken. If the boil recurs, consult a doctor.

To draw a boil to a head, cook some dried figs in milk. Next wash them and spread them on a gauze and apply to the boil. This will also work for abscesses.

BOTTOM
A spotty bottom can be the result of long periods seated on plastic-covered chairs (e.g. a car-seat) or wearing nylon pants. To prevent this wear cotton pants or cover the seat with a cotton towel.

BOWELS
Apples increase the fibre content in your diet, which improves the efficiency of bowel action and can prevent constipation and other bowel disorders. Eat an apple a day, washed but not peeled. For small children who cannot chew, grate the apple or purée it in an electric blender.

BREATH
Bad breath can quickly be remedied by crunching a clove. Your breath will have the scent of a carnation.

If your breath smells of garlic, chew a coffee bean or a stalk of parsley or celery, or better still some cardamom seeds.

BROKEN LEG CAST
When a cast on one's broken leg itches, sprinkle some baby powder down inside the cast or blow in some cool air with a hair-dryer.

BRUISES – See also Bumps
To prevent bruises appearing:
1. Take a little dry arrowroot or dry starch, moisten it with cold water and apply to the injured part as soon as possible. The sooner this is done after the injury takes place, the more effective it will be.
2. Rub the injured part firmly in a circular motion with your fingers for a

few minutes. The bruise will be less unsightly later.

3. Apply a raw piece of beef over the bruises to avoid discoloration.

4. Rub the bruise with a mixture of butter and chopped parsley.

5. Witch hazel or arnica rubbed gently on the bruise is most efficient.

6. The inside of a banana skin applied immediately to the bruise and held in position with a bandage will minimize the discoloration and dull the pain.

7. A cloth wrung out in very hot water and applied to the bruise will help also to prevent discoloration. Renew the compress frequently (as soon as it gets cold).

BUMPS (AND BRUISES)

For an instant ice-bag treatment on a minor bump or bruise, take out a loose bag of frozen vegetables (e.g. peas, beans, sweetcorn) and apply to the injured part.

BURNS

For a small burn, hold the affected part under running cold water for a while, or apply a cold compress.

For burns caused by household alkalis (e.g. ammonia, washing soda, borax etc.), wash the burn with water and apply lemon juice or vinegar to stop the effect of the alkali on the skin.

For burns caused by chemicals, the chemical should be removed before the burn is immersed in water as some chemicals react violently with water.

Sprinkle the burn with some bicarbonate of soda.

Cover small broken burns with some white of an egg. It soothes and heals. When dry, the white of egg acts as a dressing and stops the air going through.

Cover small, unbroken burns with grated raw potatoes – or some toothpaste.

CABBAGE

Cabbage is the medicine of the poor, with many healing virtues.

For gout, rheumatism, arthritis, sciatica or muscular pains, take some large cabbage leaves, cut out the hard middle vein and gently press the leaves with a medium-warm iron until they soften. Apply a few layers of the warm leaves to the sore part, securing them with a bandage or plaster. Renew twice a day.

For burns, insect bites, swellings and cuts, cabbage acts as a mild disinfectant. Clean the leaves very carefully, press them with a medium-warm iron and apply to the affected area. Crushed cabbage leaves can also be used.

For sore throats, chop some cabbage leaves (any variety), put them in a pan, pour on boiling water, cover and leave to infuse for ten minutes. Strain the infusion and gargle with it. Repeat this operation every two hours.

CAR SICKNESS

To avoid car sickness, take a bunch of fresh parsley and place it on your stomach next to the skin. Hold it with adhesive plaster. Drink a good, especially well-sugared cup of tea and leave relaxed and refreshed.

CATARRH

One can get relief from catarrh by squeezing and inhaling two drops of salted water into each nostril, morning and night (half a teaspoon of common salt to half a teacup of warm water).

CHERRIES

Do not give drinks to children when they are eating cherries or any other soft fruit. The liquid causes the pulp to swell and makes it heavy on the stomach.

CHILBLAINS

As soon as chilblains first appear, paint them over every two or three hours with tincture of iodine for quick relief.

Rub with methylated spirit or half a raw onion or soak your feet (and hands sometimes) for fifteen minutes in warm water in which one or two celery stalks have been cooked. Repeat every day.

Rub unbroken chilblains with a solution of equal parts of surgical spirit and glycerine for immediate relief.

Or bruise the leaf of a leek and rub it three times a day over the chilblain (each time using a new leaf).

The rays of an ultra-violet lamp will help get rid of your chilblains.

CHILDREN

To encourage small children to wash themselves and to prevent the water running down their arms when they do so, place a small wooden box covered with towelling in front of the basin. They can stand on it and by doing so bring themselves to the level of the basin.

If your child eats too quickly, give him only small quantities of food on his plate, and a small fork and a small spoon instead of adult cutlery.

A child will take his medicine more readily if you pour it into a glass and stir it so that it becomes frothy.

CHILDREN'S DRINK

If your child is not feeling well and has to stay in bed, keep his bedside drink in a screwtop jar with a hole in the lid to allow a straw to go through. This will avoid a lot of spilling and amuse your child at the same time.

CHILDREN'S HAIR

Let your child wear a diving mask when washing his or her hair. You will then have the child's full co-operation.

CHOKING

If a person chokes on a piece of food, act quickly. Bang him hard between the shoulder blades or, if this doesn't help, grasp him round the waist from behind, one fist clenched with the thumb towards the stomach. Clasp this fist with the other hand – the hands should be above the navel, below the rib cage – and then give a sudden squeeze, pushing the clenched fist into the upper stomach with a lifting motion. The piece of food should pop out after one or two hugs.

If a child under the age of four chokes, hold him up by his legs and bang him between the shoulders. If the child is older, put him over your knees, head downwards and slap him between the shoulders.

COCONUT

Monthly period pains will be relieved by eating freshly grated coconut.

COLD

For a heavy cold with a blocked nose, inhalations are best. Put your head over a bowl filled with boiling water to which a few drops of oil of eucalyptus (obtainable from a chemist) have been added. Cover your head and the bowl with a towel and breathe deeply, lifting your head from time to time to get some fresh air. Do this for as long as you can, and it will give you relief.

Smelling salts are a great help in unblocking the nose.

If you have a cold, warm your ears by applying a compress of very hot water (as hot as you can take it) over each ear, before going to bed. If you keep it on for at least ten minutes, your nose will unblock and you will sleep more soundly.

COLD PREVENTATIVES

Eat plenty of onions and garlic and chew a clove, or a coffee bean, or a stalk of parsley to sweeten your breath.

COLD SORE

When the swelling starts, dab it with lemon juice or apply some raw grated apple. Live plain yoghurt put on a cold sore will be very soothing.

COMPRESS

For a cold compress, put some ice-cubes and methylated spirit (five table-spoons to one pint/600 ml) into water and dip in a piece of linen or a face-towel. The evaporation of the spirit will keep the compress cold for longer. It should not be used near the eyes.

CONSTIPATION

To help constipation, use dried figs or prunes as a laxative. Soak five to six figs or prunes in water (enough to cover the fruits). First thing in the morning, drink the water and eat the prunes.

CONTACT LENSES

Do not powder your face after putting on your contact lenses. There is a risk of getting some powder between the eyes and the lenses, provoking a painful irritation.

COUGH

To cure a cough, beat until firm the white of an egg to which half a teaspoon of caster sugar has been added. Take one teaspoonful four times during the hour, every hour.

CRAMP

A towel dipped in hot water and applied to the cramp will bring immediate relief.

For cramp in the leg, simultaneously stretch out the heel and draw up the toes as far as possible, or rub hard the back of the leg.

For cramp in the instep, roll a bottle back and forward with the foot.

DANDELION

Common dandelion can be found almost anywhere – in water meadows or dry hills. Its young leaves make a delicious salad: add a touch of garlic and mustard vinaigrette. Dandelion is also considered a blood-cleanser and a diuretic.

DIABETICS

If a diabetic begins to tremble, sweat or act aggressively, it may be caused by too much, or not enough, sugar in the bloodstream. If he is able to swallow (an unconscious person should not be given anything by mouth), give plenty of sugar dissolved in a warm drink, or in lumps, or two table-spoons of powdered sugar. If the condition was caused by too little sugar, the patient will improve immediately; if there is no improvement, the sugar will not have done any harm but the person should be taken to hospital or a doctor should be called.

DIGESTION

To help digestion, eat celery at the end of a meal (e.g. with cheese). Celery is also an antacid.

DIURETIC

When water-retention is a problem, eat celery, lovage or dandelion leaves (good in soup or in salad).

DROP-FEEDER

If a drop-feeder is needed and you do not have one, take a toothpick and slowly pour the medicine over it, letting it run down the length of the toothpick.

DRY MOUTH

If you have a dry mouth because of lack of saliva, eat a prune and suck the stone. Keep sucking the stone as long as you want. Mountaineers use this old remedy against dryness in the mouth when they reach a certain altitude.

EARACHE

A doctor should be consulted for earache, but temporary relief may be obtained by resting the ear on a covered hot-water bottle.

Temporary relief may also be obtained by putting a few drops of lukewarm oil, either olive oil or ordinary cooking oil, in the ear, then plug it with cotton wool.

Put a few drops of equal quantities of ether and almond oil in each ear.

ELECTRIC SHOCK

The longer a person is attached to the current, the worse his condition will become. Switch off the current and remove the plug. If this is not possible, the person must be pulled away, but first insulate yourself or the shock will pass on to you if you touch him with bare hands, anything metal or anything damp. Wrap newspaper round your hand or use an object made of wood (a broom will do) or rubber to pull the victim clear. If he is suffering from burns, immerse the burned part in cool water, never oil or cream. If he isn't breathing, give artificial respiration and call a doctor.

EYES

Inflamed eyes should be treated by a doctor, but temporary relief may be obtained in the following way. Chop some clean parsley very finely, use it to fill two thin muslin bags large enough to cover the eyes, and tack the open end. Lie down with a bowl of cold water next to you, dip the bags in it and lay them on the eyes. Turn them from time to time and dip them in water again when they become warm. Do this for fifteen minutes. Cold damp tea-bags can be used instead of parsley.

When your eyes feel tired, bathe them morning and night with warm salted water (one teacup of warm water to half a teaspoon of salt).

Give your tired eyes some exercise while at work during the day, or while reading or looking at television: keeping your head straight, roll your eyes clockwise, then anti-clockwise for one minute.

FAINTING

An emergency method to help you stop fainting in a hot or stuffy atmosphere is to dig your fingernail firmly into the space between your nose and upper lip.

To help the blood return to the brain, bend the head down to the knees. Then put the patient down flat on his back, the legs higher than the head. Loosen his clothes.

FEET

Regularly massage your feet with baby oil or olive oil to avoid any callouses on the feet.

When summer comes, rub your feet with surgical spirit; it will refresh and harden them in preparation for wearing summer sandals.

To soothe tired feet, first walk on tiptoes for a few minutes, then shower them with water as hot as you can take it for two minutes. Follow with cold water for one minute and then dry energetically, going up the ankles.

Avoid getting blisters on a long walk by rubbing the heels of your socks with dry soap.

FEVER
If you feel feverish (hot and then cold) and are sneezing, with a nose starting to run, drink a tumbler full of hot white wine with a pinch of ground pepper added to it.

FISH BONE
If a fish bone is stuck in the throat, swallow large pieces of bread. If you have a tiny piece of cotton wool handy, swallow this first, then the bread.

GIDDINESS
To counteract giddiness, drink about two tablespoons of pure lemon juice.

GRIPE
To relieve a baby's gripe, make an infusion of fennel seeds (one pint/half a litre of boiling water, poured over one tablespoonful of fennel seeds). Leave to cool to a suitable temperature for the baby to drink. This infusion can be given (half a teacup in his feeding bottle) before and after meals.

GUMS
When the gums get too soft and the teeth loosen, rinse your mouth four times a day with the following solution: a quarter of a glass of warm water, a pinch of alum (from a chemist) and $1\frac{1}{2}$ teaspoons of bicarbonate of soda. Keep the mixture for a little while in the mouth each time.

GUMBOIL
To relieve pain in the mouth from an ulcer or a gumboil, chew some well-washed leaves from a blackberry bush.

HANGOVER
To avoid a hangover, drink several glasses of water before going to bed, or eat a tablespoonful of honey.

Another method to prevent a hangover, when you know in advance that you are going to celebrate maybe a little too much, is to drink one or two teaspoonfuls of olive oil before eating and drinking.

But if you have not followed the above advice and you are now feeling the 'punch', drink a big glass of water to which two teaspoonfuls of bicarbonate of soda have been added – or make an infusion with a big bunch of parsley and drink it hot from time to time. This is also a very efficient remedy.

If you already have a hangover, drink a glass of water to which two soluble aspirins and half a teaspoon of bicarbonate of soda have been added.

HEADACHE

The juice of a lemon to which a teaspoon of bicarbonate of soda has been added and mixed will relieve a headache.

A headache caused by foods which have fermented (e.g. chocolate, yoghurt, cheese etc.) or drinks such as beer, whisky, red wine or gin can be helped by taking as much honey as you like, a small quantity at a time.

HICCOUGHS

To stop hiccoughs, use one of these cures: eat a small piece of ice or a spoonful of sugar without drinking, or drink water from a glass after you have placed a napkin over the glass, drinking the water through the linen.

If the hiccoughs are very persistent, place a piece of sugar soaked in vinegar on your tongue and chew the sugar slowly, or drink a teaspoonful of vinegar, or drink a glass of water, holding a knife blade down in the glass, or pull out your tongue, or place some granulated sugar (one teaspoon) on your tongue and allow it to melt before swallowing.

To stop a baby hiccoughing, moisten the nipple of his feeding bottle, dip it in sugar and give it to him to suck.

INDIGESTION

A quarter of a teaspoon of bicarbonate of soda in half a glass of hot water will quickly get rid of your indigestion.

Chew raw mint leaves to get relief from indigestion.

INFLAMED NOSE

To prevent an inflamed nose when you have a cold and you blow your nose repeatedly, use silk handkerchiefs instead of tissues.

INSECT BITES

To ease the itch of an insect bite, cover with a paste made of bicarbonate of soda and water.

If you have no bicarbonate of soda, dab the bite with your own urine; this will also bring great relief.

INSOMNIA

To help you relax and go to sleep, drink a large glass or large cupful of hot lettuce juice. (Simmer two small lettuce in two pints/one litre of water for twenty minutes. Drain and drink.)

Lemon balm is extremely good for insomnia as it also acts as a tranquillizer. Take a tablespoon of chopped leaves and pour over it two teacupfuls of boiling water. Leave to infuse before drinking.

Jellyfish

If stung by a jellyfish, quickly rub the sting vigorously with wet sand. The pain will subside.

Or apply a compress of vinegar as soon as possible and renew from time to time.

Keeping Cool In Hot Weather

In hot weather wet the lobe of your ears with some saliva and fan yourself for a quick cooling. It is particularly effective when driving in a car with open windows, when the fanning is not necessary.

Running cold water over wrists and elbows is also very cooling.

Liver

Your liver may stop functioning properly after too many rich meals. This is the morning when you wake up feeling tired, with a dull-looking complexion. Do not eat any breakfast; first get your liver to function normally again by drinking the juice of three lemons (no sugar, no water) and going back to bed. Lie on your right side for at least twenty minutes, a little longer if you can.

Marigold

For wounds or skin eruptions, soak a marigold in salad oil and apply the petals. The oil will help the wound to heal more quickly.

Medicine

The medicine cabinet is usually in the bathroom, but burns and cuts most often occur in the kitchen, so keep some ointment there as well.

Remember to keep medicine locked away and out of the reach of children.

To avoid the taste of unpleasant medicine, eat a strong peppermint just before taking it, or suck an ice-cube.

Do not take pills or capsules without water. Some of them stick to the digestive tube and can perforate it. So drink, but not to excess. Too much liquid would start a quick elimination of the water, diminishing and shortening the effect of the medicine.

Crush a tablet between two teaspoons by putting the tablet in one teaspoon and pressing and grinding it with the back of the second spoon.

The instructions written on the medicine bottle by the chemist should be covered with some sellotape to prevent their fading away.

Menstruation Pains

Menstruation pains can be eased by placing a hot-water bottle on the abdomen or drinking a glass of warm water to which three drops of tincture of cinnamon (available from a chemist) have been added.

Migraine

Relieve your migraine by chewing three feverfew leaves a day. The taste is not very pleasant but it is worth it.

To get rid of a migraine after a heavy, rich meal, chew well and slowly a raw carrot and massage your eyebrows.

MORNING SICKNESS
To fight mother-to-be morning sickness, suck a wedge of lemon.

MOSQUITO BITES
Dab the bite with an equal mixture of water and ammonia as soon as possible.

To calm a mosquito bite and stop it itching, cover it with a slice of onion, a crushed clove of garlic, a slice of lemon or a compress of vinegar.

MUSCLE
When a leg muscle has been hurt, apply ice to the injured area for forty-five minutes. If there is any swelling, keep the leg elevated and keep placing cold compresses on the muscle for a few hours, then give it a warm bath.

MUSTARD PLASTER
The mustard plaster, made of equal parts of flour and mustard with a little water to make a paste, will not blister the skin if the water is replaced by some white of egg. Also a layer of gauze should be placed between the plaster and the skin.

NETTLE STINGS
When stung by nettles, rub parsley over the stung area; it will lessen the burning sensation considerably. Or rub with dock leaves, which always grow next to the nettles, or rub the area with rosemary, mint or sage leaves, or cover with egg white.

NEWSPAPERS
Fasten a large newspaper in its middle with two safety pins, to make it easier to handle for a bed-ridden elderly person.

NOSE BLEEDS
Seat the patient with his head leaning forward and with the thumb pressed firmly on the bleeding nostril. Continue this treatment for at least ten minutes. If this does not stop the bleeding, put a piece of cotton wool dipped in peroxide in the bleeding nostril.

The sudden shock of some pieces of ice (wrapped in a thin plastic bag) dropped down the spine will very often stop the bleeding instantly.

PATIENTS
Keep patients entertained by giving them a view of the outside world: hang a mirror in such a way that it reflects through the window.

Use an ironing board to serve a bed-ridden patient his meals. It can easily be adapted to the height needed.

PILLS

If you have a lot of pills to take every day, in the morning put the exact amount you need for the day in a small box. That way it will be easy to check if you have taken them or not.

An easy way to swallow a pill is to place it under the tongue and then take a big mouthful of water. Water and pill will go down together easily.

POISONING

If someone is poisoned by household products, do not panic; note the time immediately.

Do not make the patient vomit if he is not completely conscious.

Do not make the patient vomit if he has swallowed foaming or caustic products or petrol-based products. Foaming or caustic products include caustic soda, bleach, potassium chlorate and strong acids; petrol-based products include methylated spirit, white spirit and dry-cleaning fluid.

If the patient does vomit, lie him on his side.

If the patient has swallowed a foaming product, do not give him anything to drink for many hours. If it was bleach, make him drink water to dilute the product and make it less caustic.

If the poison taken is not a foaming or caustic product, empty the stomach by giving the patient a cupful of warm water mixed with one teaspoon of mustard (dry or fresh), or put your fingers down his throat.

Take the patient to the hospital without delay, also taking the container of the poisonous product.

RHEUMATISM

Warmth is very comforting during an attack of rheumatism. Apply a hot-water bottle, wrapped in a towel to avoid burning. Fill the bottle only half full so that it can be wrapped around the affected parts.

A decoction of pine needles is an effective treatment for rheumatism and gout. (Drink one or two teacupsful every day – 60 g/2 oz of pine needles to two pints/one litre of water.)

SALT

Do not put too much salt on your fresh vegetables, as this causes water-retention which will swell your tissues. Salt can be replaced with chives.

To relieve a cold or hayfever, take dry salt in the same manner as snuff.

Wash your teeth and rinse your mouth with salt water. It makes your teeth white, sweetens the breath and hardens the gums.

After tooth extraction, rinse with salt water to stop the bleeding.

SCALD

Cover the scald with a clean rag or a piece of cotton wool soaked in cold, strong tea or a strong solution of bicarbonate of soda and cold water.

SEA-SICKNESS

When feeling sea-sick, stay on the deck of the boat in the open air and look at the horizon, not at the waves, to give you a sense of stability.

SEA-URCHIN

To get rid of a sea-urchin's spikes embedded in the skin, cover the skin with warm candle wax, wait until the wax is hard, then remove; the spikes will be stuck to the wax. If the spikes are very deep in the skin, you might have to repeat the operation.

SHAVING

To stop the bleeding when you have slightly cut yourself when shaving, dip your moistened finger in a little powdered pepper and dab the cut (keep the powdered pepper handy in your bathroom in a small container).

SHOCK

Make the shocked person lie or sit down. Keep him warm with blankets or coats. If there are no injuries, give the patient a cool non-alcoholic drink (not hot) and keep comforting him by talking reassuringly. Do not let the patient go to sleep. Call for a doctor or an ambulance.

SINUS

Sinus trouble can be greatly improved by taking half a teaspoon of horse-radish sauce morning and evening. Wait ten minutes before eating or drinking anything afterwards. The treatment depends on the individual. If it is a light case, a few weeks will clear the passages; a more severe case might take a few months.

SLEEP-WALKER

A large, shallow tray full of water placed on the floor by the side of the bed will awaken the sleep-walker as soon as he puts his feet in it to start walking.

SMELLING SALTS

Smelling salts can be replaced with a little ammonia on a piece of cotton wool.

Revive your smelling salts with a few drops of ammonia when they have lost their dampness.

SNEEZING

When you feel you are going to sneeze, do not turn your head to the side, but sneeze straight in front of you (in your handkerchief if possible). Turning your head to the side twists your spine, and this movement and the vibration from the sneeze could result in a slipped disc.

To stop a sneeze, touch your palate firmly with the tip of your tongue.

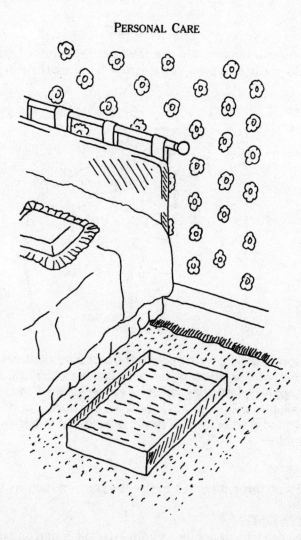

SORE THROAT

The most efficient gargle is a mixture of one teaspoon of salt to one teaspoon of bicarbonate of soda in a teacup of warm water.

Gargling with whisky (and swallowing it) will also help with a sore throat.

SPLINTERS

To draw out a splinter, cover it with a plaster which is firmly stuck to the skin. Leave it for ten to twelve hours, then peel off the plaster, bringing the splinter out at the same time, or sufficiently far out for you to finish the job with tweezers. If the splinter is very deep, you might have to do this once more. *See illustration overleaf.*

Or light a candle and let it drip a little over the splinter. Wait until the wax hardens on the skin, then remove the wax. Usually the splinter will pop out with it.

To extract a splinter quickly from a hand, especially a child's, place the affected part over a jar or wide-mouthed bottle half filled with very hot water. If a little pressure is used, the steam will induce the extraction of the splinter.

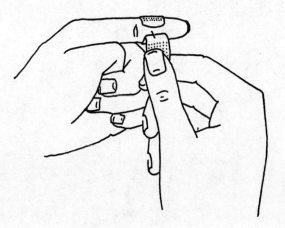

SPRAIN

For a simple sprain (ankle, wrist), cold is the best treatment. Protect the skin over the sprain with a piece of linen (a handkerchief will do) to avoid frost-bite and apply a plastic bag full of ice on the sprain. Leave for one hour. If no ice is available, soak your ankle or wrist in a bucket of cold water.

Another method is to bathe the sprain alternately in hot and cold water for fifteen minutes.

STING (FISH)

Rub the sting with turpentine to appease the pain, on the way to the doctor.

STING-RAY STINGS

A sting-ray is a fish with venomous spines in its tail, found on sandy shores. If you are stung by one, tie a scarf, a belt or a tie above the wound, making a constricting bandage, but not too tight or it will stop the circulation of the blood completely. Then as fast as possible immerse the wound in hot water – as hot as you can take it – and leave it there for thirty minutes to one hour, adding more hot water from time to time.

STITCH

Stitch in your side can be alleviated by bending forward and touching your knee with your mouth. Keep straightening up and bending until the stitch disappears.

STOMACH UPSET

Make a mixture of five tablespoons of warm water, two teaspoons of apple cider and two teaspoons of honey. Stir well before drinking. Repeat every half an hour.

STYES
Rub the styes with the juice of the houseleek plant.

SUNBATHING
The most dangerous time of the day for sunbathing is between 11 a.m. and 2 p.m. At this time, the sun is at its strongest and therefore more likely to burn the skin.

Beware of a deep suntan. It makes the features look harder and deepens lines, thus ageing the face.

Be cautious of the reflection when you are in the water; it doubles the effect of the sun and could burn your skin badly.

If you suffer from broken veins, cover your nose when lying out in the sun.

To prevent the swelling of the veins which can cause varicose veins, cover your legs in the hot sun.

The cleavage is very often susceptible to allergic reaction, and you should take care not to over-expose this area.

Do not use a deodorant soap to wash yourself before going sunbathing: it could provoke a skin rash.

Give your face a treat after sunbathing – lie down and apply a mask of mashed raw cucumber. (Do not put on eyelids or under the eyes.) Leave for twenty minutes before rinsing with warm water.

Sunbathing preparations containing oil of bergamot can leave patches on the skin: they will fade with the tan but will reappear as strongly as soon as one is the sun again. This is because oil of bergamot accelerates the pigmentation of the skin under ultra-violet rays, making the skin tan more quickly but very often patchily because the skin's pigmentation is irregular. As oil of bergamot is an ingredient in perfume, it is not recommended that you use perfume before sunbathing.

SUNBURN
For immediate relief, apply a compress dipped in a mixture of water and vinegar. Use five tablespoons of vinegar to one pint/half a litre of water. Or make a paste with bicarbonate of soda and water and apply over the burnt surface.

Five tablespoons of sugar to which a little water (just enough water to melt it into a paste) has been added will also give immediate relief to sunburn. Leave the paste to dry on the skin before dusting it off. Finish by applying a little moisturizing cream on the burnt area.

Slices of raw tomato will also relieve painful sunburn. So will the juice of the houseleek plant, or a compress dipped in strong cold tea.

Another solution is to take a bath to which one teacupful of bicarbonate of soda has been added. Dry the skin gently and apply a compress dipped in cold milk.

Some grated raw potato applied over the burn will also give immediate relief. So will a lightly beaten white of egg mixed with a few drops of olive oil and coated over the sunburn.

When the skin is very burnt or even blistered, cover it with a sterile dressing which has been soaked in a weak solution of cold tea or a weak solution of bicarbonate of soda (one tablespoonful of bicarbonate of soda to one pint/half a litre of water). When the patient complains of nausea and chills after being badly sunburnt, a doctor should treat the burn.

TEETHING BABY
To give a little relief to baby when he is teething, fill up a sterilized teat with water and freeze it. Replace it onto a feeding bottle and give to baby to suck.

THYME
Use thyme to aid the digestion of fatty food, especially pork and mutton.

THERMOMETERS
Don't put a thermometer in a young child's mouth, as he might bite and break it. The thermometer should be tucked first under the arm and then into the groin, with the knees bent up into the tummy, to get an accurate reading of the child's temperature.

TIRED LEGS
For tired legs, raise the foot of the mattress by placing some pillows under-neath, or simply place some wooden blocks or bricks or books under the bottom legs of the bed. Leave all night.

TIREDNESS
If suddenly you feel very tired during the day, strongly press the base of your nose (between your eyes) with the thumb and the forefinger and slowly count up to eight.

TONGUE-BITING
If you have just bitten your tongue or cheek, take a glass of water, add the juice of half a lemon and a teaspoon of bicarbonate of soda, stir well and rinse your mouth. Repeat often and the pain will soon subside.

TOOTHACHE
Temporary relief may be obtained by:
1. Placing a clove inside the mouth on the affected area.
2. Using the fresh crushed cleaned leaves of the yarrow herb and placing them inside the mouth on the affected area, to alleviate the pain.
3. Applying tincture of iodine on the gum around the bad tooth with a piece of cotton wool.
4. Crushing one aspirin tablet and placing it on the affected area.
5. Diluting an aspirin in two tablespoons of warm water and holding the solution in the mouth over the affected area until the pain dulls down, then spitting it out.

6. Putting a small piece of damp cotton wool, soaked in alcohol, inside your ears.

WALKING

You will walk twice as far and be less tired if you shift your weight from the heel to the ball of your front foot – your body will be lighter and the weight will be distributed naturally and more evenly over the joints. It will make a big difference to your health and efficiency.

It is also important to wear comfortable shoes.

Avoid blisters when you know you will be going on long walks by preparing your feet a week (or more if possible) before. Rub them every night and morning with surgical spirit. Leave to dry. Sprinkle talcum powder in your shoes and socks.

WARTS

To get rid of a wart, apply nail varnish once a day. Regular treatment should cause the wart to dry up and disappear after a period of time.

WASP STINGS – See Bee stings

WIND

To get rid of wind, eat burnt toast.

WOUNDS

Cuts can be very painful and bring a flood of tears from a youngster. Don't add to the pain after cleaning the wound with water by applying an antiseptic directly to the skin, but place it on the gauze.

The best way to disinfect a minor wound is to sprinkle it with sugar.

BEAUTY

AFTERSHAVE
Make him his own aftershave. Fill up an attractive smallish bottle with one-third witch hazel, two-thirds of rose water and add a few rose petals. Leave it to soak for a few days until the mixture gets to a bright pinkish colour, then get rid of the petals and the aftershave is ready to use.

ASTRINGENT
The most simple and efficient astringent to use after cleansing the face, or before making up the face, is a mixture of rosewater (two parts) and witch hazel (one part).

Make a simple, nourishing face-cream to use overnight or to leave on in the morning while having a bath. Mix one tablespoon of honey, one beaten egg white and five drops of almond oil and gently massage a thin film into the skin. Keep the cream in the fridge or a cool place.

Make a simple moisturizing lotion to apply after cleansing, after astringent and before making up. Mix six teaspoons of rosewater and five tablespoons of glycerine and apply a thin film to the face. It will help the skin hold its moisture and its smooth look.

BABY OIL
A few drops of baby oil in your bathwater will stop your skin becoming dry.

BATH
If your bathwater is very hard, add some vinegar to it (three to four tablespoons). It will soften the water, making it much more gentle on your skin.

The bathroom will not steam up when you are having a bath if the cold water is run first and then the hot.

BATH OIL
To make perfumed bath oil at home, mix $\frac{1}{2}$ pint/300 ml of almond oil with $\frac{1}{2}$ pint/300 ml of olive oil. Add ten drops of essence of jasmine – or the perfume of your choice – and shake well.

Some bath oils are so strongly scented that a few drops on the skin here and there will last all day and will cost less than perfume.

BATH RELAXATION
To relax in the bath, take a hot-water bottle, fill it up with warm water and use it as a bath pillow to rest the back of your neck.

BATH SCENT
A delightful way to scent one's bath is to make some small muslin bags, fill them up with a mixture of herbs (rosemary, lavender, mint, thyme, basil, marjoram etc.) and hang the small bags from the tap in the bathtub. Every time the bath is filled up, the little bag will scent the water. Renew the herbs from time to time.

A milk bath is sometimes very pleasing, leaving the skin soft and smooth. Use half a pound/225 g of powdered milk in your bathwater.

BEDTIME
If you want to look good in bed, apply your night cream long before going to bed. Then wipe off the excess, brush your brows, add a little touch of blusher to your cheeks, a little lip gloss to your lips, a little Kohl powder above your lower lashes, brush your hair free of any hair lacquer and do not forget the touch of perfume.

BLUSHER
To know where to start when putting blusher on your face, place your index and middle finger vertically against the side of your nose. Start putting the blusher from near the edge of the outer finger, going up to the temple.

A touch of blusher on the chin will shorten a long face or make a heavy chin look smaller.

On a square or a round face apply the blusher toward the centre area of your cheekbones. Do not go up towards your ears.

Give yourself a sunny look and put blusher where the sun would tan your skin, high on the cheekbones, going down to the bridge of the nose. Then a little blusher on the chin and forehead. The application of the blusher must be light and transparent – it has to look very natural.

When putting your hair up or if you have short hair with the earlobes showing, a touch of blusher on each earlobe will give a glow to your look.

A little lipstick in the palm of your hand mixed with a drop of foundation will do well to replace blusher on your cheekbones.

BREATH
Bad breath can quickly be remedied by crunching a clove. Your breath will have the scent of a carnation.

If your breath smells of garlic, chew a coffee bean or stalk of parsley or celery.

CHEEKS
To shade your cheeks, apply shading powder over your face powder. Suck in your cheeks to find your natural hollow and then brush on the shading

powder, starting from inside the hollow and moving outwards to the hairline.

CHIN

Double chins can be disguised by using a light colour foundation on the chin area and a dark foundation on the double chin and down into the neck area. Blend carefully to avoid any harsh lines.

Minimize a double chin by using shading blusher around the jaw bone and under the jawline.

To sleep flat without a pillow is a good practice to prevent a double chin.

CIGARETTE STAINS

To clean nicotine-stained teeth, brush them with some bicarbonate of soda.

COMPACT POWDER

The greasy film on the surface of the compact powder, which appears after using the powder for a while, can be avoided by washing the powder pad once a week or using a clean piece of cotton wool instead of the pad every day.

To get rid of the hard, greasy film on top of the compressed powder, scrape it gently with a knife.

COMPLEXION

For a good complexion drink five glasses of water a day. Let it become a habit: it will ensure good elimination and therefore encourage a good complexion.

If you have lost your youthful complexion, drink five glasses of water a day, and every morning before breakfast drink the juice of half a lemon in hot water (you will get to like it). Before going to bed, drink a cup of hot skimmed milk, mixed with half a tablespoon of wheatgerm.

Start your meal with a green salad. Eat lean meat, grilled or roasted. Use artificial sweetener instead of sugar. If you follow this diet for at least a week every month, your complexion and figure will improve greatly.

For a healthy-looking complexion, drink a glass of carrot juice with two tablespoons of lemon juice in it at breakfast time every day for five to six weeks.

For a clear complexion, to fortify the liver and to eliminate all the toxins, take one celeriac, peel it and cut it in small pieces. Place it in the blender and drink the strained juice. Take half mid-morning and the rest mid-afternoon.

To give a bloom to your complexion when tired, mix a few drops of liquid blusher with your liquid foundation and make up your face with it.

DEODORANT

If you have run out of deodorant, powder your underarms with a little bicarbonate of soda.

DRY SHAMPOO

Dry shampoo can be replaced by talcum powder to the same effect.

EAU DE COLOGNE
Cologne contains more alcohol than *eau de toilette* (toilet water) but is cooler and more refreshing. It is weaker than *eau de toilette* and perfect for providing a light touch of scent. It is good for teenagers.

EAU DE TOILETTE
Toilet water contains a higher percentage of alcohol than concentrated perfume. It evaporates more quickly, and the fragrance does not last as long as perfume, but it is more refreshing. It should be sprayed over your body and around the neck.

ELBOWS
A compress of warm olive oil held for five minutes over the rough skin on your elbows will soften them. This also applies to the skin on your heels.

ENLARGED PORES
To reduce enlarged facial pores, dab them with a piece of cotton wool dampened in a solution of borax (one tablespoon) in a teacup of warm water.

EYES
Do not apply heavy, greasy cream around your eyes at night; the skin cannot breathe properly, so you'll get puffy eyes in the morning. A light moisturizer is what you need. Keep the heavy cream for the morning when you're taking your bath.

For tired, puffy eyes which need their circulation stimulated to reduce swelling, take a piece of cotton wool big enough to cover both eyes and dip it in ice-cold water, squeeze and apply it to your eyes. As soon as the cotton wool gets warm, repeat this little operation twice.

Or use two pads of cotton wool dampened with a mixture of two tablespoons of cucumber juice and two teaspoons of witch hazel. Leave on the eyes for fifteen minutes.

Another method is to use a teabag dipped in cold water, or apply thin slices of raw potato.

A good treatment for eyes is to apply odourless castor oil around the eyes and over the lids at night when taking a bath or getting ready for bed. Blot the excess before going to sleep.

PUFFY EYES
A quick remedy for puffy eyes: place a teaspoon in the freezer. When very cold wrap the teaspoon in a tissue handkerchief and gently press the convex side of the spoon underneath your eye over the puff for a minute.

To avoid puffy eyes and for a special occasion, sleep upright. (For this place a few big pillows behind your head).

EYEBROWS
To keep the hairs in place, stroke them with a small brush dampened with hair lacquer.

When plucking eyebrows, you should pluck below and between if necessary but never above, as this would alter their natural shape. Eyebrows are the frames of your eyes: do not shave or pluck out all your eyebrows as they will grow back very untidily. Very rarely does a picture look its best without a frame.

Before plucking your eyebrows, put a small piece of cotton wool dampened in warm water over them for a few minutes. The plucking will be much easier and the little black root will come out with the hair instead of staying in the skin as it very often does otherwise.

Give your eyebrows a little gloss: brush them with vaseline.

EYEBROW PENCIL

A hard eyebrow pencil can be softened by passing it quickly over the flame of a match. Wait a few seconds for cooling before applying.

A simple way to sharpen a soft eyebrow pencil is to place it in the freezer to harden for a while.

To revive an eyeshadow dried out in its pot add a few drops of water to it and stir well.

EYELASHES

Do not make up your lashes before powdering your face. Mascara on powdered lashes will make them look thicker and longer and emphasize your eyes.

EYELASH-CURLER

Your eyelash-curler will not break or pull out your eyelashes if you cover the rubber part (the area in contact with the lashes) with a thin coat of vaseline or petroleum jelly.

EYE MAKE-UP

For a natural expression, avoid hard lines when making up your eyes. Smooth any pencil line with a matching shadow until the two blend together and look part of your eyes.

To make your eyes look brighter, darken the inner edge of your lower lid with a dark eyelid pencil or a kohl pencil.

Do not forget the mascara when making up your eyes, for an eye make-up without mascara looks unfinished.

Dark matt eye-shadow will set your eyes deeply; pale, frosted shades will make them stand out; so use a happy medium, and dark or pale shadow only where you want to emphasize.

Very pale, chalky-coloured eyeshadows look unnatural and hard when applied over the eyelid, especially in the daylight.

If your wear glasses for short-sightedness, the eye make-up needs to be a little stronger. On the other hand, glasses for long-sightedness make the eyes look bigger, so eye make-up should be light.

Eyes with little lid showing will look more open if light eyeshadow is applied on the lid and a dark line is drawn and blended into the crease of the browbone.

To make your eyes look white use blue eyeliner on the inner edge of your lower lid.

Eyes that have too much lid showing should be made to look deeper by colouring the entire lid and blending the colour into the browbone crease.

Eyes that are set too close will look wider apart if the outer corner of the lid is coloured and blended into the browbone's crease.

To widen 'close-set' eyes, apply a light foundation to the inside corner of the eyes and against the side of the nose. Apply eye-shadow to the outside of the browbone in an upward sweep and pluck the eyebrows between the eyes so that they start no closer than the inside corners of your eyes.

Protruding eyes will look less prominent if a line of colour in a medium to deep shade is drawn around the closed eye and blended to the lashes.

FACE CREAM

Liquid paraffin is as good as any face cream and much, much cheaper. Dab here and there, massage upwards into the skin and wipe off the surplus. It will leave your skin very smooth.

FACE STEAM

To clear the skin, put a handful of fresh peppermint leaves in a bowl and cover with boiling water. Immediately put your face over the bowl, cover your head and the bowl with a large towel, and steam your face for as long as the steam lasts. Then dry with a clean pad. Peppermint is antiseptic and stimulates the circulation. *See illustration overleaf.*

FACIAL MASK

A good face mask for a smooth, wrinkle-free complexion can be made by sieving some oatmeal through a coarse sieve to eliminate the large flakes, then mixing with the white of an egg to make a thick paste. Dab over the face and leave on for half an hour. Wash off with warm water and finish with a splash of cold water. Dry the face carefully.

FALSE EYELASHES

When new, soak false eyelashes for a few minutes in warm water. This will remove the stiffness and make them more supple and natural-looking.

FINGERNAILS

Dirty fingernails can be cleaned with a good brushing of bicarbonate of soda.

FOUNDATION

For a translucent look when using liquid foundation on your face, mix a little moisturizer with the foundation in the palm of your hand before applying it to your face.

SKIN FOUNDATION

If your face cream foundation is too greasy, add a little witch hazel to it. Mix well before using.

FOUNDATION THAT CHANGES COLOUR

If your foundation changes colour on your skin after a while and turns a 'strong yellowish pink' add a little talcum powder to it (a little at a time and mix well).

COLOURLESS FOUNDATION

Make a boring colourless foundation pinky and glowy by adding some pink eye shadow to it (add a drop or two of cream shadow, or scrape a little from a compact one and mix well).

HAIR

To get your hair looking very full, lean your head forward as much as you can and brush the hair from the base of the neck to the forehead. Next throw your head back and shake it gently, for the hair to fall back naturally. Finish by spraying lightly with hair lacquer.

When drying your hair, use the same process as above for a full hairstyle and extra volume.

For a silky, glossy finish on straight hair, brush it with a bristle hairbrush when the hair is nearly dry and while you are blowdrying it.

For dry, damaged hair, mix two eggs with two tablespoons of vinegar or lemon juice until fluffy. Wash your hair and rinse well. Slightly dry the hair with a towel before working the mixture into the hair. Leave for fifteen minutes. Rinse thoroughly with lukewarm water (or you would cook the eggs!).

HAIR-CONDITIONER

After shampooing your hair, use an overripe avocado for a conditioner. Mash and mix the avocado with a little water to a thick paste. Comb into your hair right to the end. Cover your head with a shower hat or plastic bag and leave on for fifteen minutes. Rinse well.

To make hair silky and easy to comb, add a little wine vinegar to the last rinse. It will remove any traces of soap left in the hair.

Yoghurt applied after the shampoo on wet hair, left for a few minutes, then thoroughly rinsed is a very good hair-conditioner.

For greasy hair add a teaspoon of starch powder to the shampoo: it will condition the hair.

Very curly, dry, difficult hair will look and feel better if conditioned with olive oil or coconut oil (obtainable from a chemist) before shampooing. Use some warm olive oil or coconut oil and cover your hair thickly with it. Next wrap your head up in a warm towel and leave for one hour before shampooing.

HAIR-CUTTING

Wet fringes should be taped in place with some wide Scotch tape before being cut. Cut them a little longer than wanted as hair, when dry, always looks slightly shorter.

HAIR LACQUER

When hair lacquer is missing but needed, make some by mixing one teacup of boiling water with one teaspoon of plain gelatine or one teacup of boiling water with two teaspoons of sugar. Leave to cool. Pour it into a spray bottle and spray lightly over the hair.

Those mixtures are also good as setting lotion. Use over wet or dry hair before setting it.

HAIR RINSES – See also **Static Hair**, p. 316

A good, efficient coloured rinse for grey hair is an infusion of sage; it will slightly darken grey hair.

To make the sage infusion, pour one pint/half a litre of boiling water over a handful of fresh sage leaves or three tablespoons of any leaves, cover the pot or pan and let it brew for twenty minutes. Strain off the liquid and pour over your hair, using two containers. Unite the infusion in one container and pour it back over your hair, three or four times, over the other, empty container.

Rinse chestnut hair with a solution made of walnut leaves and water. Throw a good handful of the walnut leaves in a pint/half a litre of cold water, boil for ten minutes, strain, leave to cool.

To intensify light tones in naturally blonde hair, use a strong infusion of camomile flowers for the final rinse. Infuse two handfuls of camomile flowers in one pint/600 ml water for thirty minutes. Let it cool a little before use.

Highlighting hair can be done easily by stroking a mixture of water (three parts) and fresh lemon juice (one part) with a piece of cotton wool onto the hair and letting it dry in the sun.

HAIR-SETTING

For a quick hair-set, dampen your dry hair with toilet water, eau de cologne or beer. Set the hair on rollers. It will dry more quickly if you use a hair-dryer for a few minutes.

HANDS

You can avoid having sweaty hands if you rub them with camphor alcohol (obtainable from a chemist) and then talcum powder.

Vegetable stains on fingers can be removed with orange skin, a piece of cut lemon or some vinegar.

If you have been doing heavy work without gloves on, make a paste with a potato peeled and boiled in water, one teaspoon of glycerine and juice of a lemon. Rub your hands with the paste for a few minutes and then rinse. Repeat his treatment a few times during the day. Your hands will become smooth again.

For an everyday hand treatment, mix equal parts of eau de cologne, rosewater, glycerine and lemon juice.

HANDS PERSPIRATION

To stop disagreeable hand perspiration, wash your hands with soap and water, dry them and rub them with an alum stone all over.

LIFTING

Open your mouth wide when lifting something heavy; it diminishes the strain by relaxing the muscles.

LIPS

Too full lips can be made to look smaller by outlining with a lip pencil only the centre of the top and bottom lips and filling the centre section of both lips with a lipstick a darker shade than the one used over the rest of the lips.

To make thin lips look fuller, outline the outside edges of the lips and fill in with lipstick and gloss.

To sharpen a lip pencil (and one needs to do so often for making a very fine line round the mouth) first place the lip pencil in the freezer for a while so the point won't break when you sharpen it.

LIP GLOSS
When applying lip gloss, do not apply it right to the edges of the mouth. It would cause the lipstick to run.

LIPSTICKS
The best place to test a lipstick is on the cushion of your finger, where the skin is, like the lips, of a pink colour.

If your mouth droops at the corners, it makes you look older. Avoid this by using a pencil to extend the outline of your lower lip upwards and by not bringing the outline of the top lip all the way into the corner.

Do not throw your nearly finished lipsticks away. Melt them together in a small jar, over a pan of hot water, and leave to set. Use it with a lip-brush to make up your lips.

Powder your lips before putting on your lipstick: it will look neater and stay that way.

Dark-red lipstick makes you look older; light colours make you look younger. Orange-red can be flattering, but it hardens the features and really suits only the exotic type. Orange and rusty colours emphasize yellow teeth.

To prevent your lipstick 'bleeding' over the edge of your lips and into the fine wrinkles around your mouth, apply it the following way. First powder the lips, then apply the lipstick; open your mouth wide and blot with a tissue. With your mouth still wide open, powder again. Relax your mouth and apply more lipstick.

MAKE-UP
If you have wrinkles, blow out your cheeks when you powder your face; look up when powdering underneath your eyes.

To test the colour of a foundation or lipstick, the best place is the inside skin of your wrist.

For a natural make-up, emphasize either the mouth or the eyes, but never both or the make-up will look heavy.

An older woman should emphasize her mouth more than her eyes; wrinkled coloured eyelids never look good.

When applying a product to your face with your hands or when cleansing with tissues, always proceed from the bottom to the top. Movements from top to bottom provoke sagging skin and wrinkles.

When applying coloured foundation to your face, dot it on first, then take some cotton wool dipped in rosewater and carefully spread the product all over your face. Using this method, you will obtain a uniform make-up which will last longer.

For a better face-coverage and a thinner, lighter make-up, blend a few drops of your foundation with a few drops of your skin-freshener in the palm of your hand before applying it to your face.

To find out if you are using the right foundation for your skin type, pour some water into a glass, put a drop of foundation on your fingertip and touch the surface of the water. If the foundation dissolves, it is oil in water and suitable for an oily skin; if it stays on your finger, it is water in oil and suitable for a dry skin.

To keep make-up fresh all day or all evening, dip a pad of cotton wool in water and squeeze out the excess moisture. When you have made up your face, dab the pad over your powdered skin and it will set the powder for many hours with no need for retouching.

For evening, a light touch of pearly white face powder on the cheek-bones, the middle of the forehead and underneath the eyebrows will give a glow to your face.

MAKE-UP PENCIL
Soften your dried make-up pencils (lip, eye pencils etc.) by standing them point down overnight in a glass with a little baby oil or salad oil.

MAKE-UP REMOVER
If you have run out of make-up remover, use a slice or two of raw potato to remove your make-up; it works wonders.

MAKE-UP TRAY
A cutlery tray, with all its divided compartments, is ideal for storing make-up.

MASCARA
Make your lashes look thicker: after the first application of mascara, when it is nearly dry, powder them with a powder puff, then apply another coat of mascara.

Add a drop of warm water to your empty mascara container; it will make it go a little further.

A gentle way of removing mascara is to use a teaspoon, a tissue and a few drops of baby oil. Put your thumb in the bowl of the spoon, take the lashes between the curved side of the spoon and the tissue to which a little oil has been added. Start at the base of the lashes and gently slide down to the tips, removing the mascara at the same time.

MASK
For a pick-me-up mask, beat the yolk of an egg with a few drops of lemon juice and half a teaspoon of olive oil. Apply the mixture to your face, leave for fifteen minutes. Rinse and dry your face gently.

For an older skin, warm some olive oil in a bowl which is standing in hot water; soak in it a piece of cotton wool large enough to cover your face.

Protect your eyes with pads of cotton wool dampened with water, then place the oily piece of cotton wool on your face and keep it on until cold. Cleanse your face with soft tissues, then pat with cotton wool dampened in cold water.

The following beauty masks can be used once a month to clean your face; they will cleanse the skin of all the impurities which block the pores. These masks should be put on a clean skin after cleansing and toning; do not put on your eyelids or under your eyes. Remove the mask with cotton wool dipped in warm water.

For greasy skin: Dilute two teaspoons of cornflour with one lightly beaten egg white and mix until creamy but not too thick. Apply gently to your face and leave to dry. When your skin starts to pull strongly, rinse with warm water.

For dry and delicate skin: Make a thin paste with the yolk of an egg, some orange juice and a few drops of lemon juice and almond oil. Apply the mask to your face, leave it on for fifteen minutes and then remove with warm water.

For all types of skin: Yoghurt makes a good, relaxing mask which leaves your face soft and fresh-looking.

MOUSTACHE

To get a splendid upturned curl, trim the top layers of the moustache shorter.

But if you want a splendid drooping moustache, trim the underneath layers shorter.

NAILS

Do not cut your nails with scissors as this can cause them to split. File them with an emery board, which is softer than a metal file.

To make your nails look longer, do not cover the entire surface of the nail with varnish but leave a space on each side.

When you are doing a dirty job without gloves on, scratch a piece of soap with your nails. The soap will stay under your nails and prevent their becoming caked with dirt.

To strengthen your fingernails and make them grow, morning and night for a fortnight paint them with white iodine. This will also prevent children biting their nails as the taste is most unpleasant.

To strengthen your nails, soak them for fifteen minutes in pineapple juice. Keep the juice in the refrigerator to use it again a few times. For a good result, apply the treatment for a fortnight. Bring the juice to room temperature before use.

Weak, broken nails will look good again after a fortnight of the potato treatment. Bury your nails in a raw peeled potato for as long as you can (e.g. at night when watching television). Then wipe your fingers and try not to wash your hands for at least half an hour after.

To strengthen your nails, soak them four times a week in warm olive oil for at least five minutes each time. Use the same olive oil over again.

The hair-dryer is great to dry nail varnish on fingernails in a hurry.

NAIL VARNISH

To prevent the lid of a bottle of nail varnish sticking, spread a little vaseline on the grooves.

Store your nail polish in the fridge or upside down in a drawer – it will last longer.

Too thick nail varnish can be made thinner by adding a few drops of nail-varnish remover to it. Acetone will also dilute nail varnish.

Gluey and sticky nail varnish will regain its liquid consistency if you dip the bottle of varnish in boiling water for a little while. But your nail varnish will not get sticky if, in the first place, you store it in the refrigerator.

Dry your nails quickly by holding your hands in the freezer for a minute or two, or if you don't like the idea, dip your nails in very cold water.

NAIL-VARNISH REMOVER

Home-made nail-varnish remover: to a small bottle of acetone (from a chemist) add four drops of castor oil (chemist). Shake and use.

NECK EXERCISE

To stretch and exercise your neck muscles, say repeatedly in a very exaggerated fashion 'O – E' for a few minutes in the morning and at night (and during the day if you can).

NOSE

If the lower part of your nose is heavy-looking, take a cream foundation two shades deeper then the one you use over your face and apply and blend a small dot on either side of the nose.

If you have a large nose, wear a fluffy fringe (not flat) or a wavy hair-do (not symmetrical hair-dos, like a centre parting).

A long nose can be given a shorter effect by using dark foundation on the nostrils and on and around the tip of the nose.

If your nose is too narrow, pluck your eyebrows to make them look set further apart and give a wider effect to your nose.

If your nose goes red and has a burning sensation, rub your ears firmly with your hands. The blood will rush to your ears and leave your nose.

PARSLEY

Parsley has a high Vitamin A content which is good for the skin, so eat as much of it as possible.

PERFUME

When choosing a perfume, smear a drop on the inside of your wrist, shake your hand a little to make the moisture evaporate, then sniff.

Perfume is very expensive and very strong, so do not shower yourself with it. A dab behind each ear, in the crook of each elbow and on the inside of your wrists – and sometimes a few dabs around the inside of the hem of your skirt – is quite sufficient.

When opened, keep the bottle in a cool place in the dark. When exposed to light and heat, perfume loses its scent.

POWDER

Apply loose powder over foundation with a powder puff, or open a pad of cotton wool, place some powder in the middle, close the pad and apply generously to the face. Brush off the excess with a tissue or very soft brush.

Powder should be one shade lighter than the foundation or translucent, so as not to affect the colour of the foundation.

Pressed powder in compacts is good for retouching your face during the day or evening.

POWDER PUFFS

Wash chamois backed or real skin powder puffs in warm soapy water; hot water would harden the skin. Add a teaspoon of glycerine to the last rinse for the puff to regain its fluffiness (this also applies to the fluffy lambswool puff).

ROSEWATER

Use rosewater after cleansing your face; it is a tonic and astringent. To make rosewater, take three handfuls of fresh rose petals, place them in a pan and pour one pint/half a litre of boiling water over them. Cover and leave for fifteen minutes, strain through a fine strainer, bottle the liquid and keep in a cool place.

RED CHEEKS

Disguise the colour of your cheeks, if they are too red, by applying a gentle touch of green-tinted moisturizer over them. It will also disguise broken veins.

SHAMPOO (DRY)

When brushing dry shampoo out of your hair, put a piece of gauze over the bristles of the hairbrush to absorb dirt and oil.

SKIN

If your skin is looking spotty, and if you are working long hours under artificial lights, you might have a vitamin deficiency. (The vitamin in your body is reduced by artificial lights.) Eat more green vegetables, milk products, tinned fish in oil, egg yolks and a lot of carrots.

SKIN CLEANSER

Once every two or three weeks get rid of all the dry dead cells which have collected on the surface of your facial skin. Rub your face gently for a few minutes with a facecloth soaked and squeezed out in warm water and sprinkled with fine kitchen soap. Rinse well in clear warm water.

To cleanse enlarged pores around the chin and nose, pat the pores with a piece of cotton wool dipped in a solution of lukewarm water (half a teacup) and borax (one heaped tablespoon).

STATIC HAIR
Hair gets very static in the mountains, especially after wearing a woollen hat while ski-ing. The static will be greatly reduced if, when you wash your hair, you use a conditioner.

SUNTAN OIL
To sunbathe without burning, fill a small bottle with refined, odourless olive oil, add a few drops of tincture of iodine (available from chemists) and shake well. Used on your skin when sunbathing, it will give a lovely golden tan.

WATER
Water on your face should never be left to dry by itself. Dry it immediately, because dampness, if left too long, irritates the skin of your face (as it does the hands).

WEIGHT
When weight-watching, remember to weigh yourself every morning. Adjust your day's food intake accordingly.

CLOTHING

BELT
Slightly soiled light-coloured kid belts can be cleaned with a pencil-eraser. Rub with a soft cloth afterwards. For suede belts use the pencil-eraser then a fine wire brush or some very fine sandpaper to raise the nap.

BERET
After washing a beret, absorb the excess water by rolling it in a bath towel, and keep its shape by stretching it over a plate of the right size.

BODY HEIGHT
If you are short and wish to look taller, avoid wearing contrasting colours on your upper and lower halves.

A short-legged woman should not wear puffed sleeves or wide jackets with square shoulders. Wide-brimmed hats are also out. Her upper half must be trim or she will look legless.

BODY WEIGHT
To look thinner, avoid tight-fitting clothes. Wear cardigans and sweaters a size larger. Wear slightly loose dresses and vertical stripes and avoid pale colours.

A narrow-shouldered and broad-hipped woman should avoid very short sleeves (puffed sleeves, long sleeves or no sleeves at all are better) and clothes with belts. She should be trim on her lower half and add width to her upper half.

If you have an over-large bust, avoid wearing high, round necklines. Instead wear Vs or square ones. These will make your bust look smaller.

BOOTS – See also **Shoes**
A boot-tree can be made quickly by introducing a thick rolled-up magazine into the leg of a boot. The magazine will unfold to the width of the boot, keeping it in good shape. You can also slide the magazine, or a piece of cardboard, into an old stocking or a long sock for a permanent shaped boot-tree.

Slide in and out of your boots easily by glueing a satin ribbon all the way down the leg inside the boot, from the top to the heel.

Never put wet leather boots (or shoes) near the fire to dry; the leather will harden.

When leather boots (or shoes) are very damp, first wash off the mud and dry a little with a clean cloth, then stuff them inside with newspaper and rub the leather with saddle soap before completely dry.

To clean rubber boots wash them in warm soapy water. To keep them supple and prevent the rubber from cracking, rub them from time to time with glycerine, the beaten white of an egg or some hot milk.

Wellington boots can be cold in winter: a few layers of newspaper cut to the shape of the sole and placed inside the boots will insulate your feet and keep them warm.

To clean patent leather boots or shoes wipe them with a wet sponge, dry with a soft cloth and rub some petroleum jelly or almond oil into them gently. Dry and shine with a soft cloth.

BUTTONHOLE FLOWER

It will keep fresh all day or all night in your buttonhole if you first burn the end of the stem with a match or dip it in melted wax.

CHIDREN'S CLOTHING

AGE	WEIGHT	CHEST	HEIGHT
3 months	5.5 kg/12 lb		62 cm/$24\frac{1}{4}$"
6 months	8 kg/18 lb		69 cm/27"
9 months	9.5 kg/21 lb		74 cm/29"
12 months	11 kg/24 lb		79 cm/31"
18 months	12.5 kg/28 lb		83 cm/33"
2 years		51 cm/$20\frac{1}{4}$"	92 cm/36"
3 years		53 cm/$20\frac{7}{8}$"	98 cm/38"
4 years		55 cm/$21\frac{1}{2}$"	104 cm/40"

CLINGING DRESS – See also **Antistatic, p. 270**

Wear a slightly starched petticoat to stop your dress clinging to your legs.

CLOTHES

Your clothes will look better and last longer if you hang them up instead of folding them. If you have the space, hang your jackets, coats and dresses on wooden or padded hangers (wire hangers will put them out of shape). Hang your blouses or shirts, as this will lessen the creases. But fold your woollens: hanging would sag them out of shape.

CLOTHES LINE

If you hang woollen shirts, dresses etc. to dry on a clothes line with clothes pegs, do not hang them by the shoulders where the pegs will leave a mark, very difficult to get rid of. Hang them from underneath the arms.

CREASES

Creases in clothes can be removed if dampened with vinegar and pressed with an iron.

To get rid of creases in a permanently pleated blouse, dress or skirt, dampen the creases with a sponge or a face cloth wrung out in warm water. Put the garment on a hanger and leave it to dry. The creases will disappear.

EVENING DRESS

To hang a long evening dress in your wardrobe without the skirt brushing the floor, sew two tape loops inside the dress at the waist on the side seams and slip the loops through the hanger.

FURS

To dry-clean your furs, warm three to four handfuls of pure bran in a baking tray in the oven, stirring often to prevent burning. When it is warm but not too hot, rub it thoroughly into the fur with your hands. Repeat three or four times if the fur is very soiled. Finally, shake the fur well and brush with a soft brush. Some resin-free sawdust (from any carpenter) heated and used in the same way as the bran or oatmeal will also clean a fur very well.

A good and cheap way to protect your furs from moths during the summer is to place them in a wooden box with a well-fitted lid or in a wooden chest or trunk. Ask the chemist for a quarter of a litre/half a pint of carbon tetrachloride (handle with care: it is not inflammable but it is very poisonous). Close the bottle with a cork, make a hole in the middle of the cork big enough to take a piece of drinking straw, through which the liquid will slowly evaporate. Tie a ribbon or a string tightly around the bottle-neck and hang it inside the box. Secure the other end of the ribbon or string to a hook outside or to the handle of the trunk. Close the lid tightly. The liquid should last the whole winter, but refill if needed. It is advisable not to keep the trunk, chest etc. in a bedroom because of the vapour.

If your fur coat is losing its hair, put it in the refrigerator overnight.

When cutting fur, put the fur side down on the table and cut the skin with a sharp razor blade, never with scissors.

GLOVES

Sew the children's gloves one at each end of a length of elastic, long enough to go through one sleeve, across the back and through the other sleeve. Then they won't lose them.

To prevent white gloves yellowing, cover them with talcum powder when not in use and keep them in a closed box.

To wash skin gloves put them on and dip your hands in warm soapy water, squeezing and rubbing your hands together. Then rinse thoroughly.

Leather gloves can be kept soft after washing if a few drops of salad oil are mixed with the soapy water. Rinse lightly in warm water and dry flat in a towel. Hang the gloves after blowing into them to give them shape.

If the gloves are still a little stiff when dry, roll them in a warm, dry towel for a while before wearing them.

Unwashable white kid gloves will clean if rubbed with a piece of cotton wool dampened with carbon tetrachloride (obtainable from a chemist). Change the piece of cotton wool when it becomes soiled. Clean your dark skin kid gloves by rubbing them with a soft cloth dipped in vaseline.

To clean kid gloves of any colour, take some skimmed milk, white soap and a sponge. Dip the sponge lightly in the skimmed milk and then rub it on the soap. Put your hand in the glove to be cleaned and rub the glove all over with the sponge, repeating this procedure twice on the dirty part. The glove will clean perfectly.

Kid gloves will also clean well if rubbed with hot sawdust. Warm the sawdust slowly in the oven and when hot put on your gloves and rub in.

Unwashable suede gloves can be cleaned by putting them on and rubbing the hands in a container full of slightly warm oatmeal. Another method is to sprinkle the gloves thoroughly with powdered French chalk or fuller's earth. Leave the gloves for an hour or two wrapped in a clean cloth. Then brush the powder off. Repeat if the gloves are very soiled.

When darning gloves, use a glass marble for a darning 'egg'.

HATS – See also **Straw hats**
To clean a hard felt hat, brush inside and outside with a soft brush dipped in benzine. Dry with a soft cloth.

To clean a soft felt hat, bring out the leather from inside and take off the trimming. Stuff the hat with clean cloths and brush the felt (following the grain of the felt) with a very soft brush with a solution of ammonia and cold water (one tablespoon of ammonia to half a litre/one pint of water). Rinse with a brush dipped in cold water and leave to dry.

To clean a white felt hat, first hold it over the steam from a kettle to restore the pile, then rub it with whiting (Spanish white). Finally brush it.

Grease will not come through the crown of a man's felt hat if a narrow piece of blotting paper is put inside, between the lining and the felt.

JEANS
New jeans should be left to soak overnight in strongly salted cold water to fix the colour.

KNITWEAR
To prevent stretching, place the knitwear in a pillowcase before putting it in the washing machine.

LACE
New lace can become antique-looking if dipped in tea or an infusion of camomile for a lighter tint. Black lace looks better after a bath in sweetened black coffee. Then press between two clean pieces of cloth.

Keep old lace in a dry warm place, airing it from time to time, if not in use often. Black lace has a tendency to mould if not aired.

LACE VEIL

To rejuvenate a lace veil, lay it flat on a towel and sprinkle with one of the following: talcum powder, French chalk, powdered magnesia, bicarbonate of soda or powder starch. Rub it into the fabric with your fingers and leave it for two hours, then shake well to remove all traces of powder.

If the veil is not too delicate, use the same products as above but place the veil in a plastic bag with the powder and shake. Spraying the veil with a dry shampoo is also a very efficient method.

LEATHER BAGS

To remove water stains, hold your bag over a pan of boiling water for a little while. Wait until the leather is dry and then apply a neutral polish.

If the colour from your leather handbag rubs off on your clothes, rub it with methylated spirit.

LINT ON DARK CLOTHES

To prevent lint sticking to dark clothes when washing them in the washing machine, turn the clothes inside out before putting them in the wash.

To prevent lint sticking when tumble drying them, place a piece of nylon net (a metre or so will do, and can be bought at any shop where they sell fabric) in the tumbler with the wet clothes.

MACKINTOSH

Do not try to remove a stain on a rubber mackintosh with a grease solvent, but cover the stain with a thick paste made of French chalk and water. Leave it to dry before brushing off.

METRIC CONVERSION CHARTS

WOMEN'S CLOTHES SIZES

SIZE	BUST	HIP	WAIST
8	76/81 cm	(30/32")	58 cm (22")
10	81/86 cm	(32/34")	61 cm (24")
12	86/91 cm	(34/36")	66 cm (26")
14	91/97 cm	(36/38")	71 cm (28")
16	97/192 cm	(38/40")	76 cm (30")
18	102/107 cm	(40/42")	81 cm (32")
20	107/112 cm	(42/44")	86 cm (34")
22	112/117 cm	(44/46")	91 cm (36")
24	117/122 cm	(46/48")	96 cm (38")

MEN'S CLOTHES SIZES

COLLAR	CHEST	WAIST
36 cm (14″)	81 cm (32″)	71 cm (28″)
38 cm (15″)	84 cm (33″)	76 cm (30″)
39/40 cm (15½″)	86 cm (34″)	81 cm (32″)
41 cm (16″)	91 cm (36″)	86 cm (34″)
42 cm (16½″)	97 cm (38″)	91 cm (36″)
43 cm (17″)	102 cm (40″)	97 cm (28″)
44 cm (17½)	107 cm (42″)	102 cm (40″)
46 cm (18″)	112 cm (44″)	107 cm (42″)

NYLON FUR

To get rid of the surface dirt on a nylon fur (collar, cuffs, etc.), spray some dry shampoo over it and follow instructions as for hair.

Or rub it gently with a sponge and some warm detergent solution, rinse and dry with a cloth.

PATENT LEATHER

To clean patent-leather shoes and handbags, rub gently with cotton wool dipped in almond oil and then shine with a soft dry cloth.

To maintain patent leather, rub vaseline into it regularly.

Marks on patent leather will come off if rubbed with methylated spirit.

Patent leather shoes that have become hard will become supple again if you cover the leather with vaseline and leave for twenty-four hours. Then rub with a clean, soft cloth.

Patent leather shoes can be kept soft and in good condition if rubbed regularly with milk or a beaten egg white or some turpentine.

When patent leather becomes dull, rub a few drops of turpentine over it, with a soft cloth.

Scratches on patent leather shoes can disappear with a coat of colourless nail varnish. Leave it to dry before polishing with a soft cloth.

PLEATED SKIRT

When packing, draw your pleated skirt through an old stocking with the foot cut off. The skirt will be uncreased when unpacked.

RIBBONS

Put a little sugar into the final rinse when washing to keep them in good condition.

To press silk, nylon or satin ribbon, place a sheet of tissue paper over it and keep the iron stationary over the tissue paper. Carefully and gradually draw the ribbon under it.

SHAWL

Clean your white woollen shawl without washing it. Lay it flat on a table-cloth, sprinkle talcum powder, powdered magnesia or powdered starch all over it. Work the powder into the wool with your fingers and roll the shawl in the tablecloth. Wait for twelve hours before taking it outdoors and shaking the powder off.

SHEEPSKIN

Keep the furry side of your sheepskin coat clean by spraying it with dry hair shampoo from time to time. Leave for at least forty-five minutes then shake and brush it, outdoors if possible or over the bathtub.

To clean white sheepskin lining, rub with a sponge dampened in liquid detergent.

SHIRTS

Shirts will not tangle together when washed in the washing machine if they are first buttoned up and the body of the shirt is turned inside out, leaving the sleeves inside.

Shirts can get very dirty round the collar and cuffs; before soaking for a wash or throwing into the washing machine, rub the dirty marks with some dry household soap.

Do not scrub the dirty creases with a brush; it will cause the shirt to tear very quickly.

SHOES – See also Boots

Try not to buy new shoes first thing in the morning when the feet are relaxed after a night's rest. Your new shoes might be too tight in the evening when your feet are tired and swollen.

Shoe trees are very important, so insert them whenever you take off your shoes. Paper stuffed into the shoe will do as second best.

Your shoes won't slip in icy weather if, before going out, you rub the soles and heels with methylated spirit.

To prevent slipping, scratch the sole of new leather-soled shoes with a knife or pair of scissors.

Stop shoes becoming slippery by sticking the rubber patch used to repair bicycle punctures onto the soles.

Relieve the friction against socks or stockings from a stiff shoe heel by rubbing the inside of the heel with soap.

When the metal or plastic end of a shoelace has come off, dip the end of the lace in clear nail varnish. Leave it to stiffen and dry.

When the inside of shoes leaves stains on socks or stockings, rub the inside of the shoes with a cloth dampened in benzine (from a chemist) or methylated spirit. Keep rubbing until no more dye comes off.

Smelly shoes will smell like new if a tablespoon of bicarbonate of soda is sprinkled inside each shoe. Shake the powder well all over the inside and leave overnight.

If a leather shoe is tight, put it on, dip a cloth in hot water and lay it across the shoe. Repeat this operation several times: the moist heat will make the leather shape itself to the foot.

Stop shoes squeaking by standing the sole in a container into which some linseed oil has been poured.

If your leather shoes become hard, rub the leather with paraffin oil and give it a regular rubbing with turpentine.

Hard leather shoes can be softened by warming the shoes in an open warm oven for a few seconds, then rubbing the leather with castor oil and wearing the shoes in the house for a little while.

Calf shoes which have become hard can be softened again if rubbed with a mixture of milk and water in equal quantities. Rub well into the leather and leave to dry in a cool, well ventilated place before polishing.

If the leather of your shoes has dried hard after a soaking in the rain rub glycerine into it with your fingertips. Leave overnight or until dry before polishing.

Very wet shoes will not become stiff while drying if they are rubbed with saddle soap when still wet and are then stuffed with newspaper. Leave them to dry away from direct heat. Replace the newspaper halfway through drying.

A few drops of paraffin oil mixed with the shoe polish when in use will give the leather a better shine.

If you want your leather shoes to shine beautifully, rub them with a cut, raw potato before polishing them.

Shoe polish that is caked, hard or lumpy can be softened with a few drops of paraffin, turpentine or olive oil.

Scuffs on shoes (especially children's shoes) will disappear if before applying the polish you rub it with a piece of raw potato, and leave it to dry before applying the polish.

When polishing and brushing children's sandals, wear an old glove, or a rubber glove or place your hand in a plastic bag before slipping it inside the sandals. This will prevent the polish staining your hands.

Water spots on leather shoes will disappear if rubbed with vaseline. Leave the vaseline to do its work. Rub and polish.

Dried rain spots on suede shoes can be removed by rubbing the stained suede with fine sandpaper, a pencil-eraser or some turpentine. Shiny marks will disappear, if rubbed gently with a new wire pad scourer.

Rain spots on suede shoes can also be removed by rubbing the shoes with fine glasspaper when they are dry.

Marks on light suede shoes can be removed by rubbing talcum powder into the stains and leaving overnight. Or rub the marks with a clean pencil-eraser.

Grease or oil on suede shoes can be difficult to remove. Cover the stain with a paste made of cleaning fluid and salt and leave it on for a few hours. Repeat if the stain is stubborn.

Sea-water or snow stains on shoes can be removed by dissolving a small piece of soda in a few tablespoons of hot milk. While the mixture is warm, apply it to the stains with a cloth, rubbing well. When dry, clean the shoes with your usual polish.

An equal part of water and vinegar will also remove sea-water stains on leather shoes.

Stains on dark leather shoes will disappear if rubbed with methylated spirit.

Stains on light leather shoes will disappear if rubbed with turpentine.

Crêpe-rubber soles will stay clean if washed regularly with warm soapy water and a nail brush. When dried off, apply glycerine over them, wait a couple of hours and sprinkle with talcum powder.

The rope heels of canvas shoes can be cleaned by brushing with a carpet shampoo. Rinse and leave to dry.

Brown shoes can be darkened and cleaned by rubbing them with the inside of a banana skin or a cut potato. Leave to dry and then polish with a soft cloth.

Milk to which a few drops of ammonia has been added will also darken shoes.

Remove stains from brown shoes with a few drops of lemon juice or vinegar mixed with a few drops of water.

White tennis shoes will keep their new look for much longer if they are sprayed generously with starch.

A clean soapy scouring pad is perfect for cleaning tennis shoes.

To clean very soiled white shoes, first rub them with an old toothbrush dipped in benzine. Leave to dry before applying any white product.

To get the whitener to coat the shoes evenly, first rub them with a raw potato or some methylated spirit.

To prevent newly whitened shoes leaving marks on clothes or other materials, spray them with hair spray after the white paste or liquid has dried thoroughly. (Do not do this to baby shoes since very often they put them in their mouth).

To clean white satin shoes, rub them with a white cotton cloth or a piece of cotton wool dipped in methylated spirit in which some soap flakes have been dissolved. Leave the shoes to dry on shoe-trees or stuff them with newspaper. For light marks on white satin shoes rub them all over with surgical spirit.

Stained lizard and skin shoes can be cleaned by dabbing the stain with hydrogen peroxide. Leave to dry and polish with a soft cloth.

SLEEVES
When pulling up your shirt/blouse sleeves, fold them, do not roll them, as that way they will be uncreased when pulled down again.

SLIMMING LOOK
For a slimming look, wear a narrow, deep V-neckline, and for the thinnest line wear a deep shawl collar down to the waist.

Raglan sleeves also belong to the slimming look. They break up a large chest frontage and cut shoulder width.

To look slimmer, avoid horizontal stripes, large prints and plaids.

If you have thick wrists or heavy forearms, do not wear three-quarter-length sleeves; they will accentuate the lower part of your arms.

If you are wide-shouldered and large-busted, do not wear a double-breasted jacket. A narrow jacket collar is a must for you.

If you want to look slimmer, do not wear a tent dress: it will have the opposite effect. A belted dress can have a slimming effect if the belt is narrow and made of the dress fabric.

When large-breasted, avoid wearing a light-coloured top with a dark skirt: it will accentuate the higher part of your body.

When wide-hipped, do not wear a light-coloured skirt with a dark top: it will accentuate the lower part of your body.

Do not wear satin if you want to look slimmer: it attracts the light over the bulging places.

On the beach wear one-piece swimsuits; avoid the shiny fabrics which reflect light in all the wrong places.

For tennis wear a clean-line dress like the princess style; if you prefer shorts, wear them well fitted at the waist and slightly loose round the thighs.

If your ankles are thick, do not wear shoes with straps across the instep: it would make them look wider; so will shoes with low-cut sides.

If you want to look taller, wear knee-high boots; mid-calf boots cut the legs and make you look smaller.

When short-waisted, avoid wearing a wide belt; wear a curved one: it lengthens the waist.

SOCKS

To buy socks of the right size for a child, ask him or her to close his fist tightly, thumb in. Next, wrap the fist with the foot of the sock. For a good fit the heel has just to touch the toe.

When darning woollen socks, add extra strength to the darn by entwining a strand of thread with the strand of wool used for darning.

Knee-high stretch-nylon socks make ideal shoebags for travelling.

STOCKINGS AND TIGHTS

Give a longer life to your stockings and tights by spraying the toes and heels with hairspray.

To dry a pair or stockings or tights in a hurry, hold them in one hand and blow them dry with a hair-dryer in the other hand.

When pegging out stockings or tights on the washing line on a windy day, peg the hanging feet together to stop the stockings wrapping around the line.

If left with odd nylon stockings of different shades, place them together in water with a mild detergent and bring to the boil. Simmer for ten minutes and rinse well. The stockings will then be of a similar shade.

Silk stockings will last longer if they are soaked in cold water.

When washing your tights, add one tablespoon of fine sugar in the last rinse; they will last longer.

A run in the stocking can be stopped with a rubbing of dry soap, a drop of clear nail varnish or a drop of clear glue.

Sew a few pairs of tights or stockings together in a ball and use it to shine the taps in your bathroom.

STRAW HATS

Methylated spirit is excellent for restoring colour and shape to straw hats. After dusting the straw, apply methylated spirit with a pad of cotton-wool – it will also give the required stiffness.

Very soiled straw hats will clean if, after removing the trimming and stuffing the crown with paper, you use a nail brush and warm soapy water to rub the straw lightly. Be careful not to wet the straw too much. Rinse and dry with a soft cloth and leave to dry outside or in a well-ventilated place.

Panama hats clean very well with the above treatment, but rinse in water to which a few drops of glycerine have been added. Blot with a soft cloth and finish drying in the sun.

White straw will stay white if rubbed from time to time with a soft brush dipped in hydrogen peroxide or lemon juice. Rinse well and leave to dry.

To clean a light straw hat, dip the hat in a bath of soap, ammonia and water (two tablespoons of soapflakes, one tablespoon ammonia, one litre/ two pints of water). Leave it for ten minutes then brush with a soft brush. Rinse with soft water (i.e. boiled water left to cool off) and leave to dry flat.

To clean a dark straw hat brush the hat, then rub it with a soft cloth dipped in a little vegetable oil.

The brim of a straw hat can be pressed flat over a damp cloth with a moderately hot iron.

STYLE IN CLOTHES

A cheap dress will look great if you add a beautiful belt to it, but you will ruin the look of an expensive dress with a plastic belt. Good-quality, well-chosen accessories (shoes, handbags, belts, scarves etc.) can give style and elegance to the most modest garment.

SUEDE

Rejuvenate your tired suede jacket; hang it in a steam-filled bathroom for an hour and leaving it to dry before brushing with a suede brush.

When your suede handbag or shoes are losing their colour all over your clothes, rub the suede lightly with a soft rag and dampen with methylated spirit.

SUIT

To rejuvenate a tired-looking suit, dampen a soft cloth in a mixture of two teaspoons of ammonia to $\frac{1}{2}$pint/300 ml of warm water; rub the suit with the cloth and leave to try.

TIES

To press a tie perfectly and avoid the seam creases marking the front of the tie with a shiny line, cut a piece of cardboard a little smaller than the tie and slide it inside the large part of the tie before pressing.

To clean a silk tie, sponge it with the juice of a raw potato (grate some raw potato, put it in a muslin cloth and drain the juice).

TIGHTS – See Stockings

TROUSERS – See also 'Shine on fabric', p. 271

When packing trousers in a suitcase, roll them instead of folding them flat.

To press trousers without an iron, lay them flat overnight underneath the mattress on your bed. In the morning you will be surprised how neat they look.

Prevent the back of a trouser leg fraying around the hem by sewing a small button half an inch up from the bottom hem inside the back of each trouser leg so that it doesn't rub on your shoes.

Creases in trousers can be sharpened by rubbing the wrong side of the crease with a dry piece of soap.

TUMBLE-DRYER CREASES

Clothes should be removed from the tumble-dryer as soon as it stops, when the items are still warm, shaken and hung to avoid creases. To get rid of creases on clothes which have been left in the tumble-dryer after it has stopped, place a wet towel which has been well wrung-out in the tumble-dryer with the wrinkled clothes and tumble them again for a short time. The creases will soon disappear.

UMBRELLA

When stained, clean your umbrella with a cloth dipped in vinegar.

UNDERWEAR

If your nylon underwear has gone grey, dye it flesh colour by dipping it in a strong, strained brew of tea. Simmer, stirring, until the underwear is the desired colour.

Do not kill your looks by wearing underwear that is too small (if it leaves a red line underneath your breasts and around your waist and thighs when you take it off, it is too small). Too small underwear makes bulges on the tummy, along the back and on the thighs, meaning visible underwear lines when you are wearing a sweater, trousers, straight skirt etc.

SEWING

BELT

To make an extra hole in your belt, take a steel needle or a skewer, get the tip red hot, and pierce the belt.

To give a backing support to a soft fabric belt, press some 'iron-on' hemming tape to the wrong side.

Stitch a matching fabric belt to the side or the back of a dress to prevent losing it or looking for it every time it is needed.

BUTTONS

When sewing buttons to thick material, a matchstick held between the button and the material will ensure the shank is long enough. It is also helpful if you use elastic thread instead of cotton.

A button will stay on a garment longer if a drop of clear nail varnish is placed on the middle of the button to hold the threads together.

Buttons sewn onto fur or leather should have a small button behind, inside the garment, to prevent the fabric tearing under the thread.

When removing a button, a fork placed between the fabric and the button will prevent the scissors cutting the material (cut the thread between the button and the fork).

Four-hole buttons will have a longer life if you saw only two holes at a time, then knot and break the thread before sewing the other two holes.

Dental floss is a good thread substitute for sewing buttons on 'hard-working' clothes.

To make a strong button loop, use a piece of shoelace.

Before cutting buttonholes in a soft fabric which frays easily, thinly coat the top and underneath of the fabric with colourless nail varnish. Wait until the varnish is dry before cutting.

DARNING

If your eyes are not very good, when doing your darning, use a lighted torch as a darning 'egg'.

Darning will be much easier if, when you have a large hole to darn, you first tack a piece of fine hairnet over the hole.

Never darn with extra-thick thread to save time, as it will tear the fabric.

DRAWING THREADS

Drawing threads can be very irritating sometimes but if you rub the fabric where the threads are to be drawn with a piece of soap first, the whole thing will become a pleasure.

DRESSMAKING PATTERNS

Paper patterns are difficult to keep still on a slippery, thin fabric while cutting. A good way of fixing the pattern is to press it lightly with a warm iron when it is placed on the fabric. The fabric will cling to the paper, making the cutting easier.

ELASTIC

Before drawing an old elastic or ribbon out of a hem to replace it, pin (with a small safety pin) or sew one end of the old piece to one end of the new one and pull the old elastic (or ribbon) out. This is a quick and simple method.

EMBROIDERY

To clean very delicate embroidery, first place it between two pieces of linen. Stitch the embroidery and the pieces of linen together loosely. Wash, rinse and press it before undoing the stitches.

To clean coloured embroidery, soak it in a solution of warm water and turpentine for twenty minutes (two litres/four pints of water to one tablespoon of turpentine). Rub the embroidery gently between your hands, then rinse.

Transfer pattern marks on embroidery which cannot be washed will disappear if rubbed with methylated spirit.

Iron embroidery face down on a bath towel placed on the ironing board to make the pattern of the embroidery stand out more.

An easy way to copy embroidery from any material is to place a piece of paper over the embroidery and rub over it firmly with the back of a spoon. The design will appear on the paper very quickly.

To draw thread in linen for embroidery (e.g. hem-stitching), use a clean toothbrush and apply some lather over the fabric where the thread will be drawn. Leave to dry before starting to pull the threads.

FITTING

To get a perfect bust line when fitting a dress or a top, remember that the bigger the bust, the shorter the bust dart below the shoulder.

HEAVY FABRIC

Heavy fabric such as canvas will be easier to sew if the hems or seams are first rubbed with soap, thus enabling the needle to pass through the fabric more easily.

HEMS

If you have no one to help you mark a skirt that you want to take up or down, stretch a string between two chairs at the height required and rub the string with a piece of chalk. Put on your dress or skirt and turn slowly and carefully, touching the string all the way round the skirt. The hem will be marked by the chalk at the perfect height.

When unpicking a hem, use a clean toothbrush to extract the small pieces of thread left caught in the fabric.

HEM LINE
To get rid of a hem line when letting down a hem, firstly wet the line with a sponge dipped in pure white vinegar, then place a dry cloth over the line on the wrong side of the fabric, and press with a hot iron. To get rid of the white hem-line apply a mixture of ink and water in equal quantities. If it is too dark, apply water with a toothbrush until you get the right colour.

HEM STITCHING
When stitching a lining to fabric, to prevent the stitches catching on the right side of the fabric, place a small piece of cardboard or a playing card between the fabric and the lining. You can slide it along as you sew.

KNITTING
To prevent two strands of yarn getting tangled when you are knitting them together, thread the strands through an empty cotton reel before starting to knit.

When knitting with different balls of wool, place the balls in a net bag or a colander and thread the yarns in different holes.

Knit the cuffs of a pullover on four needles instead of two to avoid having a seam. It looks and feels better.

To sew the hem of a knitted garment, use elasticated thread instead of an ordinary thread or wool, for a softer finish.

To teach a person how to knit, place yourself in front of a mirror and ask your pupil to look at you in the mirror while you are making your demonstration.

LINING
A shirt or a blouse with worn-out collar and cuffs can be used for lining a jacket. Cut off the collar and the cuffs, the buttons and buttonholes, turn the garment inside-out and sew it onto the jacket.

To sew a lining to the hem of a skirt without catching the underneath fabric so that it would show on the right side of the garment, place a playing card or a piece of cardboard between the lining and the fabric, sliding the card as you sew along.

MACHINE SEWING
Prevent chiffon or any fine fabric being drawn up when using the sewing machine by placing a sheet of tissue paper between the fabric and the needle. Machine through the paper and tear it delicately afterwards.

When sewing plastic with a sewing machine, put a piece of greaseproof paper between the needle and the plastic. This will stop the plastic puckering or being cut. Tear away the greaseproof paper when you have finished sewing.

MENDING

When mending old cotton table linen, tack a piece of muslin on the back where the mending is to be done before darning. That way the darn will be much stronger and after washing it will hardly show through.

To mend a sheet, use your sewing machine. Place a piece of tissue handkerchief over the hole and, with the sewing machine, go over the hole and tissue stitching forwards and backwards. Reverse the sheet and make a stitching across the hole. When laundered, the tissue will dissolve and leave a neat darn.

NEEDLES

To thread a darning needle with a thick wool quickly, fold a piece of cotton in two. Thread the loop through the eye of the needle, push the wool through the loop. Pull back the cotton, and the wool strand will come with it.

NET CURTAINS – See **Machine sewing**

OLD LINEN REPAIR

Old sheets, bedspreads, curtains and clothes need to be repaired sometimes, but matching the thread can be difficult. A good way to get the colour right is to dip white linen or cotton thread in some cold tea until it matches the colour of the old sheets, curtains etc.

PINS AND NEEDLES

A sweet-smelling soap makes a lovely pin cushion. It keeps the needles lubricated and smells good in the sewing box.

PRESS-STUD

To sew on press-studs accurately, first sew the one with the point, then touch the point with a piece of chalk, press over the material where the other part of the press-stud is to be placed and you will have the exact spot for sewing.

PVC

To stop the PVC fabric slipping when going through the sewing machine, tape (don't use pins) some tissue paper over the shiny surface before machine-sewing.

SEAM

When sewing a thick seam with the sewing machine, rub the seam first with hard, dry soap. It will become much easier to sew.

SEWING

Cotton for sewing will not knot while sewing if the loose end is threaded through the needle and the knot is made in the cut end.

To prevent your double thread tangling when sewing, knot the ends separately instead of together.

When sewing nylon lingerie which is very slippery, place a piece of blotting paper underneath the nylon and sew through the nylon and paper. Tear the paper when finished.

When sewing buttons onto thick material, a matchstick placed underneath or across the top of the button will ensure the correct shank. It is also helpful if you use elastic thread instead of cotton. If the matchstick seems too thick or too big, use a fine toothpick or a pin.

SEWING MACHINE
Run some very fine doubled sandpaper through the sewing machine to keep the needle sharp. This will prevent seams wrinkling when sewing man-made fibres.

SEWING NEEDLES
Use a discarded lipstick-holder for storing sewing needles.

SKEINS
Skeins of wool can be straightened out for knitting by placing them in a paper bag and hanging the paper bag over the steam of a pan full of boiling water for ten to fifteen minutes.

THREAD
To give a thick thread even more resistance, wax it before use with some furniture wax or rub it against a candle. Or use dental floss instead of thread.

WORKING CLOTHES
A coat of clear nail varnish applied to the edges of pockets and bottoms of trouser legs will prolong the life of working clothes. Repeat the process from time to time after a few washes.

WOOL
Thick wool is sometimes difficult to thread, but if you roll the tip on a wet piece of soap and then rub it between your fingers, the ply will stick together and won't bounce back as it does when damped with saliva.

APPENDIX:
WEIGHTS AND MEASURES
CONVERSION TABLES

CAPACITY UK (IMPERIAL) UNITS

1 fluid ounce	=	8 fluid drams
1 gill	=	5 fluid ounces
1 pint	=	4 gills
1 gallon	=	4 quarts
1 peck	=	2 gallons
1 bushel	=	4 pecks
1 quarter	=	8 bushels
1 bulk barrel	=	36 gallons

CAPACITY, METRIC UNITS

1 centilitre	=	10 millilitres
1 decilitre	=	10 centilitres
1 litre	=	10 decilitres
1 litre	=	1 cubic decimetre
1 dekalitre	=	10 litres
1 hectolitre	=	10 decalitres or 100 litres
1 kilolitre	=	10 hectolitres
1 kilolitre	=	1,000 litres
1 litre	=	100 centilitres or 1,000 millilitres

CAPACITY, METRIC CONVERSIONS

1 fl.oz.	=	2,841 centilitres
1 pint	=	0,568 litres
1 gallon	=	4,546 litres
1 centilitre (cl)	=	0,352 fl.oz.
1 litre (1)	=	1,760 pints approx. $1\frac{3}{4}$ pints

LENGTH, UK (IMPERIAL) UNITS

1 foot	=	12 inches
1 yard	=	3 feet
1 chain	=	22 yards
1 furlong	=	10 chains
1 mile	=	5,280 feet
1 mile	=	8 furlongs

LENGTH, METRIC UNITS

1 centimetre	=	10 millimetres
1 decimetre	=	10 centimetres
1 metre	=	10 decimetres
1 decimetre	=	10 metres
1 hectometre	=	10 decametres
1 kilometre	=	10 hectometres
1 megametre	=	1,000 kilometres

1 metre = 100 centimetres or 1,000 millimetres
1 kilometre = 100 decametres or 1,000 metres

LENGTH, METRIC CONVERSIONS

1 inch	=	$2\frac{1}{2}$ cm or 25 millimetres
1 foot	=	30 centimetres
1 yard	=	0.01 metre
1 mile	=	1,609 kilometres
1 metre	=	3 feet 3 inches or 1·0936 yards
1 kilometre	=	0·6214 mile
80 kilometres	=	50 miles

WEIGHT, UK (IMPERIAL) UNITS

1 ounce	=	16 drams
1 pound	=	16 ounces
1 stone	=	14 pounds
1 quarter	=	28 pounds
1 hundred weight	=	4 quarters
1 ton	=	2,240 pounds
1 ton	=	20 hundred weight

WEIGHT, METRIC UNITS

1 gram	=	1000 milligrams
1 dekagram	=	10 grams
1 hectogram	=	10 dekagrams
1 kilogram	=	10 hectograms
1 tonne	=	1,000 kilograms
1 kilogram	=	100 dekagrams or 1,000 grams

WEIGHT, METRIC CONVERSIONS

1 ounce	=	28·35 grams
1 pound	=	0·453 kilograms
1 cwt	=	50·802 kilograms
1 ton	=	1·016 tonnes

VOLUME, UK (IMPERIAL) and US UNITS

1 cubic foot	=	1,728 cubic inches
1 cubic yard	=	27 cubic feet
1 bulk barrel	=	5 cubic feet
1 ton shipping	=	40 cubic feet

VOLUME, METRIC UNITS

1 cubic centimetre	=	1,000 cubic millimetres
1 cubic decimetre	=	1,000 cubic centimetres
1 cubic metre	=	1,000 cubic decimetres
1 cubic dekametre	=	1,000 cubic metres
1 cubic rectometre	=	1,000 cubic dekametres

VOLUME, METRIC CONVERSION

1 cubic inch	=	16·39 cubic centimetres
1 cubic foot	=	28·31 cubic decimetres
1 cubic yard	=	0·764 cubic metres
1 cubic centimetre	=	0·061 cubic inches
1 cubic metre	=	35·31 cubic feet
	or	1,308 cubic yards

AREA, UK (IMPERIAL) and US UNITS

1 square foot	=	144 square inches
1 square yard	=	9 square feet
1 acre	=	4,840 square yards
1 square mile	=	640 acres

AREA, METRIC UNITS

1 square metre	=	100 square decimetres
1 acre	=	100 square metres
1 hectare	=	10,000 square metres or 100 acres
1 square kilometre	=	100 hectares

AREA, METRIC CONVERSION

1 square yard	=	0·8361 square metres
1 acre	=	0·4046 hectares
1 square mile	=	2·5899 square kilometres
1 square metre	=	1·1959 square yards
1 hectare	=	2·4710 acres
1 square kilometre	=	0·3861 square miles

TEMPERATURES

To convert approximately centigrade to Fahrenheit add 15 to the centigrade and double the sum.

CENTIGRADE	FAHRENHEIT	CENTIGRADE	FAHRENHEIT
0	32	35	95
5	40	40	105
10	50	50	122
15	60	60	140
20	70	80	175
25	75	95	203
30	86	100	212

OVEN TEMPERATURES SCALES

To convert oven temperatures approximately from Centigrade to Fahrenheit, double the sum.

CENTIGRADE SCALE	ELECTRIC FAHRENHEIT	GAS MARK
110°C	225°F	$\frac{1}{4}$
130	250	$\frac{1}{2}$
140	275	1
150	300	2
170	325	3
180	350	4
190	375	5
200	400	6
220	425	7
230	450	8
240	475	9

The following guide is to the aproximate oven temperatures

OVEN	CENTIGRADE	FAHRENHEIT
Cool (very slow)	140	275
Warm (slow)	150	325
Moderate	160	350
Moderately hot	200	400
Hot	220–230	425–450
Very hot	240	475

TABLE OF EQUIVALENTS
LIQUID MEASURES

IMPERIAL	METRIC UNITS	US
1 pint	(approx. $\frac{1}{2}$ litre) 0·568 litre	$2\frac{1}{2}$ cups

METRIC UNITS	IMPERIAL	US
1 litre	$1\frac{3}{4}$ pints	$4\frac{1}{4}$ cups or 1 quart 2 ounces

US	IMPERIAL	METRIC UNITS
1 cup	8 fl oz	$\frac{1}{4}$ litre

WEIGHT MEASURES

METRIC UNITS	IMPERIAL	US (approximate)
1 gram	0·35 oz	
30 grams	1 oz	$\frac{1}{8}$ cup
100 grams	$3\frac{1}{2}$ oz	$\frac{1}{2}$ cup
225 grams	8 oz	1 cup
1 kilogram	1 pound 4 oz	$2\frac{1}{2}$ cups

BASIC FOOD – APPROXIMATE EQUIVALENTS

	METRIC UNITS	IMPERIAL	US
Ground almonds	150 grams	$5\frac{1}{2}$ ounces	1 cup
Baking powder	4 grams	1 teaspoon	1 teaspoon
	30 grams	1 ounce	$2\frac{1}{2}$ tablespoons
Breadcrumbs, fresh	50 grams	2 oz	1 cup
dry	90 grams	$3\frac{1}{2}$ oz	1 cup
Butter	15 grams	$\frac{1}{2}$ oz	1 tablespoon
	225 grams	8 oz	1 cup
Cheese	225 grams	8 oz	$\frac{1}{2}$ pound
Grated parmesan	110 grams	4 oz	1 cup
Coffee (ground)	90 grams	$3\frac{1}{2}$ oz	1 cup
Cornflour	10 grams	$\frac{1}{3}$ oz	1 tablespoon
Cream of Tartar	4 grams	1 teaspoon	1 teaspoon
Flour	110 grams	4 oz	1 cup
Fruits (Dried)	450 grams	1 pound	2 cups
Gelatine (powdered)	150 grams	$5\frac{1}{2}$ oz	1 cup
Golden Syrup, treacle	350 grams	12 oz	1 cup
Mustard (dry)	15 grams	$\frac{1}{2}$ oz	2 tablespoons
Pepper, whole	30 grams	1 oz	$4\frac{1}{2}$ tablespoons
ground	30 grams	1 oz	4 tablespoons
Raisins	150 grams	$5\frac{1}{2}$ oz	1 cup
Rice	225 grams	8 oz	1 cup
Sugar, granulated or caster	15 grams	$\frac{1}{2}$ oz	1 tablespoon
icing	30 grams	1 oz	$\frac{1}{4}$ cup
	110 grams	4 oz	1 cup

BODY WEIGHT

STONES	KILOGRAMS
5	32
6	38
7	44.4
8	51·7
9	57·1
10	63·5
11	69·8
12	76·2

L'AGNEAU ET LE MOUTON

FRENCH WAYS OF COOKING LAMB AND MUTTON

Generally speaking lamb and mutton recipes are interchangeable. Both have their devotees and arguments abound about whether to eat underdone. A lot of people argue that mutton should be eaten well-hung and cooked pink, while lamb is best if hung less and cooked more. I like my lamb and mutton juicy and pink inside but I don't want to get into a fight about it. Mutton is better for stews because it has a fuller flavour. Cheaper cuts are most flavourful. For a stew many cooks like to blend *poitrine* and *collet*.

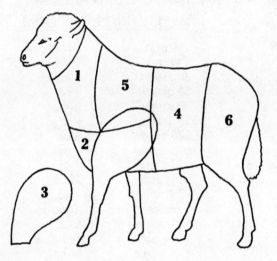

1 COLLET – NECK
Gelatinous, good for stews.

2 POITRINE – BREAST
Can be slowly roasted if all fat trimmed. Excellent for braises or stewing.

3 ÉPAULE – SHOULDER
Bone, roll and braise or roast. Serve with chestnut garnish or beans. Good for *blanquettes*, *fricassée* or stew.

4 CÔTES – SADDLE
Loin chops (*côtes*) are from here. Saddle is double-width joint of loin; it can be roasted or braised (if you have a pot big enough). Loin joints are often boned and rolled.

5 CÔTELETTES CARRÉ – BEST END OF NECK AND MIDDLE NECK (U.S. RIB)
Is usually cut into cutlets in France and then sautéed, grilled or braised. It can be a joint though if you trim fat and remove and chine bone. Roast it about 45 mins.

6 GIGOT – LEG

Can be roasted as it is, or boned and marinaded first. Mutton leg can be braised or poached in water (*gigot à l'anglaise*) and served with onion sauce.

BEUF

FRENCH WAYS OF COOKING BEEF

1 CERVELLES – BRAINS
Not as good as veal brains but very good. Soak 2 hours in cold water. Poach 45 mins. Serve with browned butter.

2 LANGUE – TONGUE
Poach 3 hours, serve hot or cold.

3 PLAT DE CÔTE – FOREQUARTER FLANK
Stock.

4 GROSSE POITRINE TENDRON – BRISKET
Pot-au-feu or stock (good cut for salt beef).

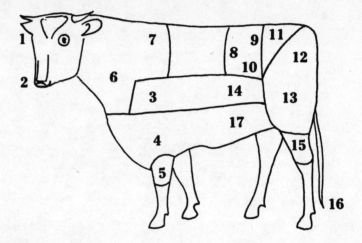

5 GÎTE – LEG
Just like rear leg but smaller.

6 MACREUSE – CLOD
Stew, braise or chop finely. *Pot-au-feu*.

7 PALERON – CHUCK
Stock, braise, stew.

8 CONTRE FILET – SIRLOIN STEAK WITHOUT FILLET
Prime cut; grill it. Can be rolled and roasted.

9 ALOYAU – SIRLOIN INCLUDING FILLET
Prime cut. Boned and trimmed of most of its fat, then rolled up and roasted.

10 ROMSTECK – RUMPSTEAK
Prime cut. Grill it.

11 AIGUILLETTE CULOTTE – RUMP
Lard it, marinade it for 6 hours then braise it or stew it. This is good for *bœuf à la mode*. (See silverside below).

12 TENDE DE TRANCHE – TOPSIDE (U.S. TOP ROUND)
Braise, stew, sometimes marinade first. If larded, can be pot-roasted.

13 GÎTE A LA NOIX – SILVERSIDE
Lard it, marinade it in red wine, then give it long slow cooking in the wine and this becomes *bœuf à la mode*. If you like salt beef this is a good cut.

14 TRANCHE GRASSE OU RONDE – SKIRT
Bottom part of the sirloin; separate lean layers for thin steaks or use whole thing for *pot-au-feu*.

15 GÎTE – LEG OF BEEF OR SHIN
Great flavour, gelatinous texure. Long (4 hours) stewing. Pies, casserole or stock.

16 QUEUE – OXTAIL
Long stewing.

17 FLANCHET – TOP RUMP OR THICK FLANK
Braise or stew, although I've heard of it being roasted.

PORC

FRENCH WAYS OF COOKING PORK

Any part of the pig can be roasted. Any part of the pig can be salted. If roasting it most French cooks would marinade it in any dry wine first for 3–6 hours or they might rub the meat with garlic, oil, salt and leave it overnight. Pork is particularly good when cooked in a closed pot.

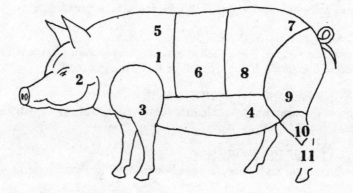

1 ÉCHINE – ENGLISH SPARE RIB (U.S. BLADE END)
Can be boned, rolled and roasted or, with all fat removed, used for *daube* or stew.

2   TÊTE OU HURE – HEAD
For brawn.

3 ÉPAULE – HAND (U.S. SHOULDER)
Bone and roll it, then roast or braise. Can be boned and cooked *en daube*.

4   POITRINE – BELLY
Gives lots of good fat. Use it for *rillettes*. Can be grilled crisp like bacon in slices. Sometimes it's salted. If smoked, it's bacon.

5 PALETTE – BLADEBONE (U.S. SHOULDER BUTT)
Bone it and braise it, or remove fat and stew it.

6 CARRÉ CÔTES DE PORC–FORE LOIN/BEST END (U.S. RIB CUT)
Classic pork chop, sauté or grill them. Boned and rolled it's good braised with turnips or cabbage.

7 POINTE DE FILET – FILLET (U.S. LOIN END)

8 MILIEU DE FILET – HIND LOIN
Just as fore-loin. Trim it of fat, bone it, roll it. Braise it with cabbage or turnip.

9 JAMBON – LARGE HALF OF LEG (U.S. FRESH HAM)
Bone it if you like, braise or roast.

10 JAMBONNEAU – KNUCKLE
Gelatinous meat, flavourful.

11 PIED – FOOT
Good for flavouring beef stews and stocks. Can be split and grilled and served with *vinaigrette* dressing. Some cooks say the fore-feet are better than the hind-feet.

VEAU

FRENCH WAYS OF COOKING VEAL

French cooks prefer braising to roasting for all meat but especially for veal.

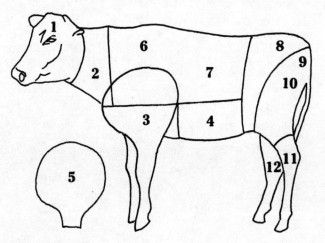

1 TÊTE – CALF'S HEAD
Buy it cleaned and blanched if possible (as pig's head for brawn), serve it sliced cold with *sauce rémoulade* or *vinaigrette* or sliced and grilled.

2 COLLET – SCRAG (U.S. NECK)
Stew it or make jellied veal (like pig's head brawn recipe).

3 POITRINE FLANCHET – BREAST
Stew, *blanquette* or boned, stuffed and braised (with sauerkraut sometimes). This is a superb but cheap cut.

4 TENDRON – BREAST (MIDDLE CUT, U.S. RIBLETS)
Contains crunchy false ribs much liked by French gourmets, but some English people don't like these sections. Slices from here can be braised slowly in butter. Can also be cut up for *blanquettes* and *fricassée*, etc.

5 ÉPAULE – SHOULDER
Meat from here plus meat from breast makes a *blanquette*. Or bone, roll and braise it. Not so good for roasting.

6 CÔTELETTES CARRÉ – BEST END OF NECK (U.S. RIB ROAST)
Luxury roasting joint. Cutlets from here can be sautéed or braised with tomato and onion in a covered pan.

7 LONGE (FILET) – LOIN
If roasted, boned, excess fat trimmed away but kidney remains inside, that's called a *rognonnade de veau*. If braised it can be left on the bone. A saddle (*selle*) is a double-width joint of loin.

8 QUASI – CHUMP END OF LOIN (U.S. HEEL OR ROUND)

Braise this or use it in a *daube*. Long (3–4 hours) cooking using a little dry white wine is good. Eat it hot or cold.

9 ROUELLES – FILLET (U.S. ROUND ROAST)

Escalope comes from this region.

10 CUISSEAU (NOIX SOUS–NOIX, FRICANDEAU)–TOPSIDE (U.S. RUMP)

Cuisseau means the leg. French butchers separate 3 joints here and slice them into escalopes. These joints can be larded and braised and sometimes are served cold. Not so good for roasting.

11 JARRET – KNUCKLE

For an unusual dish, lard it and roast it gently. Also good braised with tomatoes, garlic and onion for 2–3 hours. It's a superb thickening and enriching ingredient in any stew, e.g. beef stew, or with stuffed cabbage.

12 PIED – CALF'S FOOT

Great for thickening (as knuckle) and for making jelly for brawn, etc.